ASCENT
CENTER FOR TECHNICAL KNOWLEDGE

Autodesk® Revit® 2021
Collaboration Tools

Learning Guide

Imperial Units - 1st Edition

A AUTODESK.
Authorized Publisher

ASCENT - Center for Technical Knowledge®
Autodesk® Revit® 2021
Collaboration Tools
Imperial Units - 1st Edition

Prepared and produced by:

ASCENT Center for Technical Knowledge
630 Peter Jefferson Parkway, Suite 175
Charlottesville, VA 22911

866-527-2368
www.ASCENTed.com

Lead Contributor: Cherisse Biddulph

ASCENT - Center for Technical Knowledge (a division of Rand Worldwide Inc.) is a leading developer of professional learning materials and knowledge products for engineering software applications. ASCENT specializes in designing targeted content that facilitates application-based learning with hands-on software experience. For over 25 years, ASCENT has helped users become more productive through tailored custom learning solutions.

We welcome any comments you may have regarding this guide, or any of our products. To contact us please email: feedback@ASCENTed.com.

© ASCENT - Center for Technical Knowledge, 2020

All rights reserved. No part of this guide may be reproduced in any form by any photographic, electronic, mechanical or other means or used in any information storage and retrieval system without the written permission of ASCENT, a division of Rand Worldwide, Inc.

The following are registered trademarks or trademarks of Autodesk, Inc., and/or its subsidiaries and/or affiliates in the USA and other countries: 123D, 3ds Max, ADSK, Alias, ATC, AutoCAD LT, AutoCAD, Autodesk, the Autodesk logo, Autodesk 123D, Autodesk Alias, ArtCAM, Autodesk Forge, Autodesk Fusion, Autodesk Inventor, AutoSnap, BIM 360, Buzzsaw, CADmep, CAMduct, Civil 3D, Configurator 360, Dancing Baby (image), DWF, DWG, DWG (DWG logo), DWG Extreme, DWG TrueConvert, DWG TrueView, DWGX, DXF, Eagle, , ESTmep, FBX, FeatureCAM, Flame, FormIt 360, Fusion 360, The Future of Making Things, Glue, Green Building Studio, InfraWorks, Instructables, Instructables (Instructables logo), Inventor, Inventor CAM, Inventor HSM, Inventor LT, Make Anything, Maya, Maya LT, Moldflow, MotionBuilder, Mudbox, Navisworks, Netfabb, Opticore, PartMaker, Pier 9, PowerInspect, PowerMill, PowerShape, Publisher 360, RasterDWG, RealDWG, ReCap, ReCap 360, Remake, Revit LT, Revit, Scaleform, Shotgun, Showcase, Showcase 360, SketchBook, Softimage, Tinkercad, TrustedDWG, VRED.

NASTRAN is a registered trademark of the National Aeronautics Space Administration.

All other brand names, product names, or trademarks belong to their respective holders.

General Disclaimer:

Notwithstanding any language to the contrary, nothing contained herein constitutes nor is intended to constitute an offer, inducement, promise, or contract of any kind. The data contained herein is for informational purposes only and is not represented to be error free. ASCENT, its agents and employees, expressly disclaim any liability for any damages, losses or other expenses arising in connection with the use of its materials or in connection with any failure of performance, error, omission even if ASCENT, or its representatives, are advised of the possibility of such damages, losses or other expenses. No consequential damages can be sought against ASCENT or Rand Worldwide, Inc. for the use of these materials by any third parties or for any direct or indirect result of that use.

The information contained herein is intended to be of general interest to you and is provided "as is", and it does not address the circumstances of any particular individual or entity. Nothing herein constitutes professional advice, nor does it constitute a comprehensive or complete statement of the issues discussed thereto. ASCENT does not warrant that the document or information will be error free or will meet any particular criteria of performance or quality. In particular (but without limitation) information may be rendered inaccurate by changes made to the subject of the materials (i.e. applicable software). Rand Worldwide, Inc. specifically disclaims any warranty, either expressed or implied, including the warranty of fitness for a particular purpose.

Contents

© 2020, ASCENT - Center for Technical Knowledge®

© 2020, ASCENT - Center for Technical Knowledge®

Preface

Autodesk® Revit® is a Building Information Modeling (BIM) tool, which can be used by more than one person working on a new project. This is an important feature in collaboration within a project, between projects, and with other users, firms, and disciplines.

The objective of the *Autodesk® Revit® 2021: Collaboration Tools* guide is to enable users, who have a basic knowledge of Autodesk Revit, to increase their productivity while working with other people on a team, either in the same firm or other firms as well as with other disciplines. It also covers linking Autodesk Revit files and linking or importing other CAD files. Practices are available for each of the primary disciplines covered by Autodesk Revit: architecture, MEP, and structure.

Topics Covered

- Set up project phasing
- Use groups
- Create and display a variety of Design Options
- Link Autodesk Revit files
- Use multi-discipline coordination, including Copy/Monitor and Coordination Review
- Import and export vector and raster files, including exporting Autodesk Revit models for energy analysis
- Understand, use, and set up worksharing

Prerequisites

- Access to the 2021.0 version of the software, to ensure compatibility with this guide. Future software updates that are released by Autodesk may include changes that are not reflected in this guide. The practices and files included with this guide might not be compatible with prior versions (e.g., 2020).

- Users should be comfortable with the fundamentals of Autodesk Revit as taught in *Autodesk Revit: Fundamentals for Architecture*, *Autodesk Revit: Fundamentals for MEP*, or *Autodesk Revit: Fundamentals for Structure*. Knowledge of basic techniques is assumed, such as creating typical elements, copying and moving objects, creating and working with views, etc.

Note on Software Setup

This guide assumes a standard installation of the software using the default preferences during installation. Lectures and practices use the standard software templates and default options for the Content Libraries.

Students and Educators Can Access Free Autodesk Software and Resources

Autodesk challenges you to get started with free educational licenses for professional software and creativity apps used by millions of architects, engineers, designers, and hobbyists today. Bring Autodesk software into your classroom, studio, or workshop to learn, teach, and explore real-world design challenges the way professionals do.

Get started today - register at the Autodesk Education Community and download one of the many Autodesk software applications available.

Visit www.autodesk.com/education/home/

Note: Free products are subject to the terms and conditions of the end-user license and services agreement that accompanies the software. The software is for personal use for education purposes and is not intended for classroom or lab use.

Lead Contributor: Cherisse Biddulph

Cherisse is an Autodesk Certified Professional for Revit as well as an Autodesk Certified Instructor. She brings over 15 years of industry, teaching and technical support experience to her role as a Learning Content Developer with ASCENT. With a passion for design and architecture, she received her Associate of Applied Science in Drafting and Design and has worked in industry assisting firms with their CAD Management and software implementation needs as they modernize to a Building Information Modeling (BIM) design environment. Although her main passion is the Revit design product, she is also proficient in AutoCAD, Autodesk BIM 360, and also Autodesk Navisworks. Today, Cherisse continues to expand her knowledge in the ever-evolving AEC industry and the software used to support it.

Cherisse Biddulph has been the Lead Contributor for *Autodesk Revit: Collaboration Tools* since 2020.

© 2020, ASCENT - Center for Technical Knowledge®

In This Guide

The following highlights the key features of this guide.

Feature	Description
Practice Files	The Practice Files page includes a link to the practice files and instructions on how to download and install them. The practice files are required to complete the practices in this guide.
Chapters	A chapter consists of the following - Learning Objectives, Instructional Content, Practices, Chapter Review Questions, and Command Summary. • **Learning Objectives** define the skills you can acquire by learning the content provided in the chapter. • **Instructional Content**, which begins right after Learning Objectives, refers to the descriptive and procedural information related to various topics. Each main topic introduces a product feature, discusses various aspects of that feature, and provides step-by-step procedures on how to use that feature. Where relevant, examples, figures, helpful hints, and notes are provided. • **Practice** for a topic follows the instructional content. Practices enable you to use the software to perform a hands-on review of a topic. It is required that you download the practice files (using the link found on the Practice Files page) prior to starting the first practice. • **Chapter Review Questions**, located close to the end of a chapter, enable you to test your knowledge of the key concepts discussed in the chapter. • **Command Summary** concludes a chapter. It contains a list of the software commands that are used throughout the chapter and provides information on where the command can be found in the software.
Appendices	Appendices provide additional information to the main course content. It could be in the form of instructional content, practices, tables, projects, or skills assessment.

© 2020, ASCENT - Center for Technical Knowledge®

Practice Files

To download the practice files for this guide, use the following steps:

1. Type the URL *exactly as shown below* into the address bar of your Internet browser, to access the Course File Download page.

    Note: If you are using the ebook, you do not have to type the URL. Instead, you can access the page simply by clicking the URL below.

    ## https://www.ascented.com/getfile/id/evelynae

    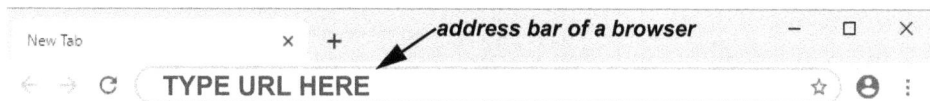

2. On the Course File Download page, click the **DOWNLOAD NOW** button, as shown below, to download the .ZIP file that contains the practice files.

3. Once the download is complete, unzip the file and extract its contents.

    The recommended practice files folder location is:
    C:\Revit 2021 Collaboration Tools Practice Files

    Note: It is recommended that you do not change the location of the practice files folder. Doing so may cause errors when completing the practices.

Stay Informed!

To receive information about upcoming events, promotional offers, and complimentary webcasts, visit:

www.ASCENTed.com/updates

© 2020, ASCENT - Center for Technical Knowledge®

Phasing, Groups, and Design Options

There are a variety of tools that can be used on complex projects:

- Phasing enables you to specify which project elements belong to a specific phase in the process of construction. You can create views that show each of these separate phases.

- Groups are sets of elements that can be inserted into a project. They can include both model and annotation elements. These groups can be saved to a separate file and then inserted or linked into multiple projects.

- Design Options enable you to create different examples for part of a building, and then display each example in separate views. Once you have decided which option to use, you can make the option part of the main model.

Learning Objectives in This Chapter

- Create and apply phases to elements.
- Create views to display different phases.
- Create groups of elements and annotations.
- Modify groups.
- Save groups as separate files.
- Create Design Options.
- Add existing and new elements to Design Options.
- Create views for Design Options.

1.1 Applying Project Phasing

Phases show distinct stages in a project's life. They are typically used with renovations and additions, as shown in Figure 1–1, or when a project involves several phases for its completion.

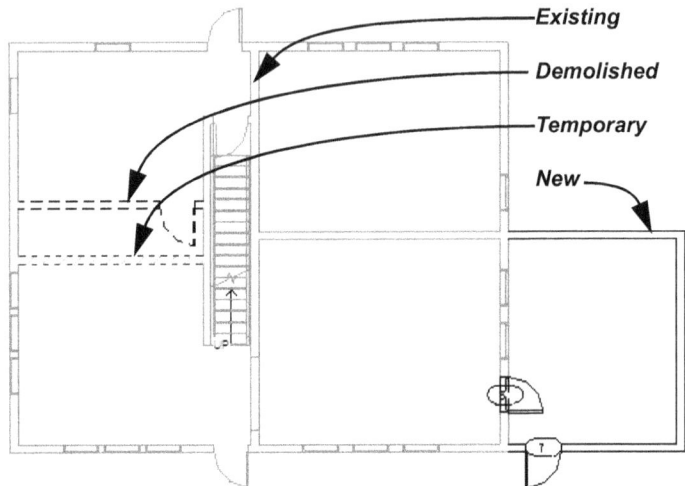

Figure 1–1

- There are two default phases included in the template files: **Existing** and **New Construction**. Many projects can be completed using just these two options, but additional phases can also be created for more complex projects.

All construction elements have two phase properties, *Phase Created* and *Phase Demolished.* This creates four potential status conditions for each element, regardless of how many phases are in a project:

- **Existing:** Created in an earlier phase and exists in the current phase.

- **New:** Created in the current phase.

- **Demolished:** Created in an earlier phase and demolished in the current phase.

- **Temporary:** Created in the current phase and demolished in the current phase.

© 2020, ASCENT - Center for Technical Knowledge®

How To: Work with Phases

1. Open the view in which you want to work.
2. Without having any elements selected, in Properties, under the *Phasing* heading, select the *Phase* from the drop-down list, as shown in Figure 1–2. This becomes the current phase for this view.

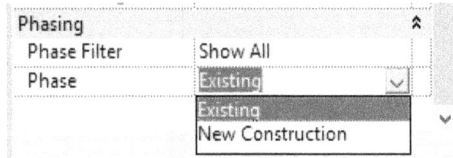

If you are working on a renovation project, start by modeling the building with the Phase set to **Existing**.

Phasing		⌃
Phase Filter	Show All	
Phase	Existing	⌄
	Existing	
	New Construction	⌄

Properties of the View

Figure 1–2

3. Start modeling the elements. They take on the phase set in the current view.

• You can change the phase of elements by changing the *Phase Created* in the element's properties, as shown in Figure 1–3. Note that you can also demolish elements.

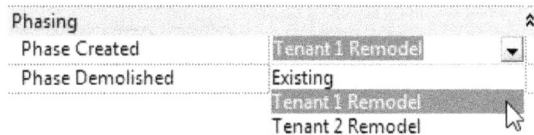

Phasing		⌃
Phase Created	Tenant 1 Remodel	▾
Phase Demolished	Existing	
	Tenant 1 Remodel	
	Tenant 2 Remodel	

Properties of the Element

Figure 1–3

Hint: Phases and Schedules

You can apply phases to schedules. When you create the schedule, include the *Phase Created* field and then use it in the *Filter* tab to limit the elements to a specific phase, as shown in Figure 1–4.

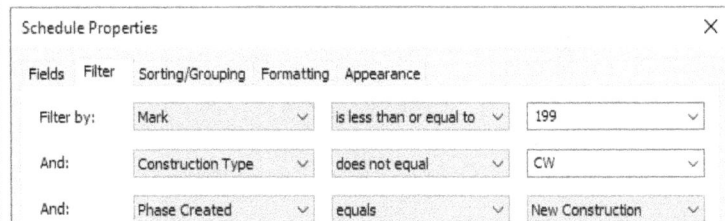

Schedule Properties				✕
Fields Filter Sorting/Grouping Formatting Appearance				
Filter by:	Mark	is less than or equal to	199	
And:	Construction Type	does not equal	CW	
And:	Phase Created	equals	New Construction	

Figure 1–4

How To: Demolish Elements

1. In the *Modify* tab>Geometry panel, click ⚒ (Demolish).
2. Click on the elements that you want to demolish in the current phase, as shown in Figure 1–5.

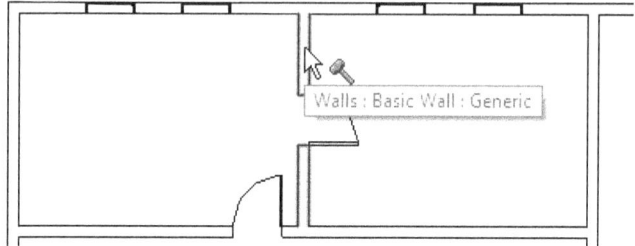

Figure 1–5

- You can also select the elements you want to demolish and, in Properties, change the *Phase Demolished* value.

- Demolishing a wall also demolishes any doors or windows associated with that wall, as shown in Figure 1–6.

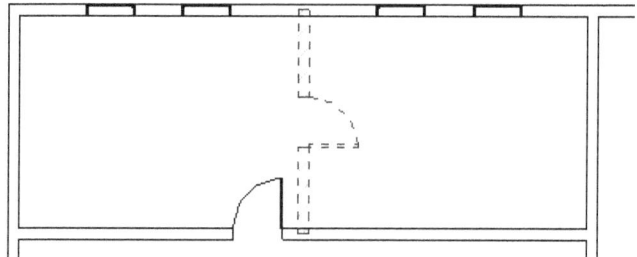

Figure 1–6

- To change an element so that it is no longer demolished, in Properties, set the *Phase Demolished* to **None**.

© 2020, ASCENT - Center for Technical Knowledge®

Hint: Elements That Do Not Have Phases

Annotations (tags, text, or dimensions), view elements (elevations, sections, and callout views), and datum elements (grids and levels) do not have phases.

Curtain walls and beam systems include sub-elements that do not have phases. You need to select the primary curtain wall or beam system to change the phase.

When selecting multiple elements to apply a phase, click

▽:37 (Filter) in the Status Bar and clear the checkbox next to any annotations and curtain wall sub-elements (as shown in Figure 1–7) before modifying the phase in the properties.

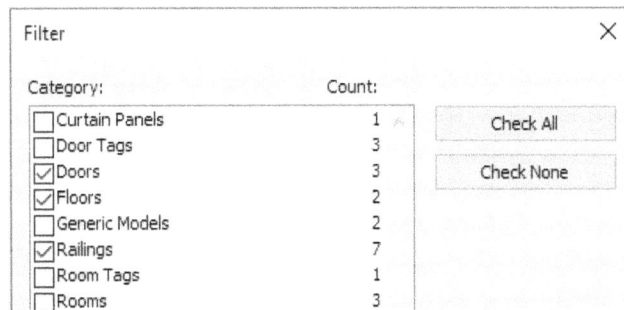

Filter		✕
Category:	**Count:**	
☐ Curtain Panels	1	Check All
☐ Door Tags	3	
☑ Doors	3	Check None
☑ Floors	2	
☐ Generic Models	2	
☑ Railings	7	
☐ Room Tags	1	
☐ Rooms	3	

Figure 1–7

- Non-phase elements can be hidden in views where you do not want them to show. For example, in Figure 1–8, hide (by element) grids 5-8 and then modify the length of grids A-C (change the 3D icon to 2D so the change only shows in the current view.) You could also change the crop region of the view.

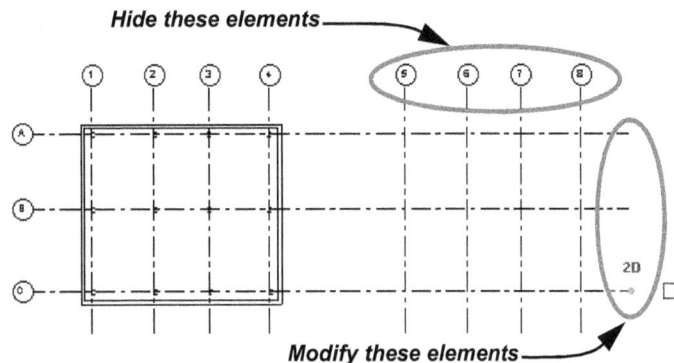

Hide these elements

Modify these elements

Figure 1–8

Phases and Views

The look of the elements is determined by graphic overrides assigned to each phase filter.

Duplicate a view for each phase you want to display. For example, you might want to show only the existing and demolished items in one view and the existing and new items, without the demolished items, in another view. You may also want to show the completed project without any of the previous phases, as shown in Figure 1–9.

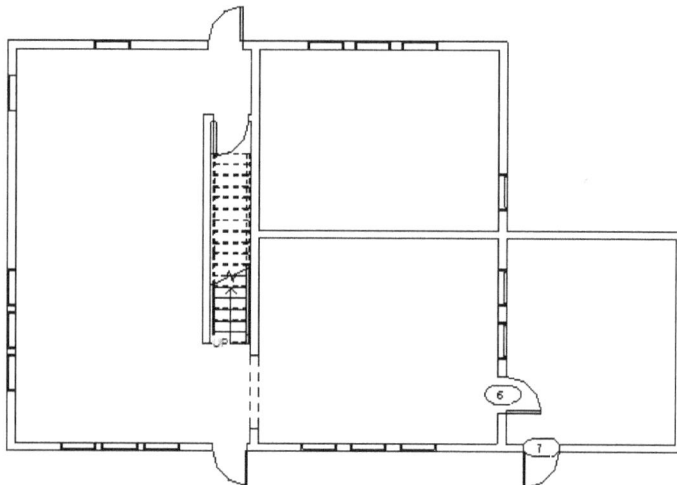

Figure 1–9

The *Phase Filter*, specified in the view properties, determines which phases display in the view relative to the current phase:

- **None:** Displays all elements regardless of the current phase.

- **Show All:** Displays all phases up to the current phase, with all except the current phase, which is grayed out.

- **Show Complete:** Displays all construction up to the current phase.

- **Show Demo + New:** Displays the current phase and any demolished elements.

- **Show New:** Displays only elements created in the current view.

- **Show Previous + Demo:** Displays elements created in previous phases and any demolished elements from the current phase.

- **Show Previous + New:** Displays elements created in the previous phase and any new elements created in the current phase.

- **Show Previous Phase:** Displays elements created in any previous phases.

© 2020, ASCENT - Center for Technical Knowledge®

Creating Phases

When you create new phases, you can specify the names and time sequence, set up phase filters, and specify graphic overrides for each phase.

How To: Create New Phases

1. In the *Manage* tab>Phasing panel, click ▦ (Phases).
2. In the Phasing dialog box, *Project Phases* tab, the existing phases display. Two phases, **Existing** and **New Construction**, come with most templates, as shown in Figure 1–10.

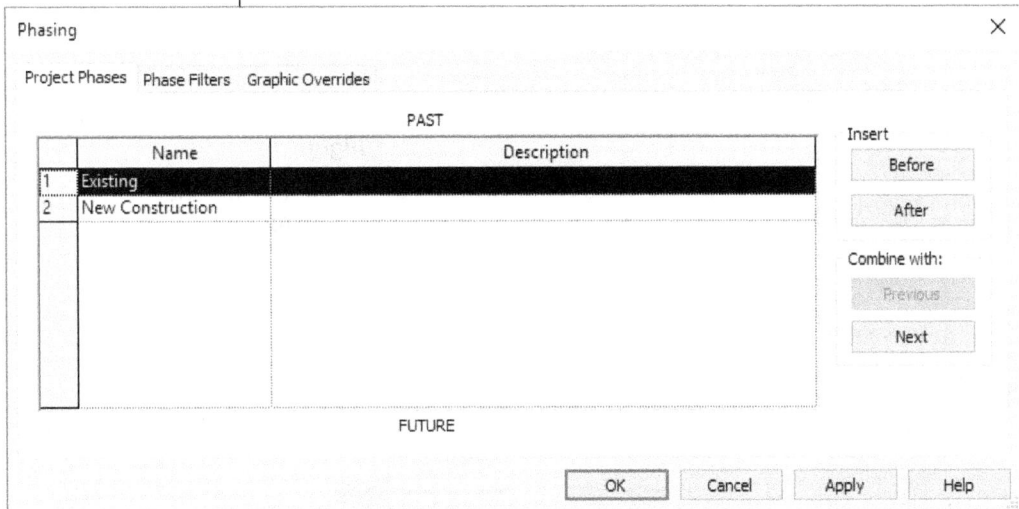

Figure 1–10

- The default phases can be renamed in this dialog box.

You need to add the phase in the correct time sequence. Past and Future notations are at the top and bottom of the dialog box.

3. In the *Project Phases* tab, select a phase in the list. In the *Insert* area, click **Before** or **After**. You cannot change the order and need to be careful as you insert phases.

- New phases are numbered (Phase 1, Phase 2, etc.). Select the name to change it. You can also add a description for each phase.
- You can combine phases, as needed. Click **Previous** or **Next**. The elements on the combined phases take on the phase properties of the phase with which they were combined.

4. Select the *Phase Filters* tab, as shown in Figure 1–11. Several phase filters are supplied with the program and you can add more. Once you have a new phase filter, you define which of the phases display. If listed as **Overridden**, the graphic overrides display for the phase.

Phasing   ×

Project Phases   Phase Filters   Graphic Overrides

	Filter Name	New	Existing	Demolished	Temporary
1	Show All	By Category	Overridden	Overridden	Overridden
2	Show Complete	By Category	By Category	Not Displayed	Not Displayed
3	Show Demo + New	By Category	Not Displayed	Overridden	Overridden
4	Show New	By Category	Not Displayed	Not Displayed	Not Displayed
5	Show Previous + Demo	Not Displayed	Overridden	Overridden	Not Displayed
6	Show Previous + New	By Category	Overridden	Not Displayed	Not Displayed
7	Show Previous Phase	Not Displayed	Overridden	Not Displayed	Not Displayed

Figure 1–11

5. Select the *Graphic Overrides* tab, as shown in Figure 1–12. Set up the overrides, as required.

Phasing   ×

Project Phases   Phase Filters   Graphic Overrides

Phase Status	Projection/Surface		Cut		Halftone	Material
	Lines	Patterns	Lines	Patterns		
Existing				Hidden	☐	Phase - Exist
Demolished	-------------		------------- Hidden		☐	Phase - Demo
New					☐	Phase - New
Temporary	....		....	///	☐	Phase - Temporary

Figure 1–12

6. Click **OK** to close the dialog box.

© 2020, ASCENT - Center for Technical Knowledge®

Practice 1a

Apply Project Phasing - Architectural

Practice Objectives

- Set custom phases in a project.
- Apply phases to elements.
- Apply phases to views.

In this practice, you will create several new phases and view the changes with the phase filters. You will also add some new elements in the existing building, as shown in Figure 1–13.

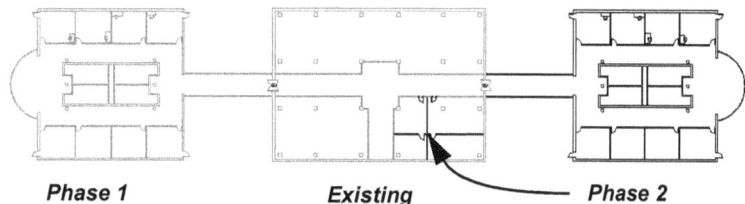

Phase 1 **Existing** **Phase 2**

Figure 1–13

Task 1 - Set up phases.

1. In the practice files folder, open **Office-Phases-A.rvt**.

2. In the *Manage* tab>Phasing panel, click ⬚ (Phases).

3. In the Phasing dialog box, in the *Project Phases* tab, rename the phase *New Construction* as **Phase 1** and add the description: **West Wing Addition**.

4. Insert an additional phase after the last one and accept the default name of **Phase 2**. Add the description: **East Wing Addition**, as shown in Figure 1–14.

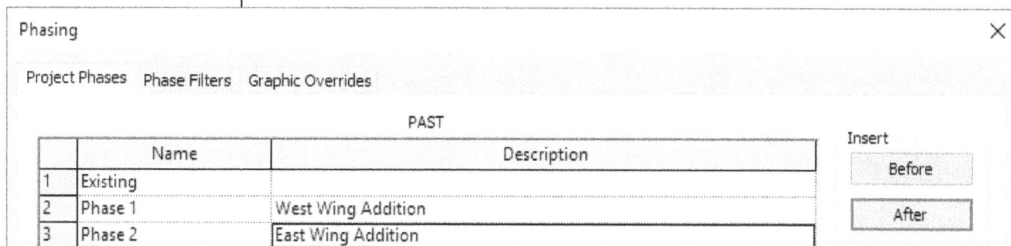

	Name	Description
1	Existing	
2	Phase 1	West Wing Addition
3	Phase 2	East Wing Addition

PAST

Insert
Before
After

Figure 1–14

5. Click **OK** to close the dialog box.

Task 2 - Apply phases to views and elements.

1. Duplicate three new views of **Level 1**. Rename them: **Level 1 - Existing**, **Level 1 - Phase 1**, and **Level 1 - Phase 2**.

2. Open the **Floor Plans: Level 1- Existing** view.

3. Select all elements in the middle building, as shown in Figure 1–15. Filter out any annotation elements, such as tags, views, and elevations.

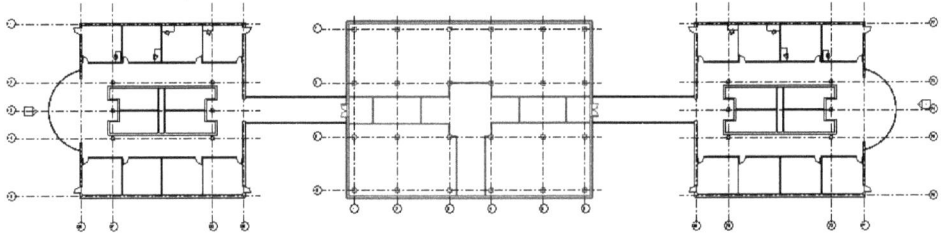

Figure 1–15

4. In Properties, change the *Phase Created* for these elements to **Existing**.

5. Click in the view to release the selection. The building elements should turn gray when you clear the selection.

6. In Properties (with no elements selected), scroll down and set *Phase Filter* to **Show Complete** and *Phase* to **Existing**, as shown in Figure 1–16.

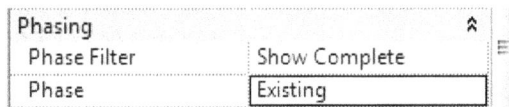

Phasing	⌃
Phase Filter	Show Complete
Phase	Existing

Figure 1–16

© 2020, ASCENT - Center for Technical Knowledge®

7. Click in the view. Only the central building displays but the grids on either side still display. Resize the crop region so only the main building displays as shown in Figure 1–17.

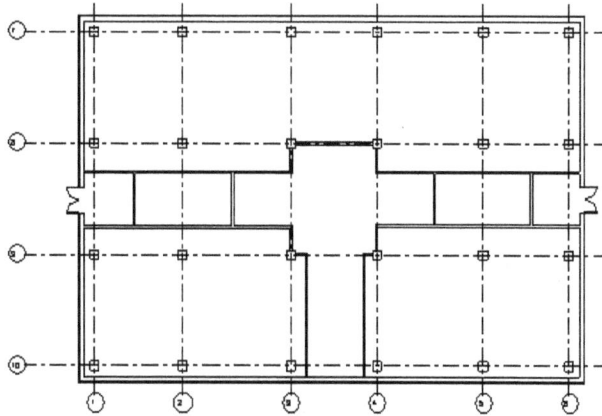

Figure 1–17

8. Open the **Floor Plans: Level 1 - Phase 1** view.

9. Select the elements in the right (east) wing, filter out any views and tags, and change the *Phase Created* of these elements to **Phase 2**. In this case, the elements are removed from the view because the *Phase* of the view is set to **Phase 1**. Resize the crop region so the east wing grids do not display, as shown in Figure 1–18.

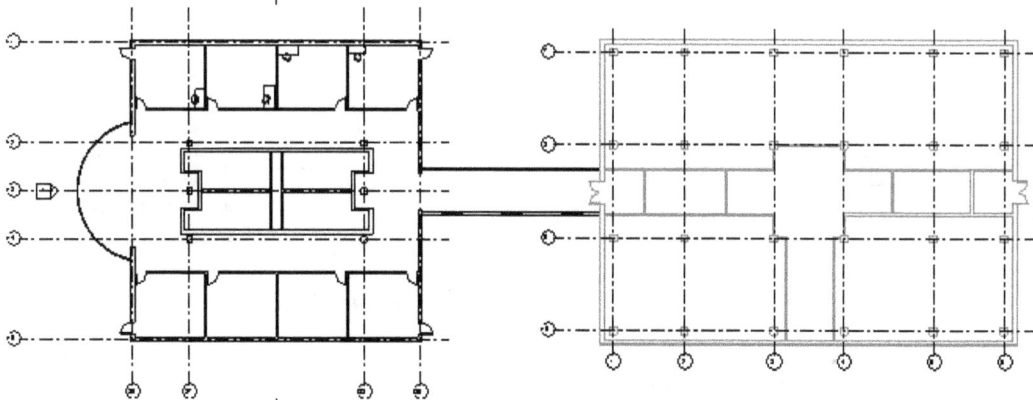

Figure 1–18

10. Without any elements selected, verify that the *Phase Filter* is set to **Show All** and the *Phase* is set to **Phase 1**.

11. In the *Modify* tab>Geometry panel, click ⚒ (Demolish). Select the four walls in the center building that cross the long horizontal hallways, as shown in Figure 1–19.

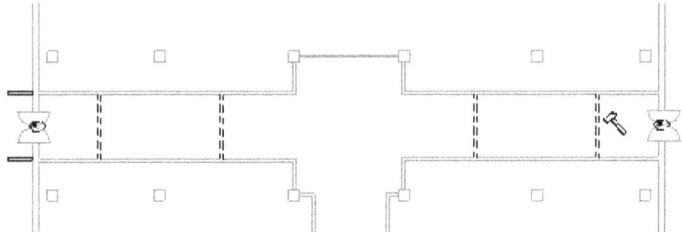

Figure 1–19

12. Click ⌕ (Modify) and select one of the demolished walls. In Properties, scroll down to the *Phasing* area. Ensure that the *Phase Created* is set to **Existing** and *Phase Demolished* is set to **Phase 1**.

13. Open the **Floor Plans: Level 1 - Phase 2** view.

14. In Properties, without any elements selected, set the *Phase Filter* to **Show All** and change the *Phase* to **Phase 2**. The East Wing is added and the demolished walls are removed, while the elements in the previous two phases are grayed out, as shown in Figure 1–20.

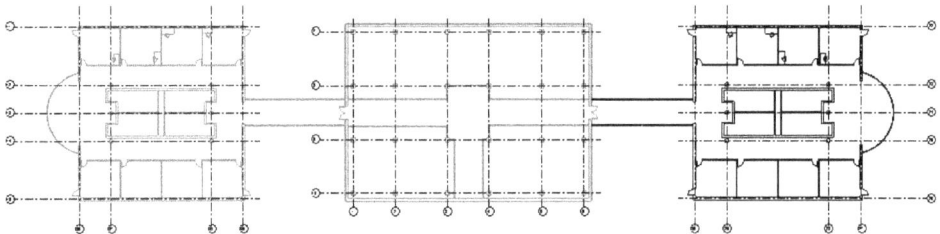

Figure 1–20

© 2020, ASCENT - Center for Technical Knowledge®

15. Modify the crop region so that it shows all of Phase 2 and part of the existing building. Hide the grids in the existing building by element, as shown in Figure 1–21.

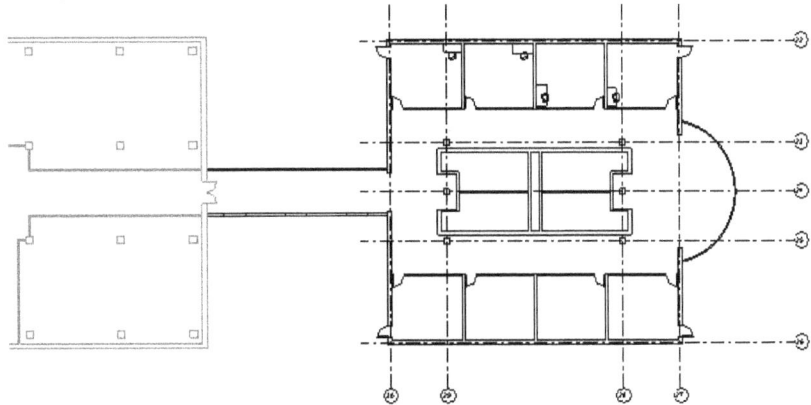

Figure 1–21

16. In the existing building add several walls and doors with some of the doors along the existing walls, as shown in Figure 1–22.

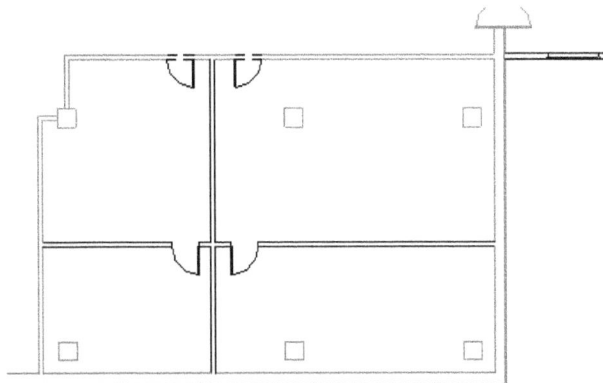

Figure 1–22

17. Open the **Floor Plans: Level 1 - Phase 1** view to see that the walls added in Phase 2 do not display.

18. Save and close the project.

Practice 1b | Apply Project Phasing - Structural

Practice Objectives

- Set custom phases in a project.
- Apply phases to elements.
- Apply phases to views.

In this practice, you will create phases and move the elements in the project to different phases. You will then view the changes with the phase filters, as shown in Figure 1–23.

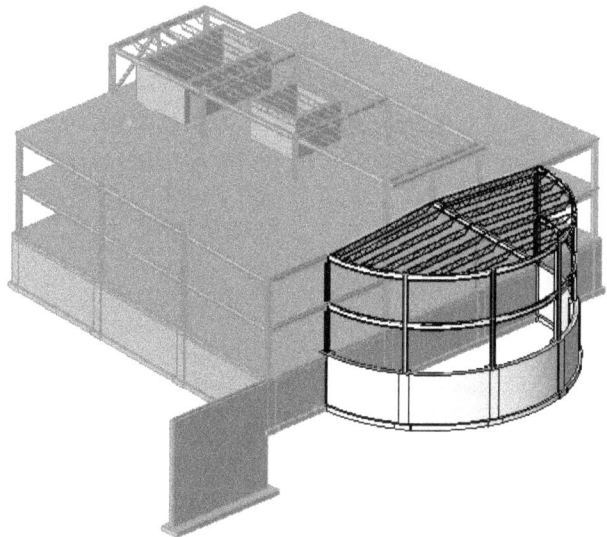

Figure 1–23

Task 1 - Set up phases.

1. In the practice files folder, open **Office-Phases-S.rvt**.

2. In the *Manage* tab>Phasing panel, click ⬚ (Phases).

3. In the Phasing dialog box there is one phase, **New Construction**. The project will now be divided into three phases. In the *Project Phases* tab, rename the phase *New Construction* as **Phase 1** and add the description **Main Building**.

© 2020, ASCENT - Center for Technical Knowledge®

4. Insert two additional phases after the last one and accept the default names of **Phase 2** and **Phase 3**. Add the description **Penthouse** to Phase 2 and **Addition** to Phase 3, as shown in Figure 1–24.

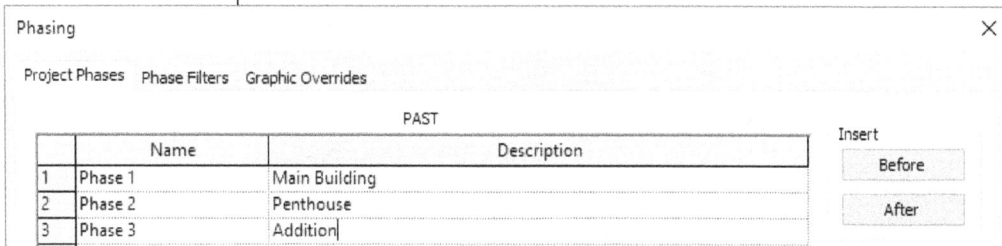

Phasing   ×

Project Phases   Phase Filters   Graphic Overrides

                              PAST   Insert

	Name	Description
1	Phase 1	Main Building
2	Phase 2	Penthouse
3	Phase 3	Addition

Before

After

Figure 1–24

5. Click **OK** to close the dialog box.

6. Select several elements from different parts of the building. They are all in Phase 1. Select in an empty area in the view to clear the selection.

7. Save the project.

Task 2 - Apply phases to elements.

1. Open the **Structural Plans: Penthouse** view. In Properties, verify that the *Phasing* area shows the *Phase* as **Phase 1**, as shown in Figure 1–25. This means that any new elements that are added will have their *Phase Created* set to Phase 1.

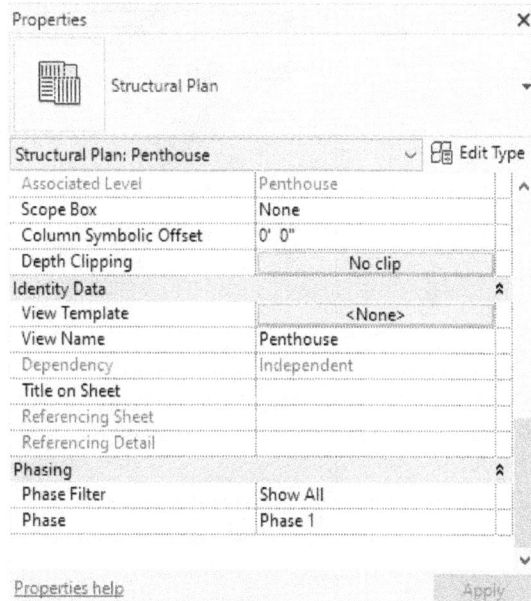

Properties   ×

Structural Plan   ▼

Structural Plan: Penthouse   ∨   Edit Type

Associated Level	Penthouse
Scope Box	None
Column Symbolic Offset	0' 0"
Depth Clipping	No clip
Identity Data	
View Template	<None>
View Name	Penthouse
Dependency	Independent
Title on Sheet	
Referencing Sheet	
Referencing Detail	
Phasing	
Phase Filter	Show All
Phase	Phase 1

Properties help   Apply

Figure 1–25

2. Select all of the structural framing girders, structural columns, and structural beam systems. To do so, perform a crossing selection and filter out everything else, as shown in Figure 1–26.

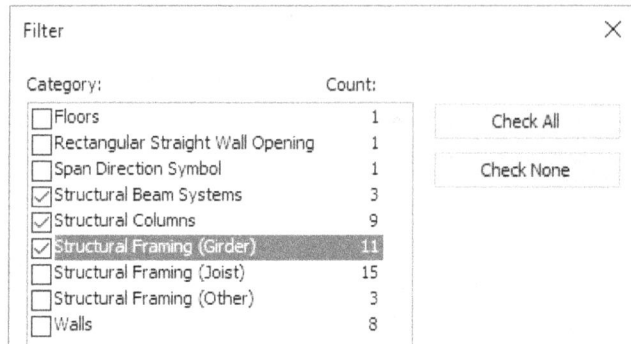

Filter			✕
Category:		Count:	
☐ Floors		1	Check All
☐ Rectangular Straight Wall Opening		1	
☐ Span Direction Symbol		1	Check None
☑ Structural Beam Systems		3	
☑ Structural Columns		9	
☑ Structural Framing (Girder)		11	
☐ Structural Framing (Joist)		15	
☐ Structural Framing (Other)		3	
☐ Walls		8	

Figure 1–26

3. In Properties, change the *Phase Created* to **Phase 2**. The Phase 2 elements are removed from the view because the view's *Phase* (in Properties) is set to Phase 1, but the elevator shaft and stair shaft remain (as shown in Figure 1–27) because their *Phase Created* is set to **Phase 1**.

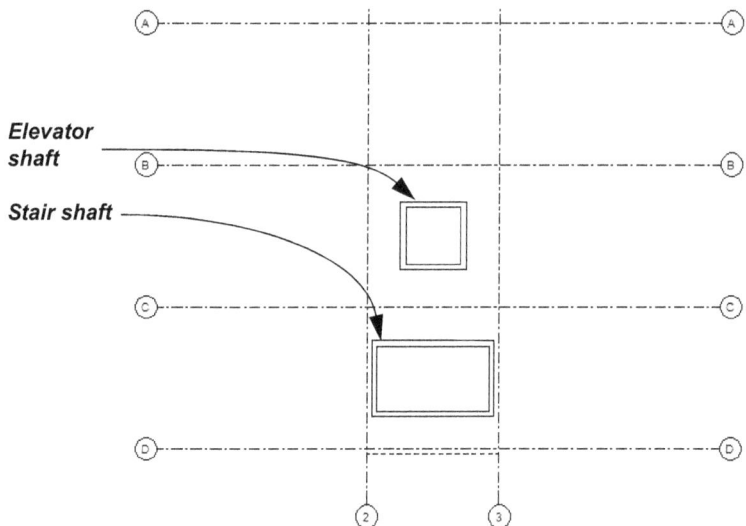

Elevator shaft

Stair shaft

Figure 1–27

4. In the *Structure* tab>Structure panel, click ⌢ (Floor: Structural). Do not use the Architectural floor tool.

© 2020, ASCENT - Center for Technical Knowledge®

5. Add two separate roof slabs to the top of the elevator and stair shafts using the **Floor: 1 1/2" Metal Roof Deck** type at a height of **8'-0"** off the Roof level. The new slabs are added to Phase 1.

   • To verify, select the new roofs. In Properties, look at the *Phasing* area and notice that the *Phase Created* is **Phase 1**.

6. Click in an empty area in the view to clear the selection.

7. With no elements selected, the Properties display the properties for the active view. Change the *Phase* to **Phase 2**. The beams and columns now display.

8. In the View Control Bar, change the *Visual Style* to **Shaded** so the roofs are easier to see.

9. In the *Modify* tab>Geometry panel, click ✎ (Demolish). Zoom in and select the metal roof decks. (Use <Tab> to select them.) Once they are demolished, they will turn red, as shown in Figure 1–28.

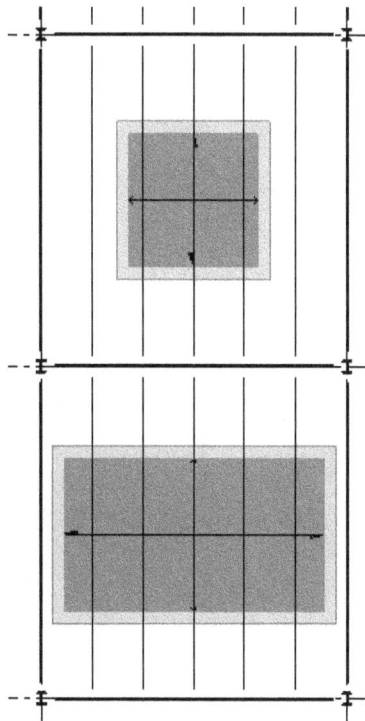

Figure 1–28

10. Select one of the now demolished metal roof decks. In Properties, note that the element is listed as *Phase Created* in **Phase 1** and *Phase Demolished* in **Phase 2**, as shown in Figure 1–29. The dashed edges do not display in the view because they overlap the walls.

Phasing		⌃
Phase Created	Phase 1	
Phase Demolished	Phase 2	

Figure 1–29

11. Open the **Structural Plans: Level 1** view.

12. Select the structural columns, structural foundations, and walls connected to the arc area, as shown in Figure 1–30. In Properties, set the *Phase Created* to **Phase 3**. Use <Shift> to remove elements and use <Ctrl> to add elements.

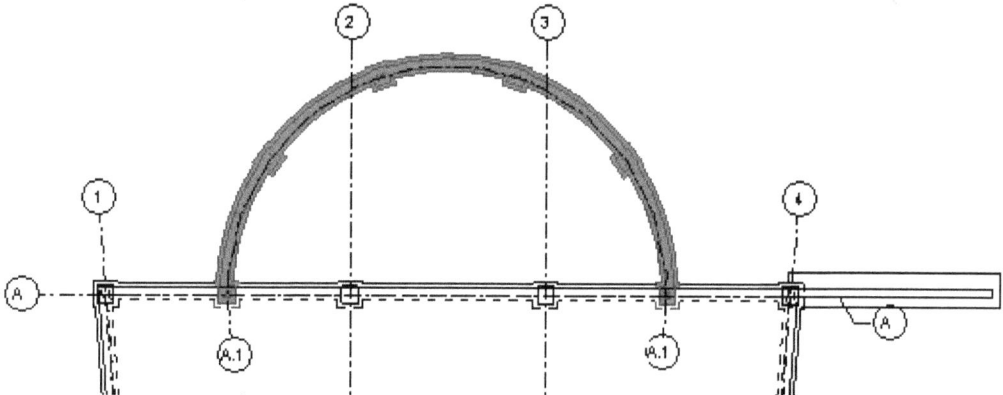

Figure 1–30

13. Select grid line A.1. Right-click and select **Hide in View by Elements**.

14. Repeat the process of assigning the arc addition elements to Phase 3 in the **Structural Plans: Level 2** and **Structural Plans: Roof** views. In the Roof view, select the beam systems first and change them to Phase 3. Then you can select the rest of the beams and columns.

© 2020, ASCENT - Center for Technical Knowledge®

15. Open the **3D Views: Front View**. It should display the existing building with the new roof slabs, as shown in Figure 1–31.

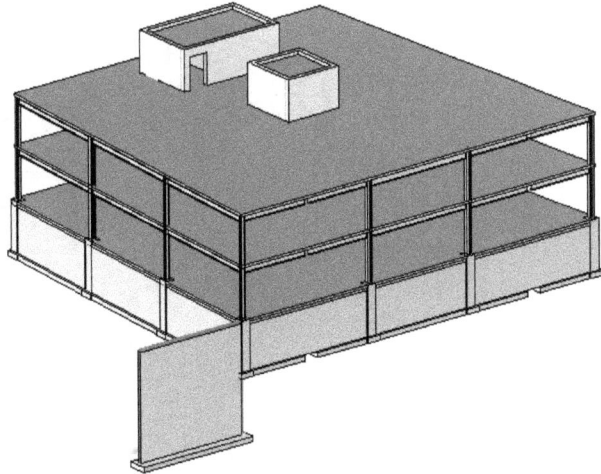

Figure 1–31

16. Save the project.

Task 3 - Apply phases to views.

1. Use **Duplicate with Detailing** and create three new views of the Front view. Rename them as **Front View - Phase 2**, **Front View - Phase 3**, and **Front View - Final**.

2. Rename Front View to **Front View - Phase 1**.

3. Open the **Front View - Phase 2** view.

4. In Properties, scroll down and change *Phase Filter* to **Show All** and *Phase* to **Phase 2** as shown in Figure 1–32.

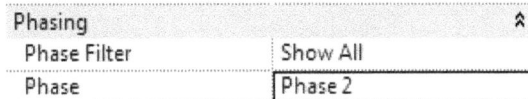

Phasing		☆
Phase Filter	Show All	
Phase	Phase 2	

Figure 1–32

5. Click in the view. The existing building is grayed out and the new Penthouse phase displays with the demolished roof slabs in red, as shown in Figure 1–33.

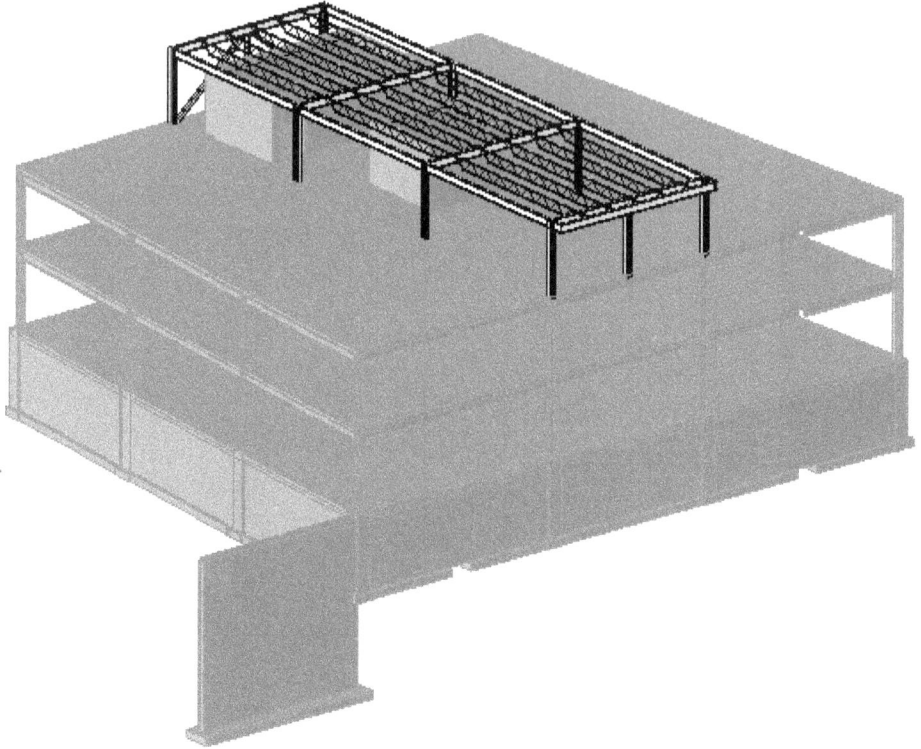

Figure 1–33

6. Open the **Front View - Phase 3** view.

© 2020, ASCENT - Center for Technical Knowledge®

7. In Properties, set *Phase Filter* to **Show All** and the *Phase* to **Phase 3**. Now the existing building and the penthouse are grayed out and the new entrance structure displays as shown in Figure 1–34.

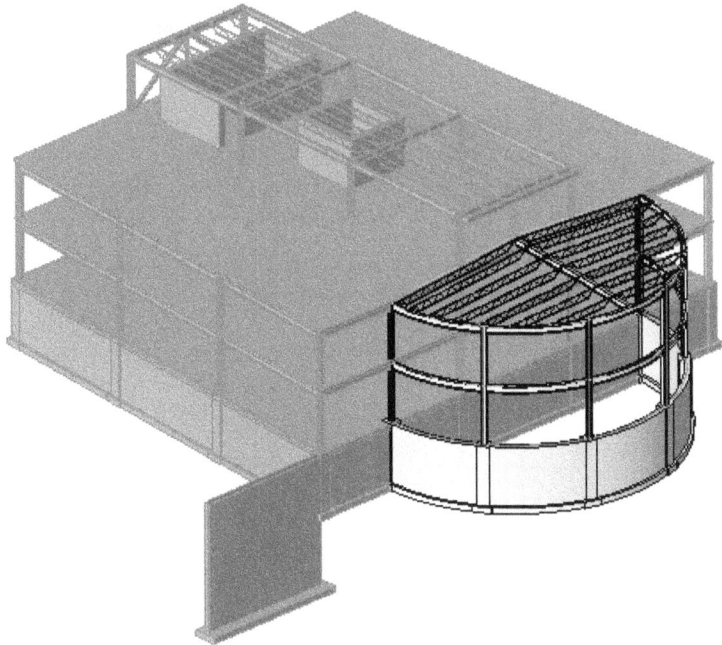

Figure 1–34

8. Open the **Front View - Final** view.

9. In Properties, set the *Phase Filter* to **Show Complete** and the *Phase* to **Phase 3**. All of the elements now display without any differences to the phases.

10. Save and close the project.

Practice 1c

Apply Project Phasing - MEP

Practice Objectives

- Set custom phases in a project.
- Apply phases to elements.
- Apply phases to views.

In this practice, you will create phases and move the elements in the project to different phases. You will also draw new elements in different phases and view the changes with the phase filters, as shown in Figure 1–35.

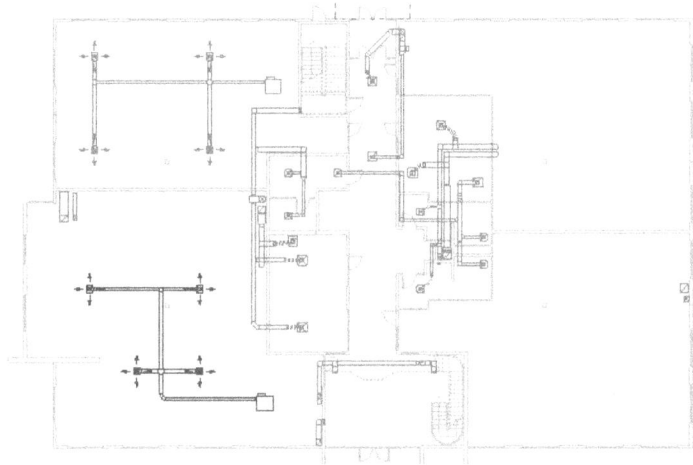

Figure 1–35

Task 1 - Set up phases.

1. In the practice files folder, open **Office-Phases-MEP.rvt**.

2. In the *Manage* tab>Phasing panel, click (Phases).

3. In the Phasing dialog box there are two phases, **Existing** and **New Construction**. You will add two phases used for tenant build out.

4. In the *Project Phases* tab, rename *New Construction* to **Tenant 1**.

© 2020, ASCENT - Center for Technical Knowledge®

5. In the *Insert* area, click **After** once and rename that phase to **Tenant 2**, as shown in Figure 1–36.

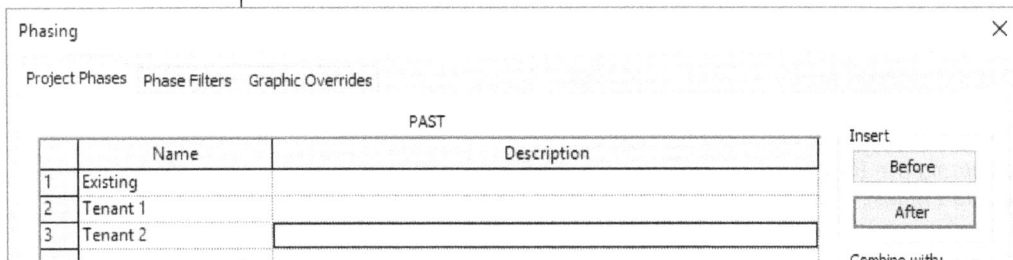

Phasing   ✕

Project Phases   Phase Filters   Graphic Overrides

PAST

	Name	Description	Insert
1	Existing		Before
2	Tenant 1		After
3	Tenant 2		

Combine with...

Figure 1–36

6. Click **OK** to close the dialog box.

7. Save the project.

Task 2 - Apply phases to elements.

1. Working in the Mechanical>HVAC>Floor Plans: **1 - Mech** view, select all of the existing ductwork and air terminals and filter out anything else, as shown in Figure 1–37.

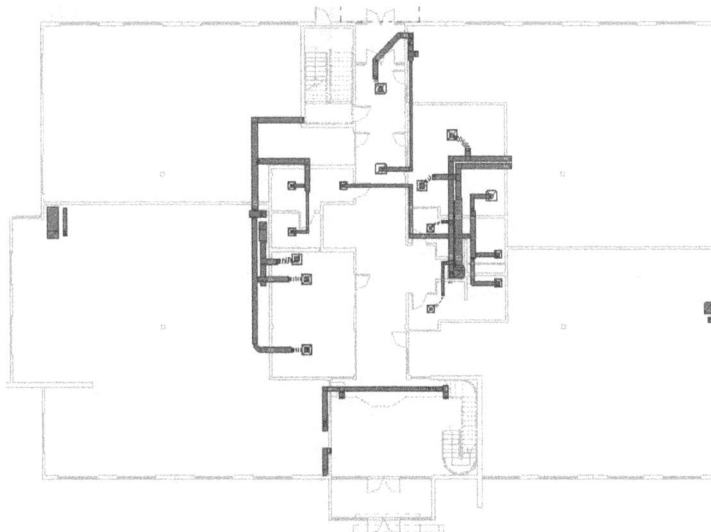

Figure 1–37

2. In Properties, change the *Phase Created* to **Existing** and note that the elements turn gray.

3. In Properties, with no element selected, note that the *Phase* is set to **Tenant 1**.

4. In the upper left area of the building, insert a VAV Unit, air terminals, and connecting ductwork, as shown in Figure 1–38.

*In this example, the VAV Unit's Elevation from Level is **10'-0"** above Level 1 and the air terminals are **8'-0"** above Level 1. The exact location is not critical.*

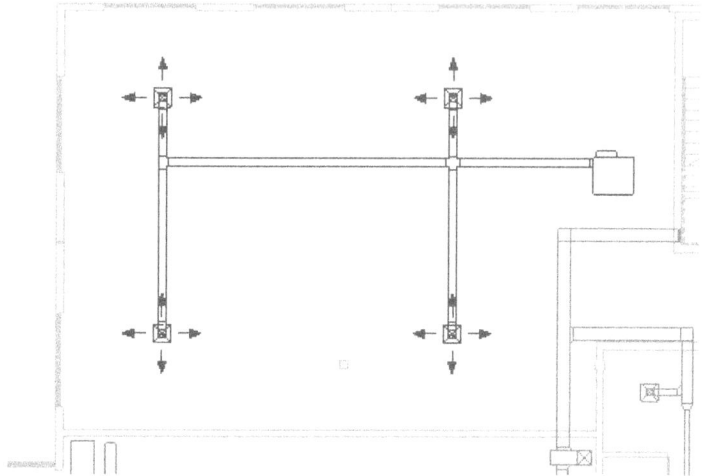

Figure 1–38

5. In Properties, with no elements selected, change the *Phase* to **Tenant 2** and draw an additional HVAC system. The Existing and Tenant 1 phases are grayed out and the current Phase displays in color, as shown in Figure 1–39.

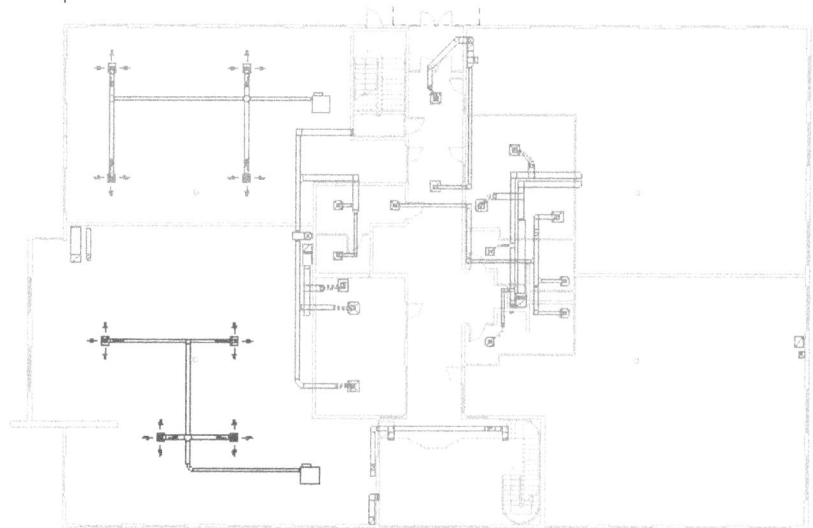

Figure 1–39

© 2020, ASCENT - Center for Technical Knowledge®

Task 3 - Apply phases to views.

1. Use **Duplicate with Detailing** and create three new views of **1- Mech** view. Rename them as **1 - Mech - Tenant 1**, **1 - Mech - Tenant 2.**, and **1 - Mech - Final**.

2. Rename *1 - Mech* to **1 - Mech - Existing** and open it.

3. In Properties, change the *Phase* to **Existing** as shown in Figure 1–40.

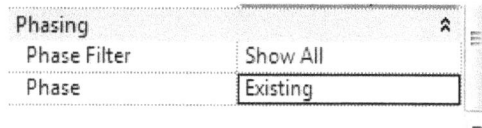

Figure 1–40

4. Open the **1 - Mech - Tenant 1** view and set the *Phase* to **Tenant 1**.

5. Open the **1 - Mech - Tenant 2** view and set the *Phase* to **Tenant 2**, if it is not already set.

6. Open the **1 - Mech - Final** view. Set the *Phase Filter* to **Show Complete** and the Phase to **Tenant 2**, as shown in Figure 1–41.

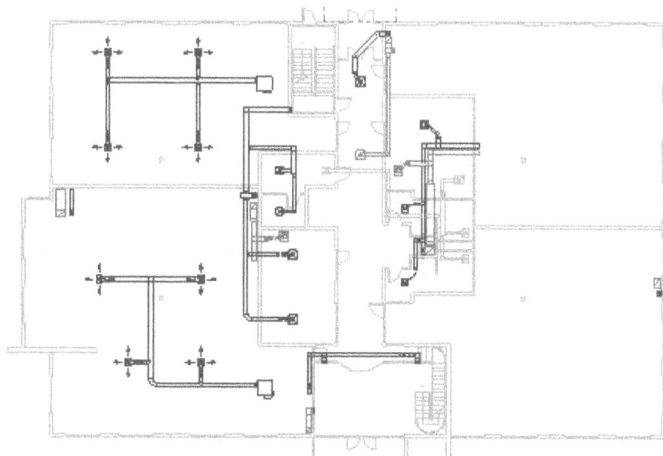

Figure 1–41

7. Save and close the project.

1.2 Working with Groups

Groups are collections of one or more components in a specific configuration. Once a group is created, it will appear in the Project Browser in the Groups section. These groups can be placed in multiple locations with a single command, similarly to placing a family. If you edit a group, those changes will reflect in every instance of that group placed in the model. For example, if you are creating a hotel lobby, you can create a seating group (as shown in Figure 1–42) and then copy the group rather than placing the individual furniture components.

Groups are rarely used in MEP projects as systems do not work in groups.

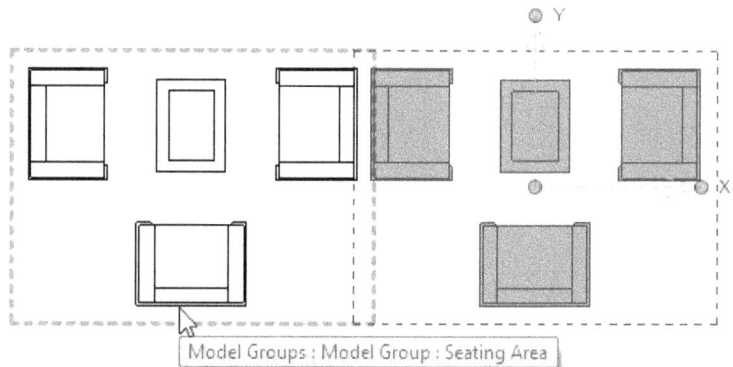

Model Groups : Model Group : Seating Area

Figure 1–42

There are three types of groups:

- **Model Groups:** Consists of model elements only.

- **Detail Groups:** Consists of detail or annotation elements only, including detail components, dimensions, tags, etc.

- **Model Groups with Attached Detail Groups:** Consists of a model group with the associated detail group attached to it.

- Model groups can be scheduled including the Count, Types, Reference Level and Origin Level Offset, as shown in Figure 1–43

<Model Groups Schedule>			
A	B	C	D
Count	Type	Reference Level	Origin Level Offset
3	Three Trees	Level 1	0' - 0"
2	Three Trees	Level 2	0' - 0"
4	Two Trees	Level 1	0' - 0"
2	Two Trees	Level 2	0' - 0"

Figure 1–43

© 2020, ASCENT - Center for Technical Knowledge®

Creating Groups

You can create groups by selecting elements and then using the **Group** command or by starting the command first and then adding the elements to the group. If you start the command first, anything you insert or draw during the process of creating the group is added to it.

How To: Create a Group Using Preselected Elements

1. Select the elements you want to include in the group.
2. In the *Modify | Multi-Select* tab>Create panel, click

   [⊡] (Create Group) or type **GP**.

If only Detail elements are selected, a similar dialog box opens. If you select both Model and Detail elements, you are prompted to name both the Model Group and the Attached Detail Group.

3. Enter a name in the Create Model Group dialog box, as shown in Figure 1–44. If you want to modify the group before creating it, select **Open in Group Editor**.

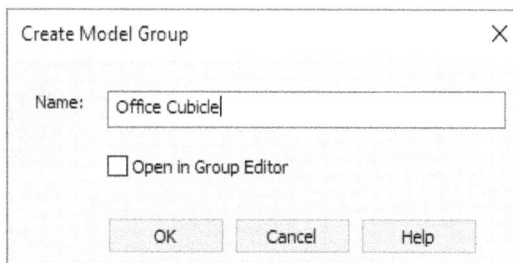

Figure 1–44

4. Click **OK** to create the group.
5. By default, the group origin is at the center of the group. Click and drag the origin to a new location, as shown in Figure 1–45. The new origin is used by any new instances of the group.

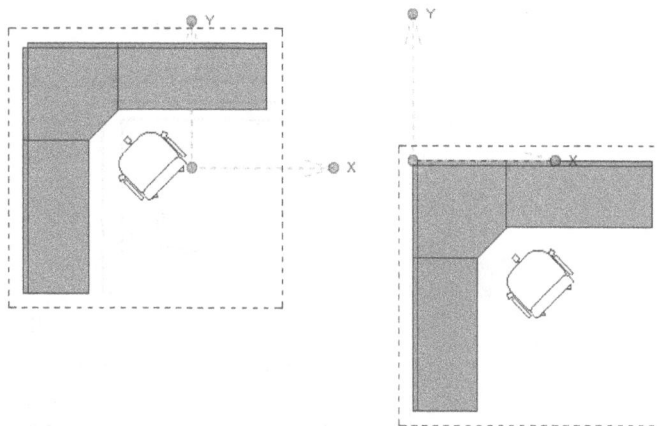

Figure 1–45

- Most elements can be grouped, including walls, components, and annotation, as long as the elements are compatible with each other.

- If you include a window, door, or other host-based element in a group, you need to place it on the type of host it is looking for.

How To: Create a Group and Add Elements

1. In the *Architecture* or *Structure* tab>Model panel, expand ⌨ (Model Group) and click ⌨ (Create Group).
2. In the Create Group dialog box, name the group and specify the type of group, either **Model** or **Detail**, as shown in Figure 1–46.

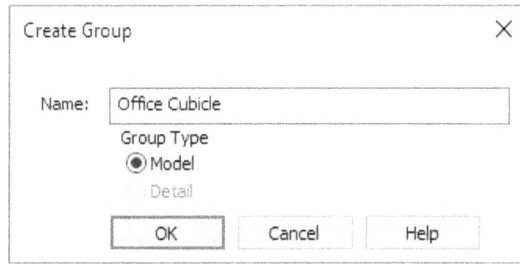

Create Group   ✕

Name: Office Cubicle

Group Type
◉ Model
　 Detail

OK   Cancel   Help

Figure 1–46

3. Click **OK**.
4. The Group Editor opens with the Edit Group panel, as shown in Figure 1–47.

Elements that are not part of the group are grayed out.

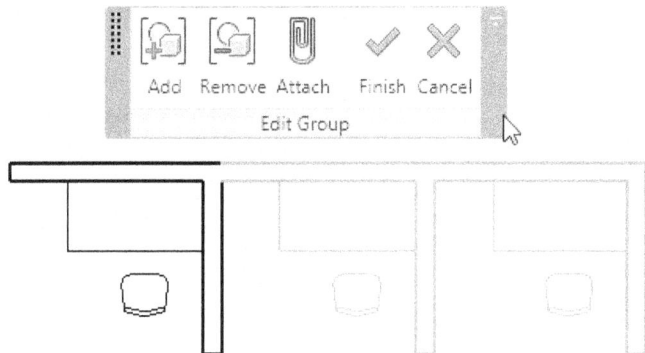

Add   Remove   Attach   Finish   Cancel

Edit Group

Figure 1–47

5. Add elements to the group.

- Click ⌨ (Add) or type **AP** and select any existing elements you want to include in the group.

© 2020, ASCENT - Center for Technical Knowledge®

*The type of elements that you can select or insert depends on the Group Type (**Model** or **Detail**).*

- Anything you draw or insert while in the Group Editor is added to the group.

- If you copy added elements, they will become a part of the group.

- Click [G] (Remove) or type **RG** to remove existing elements from the group. The elements are not removed from the project unless you delete them.

- To add or remove multiple elements from the group, hold <Ctrl> when selecting the elements.

- Click [U] (Attach) or type **AD** to add detail elements to a model group. The Create Model Group and Attached Detail Group dialog box displays as shown in Figure 1–48. The *Model Group Name* is preset and you are required to add the *Attached Detail Group Name*.

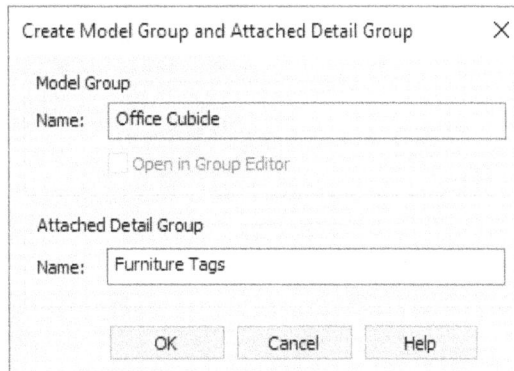

*You cannot select detail elements with **Add** when editing a model group.*

Create Model Group and Attached Detail Group

Model Group

Name: Office Cubicle

☐ Open in Group Editor

Attached Detail Group

Name: Furniture Tags

OK   Cancel   Help

Figure 1–48

Using Groups in a Project

You can add groups to a project by selecting them in the Project Browser, in the *Groups* node, and dragging them into the view, as shown in Figure 1–49. You can also use the Place Group commands.

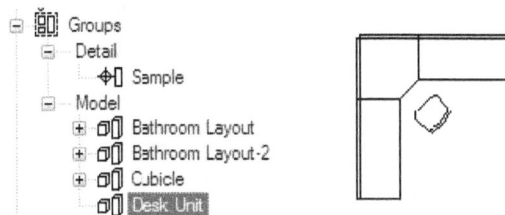

Groups
  Detail
    Sample
  Model
    Bathroom Layout
    Bathroom Layout-2
    Cubicle
    Desk Unit

Figure 1–49

- If a model group has a detail group, you need to attach it separately.

How To: Add Groups from the Ribbon

1. **Model Groups:** In the *Architecture* or *Structure* tab>Model panel, expand

   [⊡] (Model Group) and click [⊡] (Place Model Group).
   Detail Groups: In the *Annotate* tab>Detail panel, expand

   [A] (Detail Group) and click [A] (Place Detail Group).
2. In Properties, in the Type Selector, select the group you want to add.
3. Click in the drawing screen to place the group. You can add multiple copies.

- If you selected a model group with a hosted element (such as a door or window) that does not include the host (wall), you can only place one group at a time.

- In some cases, when there are hosted and non-hosted elements in the same group, pick in the model to place the group and then move it so that the hosted element is on the correct host as shown in Figure 1–50. In the *Modify | Model Groups* tab>Edit Pasted panel, click ✔ (Finish).

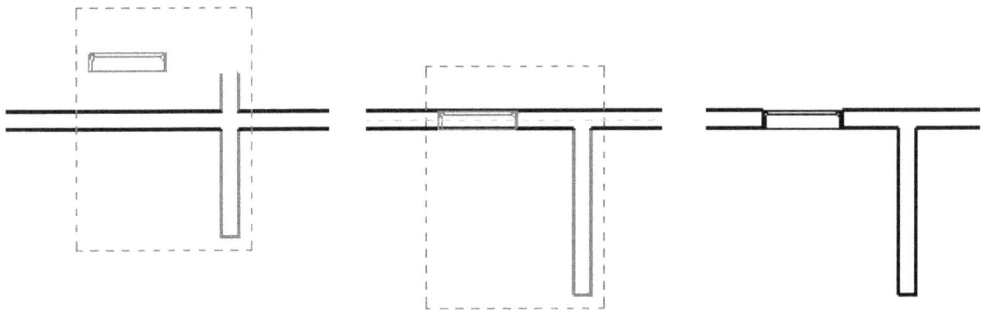

Figure 1–50

How To: Attach Detail Groups to Model Groups

1. Select a model group that has a related detail group.
2. In the *Modify | Model Groups* tab>Group panel, click

   [▦] (Attached Detail Groups).

© 2020, ASCENT - Center for Technical Knowledge®

3. In the Attached Detail Group Placement dialog box, select the detail groups that you to want attach to the model group, as shown in Figure 1–51.

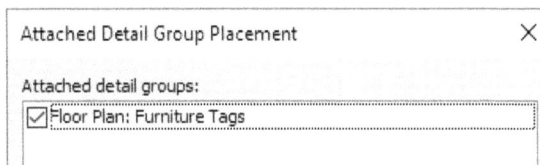

Figure 1–51

4. Click **OK**.

- Remove detail groups from the model group by following the same process, but clearing the checkmark next to the group name in the dialog box.

Modifying Groups

Groups can be copied, moved, mirrored, and rotated like most elements in the program. You can also cut, copy, and paste them to the clipboard. Some properties can be changed for individual group instances, but most changes will need to be done in Group Edit mode. Group Edit mode can be activated by selecting a group and clicking 🖉 (Edit Group) from the *Modify | Model Groups* tab>Group Panel or typing **EG**. Any changes made in Group Edit mode will be reflected in every instance of that group type.

- If you no longer want an instance of a group to act as a group, as shown in Figure 1–52, select it and click 🖉 (Ungroup) in the Group panel or type **UG**.

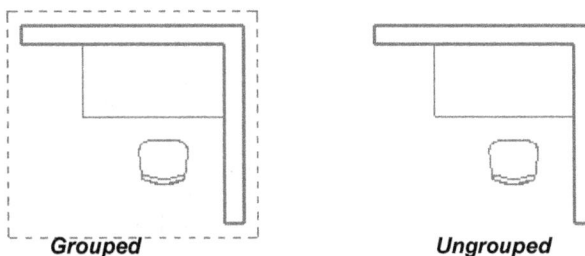

Grouped   *Ungrouped*

Figure 1–52

- To delete a group definition from the project, you must first delete all instances of the group in the project. You can then select the group name in the Project Browser, right-click, and select **Delete**.

- To modify individual instances of a group, use <Tab> to select one element in a group. Then, click on the *Group Member* icon (as shown in Figure 1–53), to remove the element from that instance of the group

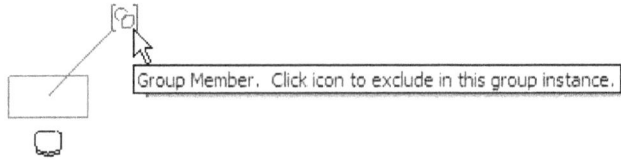

Group Member. Click icon to exclude in this group instance.

Figure 1–53

- To change a group to a different group, select one or more groups. In Properties, from the Type Selector, select another group's name, as shown in Figure 1–54.

If you are replacing groups, it helps to match the groups' origin and rotation.

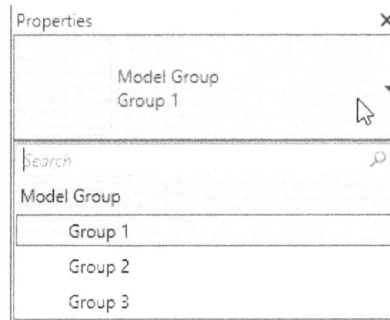

Figure 1–54

- To make duplicates of groups, in the Project Browser, *Groups* node, right-click on the group and select **Duplicate**, or in

  Properties, click ⊞ (Edit Type) and **Duplicate...**. When you have copied the new group, make any changes as shown in Figure 1–55.

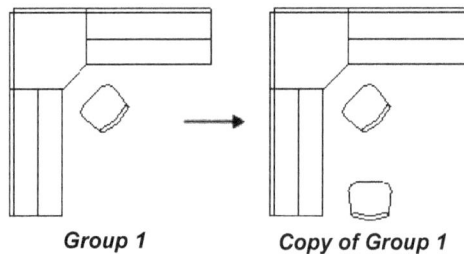

Group 1   *Copy of Group 1*

Figure 1–55

© 2020, ASCENT - Center for Technical Knowledge®

- To modify all instances of a group definition, in the *Modify |*
  Model Groups tab>Group panel, click ⬚ (Edit Group) or
  type **EG**. In the Group Editor, make changes to the group as
  required. Use the floating Edit Group toolbar to add, remove,
  and attach elements.

- To change the name of a group, right-click on the group in the
  Project Browser and select **Rename**.

Groups in Other Projects

You can save groups to a project file to use in other projects.
Groups can also be converted to links. This creates an additional
project file but also changes the group in your project to link to
the new project file.

How To: Save a Group as a File

1. In the *File* tab, expand ⬚ (Save As), expand
   ⬚ (Library), and click ⬚ (Group).
2. In the Save Group dialog box, in the Group To Save
   drop-down list, select a group as shown in Figure 1–56.

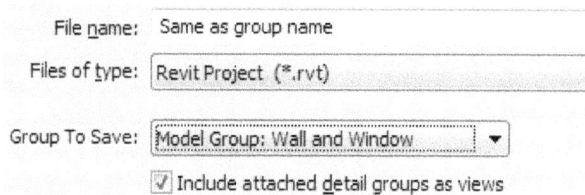

File name:	Same as group name
Files of type:	Revit Project (*.rvt)
Group To Save:	Model Group: Wall and Window ▼
	☑ Include attached detail groups as views

Figure 1–56

3. Navigate to the folder in which you want to store the group.
4. Click **Save**.

How To: Use a File as a Group in a Project

1. Open the file in which you want to load the group.

2. In the *Insert* tab>Load from Library panel, click ⬚ (Load As
   Group).
3. In the Load File as Group dialog box, navigate to the folder in
   which the file is stored and select the file.
4. Click **Open**. The file is added as a group definition in the
   current project.
5. Insert the group in the project using one of the methods for
   placing a group.

*Alternatively, right-click
on the group name in
the Project Browser and
select **Save Group**.*

- Any Autodesk® Revit® project or family file can be loaded as a group.

- Because a group can be saved as a standard RVT project file, the groups can be edited externally from any project.

- When you reload the group into a project, an alert box opens if you are loading a file with the same name as an existing group in your project, as shown in Figure 1–57.

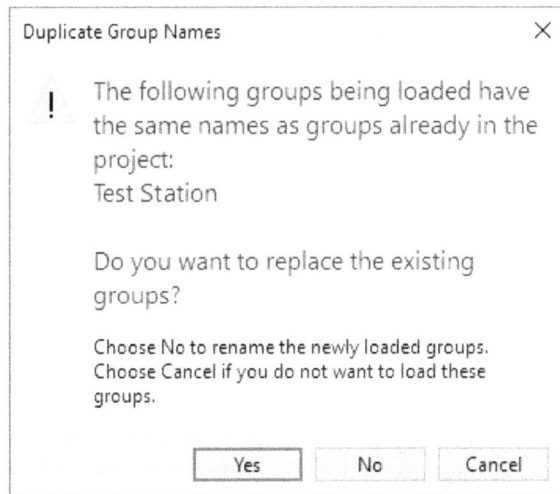

Figure 1–57

- Click **Yes** to replace all instances of the group with the new information.
- Click **No** to bring in the group with a new name incremented from the previous name.
- Click **Cancel** to stop the process.

How To: Use an Open File as a Group in Another Open File

1. Open a project file in which you want to place a group.
2. Open the file that you want to use as a group.
3. In the *Architecture* or *Structure* tab> Model panel, expand

   ![icon] (Model Group) and click ![icon] (Load as Group into Open Projects).
4. In the Load into Projects dialog box, select the projects into which you want the currently active project to be loaded as a group.
5. Click **OK**. The group is now available for use in the other projects.

© 2020, ASCENT - Center for Technical Knowledge®

How To: Convert a Group to a Link

1. Select the group that you want to convert to a link.
2. In the *Modify | Model Groups* tab>Group panel, click
   ⬚ (Link).
3. In the Convert to Link dialog box shown in Figure 1–58, select the method that you want to use.

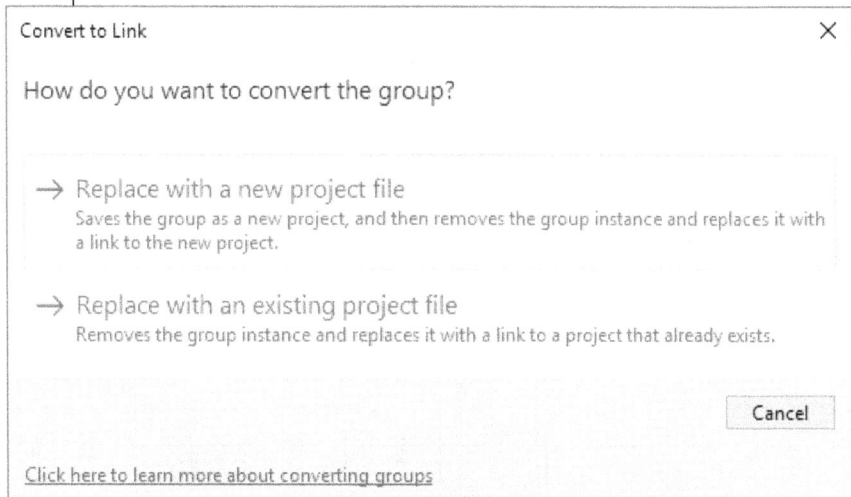

Convert to Link   ✕

How do you want to convert the group?

→ Replace with a new project file
   Saves the group as a new project, and then removes the group instance and replaces it with
   a link to the new project.

→ Replace with an existing project file
   Removes the group instance and replaces it with a link to a project that already exists.

                                                              Cancel

Click here to learn more about converting groups

Figure 1–58

4. If you create a new project file, the Save Group dialog box opens. Specify the name and location of the file and click **Save**. The group becomes a linked model in the host project.

5. If you replace it with an existing project file, the Open dialog box opens. Locate the file you want to use to replace the existing group, and click **Open**. The new project file becomes a linked model in the host project.

Practice 1d

Work with Groups - Architectural

Practice Objectives

- Create a group.
- Place instances of a group in a project.
- Edit a group definition.
- Modify an instance of a group.

In this practice, you will group components, copy the group, modify the group, and modify one instance, as shown in Figure 1–59. You will also save the group to be used in another project.

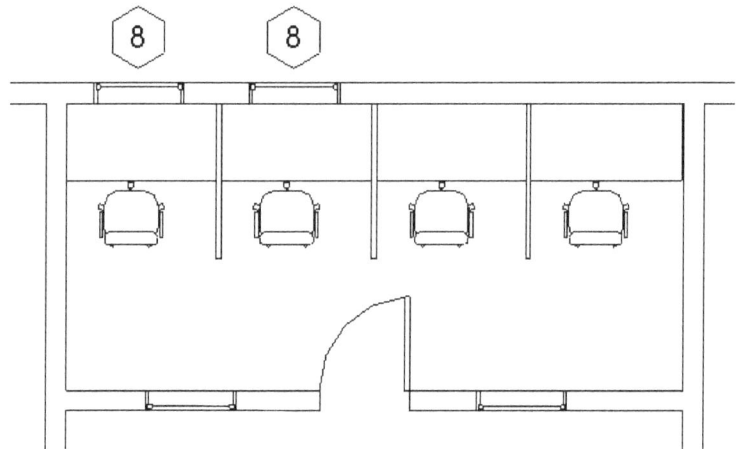

Figure 1–59

Task 1 - Create a group.

1. In the practice files folder, open **Testing-Room-A.rvt**.

2. Add the component **Desk: 60" x 30"** against the left back wall.

3. Place a **Chair-Executive** in front of the desk and a **Cube Panel: 60" x 66"** to the right of it. These components are already loaded into the project.

Click ▩ (Thin Lines) in the Quick Access Toolbar or View tab> Graphics panel to help you see the exact placement of the panel.

© 2020, ASCENT - Center for Technical Knowledge®

4. Place a window with a tag in the wall directly in front of the desk, as shown in Figure 1–60.

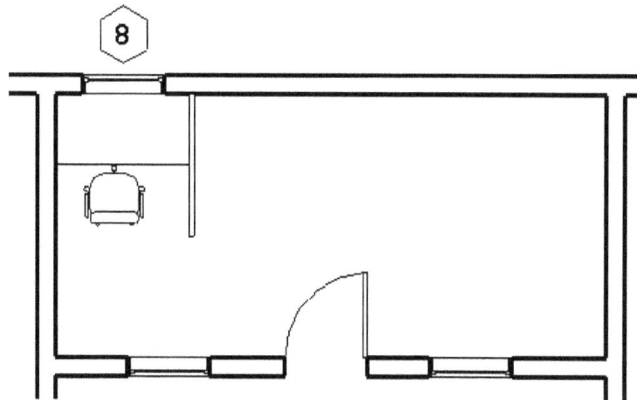

Figure 1–60

5. Select the three components, the window, and the tag.

6. In the *Modify | Multi-Select* tab>Create panel, click (Create Group).

7. Name the Model Group as **Test Station**, and the Attached Detail Group as **Tags**, as shown in Figure 1–61.

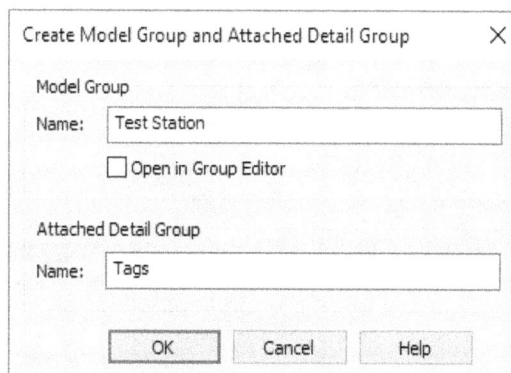

Figure 1–61

8. Click on the Modify Group Origin control and drag it to the upper left corner of the desk, as shown in Figure 1–62.

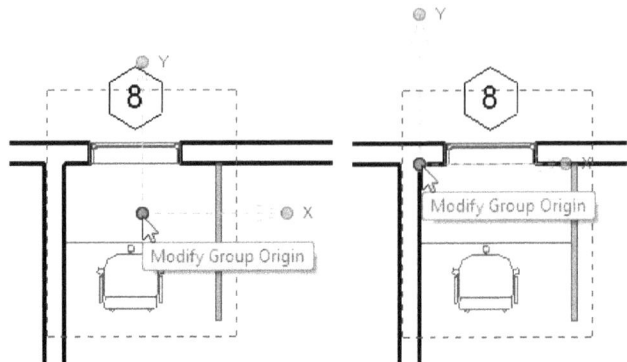

Figure 1–62

9. Click in an empty area in the view to clear the selection.

Task 2 - Place instances of the group.

1. In the *Architecture* tab>Model panel, expand (Model Group) and click (Place Model Group).

2. In the Type Selector, verify that the name of the current group is **Test Station**.

3. Place a copy of the group directly to the right of the original group. Everything but the tag should be inserted.

Because this is a model group that includes hosted elements (the window) without the host element (the wall), you can only place one group at a time.

4. Click (Finish) to complete the process.

5. Select the new group.

6. In the *Modify | Model Groups* tab>Group panel, click (Attached Detail Groups).

7. In the Attached Detail Group Placement dialog box, select the **Floor Plan: Tags** detail group and click **OK**. The tag is added to the instance of the group.

© 2020, ASCENT - Center for Technical Knowledge®

Task 3 - Edit the group definition.

1. The current group is still selected. In the *Modify | Model Groups* tab>Group panel, click [icon] (Edit Group).

2. In the Group Editor, in the floating Edit Group panel, click [icon] (Remove).

3. Select the window to remove it from the group.

4. Click [icon] (Finish).

5. The windows are no longer involved in the groups but they are still in the drawing. A warning box opens indicating that the attached detail group is removed, as shown in Figure 1–63. Click **OK**.

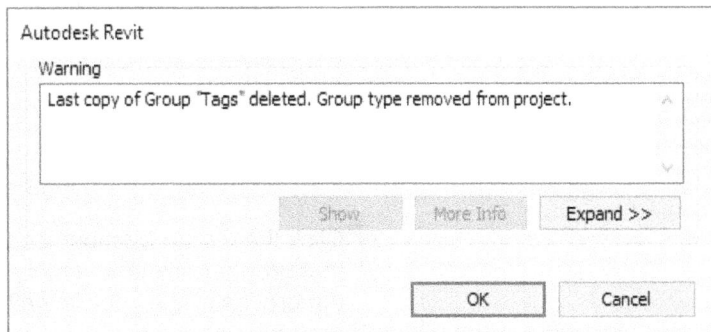

Autodesk Revit

Warning

Last copy of Group "Tags" deleted. Group type removed from project.

Show   More Info   Expand >>

OK   Cancel

Figure 1–63

6. Place two more copies of the model group **Test Station** in the project. The new groups do not include the window.

Task 4 - Modify an instance of a group.

1. The last group does not need the last cubicle wall. Hover over the element that you want to exclude, press <Tab> until it highlights, and select the element, as shown in Figure 1–64.

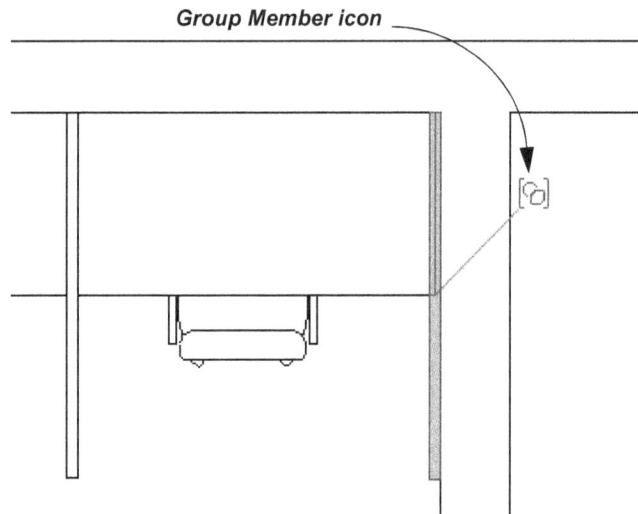

Group Member icon

Figure 1–64

2. Click the Group Member icon to only exclude the wall from that group. Click in an empty space in the view to complete the process. The cubicle wall is only excluded from that group.

Task 5 - Save the group as a file.

1. In the Project Browser, in the *Groups*>**Model** node> right-click on the **Test Station** group name and select **Save Group**.

2. In the Save Group dialog box, navigate to your practice files folder and save the group with the same name as the group. The group is now a .RVT and can be loaded as a group into other projects.

3. Save and close the project.

© 2020, ASCENT - Center for Technical Knowledge®

Practice 1e | Work with Groups - Structural

Practice Objectives

- Create a group of model and annotation elements.
- Add copies of the group to a project.
- Modify the elements of one group.

In this practice, you will place bracing in a framing elevation and then group the bracing and its associated tags as shown in Figure 1–65. You will also add the group to another bay and copy it to further bays. You will ungroup and modify one group and use the elements to create another group.

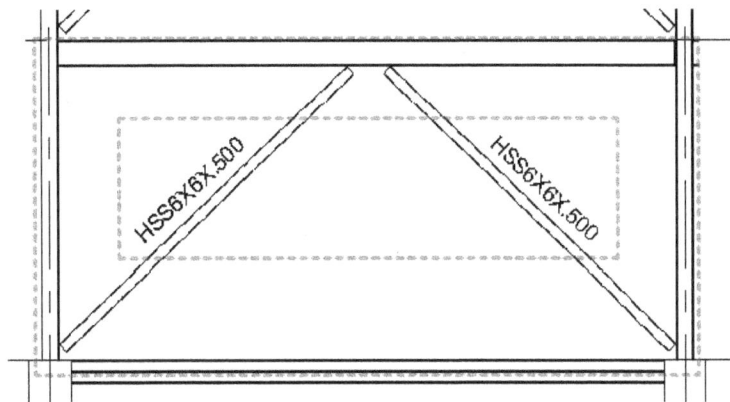

Figure 1–65

Task 1 - Add bracing.

1. In the practice files folder, open **Syracuse-Suites-Groups-S.rvt**.

2. Open the **Elevations (Framing Elevation): West Bracing** view.

3. Zoom in to display the **00 GROUND FLOOR** and **TOS-1ST FLOOR** level heads.

4. In the *Structure* tab>Structure panel, click 🔲 (Brace).

5. In the *Modify | Place Brace* tab>Tag panel, click ⌐① (Tag on Placement) to toggle it on.

6. In the Type Selector, select **HSS Hollow Structural Section: HSS6X6X.500**.

7. Draw from the midpoint of the beam located on the 1st Floor to the centerline of the column at the base, as shown in Figure 1–66. Do the same on both sides.

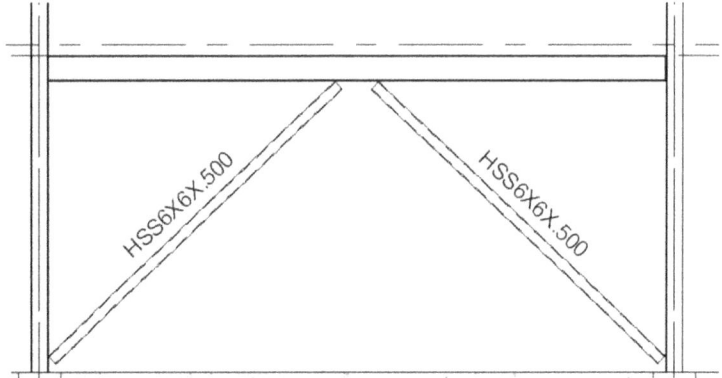

Figure 1–66

8. Press \<Esc\> or click   (Modify) to end the command.

Task 2 - Create and place groups.

1. Select the braces and the tags.

2. In the *Modify | Multi Select* tab>Create panel, click (Create Group).

3. Name the groups **Brace Frame A-Model** and **Brace Frame A-Tags**, as shown in Figure 1–67.

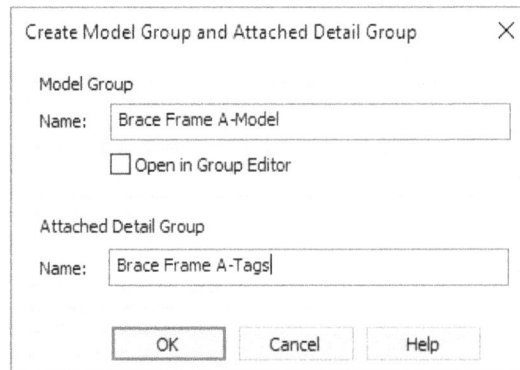

Figure 1–67

© 2020, ASCENT - Center for Technical Knowledge®

4. Click **OK**.

5. Move the Group Origin to the lower left corner, as shown in Figure 1–68, to change the insertion point of the group. Make sure to snap to the intersection of the column and beam.

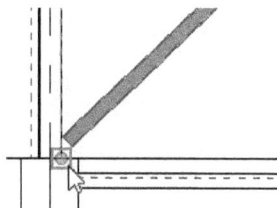

Figure 1–68

6. Place an instance of the new group. In the *Structure* tab>Model panel, expand [icon] (Model Group) and click [icon] (Place Model Group).

7. In the Type Selector, verify that the name of the current group is **Brace Frame A - Model**.

The group moves into the correct location once you complete the process.

8. In the *Modify | Model Groups* tab>Edit Pasted panel, click [icon] (Finish).

9. Select the group. In the *Modify | Model Groups* tab>Group panel, click [icon] (Attached Detail Groups).

10. In the Attached Detail Group Placement dialog box, select **Elevation: Brace Bay A-Tags**.

11. Click **OK**. The bracing is labeled.

12. Copy the group with details up to the 13th floor. Select both the brace group and the attached detail group.

13. In the *Modify | Multi-Select* tab>Modify panel, click [icon] (Copy).

14. In the Options Bar, select **Multiple** and **Constrain** (this forces the copy to only move horizontally or vertically).

15. Copy the groups to every level up to the 13th floor.

16. Zoom in on the 13th Floor bay, as shown in Figure 1–69. This bay requires a modification because of the difference in elevation.

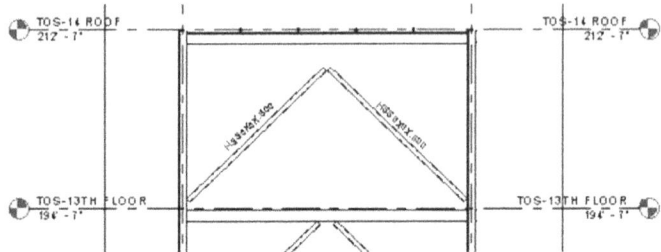

Figure 1–69

17. Select the bracing, and in the *Modify | Model Groups* tab> Group panel, click (Ungroup).

18. Modify the braces so that they extend up to the framing, as shown in Figure 1–70.

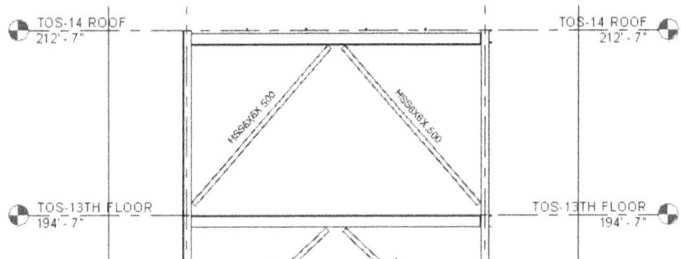

Figure 1–70

19. Select the revised braces and tags. Create two groups named **Brace Frame B-Model** and **Brace Frame B-Tags**.

20. Save and close the project.

© 2020, ASCENT - Center for Technical Knowledge®

1.3 Using Design Options

Design Options are isolated collections of model elements used to provide a variety of potential configurations for a certain area within a building model. For example, you could design several roof options, window layouts, or entry areas and view each in context with the main building.

Design Option Sets are used to gather and manage Design Options for a certain area. Areas of the building model that do not have Design Options are called the Main Model. Each Design Option Set will have a primary option that will show by default when viewing the main model. For example, you can create a Design Option Set with options for an A-frame roof (as shown in Figure 1–71) and a curved roof (as shown in Figure 1–72).

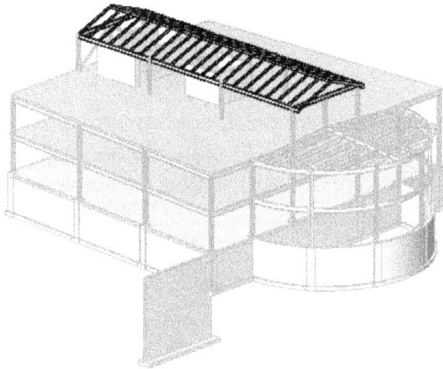

Figure 1–71

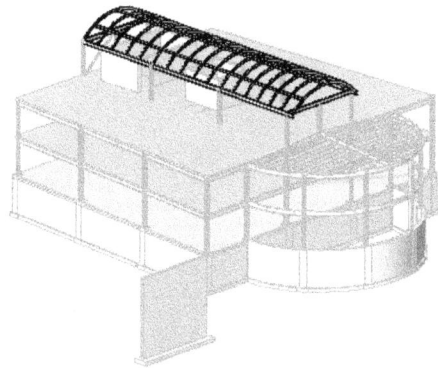

Figure 1–72

- Design Option Sets and Design Options are automatically organized alphanumerically by name. Make sure to use a clear and descriptive naming convention to help you efficiently manage your Design Option Sets.

- If the Design Option affects multiple disciplines and requires Design Options in more than one model, such as a roof that requires both architectural and structural options, coordinating these naming conventions across the models can help prevent confusion when incorporating the final decisions.

Design Options are rarely used in MEP projects as systems do not work in the options.

The Design Options tools are located in the *Manage* tab>Design Options panel, as shown in Figure 1–73, with additional tools in the Status Bar, as shown in Figure 1–74.

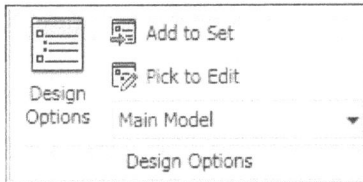

Figure 1–73

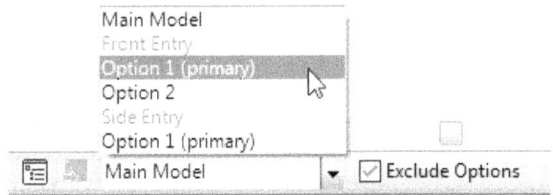

Figure 1–74

- When you have decided which Design Option will be the final configuration, you will set that option to be **primary** and accept the primary Design Option for that Design Option Set. When you accept the primary Design Option, all other Design Options within that Design Option Set will be permanently deleted and all model elements within them removed from the model.

- If other members of your team are linking your model into theirs, only the primary Design Option will be visible to them. Non-primary Design Options will not be available for interdisciplinary coordination.

How To: Set Up Design Options

1. In the *Manage* tab>Design Options panel, or in the Status Bar, click (Design Options). The Design Options dialog box opens, as shown in Figure 1–75.

© 2020, ASCENT - Center for Technical Knowledge®

You can have as many Option Sets and Options under a set, as needed. Each set always contains one primary option.

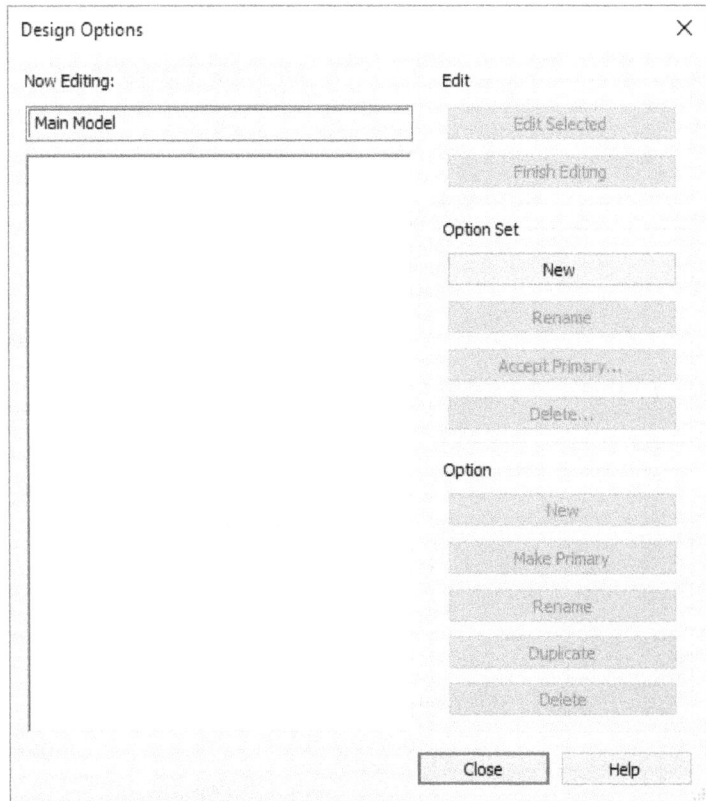

Figure 1–75

2. In the *Option Set* area, click **New**. An Option Set with a corresponding option is created, as shown in Figure 1–76.

Figure 1–76

3. To add more options, select the Option Set title. In the *Option* area in the dialog box, rename the Options so that they convey more information. In the *Option Set* or *Option* area, click **Rename** and type a new name in the Rename dialog box. As you create more Design Options and Sets, they will be automatically sorted in alphanumeric order.

4. Once you have defined the Option Sets and Options, you are ready to work on the various options. Close the dialog box.

- When you have added Design Options, you can set the current Design Option in the *Manage* tab or in the Status Bar, as shown in Figure 1–77.

Figure 1–77

How To: Add Existing Elements to Design Options

1. In the Status Bar or *Manage* tab>Design Options panel, verify that **Main Model** displays as the Active Design Option, as shown in Figure 1–78.

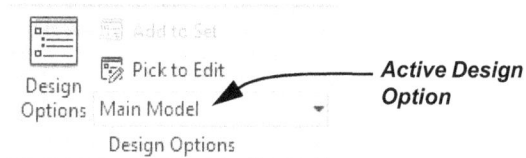

Figure 1–78

2. Select the elements that you want to include in a Design Option. The *Modify* tab displays.
3. Switch to the *Manage* tab. In the Design Options panel, click

   (Add to Set).
4. In the Add to Design Option Set dialog box, expand the drop-down list and select the **Design Option Set**. Then select the option(s) to which you want to add the selected elements, as shown in Figure 1–79. You can select more than one option.

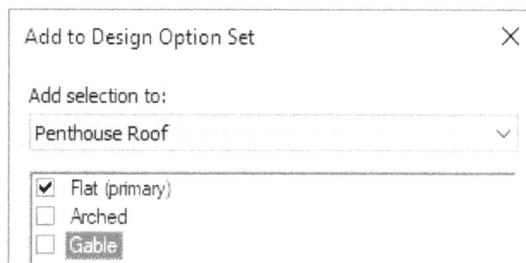

Figure 1–79

© 2020, ASCENT - Center for Technical Knowledge®

5. Click **OK** to close the dialog box. The elements are added to the option and can no longer be modified in the main model.

• Only elements in the primary Design Option display in standard views. They cannot be selected unless you clear **Exclude Options** in the Status Bar before selecting.

• **Exclude Options** is only available in the Status Bar if Design Options have been set up in the project.

How To: Add New Elements to a Design Option

1. Set a Design Option to be current in the Active Design Option drop-down list in the Status Bar or in the *Manage* tab>Design Options panel, as shown in Figure 1–80.

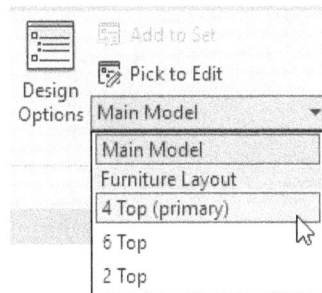

Figure 1–80

2. Only the elements that are part of the Active Design Option display in black. Elements in the main model are grayed out, as shown in Figure 1–81.

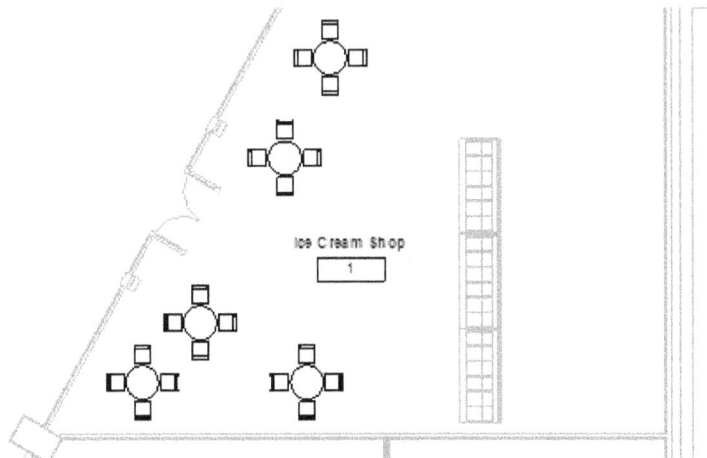

Figure 1–81

3. Use standard commands to add or modify elements in the Design Option. For example, you can move the seating and add other chairs and tables for the Ice Cream Shop shown in Figure 1–81.
4. Set the *Active Design Option* to **Main Model** when you are finished.

Viewing Design Options

You can set up views and view templates that specify Design Options. These can then be used to quickly see the various Design Options without having to edit them, as shown in Figure 1–82.

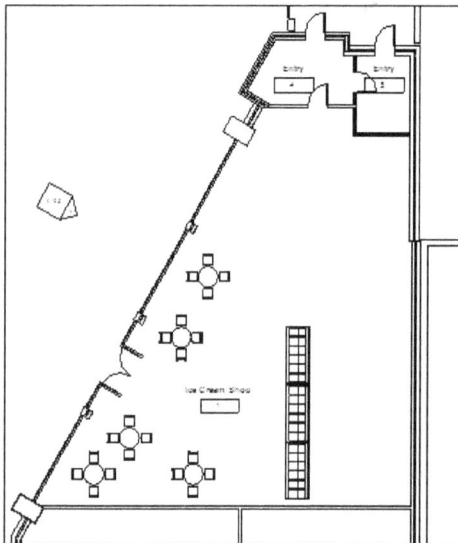

Design Option 1

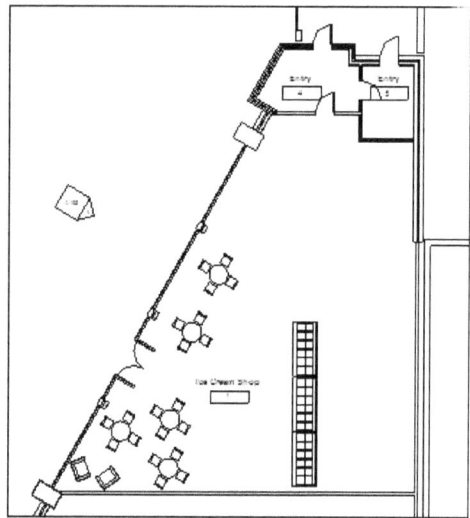

Design Option 2

Figure 1–82

How To: View Design Options

1. Create a view (a 3D view, plan, elevation, or section) that displays the information that you want to present.
2. In the view, open the Visibility/Graphic Overrides dialog box (type **VV** or **VG**) or set the current view's Design Option from the *Graphics* area in Properties.

© 2020, ASCENT - Center for Technical Knowledge®

3. In the *Design Options* tab, in the drop-down list for each Design Option Set, select a Design Option, as shown in Figure 1–83. **<Automatic>** displays the primary option or the option that is currently being edited. Setting the view to a specific choice, displays that option regardless of what is being edited.

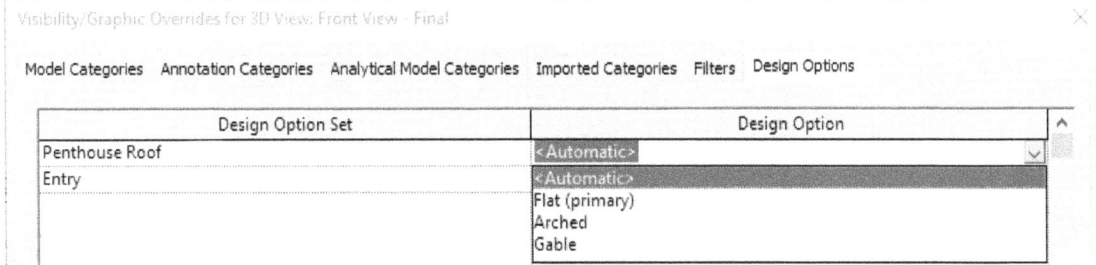

Figure 1–83

- If elements in a Design Option display in a view, you can click

   (Pick to Edit) in the Design Options panel and select one of the elements to activate that option.

How To: Incorporate Design Options into the Main Model

Once you have decided which Design Option will become part of the final model, you will incorporate it into the Main Model and remove all of the secondary Design Options within that set.

1. Set the *Active Design Option* to **Main Model**.

2. In the *Manage* tab, select (Design Options) from the Design Options panel.

3. Select the option you want to keep and click **Make Primary** from the *Options* area of the dialog box.

4. Select the Option Set and click **Accept Primary...** from the *Options Set* area of the dialog box.

*If you did not set the active option to Main Model, you must select **Finish Editing** in the dialog box to continue the process.*

5. An alert box opens as shown in Figure 1–84, warning you that all secondary options are going to be deleted. Click **Yes** if you are sure.

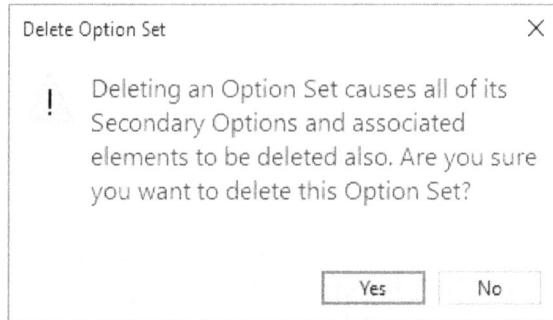

Delete Option Set	✕
❗ Deleting an Option Set causes all of its Secondary Options and associated elements to be deleted also. Are you sure you want to delete this Option Set?	
	Yes No

Figure 1–84

6. If views are associated with the option, you are prompted to delete the associated view, as shown in Figure 1–85. Select the view(s) and click **Delete**.

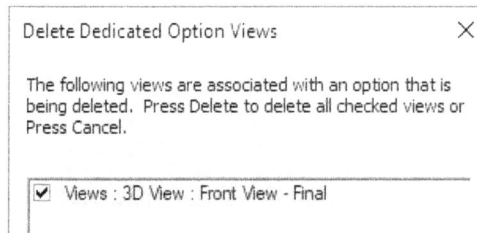

Delete Dedicated Option Views	✕
The following views are associated with an option that is being deleted. Press Delete to delete all checked views or Press Cancel.	
☑ Views : 3D View : Front View - Final	

Figure 1–85

7. Close the Design Options dialog box.

© 2020, ASCENT - Center for Technical Knowledge®

Practice 1f

Use Design Options - Architectural

Practice Objectives

- Set up Design Options.
- Draw elements in each Design Option.
- Create views that show variations on the Design Options.

In this practice, you will create two Design Option Sets and several Options for each set. You will modify the elements in each Design Option and create views that display the Options, such as the one shown in Figure 1–86.

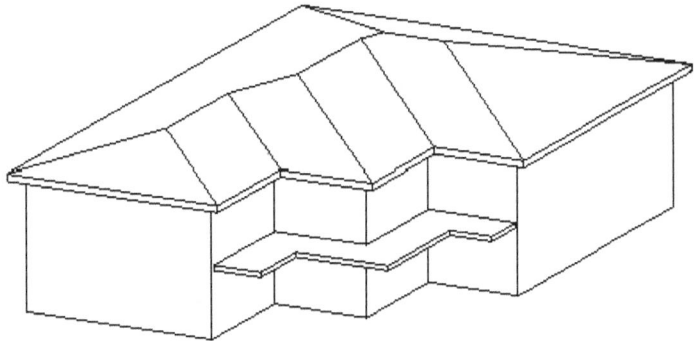

Figure 1–86

- As Design Options are rarely used with the Autodesk Revit system tools, MEP engineers can work through this practice to understand the process.

Task 1 - Set up Design Options.

1. In the practice files folder, open **Office-Entry-A.rvt**.

2. In the *Manage* tab>Design Options panel or in the Status Bar, click ▤ (Design Options).

3. In the Design Options dialog box, in the *Options Set* area, click **New**. A new Option Set and a primary option is created, as shown in Figure 1–87.

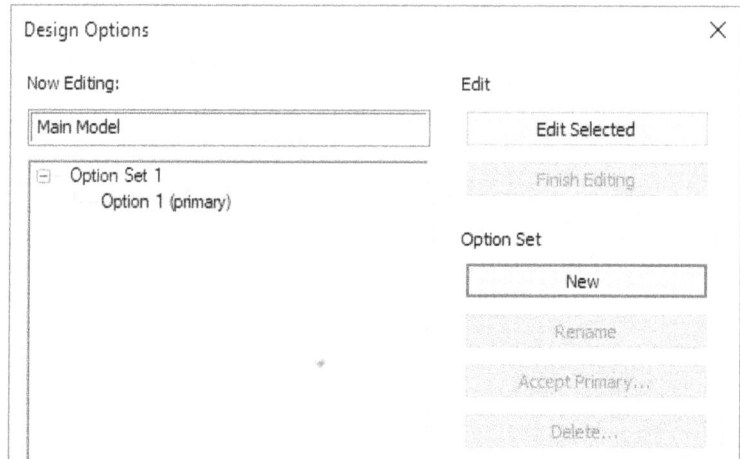

Figure 1–87

4. Select **Option Set 1** and in the *Option Set* area, click **Rename**. In the Rename dialog box set its name as **Main Roof** and click **OK**.

5. Select **Option 1 (primary)** and in the *Option* area, click **Rename**. Set its name as **Shallow Slope**.

6. In the *Option* area, click **New** twice to add two more options and name them as **Medium Slope** and **Steep Slope**.

7. Create an additional Option Set as **Entry Roof** and three options, as shown in Figure 1–88.

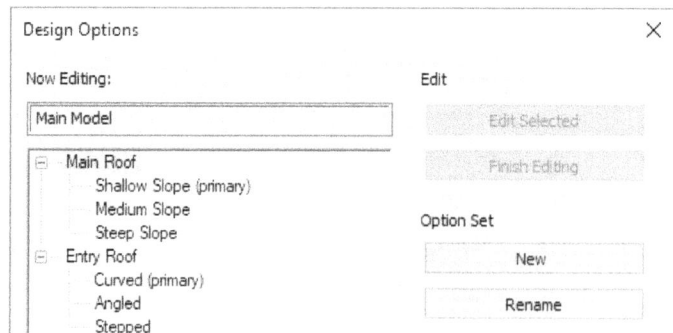

Figure 1–88

8. In the **Main Roof** option set, select **Medium Slope** and click **Make Primary**.

9. Close the Design Options dialog box.

© 2020, ASCENT - Center for Technical Knowledge®

Task 2 - Create main roof Design Options.

1. In the Design Options panel or in the Status Bar, in the Active Design Option drop-down list, activate the **Main Roof> Medium Slope (primary)** option. The main model is grayed out.

2. Open the **Floor Plans: Roof** view.

3. Draw a **Roof by Footprint** with a deep overhang, all edges sloped, and a medium slope angle, as shown in Figure 1–89.

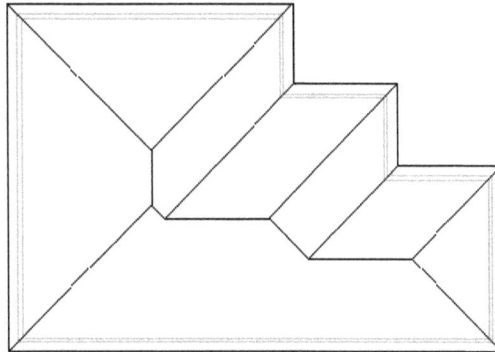

Figure 1–89

4. When prompted to attach highlighted walls to the roof, select **Don't Attach**.

5. View the roof in a 3D view.

6. Return to the **Floor Plans: Roof** view. Set the *Active Design Option* to **Main Roof>Steep Slope**. The main model is grayed out and the medium sloped roof is toggled off.

7. Draw a **Roof by Footprint** using a steep slope angle.

8. Repeat the process using the **Shallow Slope** Design Option and a shallow roof slope.

9. Set the *Active Design Option* to **Main Model**. The primary **Medium Slope** design option displays.

10. Duplicate the default 3D view three times and rename them as **3D Steep Roof**, **3D Medium Roof**, and **3D Shallow Roof**.

11. Within each of the new 3D views, open the Visibility/Graphic Overrides dialog box and click on the *Design Options* tab. Set the Design Option Set **Main Roof** to each of the entry roof option types.

12. Save the project.

Task 3 - Create entry roof Design Options.

1. Return to the **Floor Plans: Roof** view.

2. Set the *Active Design Option* to **Entry Roof>Curved**. The main model and main roof are grayed out.

3. Open the **Floor Plans: Level 2** view.

4. Use **Roof by Footprint** to draw a curved flat roof over the entry area, as shown in Figure 1–90. You can use the **Spline** or **Arc** sketch options. Use a generic roof type.

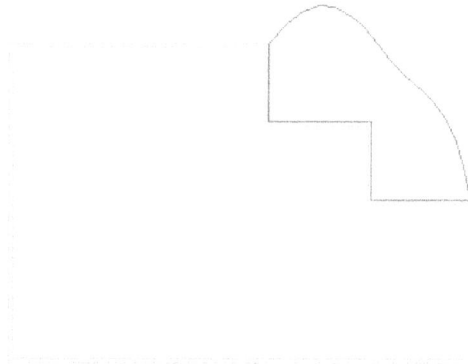

Figure 1–90

5. Create additional flat roofs similar to those shown in Figure 1–91 for the **Angled** and **Stepped** entry roof options.

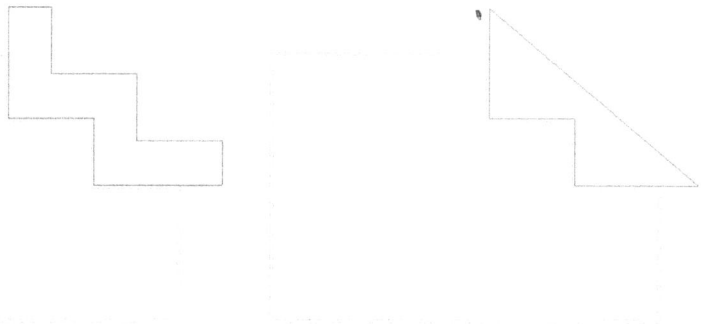

Figure 1–91

6. Return the Design Option to the **Main Model**. The curved roof displays as it is the primary design option that shows at this level.

7. Save the project.

© 2020, ASCENT - Center for Technical Knowledge®

Task 4 - Create views of Design Options.

1. Switch to the **3D Medium** view that displays both the main and entry roofs. Type **VV** to open the Visibility/Graphic Overrides dialog box.

2. In the *Design Options* tab, specify the Design Options for the sets as follows and click **OK**:

   • Main Roof - Medium Slope (primary)
   • Entry Roof - Curved (primary)

3. The 3D view should show the curved and medium sloped roofs, as shown in Figure 1–92.

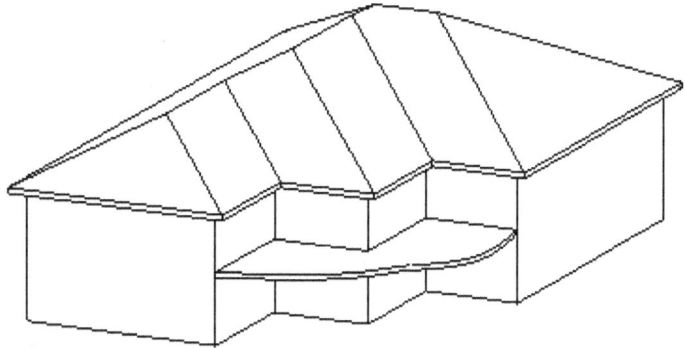

Figure 1–92

4. Open the Visibility/Graphic Overrides dialog box and in the *Design Options* tab, specify the Design Options for the sets as follows and click **OK**. The new layout displays as shown in Figure 1–93.

- Main Roof - Shallow Slope
- Entry Roof - Stepped

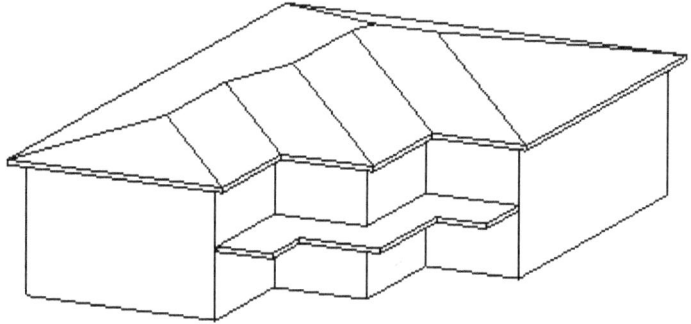

Figure 1–93

5. Repeat this with other combinations of the options if you have time.

6. Switch between the various views to see the differences.

7. Save and close the project.

© 2020, ASCENT - Center for Technical Knowledge®

Practice 1g | Use Design Options - Structural

Practice Objectives

- Set up Design Options.
- Draw elements in each Design Option.
- Create views that show variations on the Design Options.

In this practice, you will create two Design Options. You will modify the elements in each Design Option and create views that display the Options, such as the one shown in Figure 1–94.

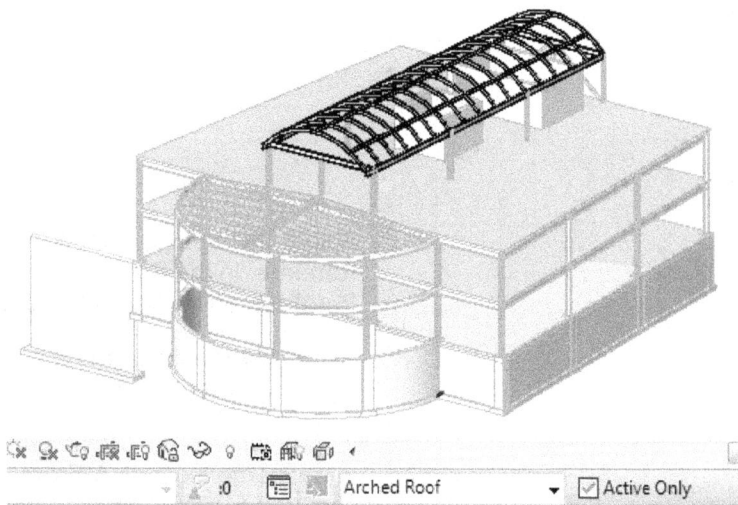

Figure 1–94

Task 1 - Set up Design Options.

1. In the practice files folder, open **Office-Options-S.rvt**.

2. In the *Manage* tab>Design Options panel or in the Status Bar, click (Design Options).

3. In the Design Options dialog box, in the *Options Set* area, click **New**. A new Option Set and a primary option are created, as shown in Figure 1–95.

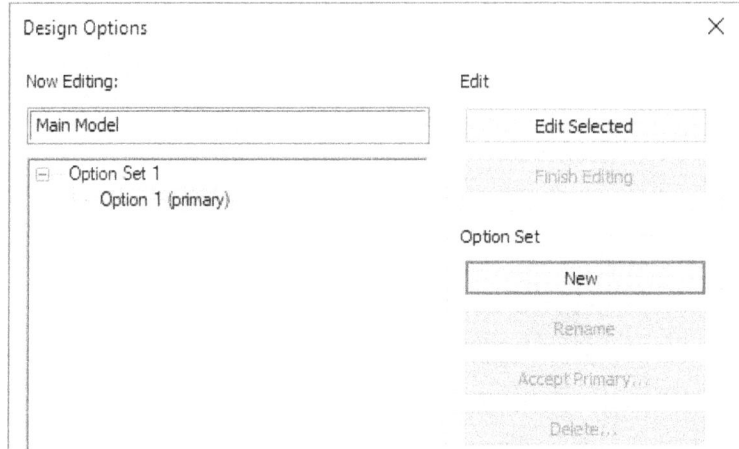

Figure 1–95

4. Select **Option Set 1** and in the *Option Set* area, click **Rename**. In the Rename dialog box, set the new name as **Penthouse Roof** and click **OK**.

5. Select **Option 1 (primary)** and in the *Option* area, click **Rename**. Set the name as **Flat Roof**.

6. In the *Option* area, click **New** twice to add two more options and rename them as **A-Frame Roof** and **Arched Roof**, as shown in Figure 1–96.

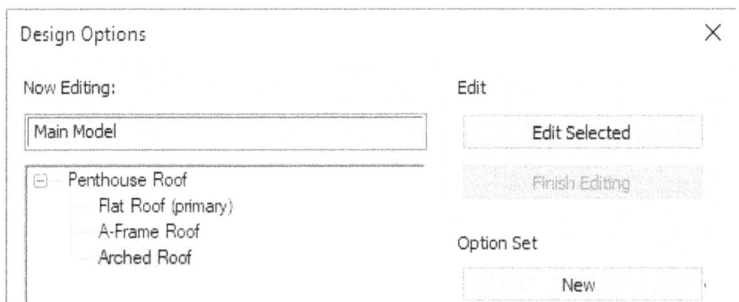

Figure 1–96

7. Close the Design Options dialog box.

8. Save the project.

© 2020, ASCENT - Center for Technical Knowledge®

Task 2 - Add structural elements to Design Options.

1. In the Design Options panel or in the Status Bar, in the Active Design Option drop-down list, activate the **Flat Roof (primary)** option. The model is grayed out.

2. Open the **Structural Plans: Penthouse** view.

3. In the Status Bar, clear the **Active Only** option. This enables you to select elements that are not in the current Design Option.

4. Select all of the structural elements but not the tags, openings, and walls, as shown in Figure 1–97.

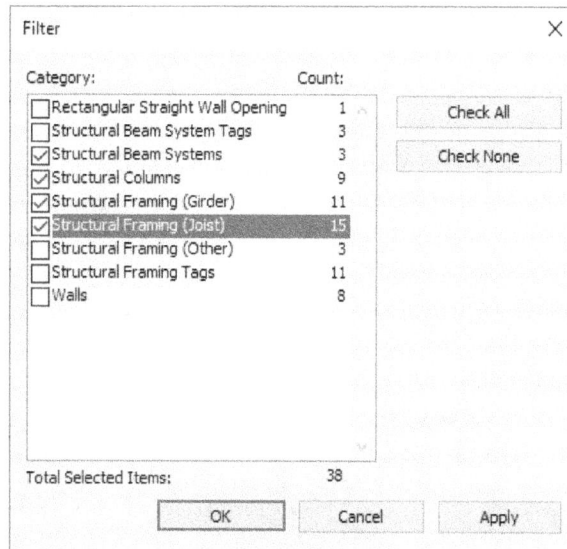

Filter		×
Category:	**Count:**	
☐ Rectangular Straight Wall Opening	1	Check All
☐ Structural Beam System Tags	3	
☑ Structural Beam Systems	3	Check None
☑ Structural Columns	9	
☑ Structural Framing (Girder)	11	
☑ Structural Framing (Joist)	15	
☐ Structural Framing (Other)	3	
☐ Structural Framing Tags	11	
☐ Walls	8	
Total Selected Items:	38	
OK	Cancel	Apply

Figure 1–97

5. In the *Manage* tab>Design Options panel or in the Status Bar, click 🔲 (Add to Set). If needed, close the Warning dialog box.

6. Switch to a 3D view that displays the elements in this design option, as shown in Figure 1–98.

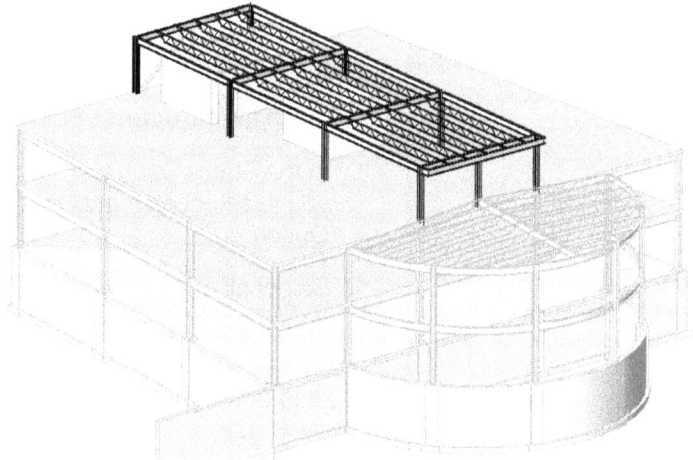

Figure 1–98

7. While still in the 3D view, switch to the **A-Frame Roof** design option. The elements in the previous design option are also available for this design option.

8. Create two additional penthouse roofs similar to those shown in Figure 1–99 for the **A-Frame Roof** and **Arched Roof** options.

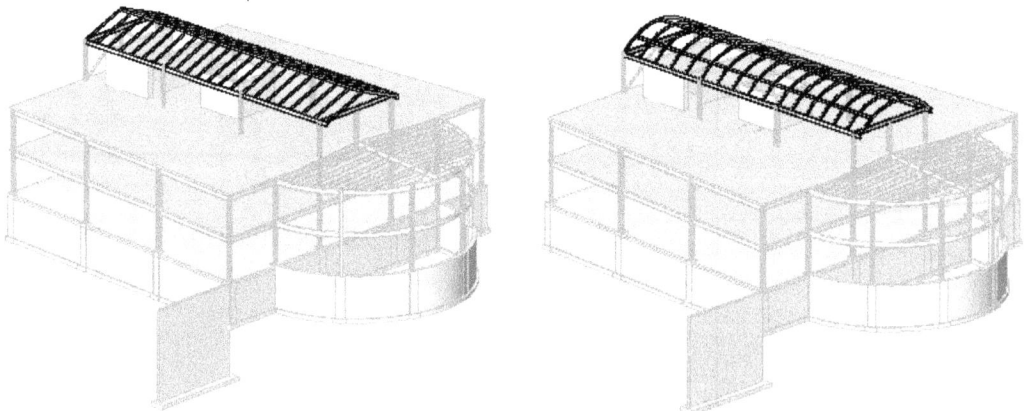

Figure 1–99

9. Return the Design Option to the **Main Model**. The flat roof displays as it is the primary design option that shows at this level.

10. Save the project.

© 2020, ASCENT - Center for Technical Knowledge®

Task 3 - Create views of Design Options.

1. Open the 3D view **Front View**. All of the building with the Flat Roof (primary) design option should display.

2. Duplicate the view and rename it **3D Flat Roof**.

3. Type **VV** to open the Visibility/Graphic Overrides dialog box.

4. In the *Design Options* tab, set the Design Option for the Penthouse roof to **Flat Roof (primary)**. Click **OK** and the view remains as is.

5. Duplicate this 3D view and rename it **3D A-Frame Roof**.

6. In the Visibility/Graphic Overrides dialog box, change the Design Option to **A-Frame Roof**. Click **OK** and note that the building updates with the A-Frame Roof design option in place of the flat roof as shown in Figure 1–100.

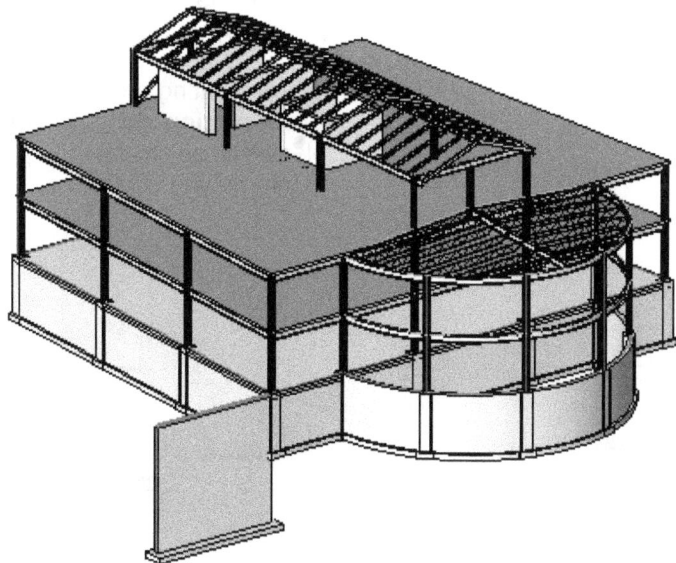

Figure 1–100

7. Repeat one more time creating a 3D View for the **Arched Roof** design option.

8. Switch between the various views to see the differences.

9. Save the project.

Chapter Review Questions

1. When you want to demolish some elements, as shown in Figure 1–101, in what phase should the elements be?

    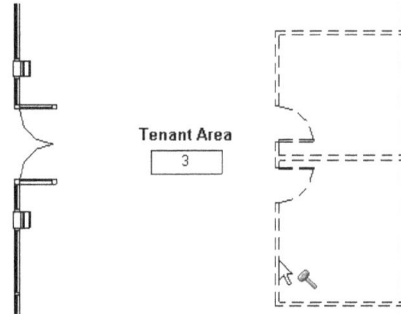

    Figure 1–101

    a. New Construction

    b. Existing

    c. Demolition

2. When creating a view that displays the *Phase* **New Construction** along with the existing and demolished elements, as shown in Figure 1–102, which of the Phase Filters do you use?

    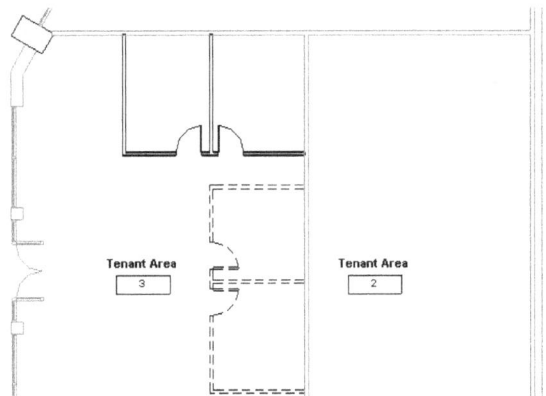

    Figure 1–102

    a. Show All

    b. Show Complete

    c. Show Previous + New

    d. Show Previous Phase

© 2020, ASCENT - Center for Technical Knowledge®

3. Which statement is true regarding *Option Set* and *Option*, as shown in Figure 1–103?

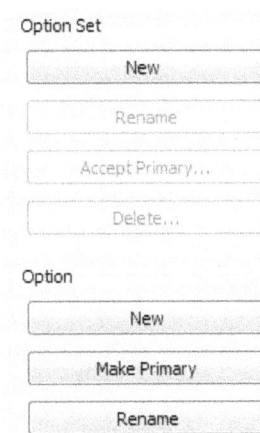

Option Set

> New
>
> Rename
>
> Accept Primary...
>
> Delete...

Option

> New
>
> Make Primary
>
> Rename

Figure 1–103

a. You can have multiple Options but only one Option Set.

b. You can have multiple Options without any Option Set.

c. You can have multiple Option Sets without any Options.

d. You can have multiple Option Sets with multiple Options in each set.

4. What method do you use to set up a view to display specific Design Options?

a. Set the Active Design Option.

b. Select the Primary Design Option in the Design Options dialog box.

c. Open the Visibility/Graphic Overrides dialog box and select the option from the *Design Options* tab.

d. Right-click in the view and select **Override Graphics** in view>By Element.

5. Which are the type of groups that can be created in the Autodesk Revit software? (Select all that apply.)

a. Annotative

b. Component

c. Detail

d. Model

6. While in the Group Editor, how do you add tags to an existing group, as shown in Figure 1–104, so that it creates a related detail group?

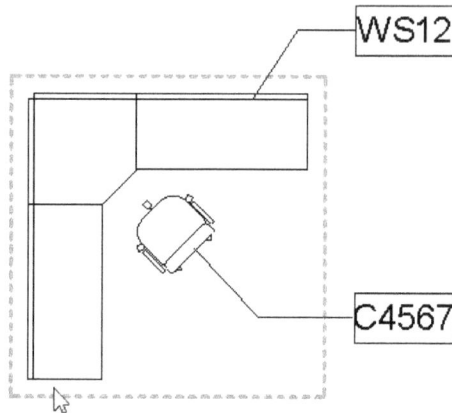

Figure 1–104

a. Drag and drop the tags group from the Project Browser on to the group.

b. In the Edit Group panel, click [icon] (Add) and select existing tags.

c. In the Edit Group panel, click [icon] (Attach) and specify the tags group.

d. Add the tags using [icon] (Tag by Category).

7. You can use the contents of an entire open project as a group in another project.

a. True

b. False

© 2020, ASCENT - Center for Technical Knowledge®

Command Summary

Button	Command	Location
Phases		
	Demolish	• **Ribbon**: *Modify* tab>Geometry panel
	Phases	• **Ribbon**: *Manage* tab>Phasing panel
Design Options		
Main Model ▾	**Active Design Option**	• **Ribbon**: *Manage* tab>Design Options panel • **Status Bar**
	Add to Set	• **Ribbon**: *Manage* tab>Design Options panel • **Status Bar**
	Design Options	• **Ribbon**: *Manage* tab>Design Options panel • **Status Bar**
	Pick to Edit	• **Ribbon**: *Manage* tab>Design Options panel
Groups		
	Add to Group	• **Floating Panel**: Edit Group • **Shortcut**: AP (when a group is in edit mode)
	Attach Detail	• **Floating Panel**: Edit Group • **Shortcut:** AD (when a group is in edit mode)
	Attached Detail Groups	• **Ribbon**: *Modify	Model Groups* tab> Group panel
	Create Group (Detail)	• **Ribbon**: *Annotate* tab>Detail panel> expand Detail Group • **Shortcut: GP**
	Create Group (elements selected)	• **Ribbon**: *Modify* contextual tab>Create panel • **Shortcut: GP**
	Create Group (Model)	• **Ribbon**: *Architecture* or *Structure* tab> Model panel>expand Model Group • **Shortcut: GP**
	Edit Group	• **Ribbon**: *Modify	Model (or Detail) Groups* tab>Group panel • **Shortcut:** EG (when a group is selected)

	Load as Group	• **Ribbon:** *Insert* tab>Load from Library panel
	Load as Group into Open Projects	• **Ribbon:** *Architecture* or *Structure* tab>Model panel> expand Model Group
	Place Detail Group	• **Ribbon:** *Annotate* tab>Detail panel> expand Detail Group
	Place Model Group	• **Ribbon:** *Architecture* or *Structure* tab>Model panel> expand Model Group
	Remove from Group	• **Floating Panel:** Edit Group • **Shortcut: RG** (when a group is in edit mode)
	Ungroup	• **Ribbon:** *Modify	Model* (or *Detail*) *Groups* tab>Group panel • **Shortcut: UG** (when a group is selected)

© 2020, ASCENT - Center for Technical Knowledge®

Linking Models

Linking Autodesk® Revit® models into other models is a common practice for many reasons and can provide a variety of benefits. The most common reasons to link one model into another are:

- Interdisciplinary coordination, such as linking an architectural model into a structural model to reference during the Structural Design process.

- Having multiple buildings on a single site, such as a college campus that has a variety of different buildings.

- Having identical buildings in multiple locations on a single site, such as an office park where the same building is used, but may be oriented differently.

- Having units that are used multiple times within a single project, such as patient rooms in a hospital, or multiple times across more than one project, such as a prototypical hotel guest room or lobby layout.

Linking models allows you to check for interferences in the design across multiple models, view information through a linked model, share information to any parties linking your model into theirs, and quickly identify or communicate design revisions. The Copy/Monitor tool will enable you to copy elements from a linked model into your own and will monitor them for any changes made to those elements in the original model so that you are alerted in the event of a revision.

Learning Objectives in This Chapter

- Link Autodesk Revit models into a host project.
- Modify link display settings in views.
- Copy and monitor elements from linked models.
- Use a Coordination Review to identify breaks in monitoring.
- Check interferences between elements in linked projects.

2.1 Linking Models

You can link an Autodesk® Revit® project into any other project. A linked model automatically updates if the original file is changed. This method can be used in many ways. For example, use this method when you have a number of identical buildings on one site plan, as shown in Figure 2–1. When you link one Revit model into another, the model that you are working in is called the *host* or *hosting* model, and the model that has been linked into the host model is called the *linked* model.

Figure 2–1

It is important to understand that when models are linked into a Revit project, that project remembers the paths so that the user does not have to relink the models every time they reopen their own model. This saves the user a great deal of time over the course of a project; however, it can also increase the amount of time it takes to open a model. The more linked models in a project, the longer it will take to open.

It is best practice, when linking models into one another, to use the same Revit version across all of the models.

Structural and MEP projects typically use the architectural model as the base for their projects. But there are times when an architect will link consultants' files into the architectural file as well.

© 2020, ASCENT - Center for Technical Knowledge®

- Architectural, structural, and MEP models created in the Autodesk® Revit® software can be linked to each other as long as they are from the same release cycle.

- When you use linked models, clashes between disciplines can be detected, and information can be passed between disciplines.

- Elements can be copied and monitored for even better coordination.

- Linked models can be constrained to elements in the host project and to each other. You can select references in linked models as a work plane and can schedule elements from the linked model in the host project.

Hint: Project Base Point

The origin of a project coordinate system is specified by the project base point, as shown in Figure 2–2. This should be set early in the project and before you start linking files together. It can be (but is not always) connected with the Survey Point, a secondary coordinate system used with shared coordinates. The internal origin, or startup location, never moves and is the internal coordinate system used for the base position for all of the model's elements.

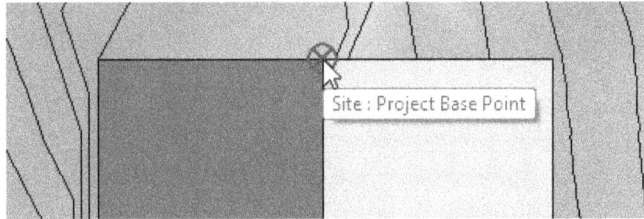

Site : Project Base Point

Figure 2–2

- Project base points and survey points are visible in the Site view of the default architectural template. You can toggle them on in any view. In the Visibility/Graphic Overrides dialog box, in the *Model Category* tab, expand the **Site** category.

- The Internal Origin is typically off in all views, but it can be toggled on through the Visibility/Graphic Overrides dialog box, in the *Model Category* tab under the **Site** category.

- A linked model's project base, survey, and internal origin points will be grayed out in the view, indicating they belong to the linked model. The host model's points display in color, as shown in Figure 2–3.

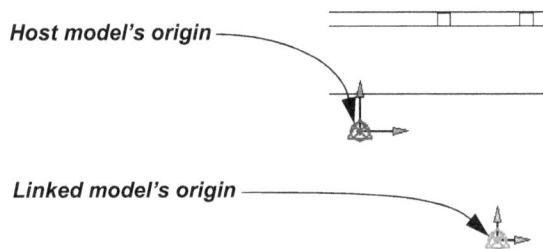

Host model's origin —

Linked model's origin —

Figure 2–3

- Spot Coordinates and Spot Elevations are relative to the project base point.

© 2020, ASCENT - Center for Technical Knowledge®

How To: Add a Linked Model to a Host Project

1. In the *Insert* tab>Link panel, click ⬛ (Link Revit).
2. In the Import/Link RVT dialog box, select the file that you want to link. Before opening the file, set the *Positioning*, as shown in Figure 2–4, and click **Open**.

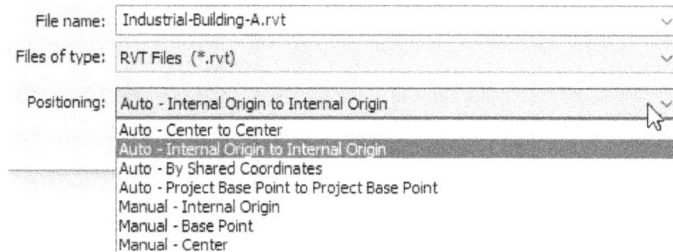

File name:	Industrial-Building-A.rvt
Files of type:	RVT Files (*.rvt)
Positioning:	Auto - Internal Origin to Internal Origin

Auto - Center to Center
Auto - Internal Origin to Internal Origin
Auto - By Shared Coordinates
Auto - Project Base Point to Project Base Point
Manual - Internal Origin
Manual - Base Point
Manual - Center

Figure 2–4

- Depending on how you decide to position the file, it is automatically placed in the file or you can manually place it with the cursor.

- The default positioning is **Auto - Internal Origin to Internal Origin**. The center of a linked model is the center of the geometry. Therefore, if you modify the extents of the original model, its exact location changes in the host project if you link **Center to Center**.

- **Auto - Project Base Point to Project Base Point** aligns the base points of the projects rather than the default origins.

- The software remembers the most recently used positioning type as long as you are in the same session of Autodesk Revit. (The CAD Links dialog box remembers the last positioning used as well, but separately from RVT Links)

- As the links are loading, do not click on the screen or click any buttons. The more links that are present in a project, the longer it takes to load.

- Linked models can be moved once you have placed them in the project. If you want to return them to the original location, right-click on the link and select either **Reposition to Project Base Point** or **Reposition to Internal Origin**, as shown in Figure 2–5

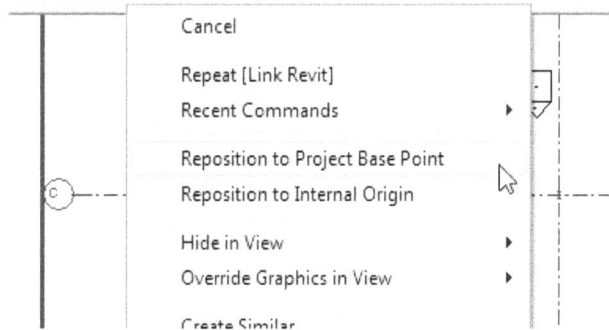

Figure 2–5

Hint: Preventing Linked Model from Being Moved

Once a linked model is in the correct location, you can lock it in place to ensure that it does not get moved by mistake, or prevent the linked model from being selected.

- To toggle off the ability to select links, in the Status Bar, click 🕱 (Select Links).

- To pin the linked model in place, select it and in the *Modify* tab>Modify panel, click 📌 (Pin).

- To prevent pinned elements from being selected, in the Status Bar, click 🕱 (Select Pinned Elements).

Multiple Copies of Links

Copied instances of a linked model are typically used when creating a master project with the same building placed in multiple locations, such as a university campus with several identical student residences, or with identical units, such as hospital rooms used multiple times within one building.

- Linked models can be copied, rotated, arrayed, and mirrored.

© 2020, ASCENT - Center for Technical Knowledge®

- You only link a model once, but you can place as many copies as are required into the host project. The copies are numbered automatically, and the name can be changed in Properties when the instance is selected. There is only one linked model, and the copies are additional instances of that link.

- When you have placed a link in a project, you can use the Project Browser, as shown in Figure 2–6, to drag and drop additional copies of the link into the project.

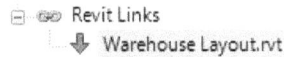

Figure 2–6

Annotation and Linked Models

Many annotations can be added to the host model that reference elements in the linked model. For example, in Figure 2–7, the walls columns and grids are part of the linked model but the dimensions and tags are placed in the host project.

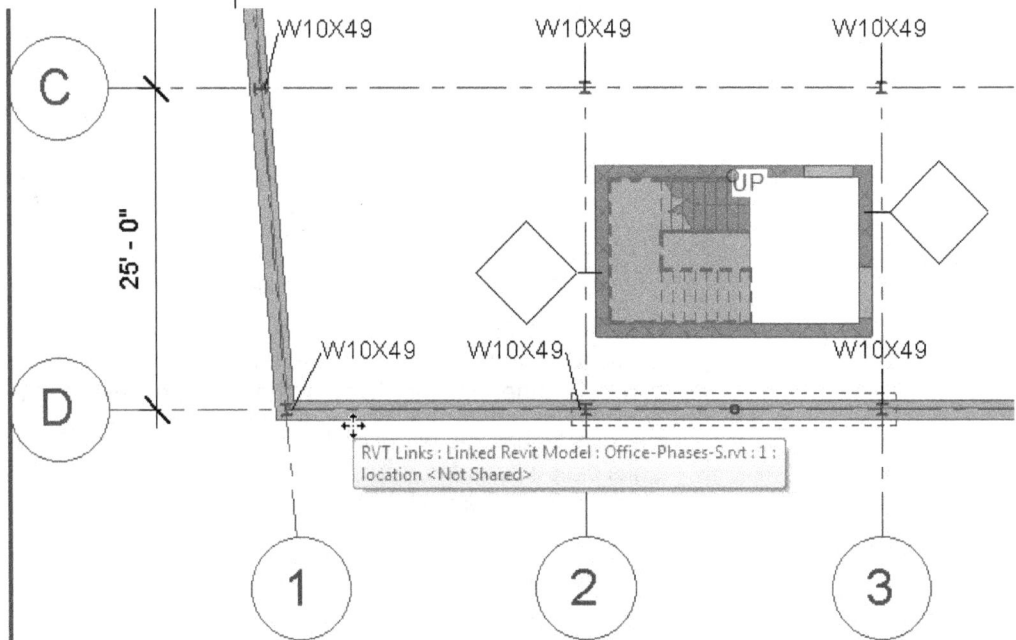

Figure 2–7

- Elements in the linked model can also be scheduled in the host project.

- The information annotated or scheduled for elements in a linked model cannot be controlled through the host model. Therefore, it is best to coordinate what information needs to be used in the hosting model annotation at the beginning of the project rather than waiting until it is necessary.

Managing Links

A linked model reloads each time the host project is opened. You can also reload the model by right-clicking on the Revit Link in the Project Browser, and then selecting **Reload** or **Reload From**, as shown in Figure 2–8.

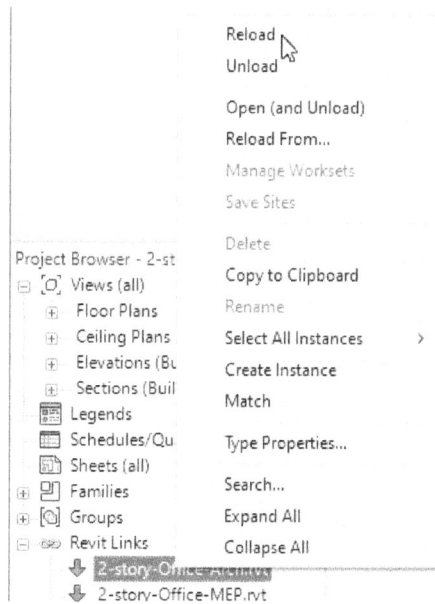

Figure 2–8

The Manage Links dialog box (shown in Figure 2–9) enables you to reload, unload, add, and remove links. Additionally, it provides access to other options. To open the Manage Links dialog box, in the *Insert* tab>Link, panel click ⬚ (Manage Links). The Manage Links dialog box also displays when you select a link in the *Modify | RVT Links* tab.

© 2020, ASCENT - Center for Technical Knowledge®

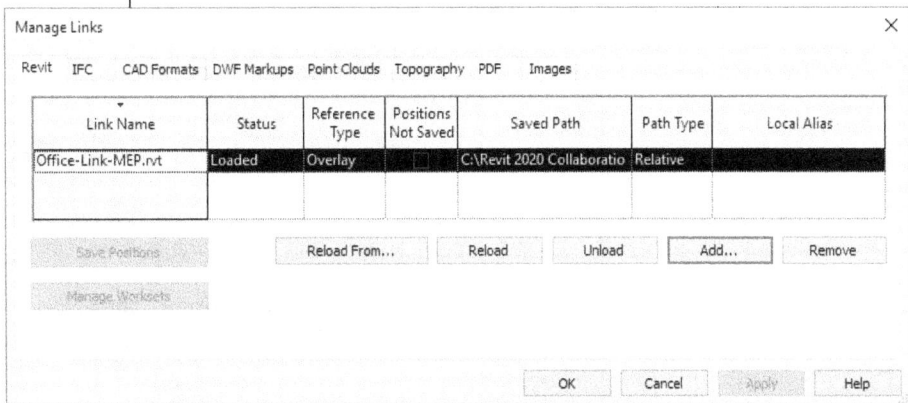

Figure 2–9

The options available in the Manage Links dialog box include the following:

- **Reload From:** Opens the Add Link dialog box, which enables you to select the file you want to reload. Use this if the linked file location or name has changed.

- **Reload:** Reloads the file without additional prompts.

- **Unload:** Unloads the file so that it the link is kept, but the file is not displayed or calculated in the project. Use **Reload** to restore it.

- **Add:** Opens the Import/Link RVT dialog box, which enables you to link additional models into the host project.

- **Remove:** Deletes the link from the file.

Links can be nested into one another. How a link responds when the host project is linked into another project depends on the option in the *Reference Type* column:

- **Overlay:** The nested linked model is not referenced in the new host project.

- **Attach:** The nested linked model displays in the new host project.

The option in the *Path Type* column controls how the location of the link is remembered:

- **Relative**

  - Searches the root folder of the current project.
  - If the file is moved, the software still searches for it.

- **Absolute**

  - Searches the entire file path where the file was originally saved.
  - If the original file is moved, the software is not able to find it.

- Other options control how the linked file interfaces with Worksets and Saved Positioning.

- In the Manage Links dialog box, when you have multiple links, you can sort rows by clicking the column header.

Linked Model Properties

Linked models have both instance properties and type properties. Instance Properties, as shown in Figure 2–10, include the *Name* for the individual copy of the link. This is automatically updated as you insert more than one. You can also change the name to help you identify it later. It also shows if it is part of a *Design Option* and if it is set to a *Shared Site*.

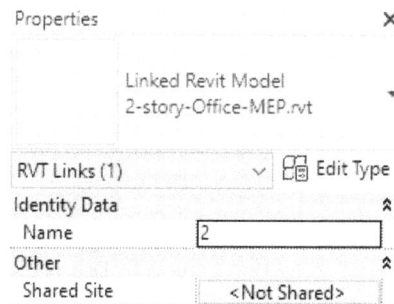

Figure 2–10

Type Properties, as shown in Figure 2–11, include *Room Bounding* which is required if you want to be able to place rooms or spaces from the information in the linked model. It also includes *Reference Type* (Overlay or Attachment) and *Phase Mapping* as well as workset information if the project is workshared.

© 2020, ASCENT - Center for Technical Knowledge®

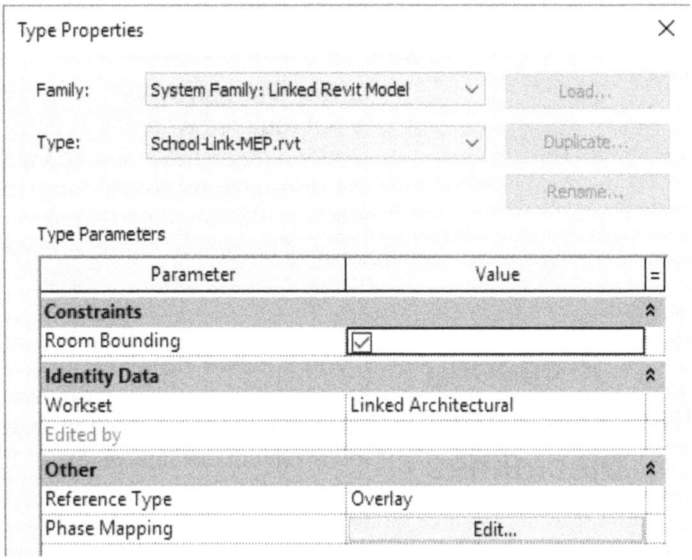

Type Properties   ×

Family: System Family: Linked Revit Model   ∨   Load...

Type: School-Link-MEP.rvt   ∨   Duplicate...

                                                         Rename...

Type Parameters

Parameter	Value	=
Constraints		⌃
Room Bounding	☑	
Identity Data		⌃
Workset	Linked Architectural	
Edited by		
Other		⌃
Reference Type	Overlay	
Phase Mapping	Edit...	

Figure 2–11

The phases in linked models can be mapped to the host project phasing so that the phasing schemes from different projects can be displayed consistently. Edit the Type Properties of the linked model and next to *Phase Mapping*, click **Edit....** In the Phases dialog box, as shown in Figure 2–12, select the Phase from the linked model to match the corresponding phase in the host project.

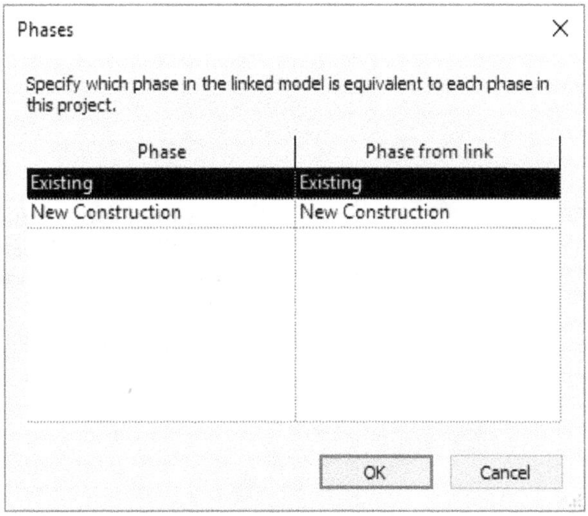

Phases   ×

Specify which phase in the linked model is equivalent to each phase in this project.

Phase	Phase from link
Existing	Existing
New Construction	New Construction

                                          OK   Cancel

Figure 2–12

2.2 Views and Linked Models

Linked files can be very large and include a lot of information that is not required when all you want is the base building model. Depending on the standards of your office, it can help to clean up the linked file by deleting unnecessary views or sheets and purging out all unused families. If required, you can request the original creator to set up coordination views that can be used specifically as a base view in the project.

Preparing Views for Other Disciplines

If you are working with consultants from other disciplines, it can be helpful to create coordination views for them that include only the element types that they require. For example, in Figure 2–13, the architect created plans for the first and second floors as a base for MEP and Structural projects. These views display only the architectural elements that other disciplines require as a background for their own elements.

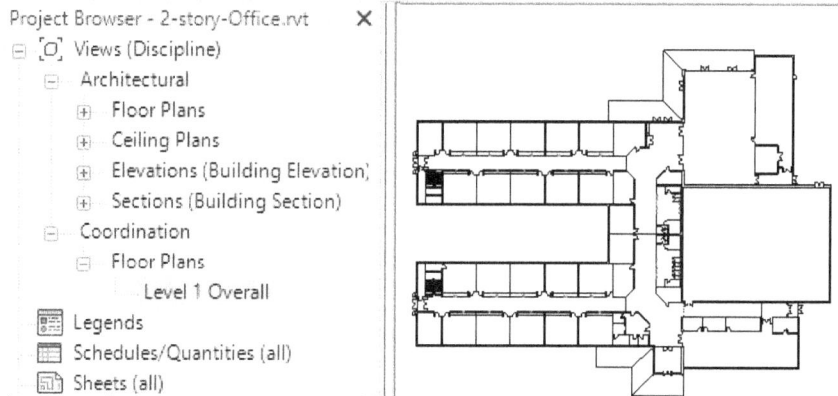

Figure 2–13

- When a model is linked to a host project, any changes you make in the Visibility/Graphic Overrides dialog box are also made in the linked model by default. For example, if you toggle off the visibility of the grids in the host project, it also toggles off the visibility of the grids in linked models.

© 2020, ASCENT - Center for Technical Knowledge®

Hint: Hiding Individual Elements in Linked Models

Individual elements in linked models can be hidden in the host project as shown in Figure 2–14. To select an element in a linked model, hover the cursor over the element and press <Tab> until only that element highlights. Then, right-click and select **Hide in View>Elements**. You can do this in plans, sections, elevations, and 3D views.

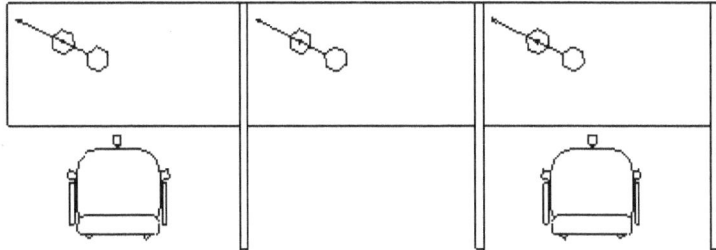

Three instances of a linked model with the chair hidden in one instance

Figure 2–14

- You can only modify the graphic overrides of elements in linked models by category, not by element.

- Hiding elements in the linked model By Category, has the same effect as hiding elements By category in the Main Model. All elements of that category are hidden in the Main Model and in all instances of all links, unless other link(s) have overrides attached to them.

Display Settings in Linked Models

To further customize views in projects with links, you can modify the Display Settings of the link. By default, the link displays using the host view parameters, but you can change it to use a view in the linked file or a custom view where you can specify every aspect of its appearance.

For example, in Figure 2–15, an MEP model has been linked into an architectural model and the Display Settings are set to **By Host View**. Only a couple of MEP elements display by default, such as the lights and some piping.

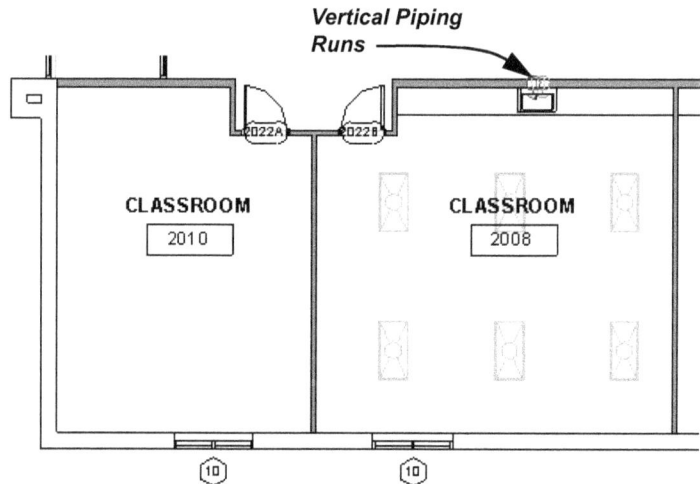

*If a graphic override has been applied to categories in a project, the linked files are also modified if their display setting is set to **By host view**.*

Figure 2–15

In Figure 2–16, the Display Settings have been changed to **By Linked View** with a mechanical view selected. The duct work and air terminals display, the lights remain grayed out and piping is toggled off.

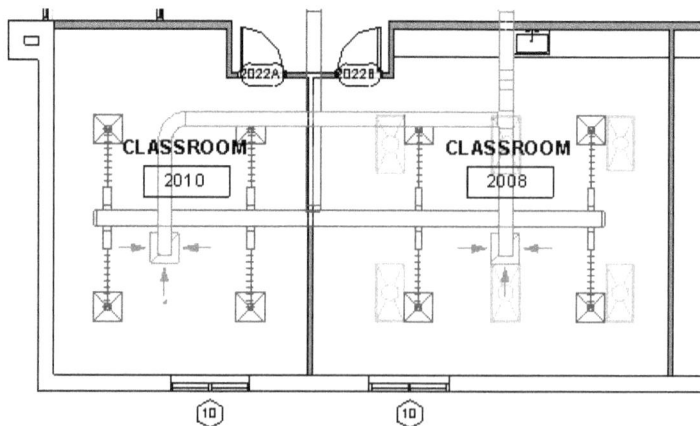

Figure 2–16

© 2020, ASCENT - Center for Technical Knowledge®

In Figure 2–17, the Display Settings have been customized. The Mechanical view is still selected but all of the duct elements are toggled off while the air terminals display.

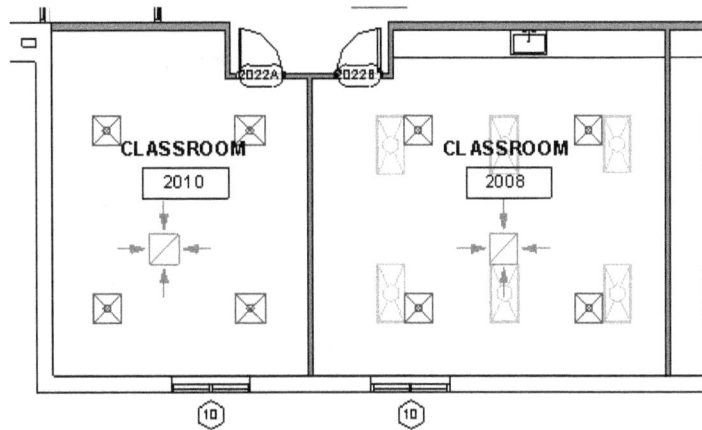

Figure 2–17

How To: Modify Display Settings in a Linked View

1. Type **VV** or **VG** to open the Visibility/Graphic Overrides dialog box.
2. Switch to the *Revit Links* tab.
3. Set the *Display Settings* for the linked model or an instance of the linked model, as shown in Figure 2–18.

If you have more than one copy of a link, you can have them all update together by clicking on the Display Settings next to the link name rather than the instance name.

Figure 2–18

4. In the RVT Link Display Settings dialog box, in the *Basics* tab, select **By linked view** or **Custom**.

- If you select **By linked view**, you can select from a list of views in the linked model, as shown in Figure 2–19.

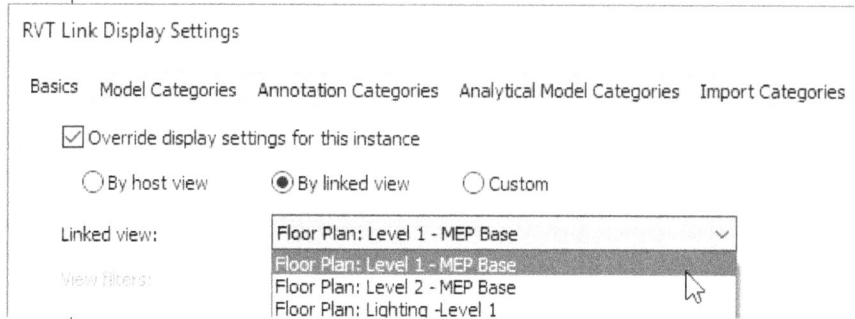

RVT Link Display Settings

Basics   Model Categories   Annotation Categories   Analytical Model Categories   Import Categories

☑ Override display settings for this instance

◯ By host view   ◉ By linked view   ◯ Custom

Linked view: Floor Plan: Level 1 - MEP Base   ⌄

View filters: Floor Plan: Level 1 - MEP Base
                    Floor Plan: Level 2 - MEP Base
                    Floor Plan: Lighting -Level 1

Figure 2–19

- If you select **Custom**, you can specify each setting independently, as shown in Figure 2–20.

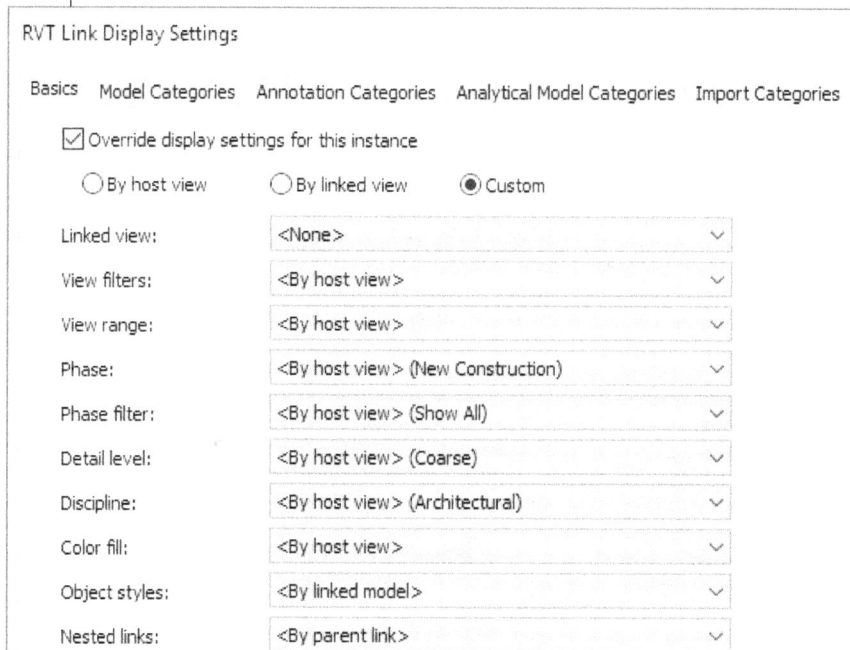

RVT Link Display Settings

Basics   Model Categories   Annotation Categories   Analytical Model Categories   Import Categories

☑ Override display settings for this instance

◯ By host view   ◯ By linked view   ◉ Custom

Linked view:	<None>	⌄
View filters:	<By host view>	⌄
View range:	<By host view>	⌄
Phase:	<By host view> (New Construction)	⌄
Phase filter:	<By host view> (Show All)	⌄
Detail level:	<By host view> (Coarse)	⌄
Discipline:	<By host view> (Architectural)	⌄
Color fill:	<By host view>	⌄
Object styles:	<By linked model>	⌄
Nested links:	<By parent link>	⌄

Figure 2–20

- When **Custom** is selected, you can also customize the display of specific categories using other tabs in the RVT Link Display Settings dialog box.

- If a linked model contains phases that are not in the host project, they can still be displayed by overriding the display settings for that instance of the linked model. The phases from the linked model display in the Phase drop-down list.

© 2020, ASCENT - Center for Technical Knowledge®

Practice 2a

Link Models - All Disciplines

Practice Objectives

- Link several models into a host project.
- Make copies of linked models in a project.
- Modify the Visibility/Graphic Overrides of the copied links.

In this practice, you will link architectural, structural, and MEP models into a host building site project. You will make copies of the linked models and modify the Visibility/Graphic Overrides for several of the instances. You will also modify one of the linked models and then reopen the site model to see how the changes automatically update in the final project, as shown in Figure 2–21.

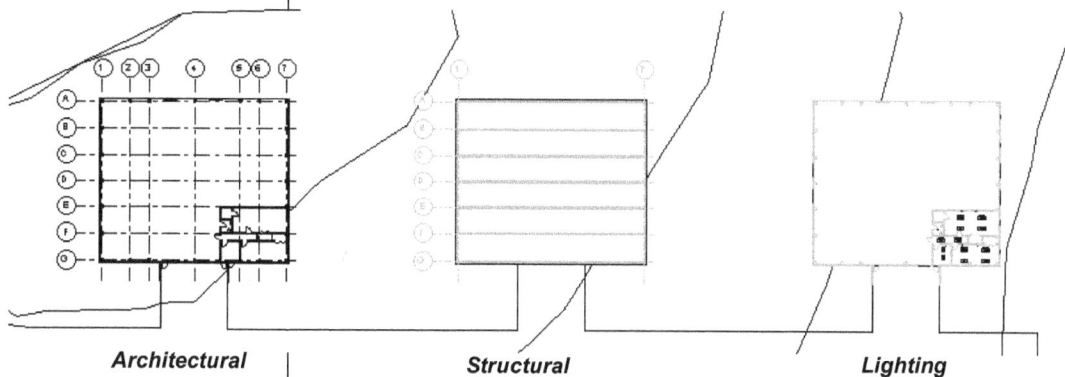

Architectural   Structural   Lighting

Figure 2–21

Task 1 - Link several models into a host project.

1. In the practice files folder, open **Industrial-Park.rvt**. The site has six rectangular pads for warehouse buildings.

2. In the *Insert* tab>Link panel, click (Link Revit).

3. In the Import/Link RVT dialog box, select the file **Industrial-Building-A.rvt**. Verify that the Positioning is set to **Auto - Internal Origin to Internal Origin.**

4. Click **Open**.

5. Select the new link. In Properties, verify that the *Name* of this instance is **1**. This makes tracking the rest of the instances easier.

6. Click ![Link Revit icon](Link Revit) again and link in **Industrial-Building-MEP.rvt** at the same position.

7. An alert box opens, warning you that the model has another model linked to it and that it is not visible in this project. This is because it was linked in that file as an overlay rather than an attachment. Close the dialog box.

8. Repeat the process one more time and link in **Industrial-Building-S.rvt** at the same position.

9. The links do not come in directly on a pad. They need to be moved to the correct location. Select all of the linked models that are on top of each other and move them to one of the pads at the top of the site. You might need to zoom in to place it precisely.

10. Copy the linked models to the other pads on the same side of the parking lot.

11. Mirror the links from the north side of the parking to the south side and move them into place, as shown in Figure 2–22.

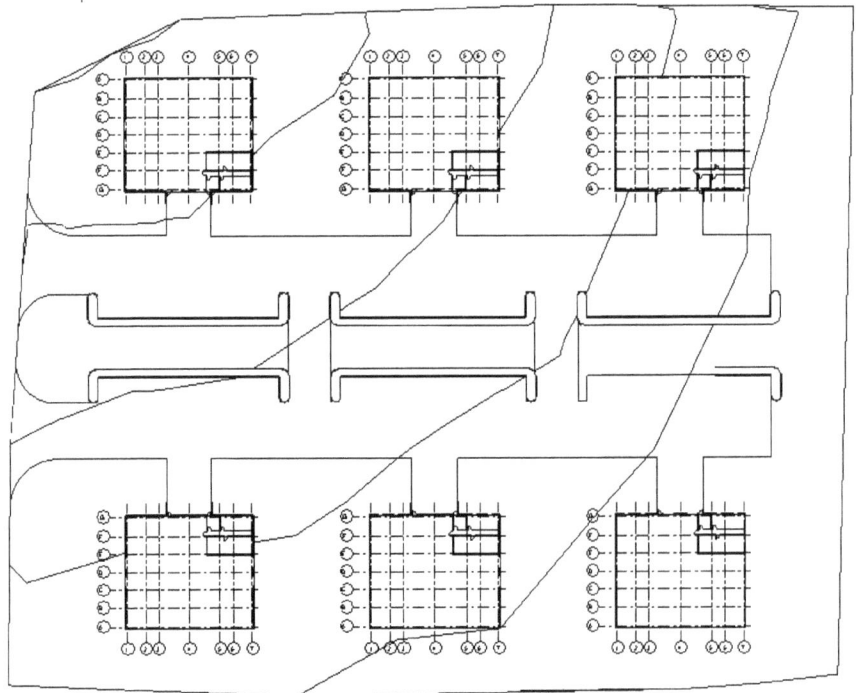

Figure 2–22

12. Save the project.

Task 2 - Modify the Visibility/Graphic Overrides of the links.

1. Zoom in to see the top group of warehouses.

2. Type **VV** to open the Visibility/Graphic Overrides dialog box. In the *Revit Links* tab, next to the main MEP and S links, select **Halftone**. Click **Apply** and move the dialog box out of the way slightly so that you can see the changes, as shown in Figure 2–23.

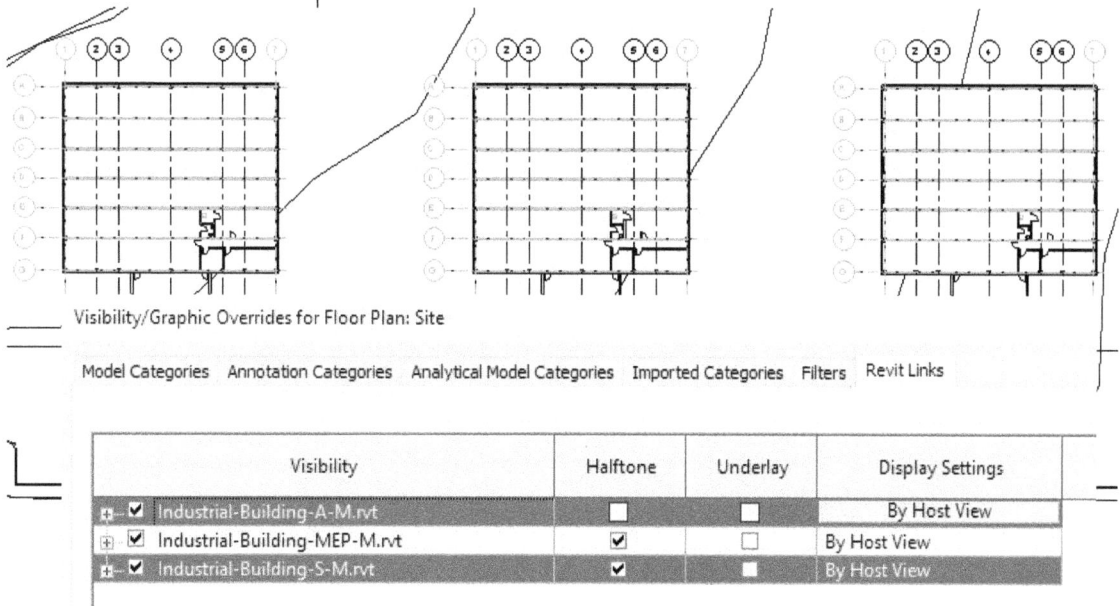

Visibility/Graphic Overrides for Floor Plan: Site

Model Categories   Annotation Categories   Analytical Model Categories   Imported Categories   Filters   Revit Links

Visibility	Halftone	Underlay	Display Settings
☑ Industrial-Building-A-M.rvt	☐	☐	By Host View
☑ Industrial-Building-MEP-M.rvt	☑	☐	By Host View
☑ Industrial-Building-S-M.rvt	☑	☐	By Host View

Figure 2–23

3. Remain in the Visibility/Graphic Overrides dialog box, *Revit Links* tab. Set up the first pad location so that it displays the architectural information, as shown in Figure 2–24. Expand the lists beside each of the links and clear the first instance of MEP (2) and S (3) links. Click **Apply**. Only the architectural information displays in this one instance

4. Set up the second pad location to display only the structural information, as shown in Figure 2–24. Clear the second architectural instance (4) and the second MEP instance (5). Click **Apply**. Only the structural information displays in this instance.

5. Set up the third pad location to display the MEP lighting information. Clear the third architectural (7) and structural (9) instances. Click **Apply**. Not enough information displays in this instance, as shown in Figure 2–24.

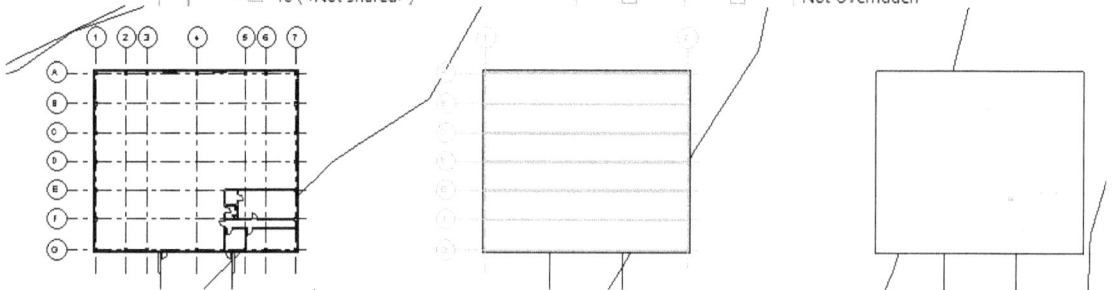

Figure 2–24

6. Select the third architectural instance (7) again and change only this one instance to **Halftone**.

© 2020, ASCENT - Center for Technical Knowledge®

7. Clear the **Halftone** option for the main MEP link.

8. Override the Display Settings of the third MEP instance (8). In the RVT Link Display Settings dialog box, in the *Basics* tab, select **Override display settings for this instance**. Set it to **By linked view** and select **Floor Plan: 1 - Lighting** for this view, as shown in Figure 2–25.

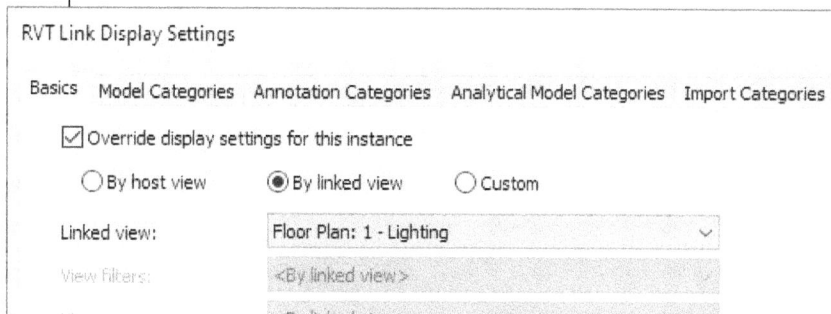

Figure 2–25

9. Click **OK** twice to close the dialog boxes.

10. Zoom in to see the lighting layout in the office area as shown in Figure 2–26.

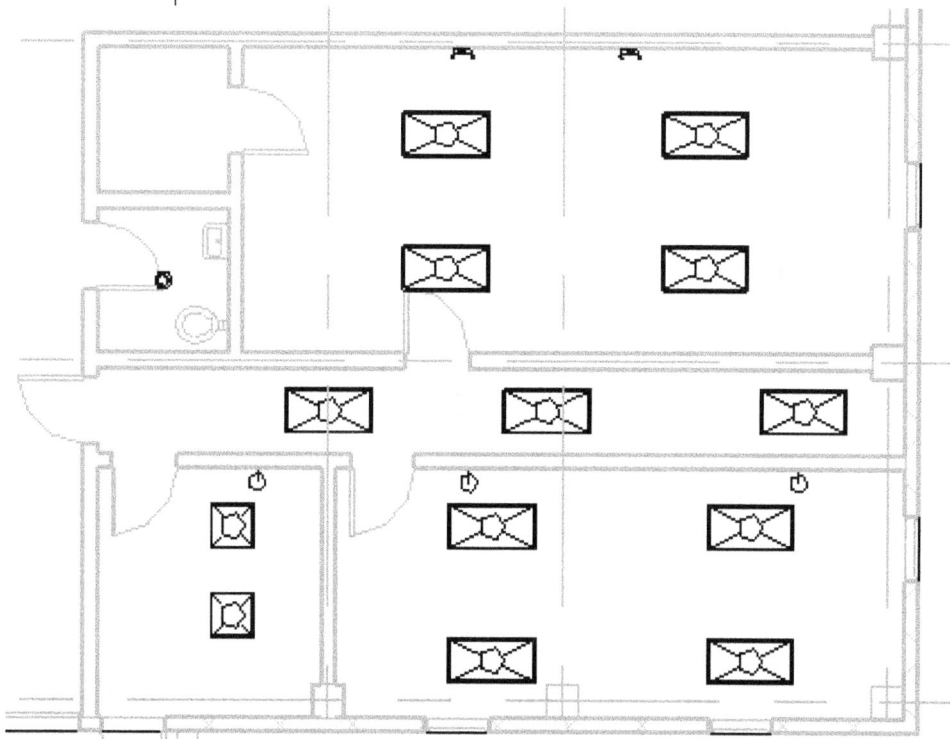

Figure 2–26

11. If you have time you can repeat the MEP steps for another instance and set up one using the view **Floor Plans: 1 - Mech**.

12. Save and close the project.

Task 3 - Modify linked models.

1. Open **Industrial-Building-A.rvt** from your practice files folder.

2. Add several other interior walls and doors to the office area of the warehouse, similar to that shown in Figure 2–27.

3. Duplicate the **Floor Plan: Level 1** view and rename it to **Level 1 - Coordination**. Verify that the tags and grids are not displaying, as shown in Figure 2–27.

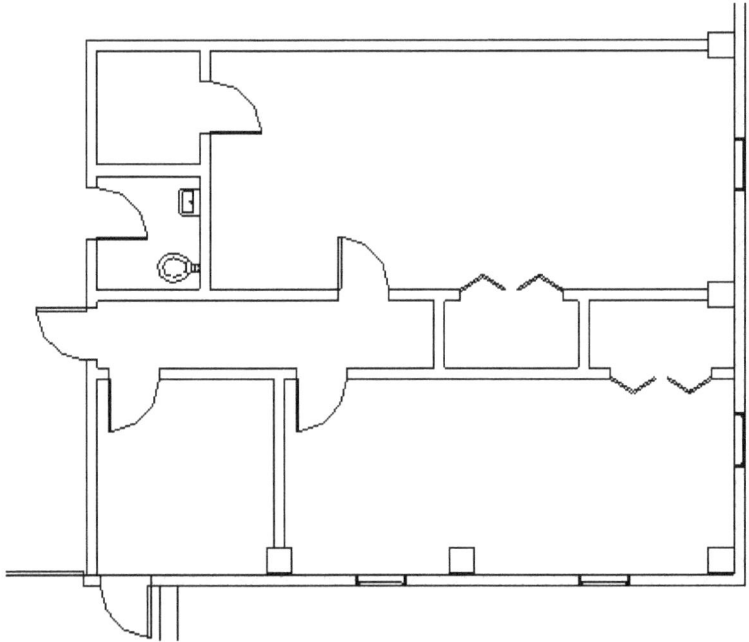

Figure 2–27

4. Save and close the project.

5. Open **Industrial-Building-MEP.rvt** from your practice files folder. The linked architectural model is automatically updated in this project.

6. Open the Electrical>Lighting>**Ceiling Plans: 1 - Ceiling Elec** view.

© 2020, ASCENT - Center for Technical Knowledge®

7. Depending on where you added walls, modify the lighting locations.

8. Save and close the file.

9. Reopen the project **Industrial-Park.rvt**. The new walls and the modified lighting locations display in the linked files, as shown in Figure 2–28 for the office section at the third pad location.

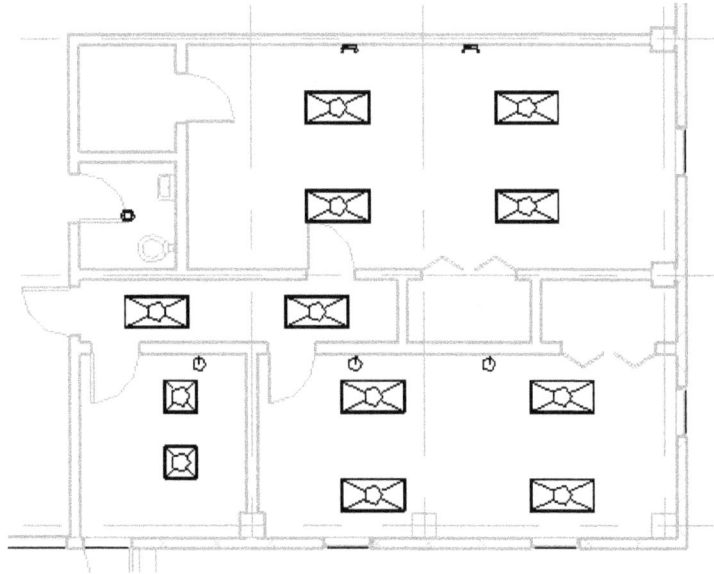

Figure 2–28

10. Type **VV** and for the third architectural instance (7), override the Display Settings by linked view. Select **Floor Plan: Level 1 - Coordination**. The grids no longer display in this instance.

11. Save and close the project.

12. If you have time, you can link the structural model into the architectural model and delete the columns and extra grids because the structural model uses a wide-span structural system.

13. In the structural model, you can also add more beams and other structural elements to finish the project. Test it in the Industrial Park project.

2.3 Copying and Monitoring Elements

When working with linked files, such as an architectural model linked into a structural or MEP project, you can coordinate information between the files using the **Copy/Monitor** tool. When you monitor an item in the linked file with an identical or similar one in the host project, the program tracks these two items, looking for changes in location, existence, height, etc. It always requires two elements to compare.

Items that are monitored display the ⬚ icon when selected, as shown in Figure 2–29.

Copy/Monitor works with grids, levels, columns, walls, and floors, as well as MEP fixtures in the same file or in a linked file.

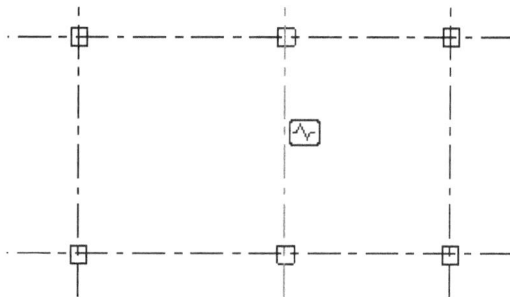

Figure 2–29

When starting the Copy/Monitor command, you can choose **Use Current Project** or **Select Link**. Use Select Link to monitor a linked file's elements if they could potentially be moved and affect your system.

- **Copy:** Copies the selected element from the linked model to the current model or host model, then monitors the element for any changes that may happen in the linked model.

- **Monitor:** Compares two elements of the same type against each other, either from a linked model to the current project (as shown in Figure 2–30) or in the current project.

© 2020, ASCENT - Center for Technical Knowledge®

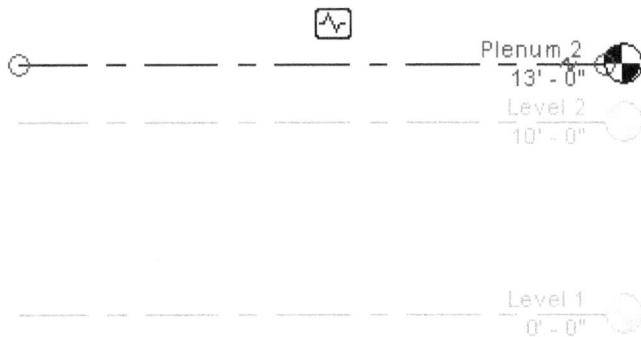

Figure 2–30

What Is Typically Copied/Monitored:

- **Architecture:** The **Copy/Monitor** tool is not heavily used by architects, although they might on occasion monitor elements in their project. For some projects they might use the structural engineer's linked model to control the grids and column locations or the plumbing engineer's linked model to control the location of the plumbing fixtures.

- **Structure:** Structural consultants copy/monitor levels, grids, columns, floors, and bearing walls from the architectural project.

- **MEP:** Mechanical consultants monitor levels and grids from the architectural model. They also copy/monitor some elements including plumbing and lighting fixtures.

- It is especially important to agree who controls datum elements, such as levels and grids, and not to modify them without explicit communication with others using that project as a link.

How To: Copy and Monitor Elements from a Linked File

1. In the *Collaborate* tab>Coordinate panel, expand

   (Copy/Monitor) and click (Select Link).

2. Select the link.

3. In the *Copy/Monitor* tab>Tools panel, click (Copy) or

   (Monitor).

4. If copying from the linked file, select each element that you want to copy. Alternatively, use the **Multiple** option:

- In the Options Bar, select **Multiple**, as shown in Figure 2–31.

Copy/Monitor ☑ Multiple Finish Cancel

Figure 2–31

- Hold <Ctrl> and select the elements that you want to copy into your model individually, or use a pick and drag window around multiple elements.
- In the Options Bar, click **Finish**.

- If monitoring elements in the current project with elements in the linked model, first select the element in the current project and then select the element in the linked model.

Warnings about duplicated or renamed types might display.

5. Click ✓ (Finish) to end the session of Copy/Monitor.

How To: Copy and Monitor Elements in the Current Project.

1. In the *Collaborate* tab>Coordinate panel, expand

   (Copy/Monitor) and click (Use Current Project).

2. In the *Copy/Monitor* tab>Tools panel, click (Copy) or

   (Monitor).

3. Select the two elements you want to monitor.
4. Repeat the process for any additional elements.

5. Click ✓ (Finish) to end the command.

- The elements do not have to be at the same elevation or location for the software to monitor them.

© 2020, ASCENT - Center for Technical Knowledge®

Copy/Monitor Options

Before starting the copy/monitor process, you can modify settings for the types of elements. In the *Copy/Monitor* tab>Tools panel, click ✎ (Options). In the Copy/Monitor Options dialog box, select the tab for the type of element that you want to copy: *Levels*, *Grids*, *Columns*, *Walls*, or *Floors*, as shown in Figure 2–32.

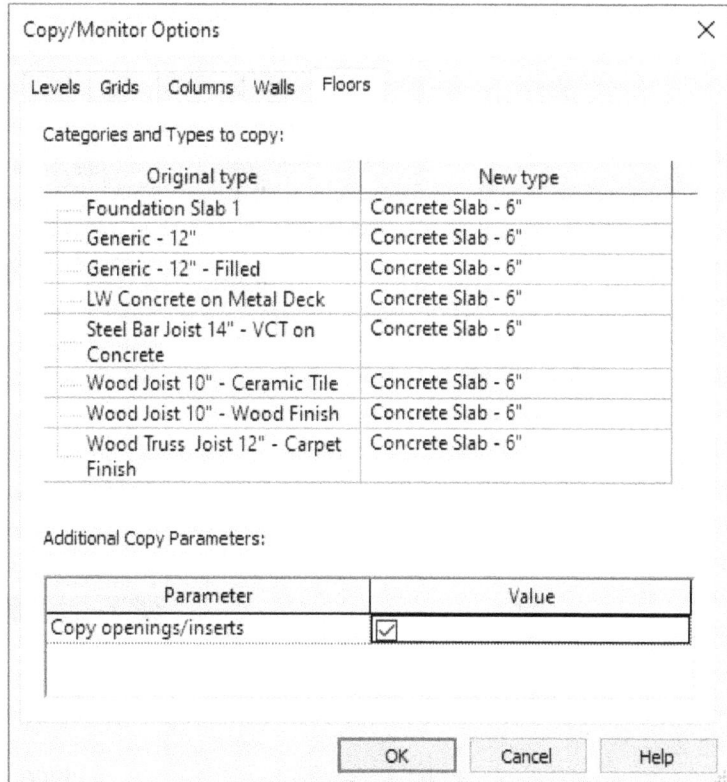

Tabs display for the categories that exist in the linked project.

Copy/Monitor Options   ✕

Levels   Grids   Columns   Walls   Floors

Categories and Types to copy:

Original type	New type
Foundation Slab 1	Concrete Slab - 6"
Generic - 12"	Concrete Slab - 6"
Generic - 12" - Filled	Concrete Slab - 6"
LW Concrete on Metal Deck	Concrete Slab - 6"
Steel Bar Joist 14" - VCT on Concrete	Concrete Slab - 6"
Wood Joist 10" - Ceramic Tile	Concrete Slab - 6"
Wood Joist 10" - Wood Finish	Concrete Slab - 6"
Wood Truss Joist 12" - Carpet Finish	Concrete Slab - 6"

Additional Copy Parameters:

Parameter	Value
Copy openings/inserts	☑

OK   Cancel   Help

Figure 2–32

- By default, hosted elements such as shaft openings in floors and door, and window openings in walls (as shown in Figure 2–33) are automatically copied with their host elements. You can change this response in the Copy/Monitor Options dialog box, in the *Floors* tab *Additional Copy Parameters* area, as shown above in Figure 2–32.

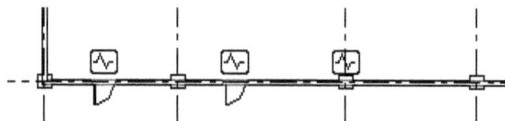

Figure 2–33

- MEP projects have additional options for Coordination Settings where you specify the copy and mapping behavior for different HVAC, Plumbing, Electrical equipment and fixtures, and other related devices, as shown in Figure 2–34. These elements can also be batch copied into the host project from the linked model.

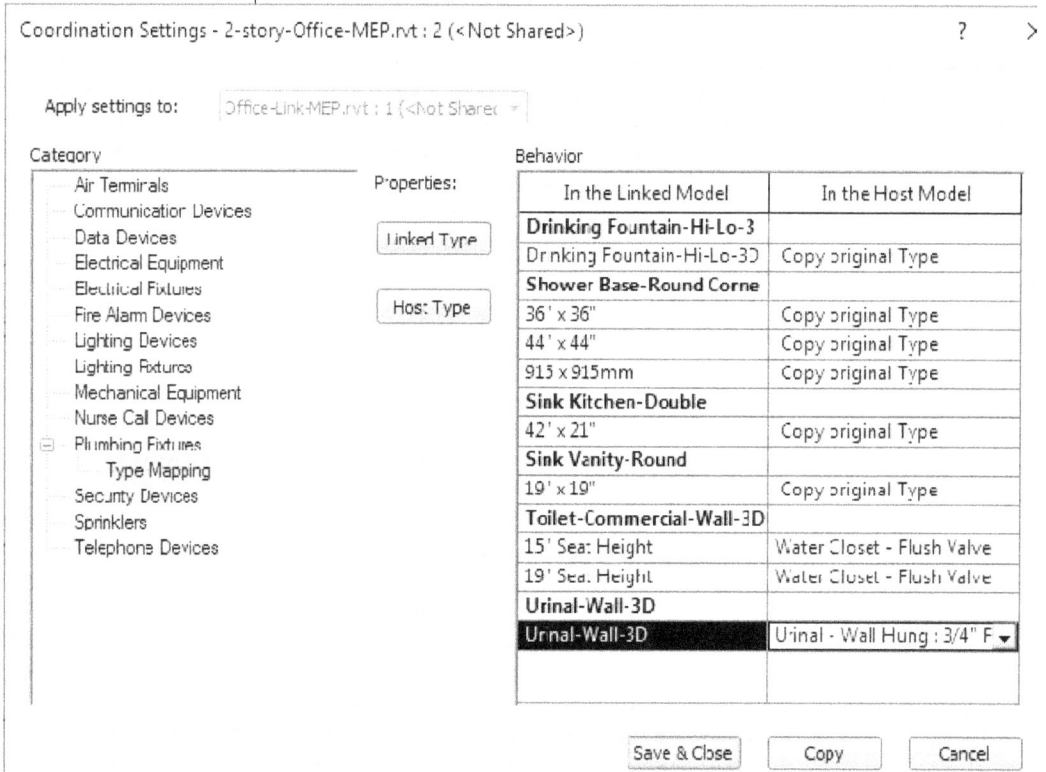

Figure 2–34

© 2020, ASCENT - Center for Technical Knowledge®

2.4 Coordinating Linked Models

Monitoring elements identifies changes in the data and changes in placement. For example, if you move a grid line, a Coordination Monitor alert displays, as shown in Figure 2–35. You can run a Coordination Review to correct or accept these changes.

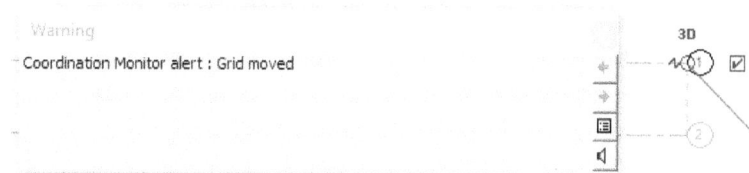

Figure 2–35

- If you open a project with a linked file containing elements that have been modified and monitored, the Warning shown in Figure 2–36 displays.

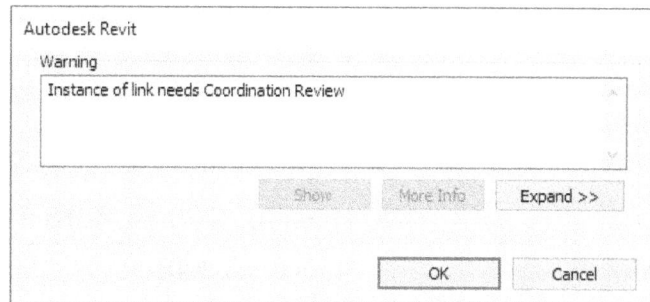

Figure 2–36

- Warnings do not prevent you from making a change, but rather alert you that the element is monitored and requires further coordination.

- If you no longer want an element to be monitored, select it and in the associated *Modify* tab>Monitor panel, click

  (Stop Monitoring).

- When you work in a host project and move an element that is copied into the host file, a warning displays as shown in Figure 2–37. This does not prevent you from making the change, but alerts you that this is a monitored element that requires further coordination with the other disciplines involved.

Figure 2–37

- If you make a change to a monitored host element, such as adding a door in a wall, a warning opens as shown in Figure 2–38.

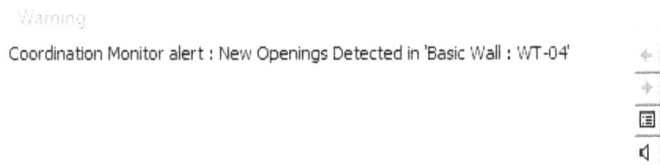

Figure 2–38

How To: Run a Coordination Review

1. In the *Collaborate* tab>Coordinate panel, expand (Coordination Review) and click (Use Current Project) or (Select Link). The Coordination Review dialog box lists any conflicts detected, as shown in Figure 2–39.
   - If there are no conflicts, the *Message* area is empty.

© 2020, ASCENT - Center for Technical Knowledge®

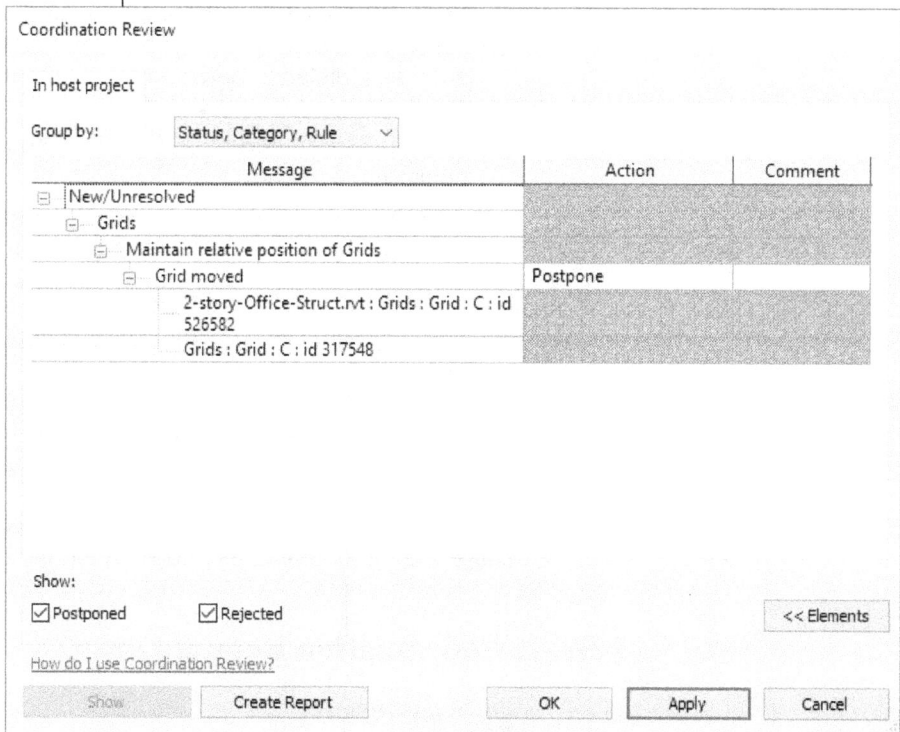

Figure 2–39

2. Use the Group by: drop-down list to group the information by **Status**, **Category**, and **Rule** in a variety of different ways. This is important if you have many elements to review.

3. Select an *Action* for each conflict related to the elements involved, as shown in Figure 2–40.

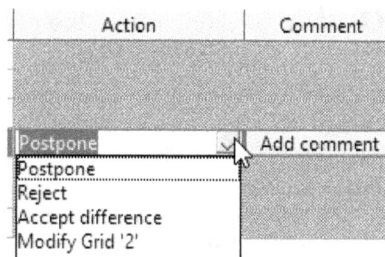

Figure 2–40

- **Postpone:** Do nothing, but leave it to be handled later.
- **Reject:** Do not accept the change. The change needs to be made in the other model.

- **Accept Difference:** Make no change to the monitored element in the current project, but accept the change (such as a distance between the elements) in the monitor status.
- **Rename/Modify/Move:** Apply the change to the monitored element.
- Other options display when special cases occur. For more information, see the Autodesk Revit help files.

4. Add a comment by clicking **Add comment** in the column to the right. This enables you to make a note about the change, such as the date of the modification.
5. Select the element names or click **Show** to display any items in conflict. Clicking **Show** changes the view to center the elements in your screen. Selecting the name does not change the view.
6. Click **Create Report** to create an HTML report that you can share with other users, as shown in Figure 2–41.

Revit Coordination Report

In host project

New/Unresolved	Plumbing Fixtures	Maintain relative position of Fixtures	Relative position of two Fixtures changed	Plumbing Fixtures : Sink_Kitchen-Single[1] : Mark 1 : id 734856 MEP-Elementary-School-Architectural.rvt : Plumbing Fixtures : Sink_Kitchen-Single[1] : Mark 80 : id 329165

Figure 2–41

Reconciling Hosts

If the owner of a linked file deletes or moves a host, such as a wall and the current project had elements hosted to it, such as a light fixture, the connection between the two is lost, as shown in Figure 2–42.

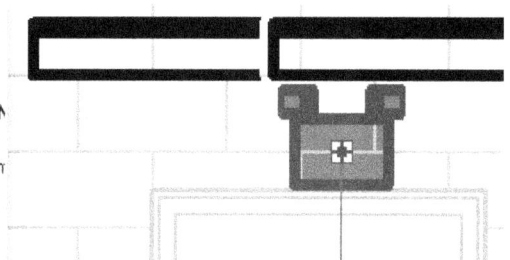

Figure 2–42

© 2020, ASCENT - Center for Technical Knowledge®

How To: Reconcile Hosting

1. When you open a project or reload a linked file, an alert box might be displayed, as shown in Figure 2–43.

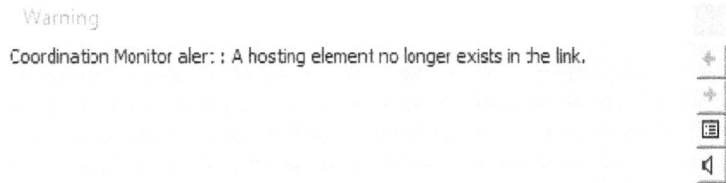

Warning

Coordination Monitor aler: : A hosting element no longer exists in the link.

Figure 2–43

2. In the *Collaborate* tab>Coordinate panel, click (Reconcile Hosting).
3. The Reconcile Hosting palette displays as shown in Figure 2–44.
4. Expand the list, select the element, and click **Show** to zoom in on the element that is orphaned.
5. To correct the issue, right-click on the element name, as shown in Figure 2–44, and select **Pick Host** or **Delete**.

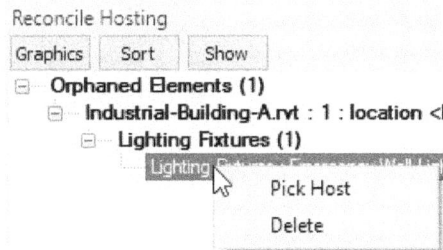

Reconcile Hosting

| Graphics | Sort | Show |

⊟ **Orphaned Elements (1)**
  ⊟ **Industrial-Building-A.rvt : 1 : location <N**
    ⊟ **Lighting Fixtures (1)**
      Lighting

        Pick Host

        Delete

Figure 2–44

- You can also select the element and in the *Modify*

  contextual tab>Work Plane panel, click (Pick New) and select a new host or delete it.

6. When you are finished correcting the elements, close the Reconcile Hosting palette.

- If you have control of the host elements in your project and you want to use a different wall type, do not delete and redraw the wall, just select it and in the Type Selector, select the new type. This does not create issues for others who are using the model as a link which has objects hosted on it.

- Because of this issue, many hosted elements are face-based rather than wall (or other host type) based. These elements do not notify you if a host is moved so you need to be aware to look for these orphaned elements.

Interference Checking

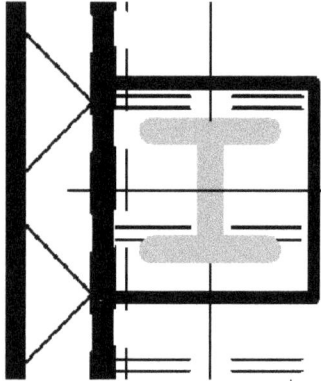

Interference Checking can be used when there are potential overlaps between disciplines, such as the structural column and ducts shown in Figure 2–45.

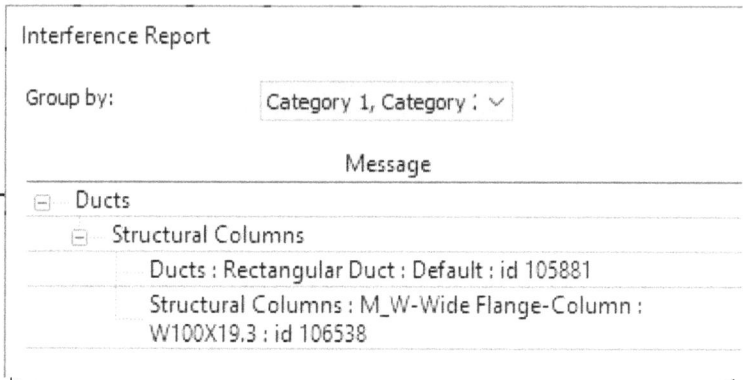

Interference Report

Group by: Category 1, Category ⌄

Message
⊟ Ducts
⊟ Structural Columns
Ducts : Rectangular Duct : Default : id 105881
Structural Columns : M_W-Wide Flange-Column : W100X19.3 : id 106538

Figure 2–45

- Typical items to check include structural elements against architectural columns, walls, door or window openings, floors and roofs, specialty equipment and floors, and any elements in a linked file with the host file.

- For more complex projects and those that include files from other software, the Navisworks software provides a much more powerful solution than this basic interference checking.

How To: Run an Interference Check

1. In the *Collaborate* tab>Coordinate panel, expand (Interference Check) and click (Run Interference Check).
   - To filter out unneeded elements, select the elements first and then run the interference check.

2. In the Interference Check dialog box, as shown in Figure 2–46, in the *Categories From* drop-down list, select the projects that you want to compare. This can be the same project or any linked projects.

Select only the categories that you need to review. In a large project, selecting all categories can take a very long time to process.

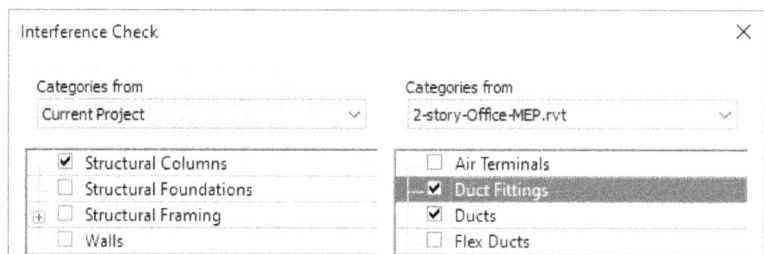

Interference Check   ✕

Categories from	Categories from
Current Project ⌄	2-story-Office-MEP.rvt ⌄
☑ Structural Columns	☐ Air Terminals
☐ Structural Foundations	☑ Duct Fittings
⊞ ☐ Structural Framing	☑ Ducts
☐ Walls	☐ Flex Ducts

Figure 2–46

© 2020, ASCENT - Center for Technical Knowledge®

3. Select the element types that you want to compare.
4. Click **OK**.
5. If there are interferences, the Interference Report dialog box opens as shown in Figure 2–47.

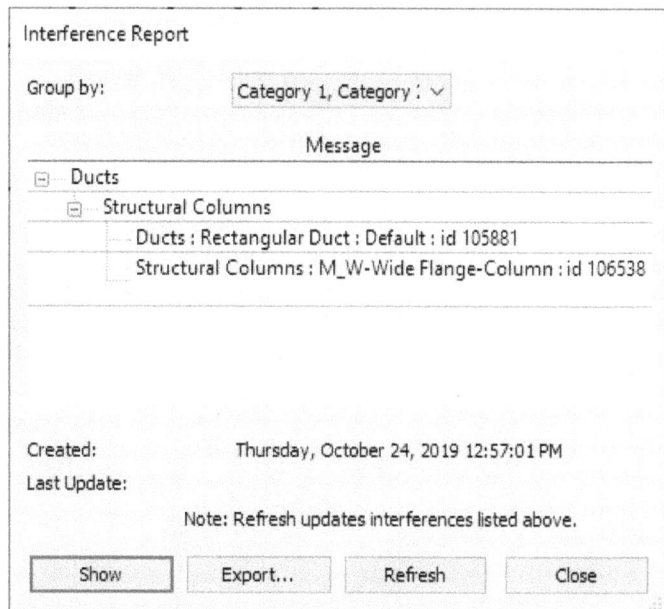

Interference Report

Group by: Category 1, Category ⋮ ∨

                                         Message
⊟ Ducts
   ⊟ Structural Columns
         Ducts : Rectangular Duct : Default : id 105881
         Structural Columns : M_W-Wide Flange-Column : id 106538

Created: Thursday, October 24, 2019 12:57:01 PM
Last Update:

         Note: Refresh updates interferences listed above.

   Show   Export...   Refresh   Close

Figure 2–47

6. To see the elements that are interfering, select an element in the list and click **Show**.
7. If you need to create a report that can be viewed by other users, click **Export....** This creates an HTML file listing the conflicts.
8. The dialog box can remain open while you make changes or you can click **Close** and then expand 📄 (Interference Check) and click 📄 (Show Last Report) to see the report again.
9. In the Interference Report dialog box, click **Refresh** to display any changes.
10. Refreshing the report only reviews the elements selected when the report was first run. If you need to select other elements, run a new report.

Practice 2b

Coordinate Linked Projects - Architectural and Structural

Practice Objectives

- Copy and monitor elements.
- Review and correct issues when coordination relationships established with Copy/Monitor are broken.

In this practice, you will start a new structural project and link in an architectural model. You will then Copy/Monitor the grids, set up Column options to use structural columns, and Copy/Monitor in the columns, as shown in Figure 2–48. Finally, you will make changes to the architectural project and then use Coordination Review to match the structural project with the link.

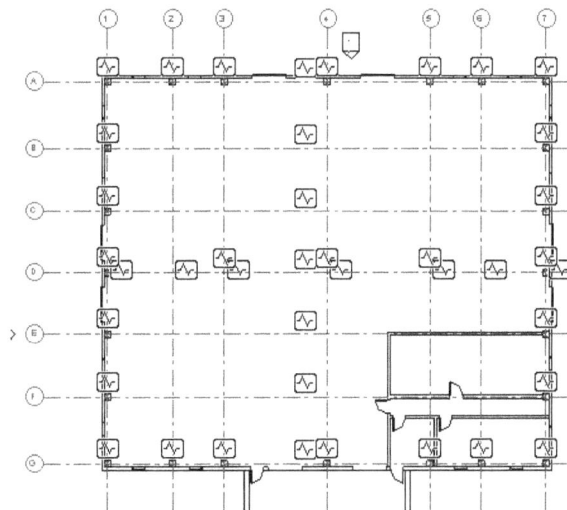

Figure 2–48

Task 1 - Link a file and copy/monitor elements.

1. Start a new project based on the Structural template and save the project as **Warehouse-Structural.rvt** in your practice files folder.

2. Open the **Structural Plans: Level 1** view.

© 2020, ASCENT - Center for Technical Knowledge®

3. In the *Insert* tab>Link panel, click 🔳 (Link Revit).

4. In the Import/Link RVT dialog box, navigate to the practice files folder and select **Warehouse-A.rvt**. Verify that the *Positioning* is set to **Auto - Internal Origin to Internal Origin** and click **Open**.

5. The columns and grids of the linked model, and the doors and foundation elements display, while the walls do not because they are not structural.

6. In the View Control Bar, click 📷 (Temporary View Properties) and select **Temporarily Apply Template Properties**.

7. In the Temporarily Apply Template Properties dialog box select **Architectural Plan** and click **OK**.

8. In the *Collaborate* tab>Coordinate panel, expand 📷 (Copy/Monitor) and click 📷 (Select Link).

9. Select the linked warehouse model.

10. In the *Copy/Monitor* tab>Tools panel, click 📷 (Copy).

11. In the Options Bar, select **Multiple**. Select all of the grids using any selection method, such as that shown in Figure 2–49. Hold <Ctrl> to select additional grids, if needed. In the Options Bar, click **Finish**.

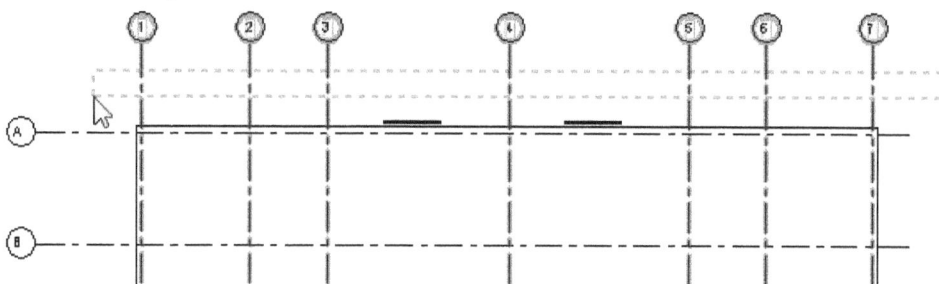

Figure 2–49

12. The grids are copied into the host project and monitored in place, as shown in Figure 2–50.

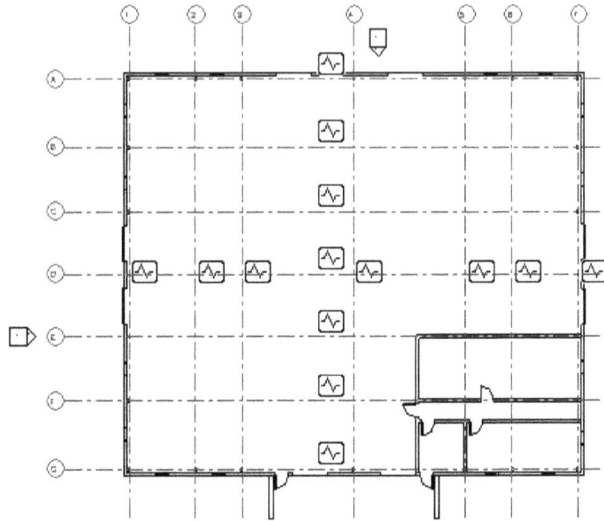

Figure 2–50

13. Click ⟍ (Modify) to release the grids.

14. Return to the *Copy/Monitor* tab. In the Tools panel, click 🔧 (Options).

15. In the Copy/Monitor Options dialog box, select the *Columns* tab. The types of columns in the linked file are listed on the left. Verify that the architectural columns are set to a structural column type. For the *Pipe-Column*, select **Copy original Type** as shown in Figure 2–51.

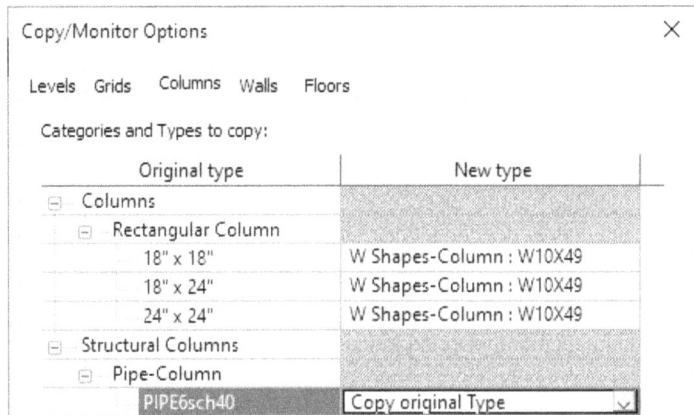

Figure 2–51

© 2020, ASCENT - Center for Technical Knowledge®

16. Click **OK**.

17. In the *Copy/Monitor* tab>Tools panel, click ⌔ (Copy).

18. In the Options Bar, select **Multiple**.

19. Create a window around the entire building to select everything but the grids.

20. In the Status Bar or Options Bar, click ▽ (Filter).

21. In the Filter dialog box, select **Columns** and **Structural Columns**. Clear **Walls** as shown in Figure 2–52 and click **OK**.

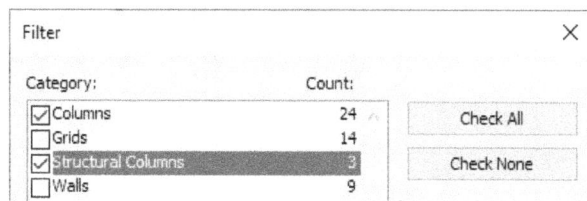

Filter			✕
Category:		Count:	
☑ Columns		24	Check All
☐ Grids		14	
☑ Structural Columns		3	Check None
☐ Walls		9	

Figure 2–52

22. In the Options Bar, click **Finish**.

23. The columns are copied into the project as shown in Figure 2–53.

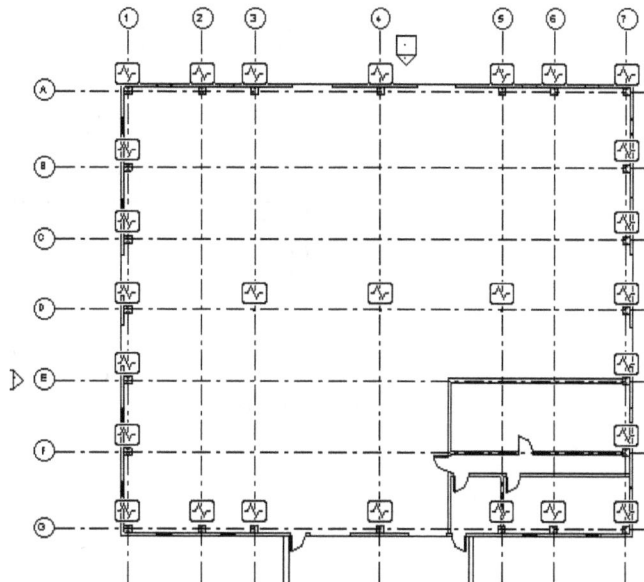

Figure 2–53

24. In the *Copy/Monitor* tab, click ✔ (Finish).

25. Zoom into the columns. There should be structural columns at the location of the square architectural columns, as shown in Figure 2–54, and pipe columns in the center of the building.

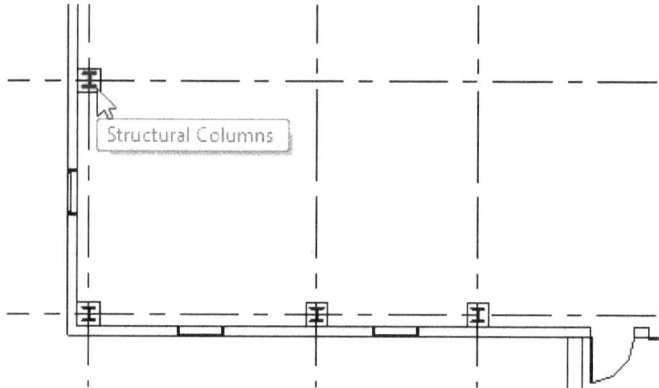

Figure 2–54

26. Save and close the project.

Task 2 - Modify the Architectural project.

1. Open **Warehouse-A.rvt** from your practice files folder.

2. Zoom in to check that there are no structural columns where the architectural columns are, as shown in Figure 2–55.

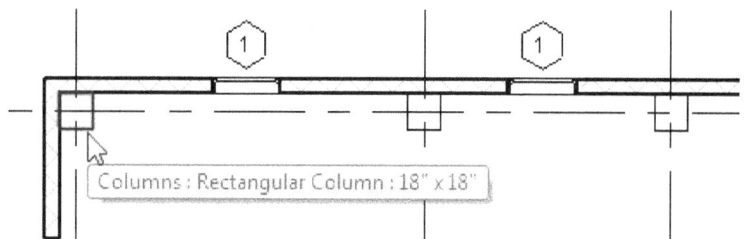

Figure 2–55

3. Zoom out.

© 2020, ASCENT - Center for Technical Knowledge®

4. Select grid line 3 and change it so it is **12'-0"** from grid line 2, as shown in Figure 2–56.

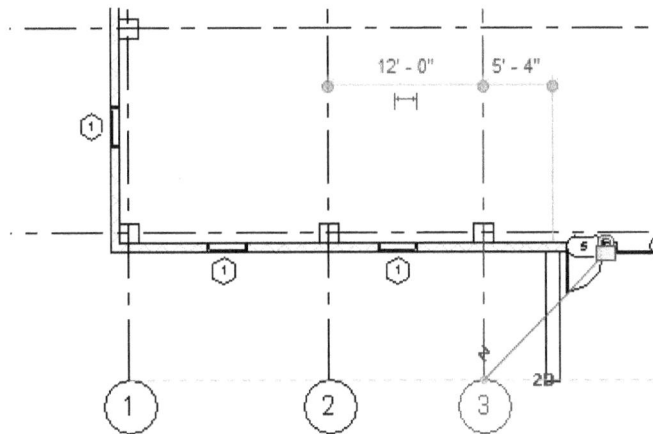

Figure 2–56

5. Repeat the process with grid line 5 and move it **12'-0"** from grid line 6. The associated architectural columns move with the grid line.

6. Save and close the project.

Task 3 - Coordinate the host file with the linked file.

---

1. Open the project **Warehouse-Structure.rvt** that you created earlier. The warning about needing a coordination review, as shown in Figure 2–57, displays.

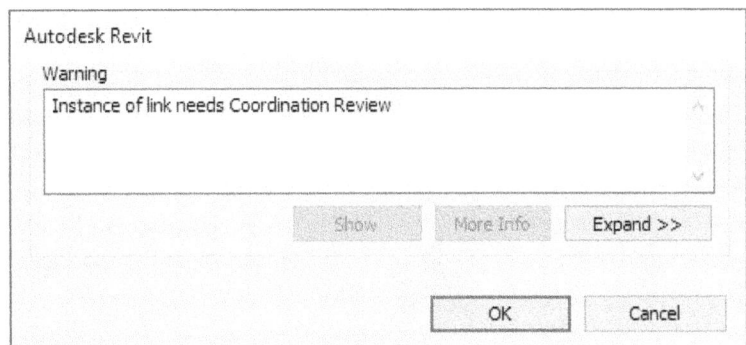

Figure 2–57

2. Click **OK**.

3. You can see the change between the host project and linked model as shown in Figure 2–58.

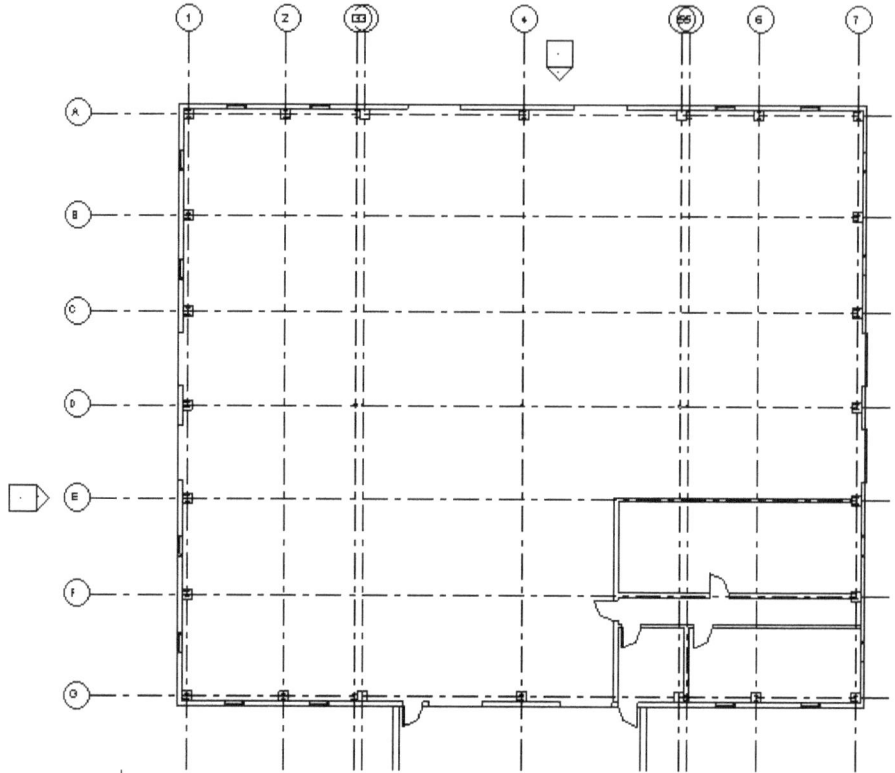

Figure 2–58

4. In the *Collaborate* tab> Coordinate panel, expand (Coordination Review) and click (Select Link).

5. Select the linked model.

© 2020, ASCENT - Center for Technical Knowledge®

6. In the Coordination Review dialog box, review the issues as shown in Figure 2–59.

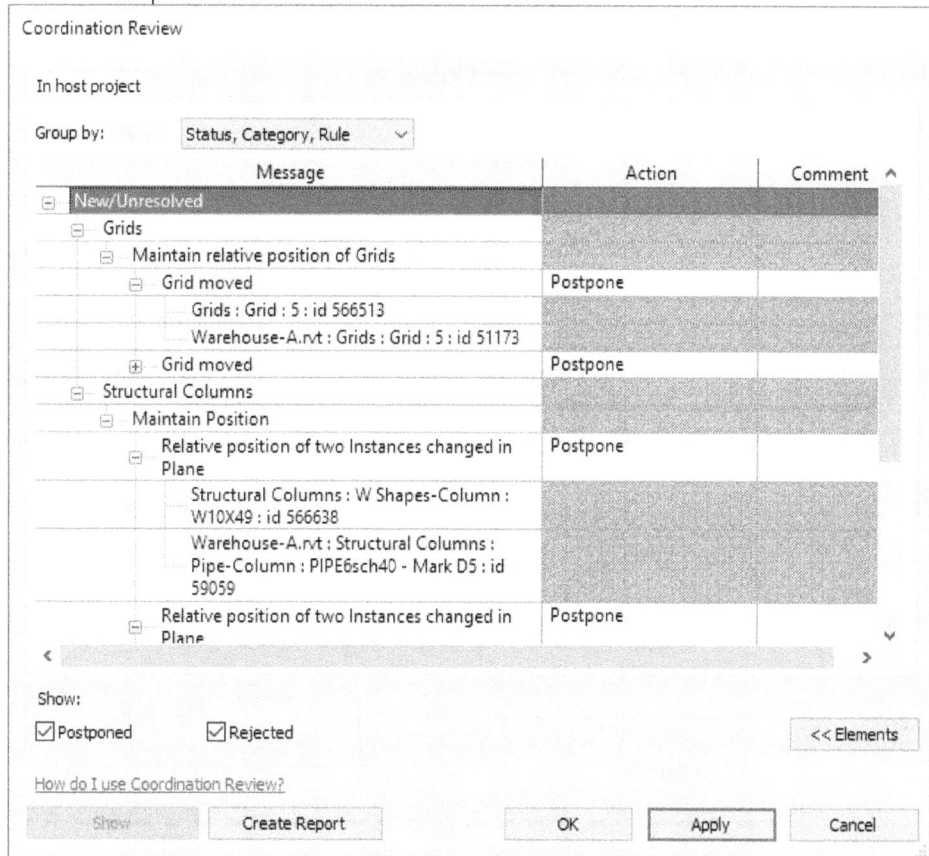

Coordination Review

In host project

Group by: Status, Category, Rule

Message	Action	Comment
New/Unresolved		
Grids		
Maintain relative position of Grids		
Grid moved	Postpone	
Grids : Grid : 5 : id 566513		
Warehouse-A.rvt : Grids : Grid : 5 : id 51173		
Grid moved	Postpone	
Structural Columns		
Maintain Position		
Relative position of two Instances changed in Plane	Postpone	
Structural Columns : W Shapes-Column : W10X49 : id 566638		
Warehouse-A.rvt : Structural Columns : Pipe-Column : PIPE6sch40 - Mark D5 : id 59059		
Relative position of two Instances changed in Plane	Postpone	

Show:
☑ Postponed   ☑ Rejected   << Elements

How do I use Coordination Review?

Show | Create Report | OK | Apply | Cancel

Figure 2–59

7. In the *Action* column, next to the grid issues, select **Modify Grid '5'** and **Modify Grid '3'**.

8. Click **Apply**. The grid lines move over, and because columns move with grid lines, the issues with the structural columns are resolved and are not listed in the Coordination Review dialog box.

9. Click **OK** and the host file matches up with the linked file.

10. Save and close the project.

Practice 2c

Coordinate Linked Projects - MEP and Architectural

Practice Objectives

- Copy and monitor elements.
- Review and correct issues when coordination relationships that were established with **Copy/Monitor** are broken.

In this practice, you will create a new systems project and link in an architectural model. You will then Use Copy/Monitor to monitor levels and draw some ductwork that references one of the levels as shown on the top in Figure 2–60. You will then change the level in the architectural model and use Coordination Review to update the change in the systems model as shown on the bottom in Figure 2–60.

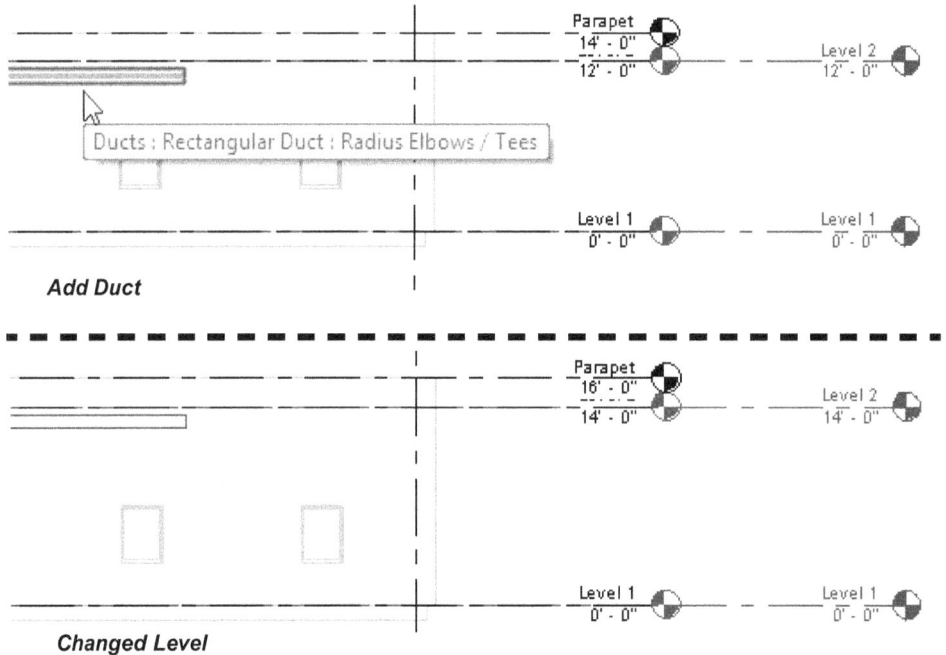

Figure 2–60

Task 1 - Link a file and copy/monitor elements.

1. Start a new project based on the Mechanical or Systems template and save the project as **Warehouse-MEP.rvt** in your practice files folder.

© 2020, ASCENT - Center for Technical Knowledge®

2. In the *Insert* tab>Link panel, click ▣ (Link Revit).

3. In the Import/Link RVT dialog box, navigate to the practice files folder and select **Warehouse-A.rvt**. Verify that the *Positioning* is set to **Auto - Internal Origin to Internal Origin** and click **Open**.

4. Open the Mechanical>HVAC>**Elevations (Building Elevation): South - Mech** view. The host project has two levels and the architectural model has three, as shown in Figure 2–61. Hint: Select the linked file in the view and everything in the linked model will turn blue.

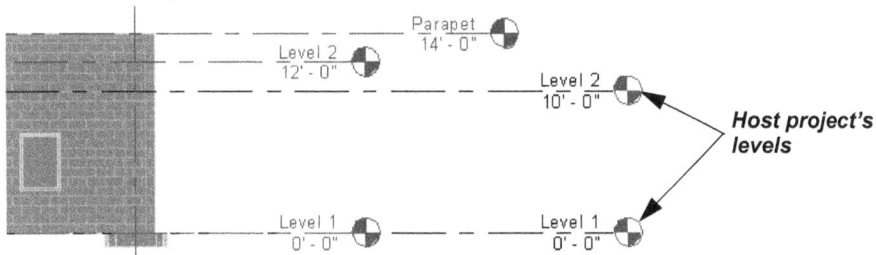

Figure 2–61

5. Align Level 2 of the current project with Level 2 of the linked project.

6. In the *Collaborate* tab>Coordinate panel, expand ▣ (Copy/Monitor) and click ▣ (Select Link).

7. Select the linked warehouse model.

8. In the *Copy/Monitor* tab>Tools panel, click ▣ (Monitor).

9. Select Level 1 in the host project and then Level 1 in the linked model.

10. Repeat the process with Level 2 and click ✓ (Finish).

Task 2 - Add ductwork (and lighting).

1. Open the Mechanical>HVAC>Floor Plans>**1 - Mech** view.

2. In the *Systems* tab>HVAC panel, click ▣ (Duct).

3. In Properties, set the *Reference Level* to **Level 2** and the *Middle Elevation* to (negative) **-1'-0"**. Draw several ducts.

4. Return to the elevation view to see the location of the ducts, as shown in Figure 2–62.

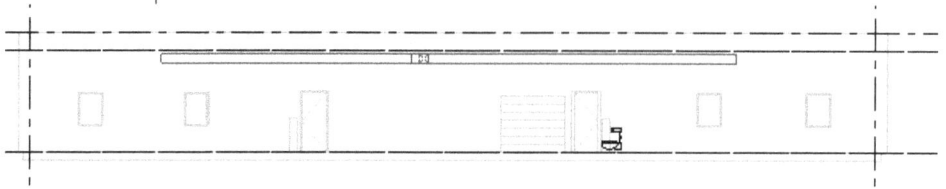

Figure 2–62

5. Save and close the project.

Task 3 - Modify the Architectural project.

1. Open **Warehouse-A.rvt** from your practice files folder.

2. Open the **Elevations: South** view.

3. Change the height of Level 2 to **14'-0"**.

- The parapet level automatically changes height because it has been dimensioned and locked to Level 2.

4. Save and close the project.

Task 4 - Coordinate the host file with the linked file.

1. Open the project **Warehouse-MEP.rvt** that you created earlier. The warning about needing a coordination review displays, as shown in Figure 2–63.

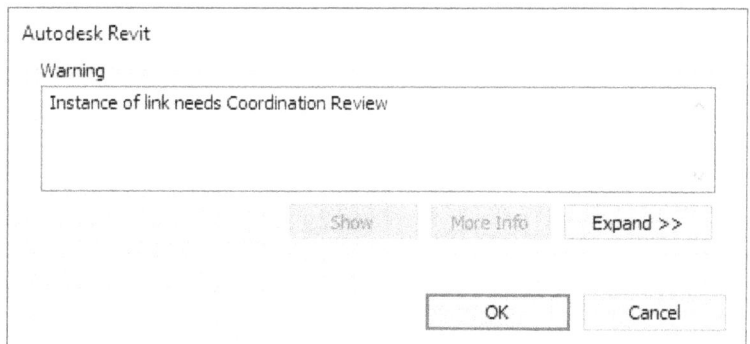

Figure 2–63

2. Click **OK**.

© 2020, ASCENT - Center for Technical Knowledge®

3. You can see the change between the host project and linked model as shown in Figure 2–64.

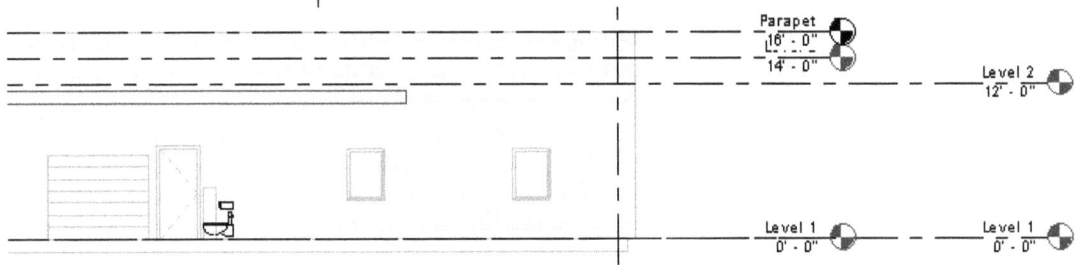

Figure 2–64

4. In the *Collaborate* tab> Coordinate panel, expand ![icon](Coordination Review) and click ![icon](Select Link).

5. Select the architectural link.

6. In the Coordination Review dialog box, expand the options in the *Action* column and select **Move Level 'Level 2'**, as shown in Figure 2–65.

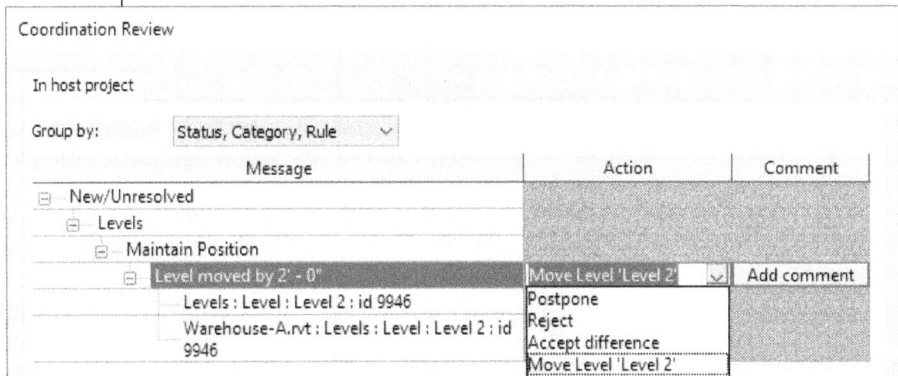

Figure 2–65

7. Click **OK** and the host file matches up with the linked file. The duct work moves as well because it was referenced to the level that was changed.

8. Save and close the project.

Chapter Review Questions

1. When linking an Autodesk Revit model into another project, which of the positioning methods keeps the model in the same place if the extents of the linked model changes in size?

   a. Auto - Center to Center

   b. Auto - Internal Origin to Internal Origin

   c. Manual - Base Point

   d. Manual - Center

2. If you want to toggle off all the grids in a linked file but still display them in the host file, what do you need to do?

   a. Select one of the grids in the linked file and select **Hide in View>Category**.

   b. Select one of the grids in the host file and, in the View Control Bar, expand ✎ (Temporary Hide/Isolate) and select **Isolate Category**.

   c. In the Visibility/Graphic Overrides dialog box, change the link's *Display Settings* to **Custom** and in the *Annotation Categories* tab, clear **Grids**.

   d. In the Visibility/Graphic Overrides dialog box, in the *Annotation Categories* tab, clear **Grids**.

3. Which of the following elements, as shown in Figure 2–66, can be copied and monitored? (Select all that apply.)

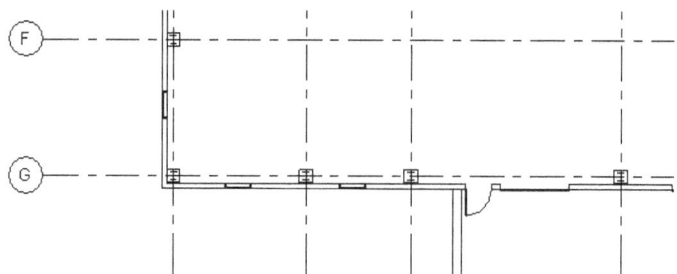

Figure 2–66

   a. Grids

   b. Walls

   c. Columns

   d. Doors

© 2020, ASCENT - Center for Technical Knowledge®

4. When working with nested links, which of the following describes the Reference Type that is NOT included when its host project is linked into another project?

    a. Attach

    b. Bind

    c. Import

    d. Overlay

5. What type of element(s) is created when you bring links permanently into a host file?

    a. The elements come in individually

    b. A block

    c. A group

    d. An import

6. When working with a linked file, as shown in Figure 2–67, what property do you need to set to be able to add rooms or spaces?

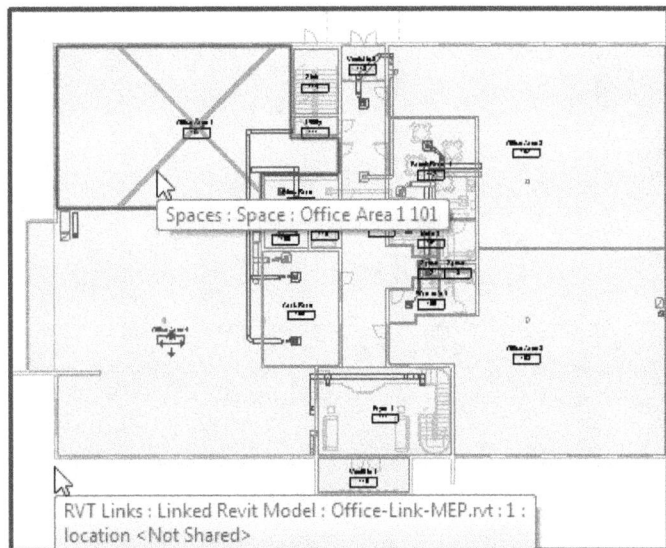

Figure 2–67

    a. Reference Type

    b. Room Bounding

    c. Phase Mapping

    d. Shared Site

7. In Figure 2–68, a wall in the link has been moved but the monitored wall in the host file has not been moved. How do you align the wall in the host file with the wall in the linked file? (Select all that apply.)

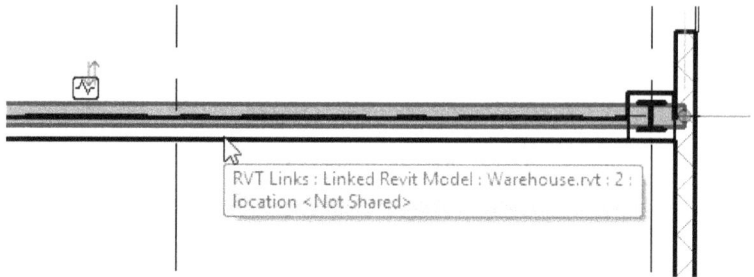

RVT Links : Linked Revit Model : Warehouse.rvt : 2 : location <Not Shared>

Figure 2–68

a. Move the wall in the host file so it matches the location in the linked file.

b. Run Coordination Review and select **Accept the difference**.

c. Run Coordination Review and select **Modify Wall**.

d. Run Interference Check and select **Match Centerlines**.

© 2020, ASCENT - Center for Technical Knowledge®

Command Summary

Button	Command	Location
	Bind Link (convert link to group)	• **Ribbon**: *Modify	RVT Links* tab>Link panel>Bind Link
	Copy/Monitor	• **Ribbon**: *Collaborate* tab>Coordinate panel
	Coordination Review	• **Ribbon**: *Collaborate* tab>Coordinate panel
	Interference Check	• **Ribbon**: *Collaborate* tab>Coordinate panel
	Link (convert group to link)	• **Ribbon**: *Modify	Model Groups* tab> Group panel>Link • **Shortcut**: LG (when a group is selected)
	Link Revit	• **Ribbon**: *Insert* tab>Link Panel>Link Revit
	Manage Links	• **Ribbon**: *Insert* tab>Link panel> Manage Links or *Modify RVT Links* tab> Link panel>Manage Links (if selected)
	Reconcile Hosting	• **Ribbon**: *Collaborate* tab>Coordinate panel>Reconcile Hosting

© 2020, ASCENT - Center for Technical Knowledge®

Chapter 3

Importing and Exporting

Files from other CAD programs can be linked and imported into an Autodesk® Revit® project. These elements can be traced over or used as is to create a hybrid project. Imported CAD files can be manipulated and even exploded into individual elements, which can then take on Revit properties. Raster images and PDF files can also be linked and imported into a Revit project. Information stored in Autodesk Revit files can also be exported for use in other CAD programs. The detailed building information that is stored in a project can be exported to other file formats that include DWF, DGN, and IFC. Further, information that is exported to a gbXML file can be used in energy analysis programs.

Learning Objectives in This Chapter

- Import or link files that were created in other CAD programs into an Autodesk Revit project.
- Query elements and delete layers in imported/linked CAD files.
- Explode imported CAD files.
- Import/link and modify raster images.
- Import/link PDF files.
- Export Autodesk Revit projects to other file formats, including CAD formats and DWF files.
- Export information contained in a project to gbXML that can be used in other energy analysis software.

3.1 Importing and Linking Vector Files

You can print a hybrid drawing - part Autodesk Revit project and part imported/linked drawing.

Many firms have legacy drawings from vector-based CAD programs and could be working with consultants that use them. For example, you may want to link a DWG plan into your project, as shown in the Link CAD Formats dialog box in Figure 3–1, that you would then trace over using Autodesk Revit tools. Other non-CAD specific file formats, including coordination models from Navisworks, IFC files and point clouds, can also be opened or linked into Autodesk Revit projects.

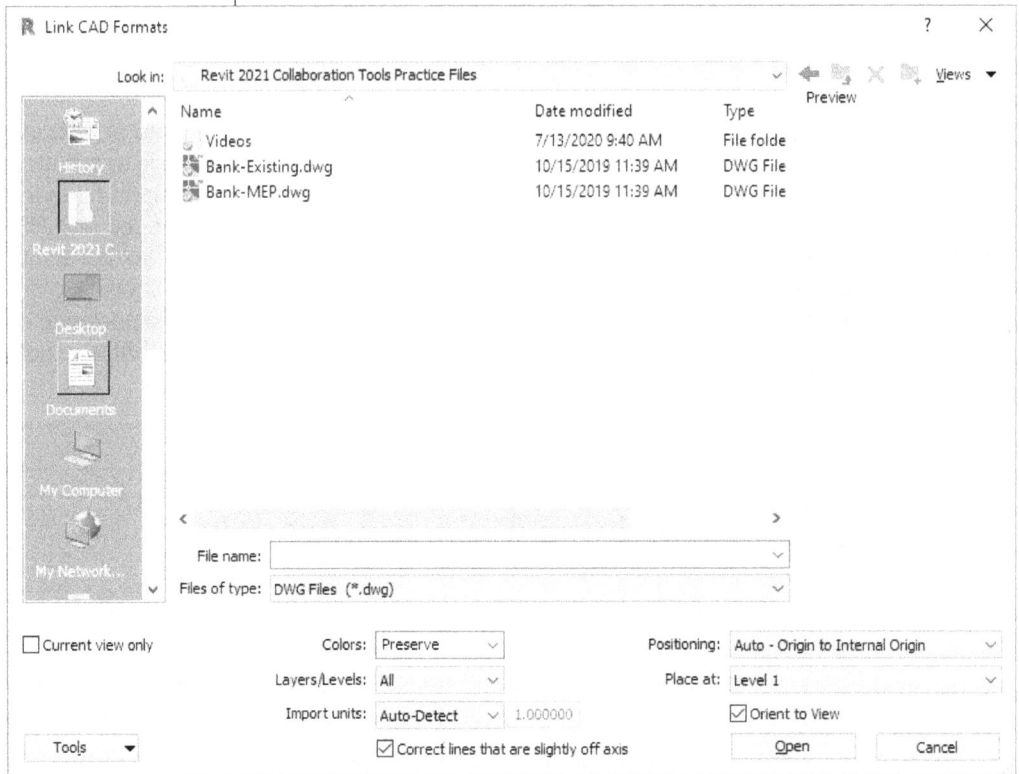

Figure 3–1

CAD file formats that can be imported or linked include AutoCAD® (DWG and DXF), MicroStation® (DGN), 3D ACIS modeling kernel (SAT), and Trimble® SketchUp® (SKP). Note that files from Rhinoceros® (3DM) can only be imported.

© 2020, ASCENT - Center for Technical Knowledge®

Linking vs. Importing

- **Link:** A connection is maintained with the original file and the link updates if the original file is updated.
- **Import:** No connection is maintained with the original file. It becomes a separate element in the Autodesk Revit model.

How To: Import or Link a CAD File

1. The dialog boxes for Link CAD and Import CAD formats are the same except for the Positioning method. Proceed as follows:

To...	Then...
Import a CAD file	In the *Insert* tab>Import panel, click (Import CAD).
Link a CAD file	In the *Insert* tab>Link panel, click (Link CAD).

2. Fill out the Import CAD (or Link CAD) dialog box. The top part of the dialog box holds the standard select file options. The bottom outlines the various options for importing or linking, as shown in Figure 3–2.

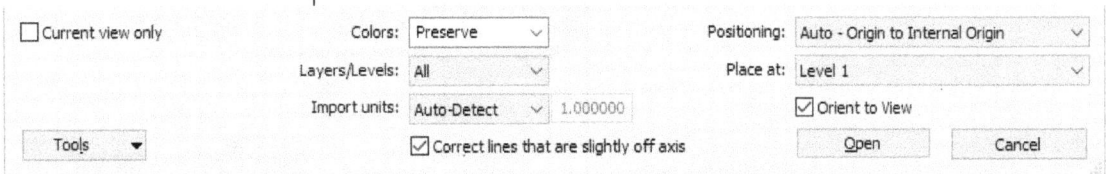

Current view only		Colors:	Preserve		Positioning:	Auto - Origin to Internal Origin	
		Layers/Levels:	All		Place at:	Level 1	
		Import units:	Auto-Detect	1.000000		☑ Orient to View	
Tools ▾			☑ Correct lines that are slightly off axis			Open	Cancel

Figure 3–2

3. Click **Open**.

Depending on the selected Positioning method, the file is automatically placed or you can place it with the cursor.

Link and Import Options

Current view only	If selected, the file is imported/linked into the current view and not into other views. You might want to enable this option if you are just working on a floor plan and do not want the objects to display in 3D and other views.
Colors	The Autodesk Revit software works mainly with black lines of different weights on a white background to describe elements, but both AutoCAD and MicroStation use a variety of colors. To make the move into the Autodesk Revit software easier, you can select to turn all colors to Black and White, Preserve colors, or Invert colors
Layers	You can select which layers from the original drawing are imported/linked. The options are All, Visible (those that are not off or frozen), and Select. Select opens a list of layers or levels from which you can select when you import the drawing file.
Import units	Autodesk Revit software can auto-detect the units in the imported/linked file. You can also specify the units that you want to use from a list of typical Imperial and Metric units or set a Custom scale factor.
Correct lines that are slightly off axis	Corrects lines that are less than 0.1 degree of axis so that any elements based on those line are created correctly. It is on by default. Toggle it off if you are working with site plans.
Positioning	Select from the methods to place the imported/linked file in the Autodesk Revit host project. If linking the file, Auto - By Shared Coordinates is available. Positioning: Auto - Origin to Internal Origin Place at: Auto - Center to Center Auto - Origin to Internal Origin Manual - Origin Manual - Center
Place at:	Select a level in the drop-down list to specify the vertical positioning for the file. This is grayed out if you have selected Current view only.
Orient to View	Select this to place the file at the same orientation as the current view.

- The default positioning is **Auto - Origin to Internal Origin**. The software remembers the most recently used positioning type as long as you are in the same session of Autodesk Revit. (The CAD Links dialog box remembers the last positioning used separately from the RVT Links dialog box.)

© 2020, ASCENT - Center for Technical Knowledge®

- If you are linking a file, an additional Positioning option, **Auto-By Shared Coordinates**, is available. It is typically used with linked Autodesk Revit files. If you use it with a CAD file, an alert box opens, as shown in Figure 3–3, containing information about the coordinate systems and what the Autodesk Revit software does.

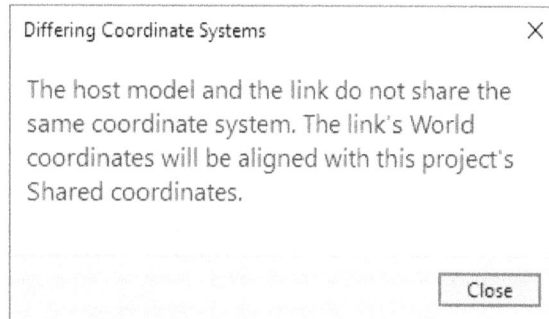

Differing Coordinate Systems ✕

The host model and the link do not share the same coordinate system. The link's World coordinates will be aligned with this project's Shared coordinates.

Close

Figure 3–3

- When you link a DWG file that includes reference files (XREFs), as shown in AutoCAD's External References palette in Figure 3–4, only files whose *Type* is set to **Attach** will display. Files whose *Type* is set to **Overlay** do not display.

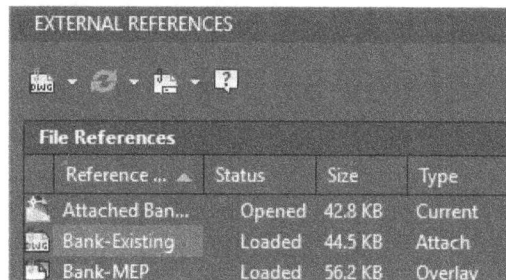

Figure 3–4

- When you import a DWG file, all XREFs display no matter how they are set up in the DWG file.

Importing Line Weights

One significant setting for imported drawings is the line weight. Both AutoCAD and MicroStation can use line weights as well as colors. Typically, AutoCAD line weights are associated with a color. Therefore, the Autodesk Revit software imports them by color.

How To: Import Line Weights

1. Before you import a CAD file, in the *Insert* tab>Import panel, click ⌐ (Import Line Weights), as shown in Figure 3–5.

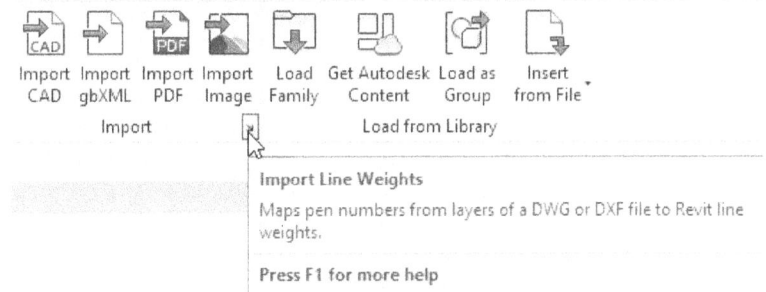

Clicking ⌐ in the title bar of a panel typically opens a settings dialog box related to the commands in the panel.

Import Line Weights

Maps pen numbers from layers of a DWG or DXF file to Revit line weights.

Press F1 for more help

Figure 3–5

2. In the Import Line Weights dialog box, shown in Figure 3–6, load a text file that holds the relationships or type them in the dialog box. You can then save them for later use.

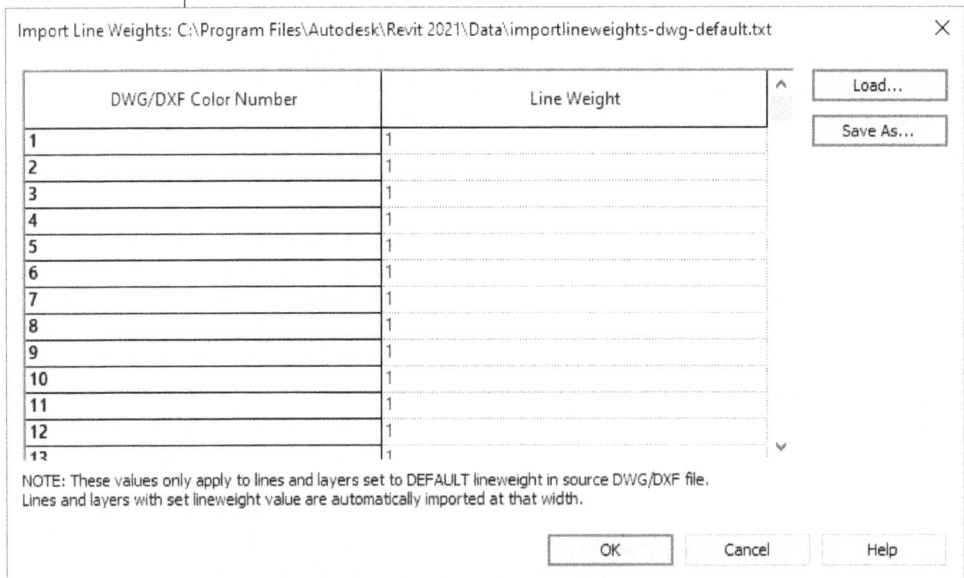

Import Line Weights: C:\Program Files\Autodesk\Revit 2021\Data\importlineweights-dwg-default.txt ✕

DWG/DXF Color Number	Line Weight		
1	1		Load...
2	1		Save As...
3	1		
4	1		
5	1		
6	1		
7	1		
8	1		
9	1		
10	1		
11	1		
12	1		
13	1		

NOTE: These values only apply to lines and layers set to DEFAULT lineweight in source DWG/DXF file. Lines and layers with set lineweight value are automatically imported at that width.

OK Cancel Help

Figure 3–6

3. Click **OK** and then import the CAD file.

© 2020, ASCENT - Center for Technical Knowledge®

- To load information from an existing text file, click **Load...** and select the file that you want to use. Several files are included in the *Data* folder, as shown in Figure 3–7.

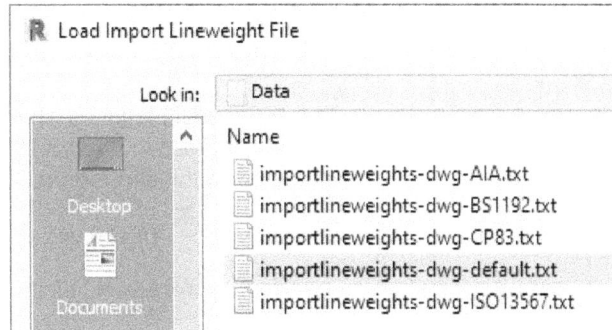

Figure 3–7

- To create a custom text file for specific projects, set up a sequence and click **Save As...**.

- Save your custom import line weight text files to a folder that is accessible to everyone that might need to use it. Do not save any custom files to the Autodesk Revit folders because they might be deleted if the program is upgraded or reinstalled.

> **Hint: Linking AutoCAD Civil 3D DWG Files**
>
> AutoCAD Civil 3D creates DWG files but the process of using them accurately in Autodesk Revit requires some extra steps. The Project Base Point in Revit is basically the same as the 0,0,0 origin point in an AutoCAD DWG. However, Civil 3D files typically use real world site locations established by surveyors. You can request a reference point (Northing, Easting, Elevation) from the civil engineer and add that information to the Survey Point in the Revit project before linking the site into the model.
>
> - Since the update to Autodesk Revit 2019.1, Civil 3D topography can be published to BIM 360 and then linked into Autodesk Revit. You must have BIM 360 to use this process.

Working with Other File Formats

There are additional file formats that can be opened or linked into Autodesk Revit projects, including IFC (Industry Foundation Class) elements, point clouds and coordination models. ADSK (Autodesk Exchange) files can be loaded and used as a family.

IFC (Industry Foundation Classes)

The IFC specification is an international data neutral format. Models created in any building design program can be saved or exported to this file format. You can open IFC files directly (*File* tab>Open> ✳ (IFC)) or link them into the current project (in the *Insert* tab>Link panel, click ⌐ (Link IFC)).

- If you are opening an IFC file, first set up the default template and manage the mapping of IFC classes to Revit Categories (*File* tab>Open> ✳ (IFC Options).

- Autodesk Revit models can be exported to IFC.

Autodesk Exchange Files

Building Component files, such as the blower created in Inventor shown in Figure 3–8, can be loaded and used as a family into an Autodesk Revit project. They display the real size of the equipment and can also include connectors to related MEP elements. They must first be saved in the original program as an Autodesk® Exchange (ADSK) file.

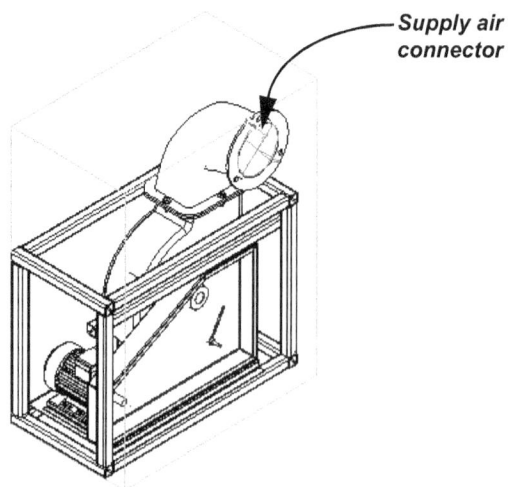

Supply air connector

Figure 3–8

© 2020, ASCENT - Center for Technical Knowledge®

- To use an ADSK file, first load it into the project (*Insert* tab> Load from Library panel, click ⬇ (Load Family)) and then use the **Component** command to place it.

- ADSK files can be saved as an RFA family file. In the *File* tab, expand 📂 (Open), expand 🗄 (Building Component) and select the ADSK file to open. Then, in the *File* tab, expand 💾 (Save As) and click 🗔 (Family).

Point Clouds

Point clouds are created using 3D laser scanners and are frequently used to establish accurate existing information. Once you link a point cloud (in the *Insert* tab>Link panel click

🔘 (Point Cloud)) into a project, as shown in Figure 3–9, you can snap to alignment planes and individual points.

Figure 3–9

There are three file formats that you can link:

- **RCS** - Individual indexed scanned models.
- **RCP** - Groups of indexed scanned models.
- Raw format point clouds must first be converted to RCS or RCP files using Autodesk® Recap® before being imported into Autodesk Revit.

How To: Link a Point Cloud

1. In the *Insert* tab>Link panel, click ⬡ (Point Cloud).
2. In the Link Point Cloud dialog box, specify the Positioning (Auto - Center to Center, Auto - Origin to Internal Origin, or Auto - By Shared Coordinates), as shown in Figure 3–10, and click **Add...**.

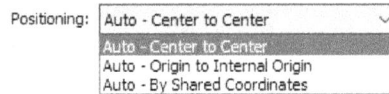

Positioning: | Auto - Center to Center ⌄
Auto - Center to Center
Auto - Origin to Internal Origin
Auto - By Shared Coordinates

Figure 3–10

- In the Visibility/Graphic Overrides dialog box, in the P*oint Clouds* tab, you can change the visibility and set a color mode. Each individual scan can be controlled individually.

Coordination Models

Many construction projects include designs from a variety of software programs. Autodesk® Navisworks® enables you to link together files from these different programs to create a coordination model. You can then link the models saved in Navisworks as a NWD or NWC file into your Autodesk Revit model, to help you coordinate the larger project, as shown in Figure 3–11.

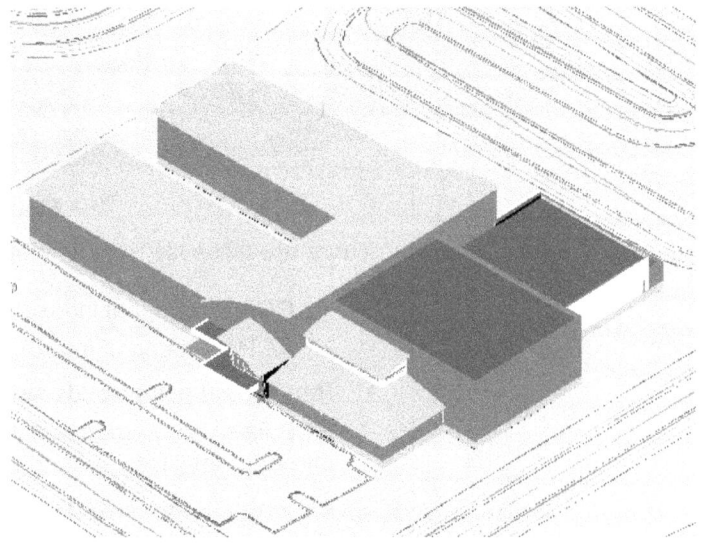

Figure 3–11

© 2020, ASCENT - Center for Technical Knowledge®

How To: Link a Coordination Model

1. In the *Insert* tab>Link panel, click (Coordination Model).
2. In the Coordination Model dialog box, specify the *Positioning* (**Origin to Internal Origin** or **By Shared Coordinates**), as shown in Figure 3–12, and click **Add...**.

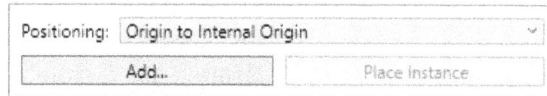

Positioning:	Origin to Internal Origin ⌄
Add...	Place Instance

Figure 3–12

3. Navigate to the correct file folder, select the Navisworks document (NWD or NWC), and click **Open**.
4. In the Coordination Model dialog box (shown in Figure 3–13), modify the *Path Type* if required and click **Apply** if you want to remain in the dialog box. Otherwise, click **OK**.

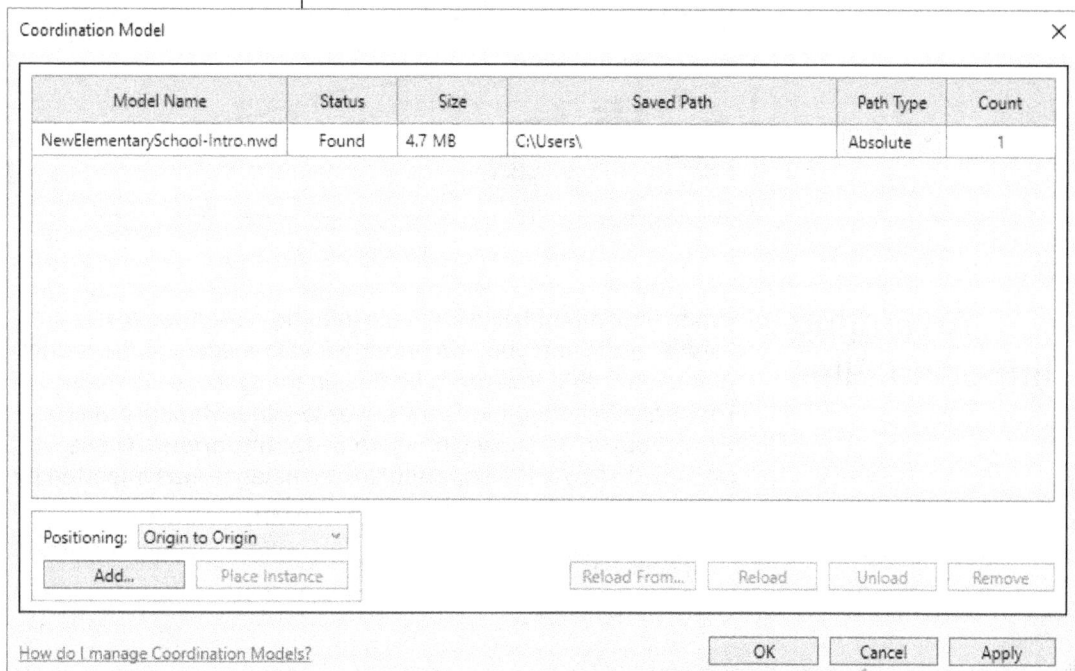

Coordination Model ✕

Model Name	Status	Size	Saved Path	Path Type	Count
NewElementarySchool-Intro.nwd	Found	4.7 MB	C:\Users\	Absolute ⌄	1

Positioning: Origin to Origin ⌄

| Add... | Place Instance | | Reload From... | Reload | Unload | Remove |

How do I manage Coordination Models?   OK   Cancel   Apply

Figure 3–13

- You can add copies of the coordination model if needed. Select the *Model Name*, specify the *Positioning* and click **Place Instance**.

- You can also use the buttons to **Reload From...**, **Reload**, **Unload**, and **Remove** coordination models.

3.2 Modifying Imported Files

When you select an imported/linked file, you can modify it by arranging the Foreground/Background status, modifying its Type Properties, querying information about elements in the file, and deleting layers. You can also modify the Visibility/Graphic Overrides of each imported/linked instance.

- An imported/linked file is called an Import Symbol once it is inserted into a project, as shown in Figure 3–14.

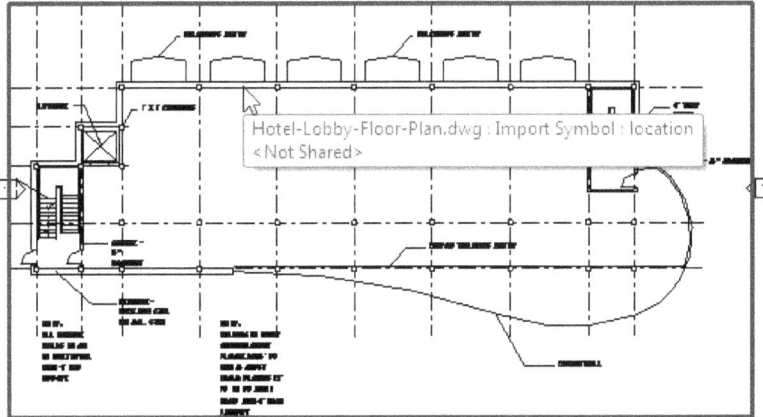

Figure 3–14

Arranging Imported Files

When you import/link a CAD file into the current view, it is view-specific and you can arrange it with respect to the model elements in the project. To do this, in the Options Bar or in Properties, change the *Draw Layer* to either **Background** or **Foreground**, as shown in Figure 3–15. **Important:** These options display if the imported/linked instance was imported by **Current View Only** or into a drafting view.

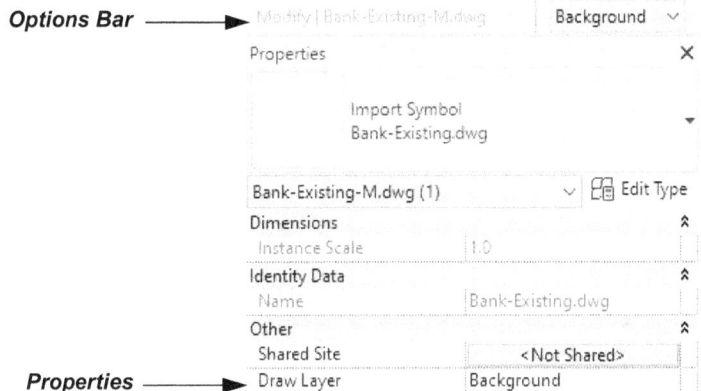

Figure 3–15

© 2020, ASCENT - Center for Technical Knowledge®

- If a file is linked/imported with Current View selected, you can also move imported/linked files incrementally using **Bring to Front** and **Send to Back** in the Arrange panel, as shown in Figure 3–16.

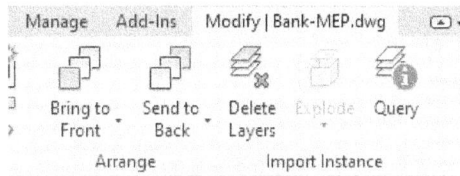

Figure 3–16

Modifying Type Properties

The *Instance Scale* and the *Name* of the file are Type Properties. Select the import/inked instance you want to modify and click

(Edit Type) to open the Type Properties dialog box, as shown in Figure 3–17.

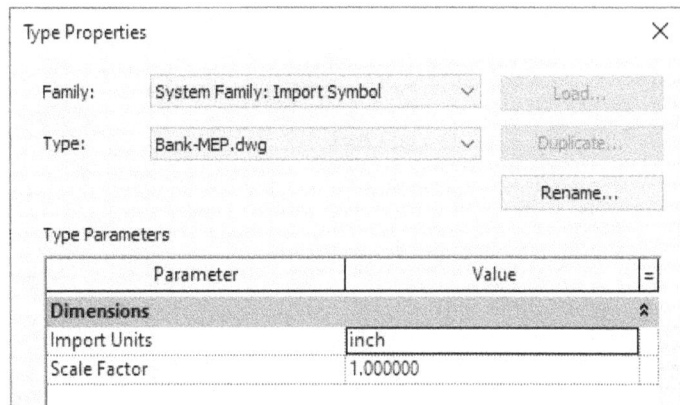

Figure 3–17

- If you change the *Import Units*, the *Scale Factor* is automatically updated. If the *Import Units* are the same type as the host units, you can change the *Scale Factor* independently. You might need to do this if the original file was scanned and not necessarily accurately to scale.

- You can also change the scale using (Scale). This command is not typically used on other Autodesk Revit elements.

- Imported/linked instances can be part of a group. If they are placed in the current view, they are the only ones to be considered detail elements, otherwise they will be considered model elements.

Querying Imported Files

When working with imported/linked files, it often helps to know what type of objects you are dealing with, without having to modify the file in any way. The **Query** command gives you this information and also enables you to delete or hide the layer of the selected object.

How To: Query Imported/Linked Files

1. Select the imported/linked file that you want to query.
2. In the *Modify* contextual tab>Import Instance panel, click

   (Query).
3. Select the element in the imported/linked file about which you want to inquire. The Import Instance Query dialog box displays information about the objects, as shown in Figure 3–18.

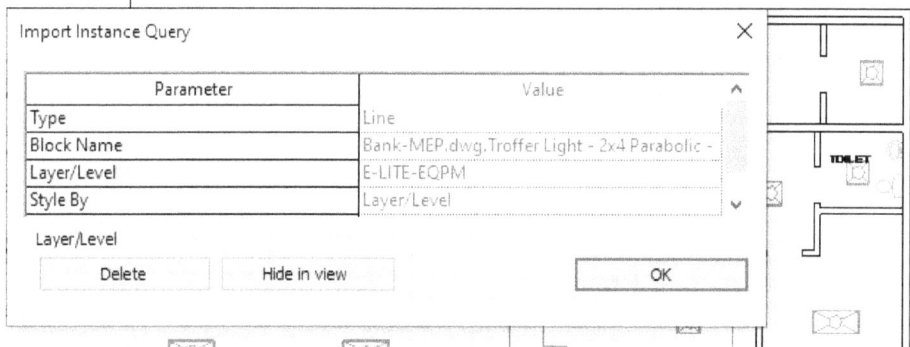

Figure 3–18

- Click **OK** if you just want to look at the object's information.
- Click **Delete** to remove all objects on the layer referenced by the selected object.
- Click **Hide in View** to hide (but not delete) all objects on the layer referenced by the selected object.
4. You are still in the **Query** command and can select other items in the file.
5. Press <Esc> to end the command.

© 2020, ASCENT - Center for Technical Knowledge®

Deleting Layers

If you are creating a hybrid file and there are layers or levels in the imported/linked file that you do not need in the project, you can delete them without exploding the imported file.

- Only items on the selected layers are removed. What is actually on those layers depends on how well the original drafters followed the layering guidelines.

- If deleting layers from a linked file, the layers and items on them are deleted inside the Autodesk Revit project only. The original file is not changed.

How To: Delete Layers in Imported/Linked Files

1. Select the imported/linked file.
2. In the *Modify* contextual tab>Import Instance panel, click

   (Delete Layers).
3. The Select Layers/Levels to Delete dialog box displays a list of all layers or levels in the drawing, as shown in Figure 3–19.

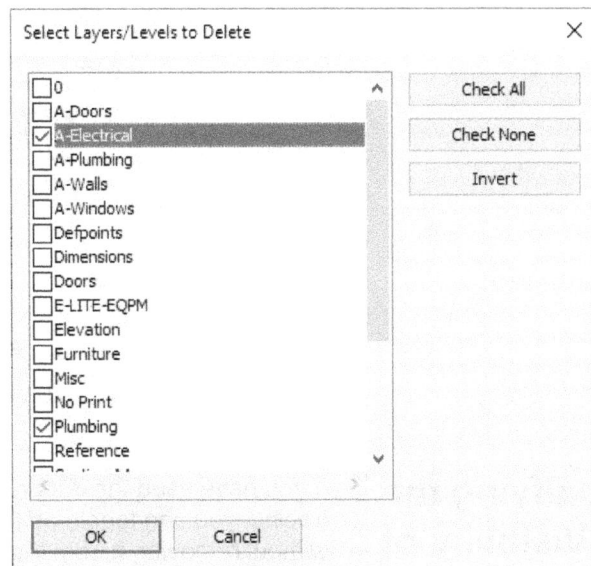

Figure 3–19

- Select the layers or levels that you want to delete from the imported/linked file and click **OK**.

Hint: Exploding Imported Files

Exploding CAD files is a dangerous action and is not recommended in most situations as it increases the file size of the project and leaves behind a variety of undesirable 2D elements. However, if this action is absolutely necessary, there are several commands to help. Select the imported file and in the *Modify* contextual tab>Import Instance panel, expand

Explode and click ⬜ (Full Explode) or ⬜ (Partial Explode).

- Full Explode converts everything to Autodesk Revit objects.

- Partial Explode converts all top-level objects but does not explode reference files or blocks in the imported drawing, as shown in Figure 3–20.

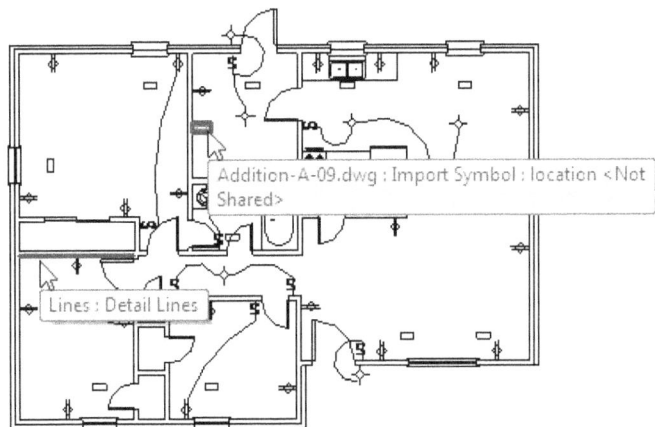

Figure 3–20

- Linked files cannot be exploded.

Modifying the Visibility of Imported Files

If you have used the imported/linked file as a guideline for tracing, you can toggle off the visibility of the entire image without removing it from the project in case you need it later. You can also toggle off individual layers or levels.

How To: Hide individual Layers

1. Open the Visibility/Graphic Overrides dialog box.
2. Switch to the *Imported Categories* tab. It displays a list for each imported instance, as well as its layers/levels, as shown in Figure 3–21.
3. To have the linked/imported file display in halftone, check the box in the **Halftone** column.

© 2020, ASCENT - Center for Technical Knowledge®

Click to have the imported/linked file display in halftone

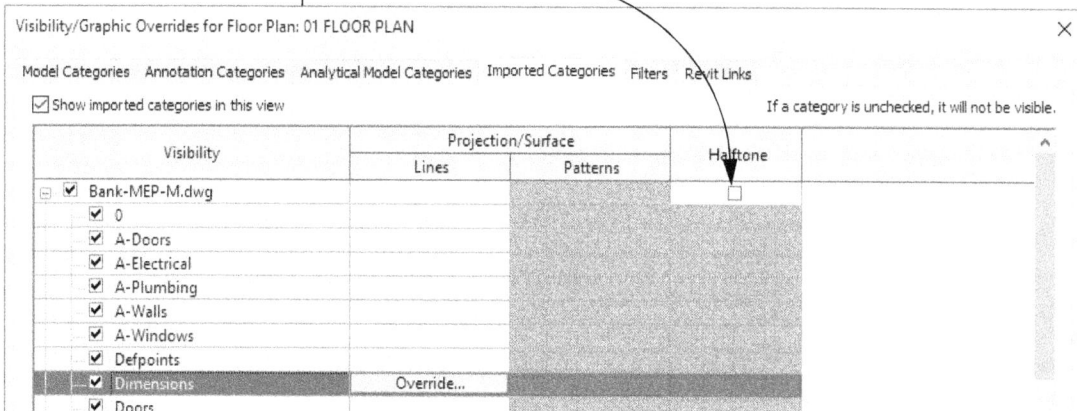

Visibility/Graphic Overrides for Floor Plan: 01 FLOOR PLAN				✕

Model Categories   Annotation Categories   Analytical Model Categories   Imported Categories   Filters   Revit Links

☑ Show imported categories in this view   If a category is unchecked, it will not be visible.

Visibility	Projection/Surface		Halftone
	Lines	Patterns	
☐ ☑ Bank-MEP-M.dwg			☐
☑ 0			
☑ A-Doors			
☑ A-Electrical			
☑ A-Plumbing			
☑ A-Walls			
☑ A-Windows			
☑ Defpoints			
☑ Dimensions	Override...		
☑ Doors			

Figure 3–21

4. Click the plus sign beside the file name to expand a list of the layers or levels in that file.

5. Clear the checkmark from the individual layers that you do not want to display.

   - Typically, these layers contain similar information, such as all windows or all notes in a drawing. However, it is not as definite as using Autodesk Revit elements. An item might have been misplaced on a different layer and if so, it does not toggle off.

6. Close the dialog box.

   - To toggle off the entire file, clear the checkmark next to the file name.

   - You can also use ♀ (Hide in View) and ✎ (Override Graphics in View) in the View Graphics panel or in the shortcut menu to modify the view graphics of an imported/linked file.

Practice 3a

Work with Vector Files - Architectural

Practice Objectives

- Link an AutoCAD file into an Autodesk Revit project and use it as a basis to add elements for a hybrid drawing.
- Query elements in the linked file and delete extraneous layers.

In this practice, you will create a hybrid CAD/Autodesk Revit project for an addition to an existing building. You will link an AutoCAD file into a project and add some Autodesk Revit elements, as shown in Figure 3–22. You will then query elements in the linked file, toggle off layers, and delete layers from the project.

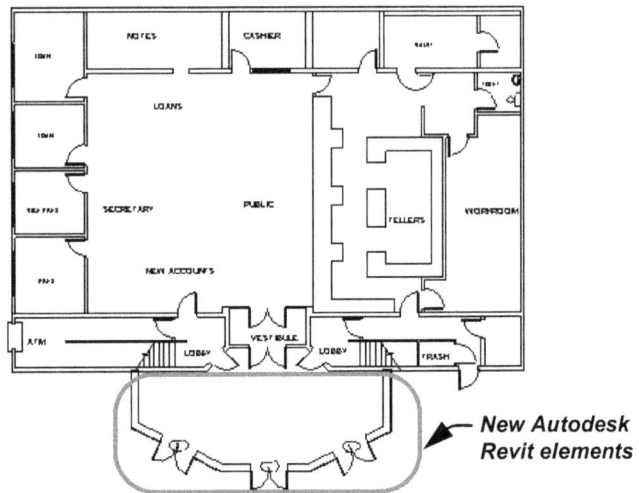

New Autodesk Revit elements

Figure 3–22

Task 1 - Link a CAD file and add Revit elements.

1. Start a new project based on the default Architectural template.

2. Save the project as **Bank Addition Architectural.rvt** in your practice files folder.

© 2020, ASCENT - Center for Technical Knowledge®

3. Verify that you are in the **Floor Plans: Level 1** view.

4. In the *Insert* tab>Link panel, click 🗋 (Link CAD).

5. In the Link CAD dialog box, in the practice files folder, select the AutoCAD drawing file **Bank-Existing.dwg** and set the following options:

   - Select **Current View Only**
   - *Colors*: **Black and White**
   - *Layers:* **All**
   - *Import Units:* **Auto-Detect**
   - Select **Correct lines that are slightly off axis**
   - *Positioning*: **Auto - Center to Center**

6. Click **Open**.

7. Switch to an elevation view. No elements are in that view—the imported information is 2D only. Switch to **Floor Plans: Level 2**. You will not see the linked file because it was linked in **Floor Plans: Level 1** with **Current View Only** selected.

8. Switch back to the **Floor Plans: Level 1** view.

9. Use the outline in front of the lobby and vestibule to draw exterior walls (with a Height to Level 2). Add doors (you will need to load a double door) and windows in front of the existing entrance of the building as a new entrance, similar to that shown in Figure 3–23.

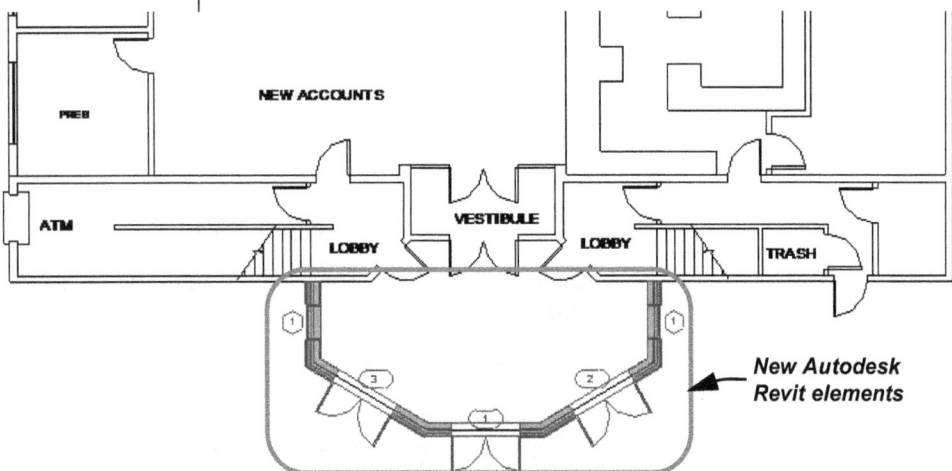

NEW ACCOUNTS

PREB

ATM

VESTIBULE

LOBBY   LOBBY

TRASH

New Autodesk Revit elements

Figure 3–23

10. Switch to the **Elevations (Building Elevations): South** view. You should see the Autodesk Revit objects in the view.

11. Save the project.

Task 2 - Query and modify the visibility of elements in the linked CAD file.

---

1. Return to the **Floor Plans: Level 1** view.

2. Select the linked CAD file. In the *Modify | Bank-Existing.dwg* tab>Import Instance panel, click 🔲 (Query).

3. Select the toilet bowl in the Toilet room. It is a block from AutoCAD on the layer **Plumbing**, as shown in Figure 3–24.

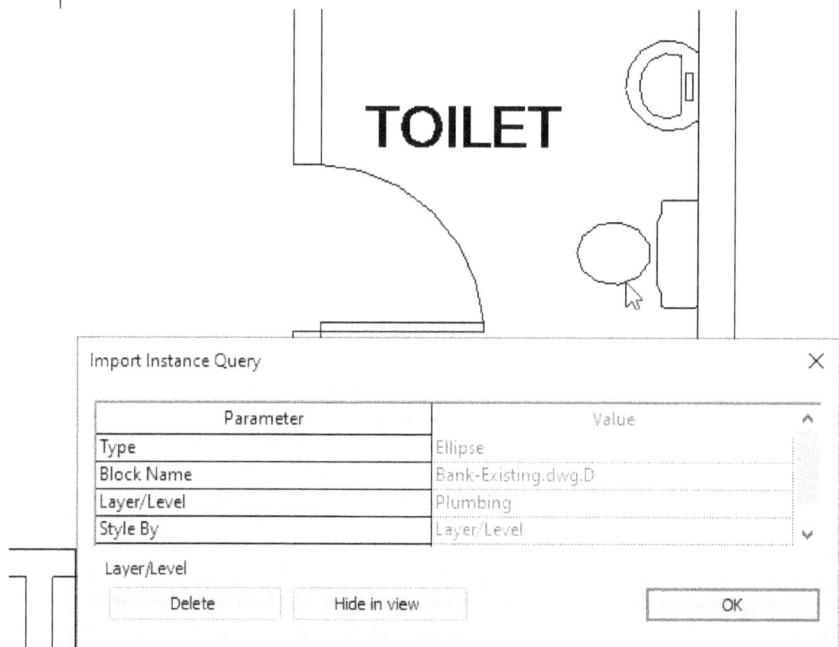

Figure 3–24

4. Click **Hide in View**. This and the other block are removed from the view.

5. Press <Esc> to end the query.

6. Type **VV** to open the Visibility/Graphic Overrides dialog box. Switch to the *Imported Categories* tab.

© 2020, ASCENT - Center for Technical Knowledge®

7. Click the "+" next to **Bank-Existing.dwg** to expand the layers. Toggle off the **Text** and **Furniture** layers. Click **OK**.

8. The cabinetwork of the tellers' booths is toggled off but the text still displays, as shown in Figure 3–25. Note that the text that was supposed to be on this layer, is actually on a different layer.

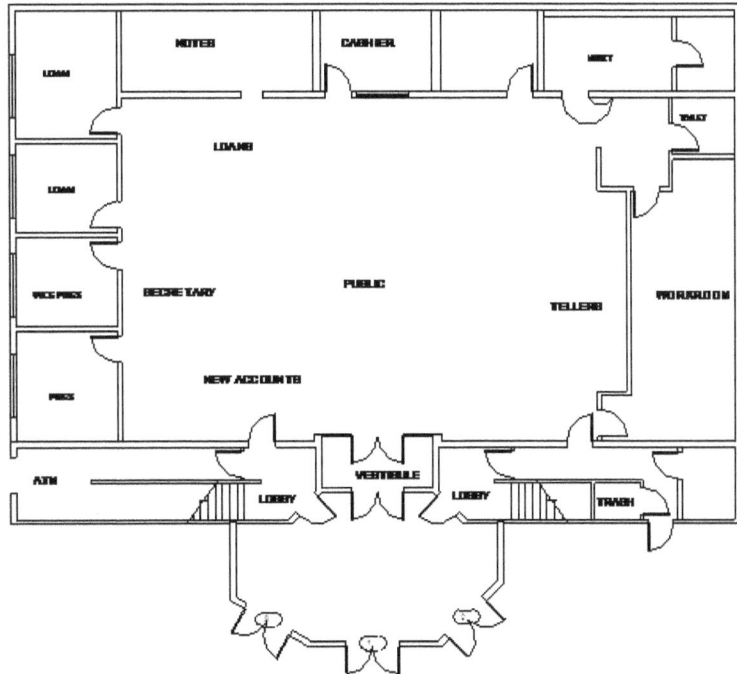

Figure 3–25

9. Select the linked CAD file and use $\stackrel{\textstyle\square}{\textstyle\circ}$ (Query) to find out which layer the text is on and hide it in the view.

10. Press <Esc> to end the query.

11. Elements on several layers are not required for this project. Select the linked CAD file in the project. In the *Modify | Bank-Existing.dwg* tab>Import Instance panel, click

$\stackrel{\textstyle\square}{\textstyle\times}$ (Delete Layers).

12. Select the layers **Header**, **Furniture**, and **Plumbing** in the dialog box, as shown in Figure 3–26, and click **OK**.

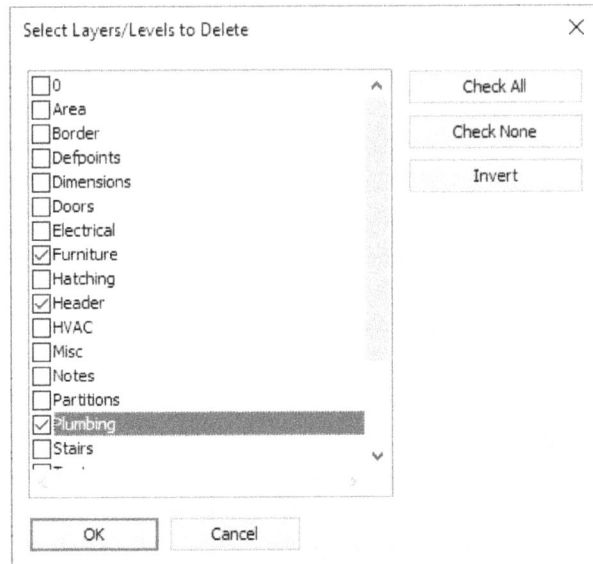

Figure 3–26

13. Save and close the project.

Practice 3b

Work with Vector Files - Structural

Practice Objectives

- Link an AutoCAD file into an Autodesk Revit project and use it as a basis to add elements for a hybrid drawing.
- Query elements in the imported file and delete extraneous layers.

In this practice, you will create a hybrid CAD/Autodesk Revit project for an addition to an existing building. You will link an AutoCAD file into a project and add some Autodesk Revit elements, as shown in Figure 3–27. You will then query elements in the linked file, toggle off layers, and delete layers from the project.

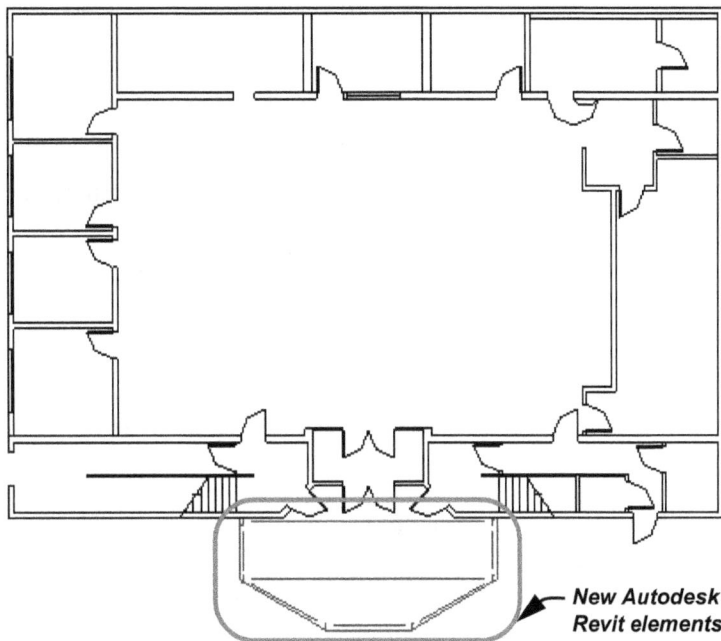

New Autodesk Revit elements

Figure 3–27

Task 1 - Link a CAD file.

1. Start a new project based on the default Structural template.

2. Save the project as **Bank Addition Structural.rvt** in your practice files folder.

3. Verify that you are in the **Structural Plans: Level 2** view.

4. In the *Insert* tab>Link panel, click ⬚ (Link CAD).

5. In the Import CAD dialog box, in the practice files folder, select the AutoCAD drawing file **Bank-Existing.dwg** and set the following options:

   - Select **Current View Only**
   - *Colors*: **Black and White**
   - *Layers:* **All**
   - *Import Units:* **Auto-Detect**
   - Select **Correct lines that are slightly off axis**
   - *Positioning*: **Auto - Center to Center**

6. Click **Open**.

7. Switch to an elevation view. No elements are in that view—the imported information is 2D only. Switch to **Structural Plans: Level 1**. You will not see the linked file because it was linked in **Structural Plans: Level 2** with **Current View Only** selected.

8. Switch back to the **Structural Plans: Level 2** view.

9. Change the imported CAD file to halftone in the Visibility/Graphic Overrides dialog box.

10. Add structural columns (with a *Depth* set to **Level 1**) and beams to the top of them using the outline in front of the vestibule and lobbies for a new entrance, similar to that shown in Figure 3–28.

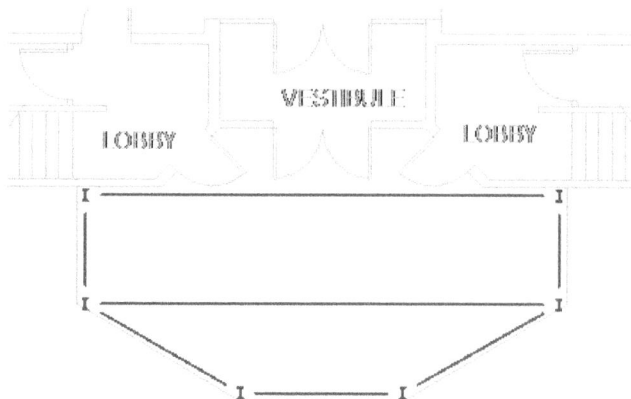

Figure 3–28

© 2020, ASCENT - Center for Technical Knowledge®

11. Switch to the **Elevations (Building Elevations): South** view. You should see the Autodesk Revit objects in the view.

12. Save the project.

Task 2 - Query and modify the visibility of elements in the linked CAD file.

---

1. Return to the **Structural Plans: Level 2** view.

2. Select the linked CAD file. In the *Modify | Bank-Existing.dwg* tab>Import Instance panel, click 📦 (Query).

3. Select the toilet bowl in the Toilet room. It is a block from AutoCAD on the layer **Plumbing**, as shown in Figure 3–29.

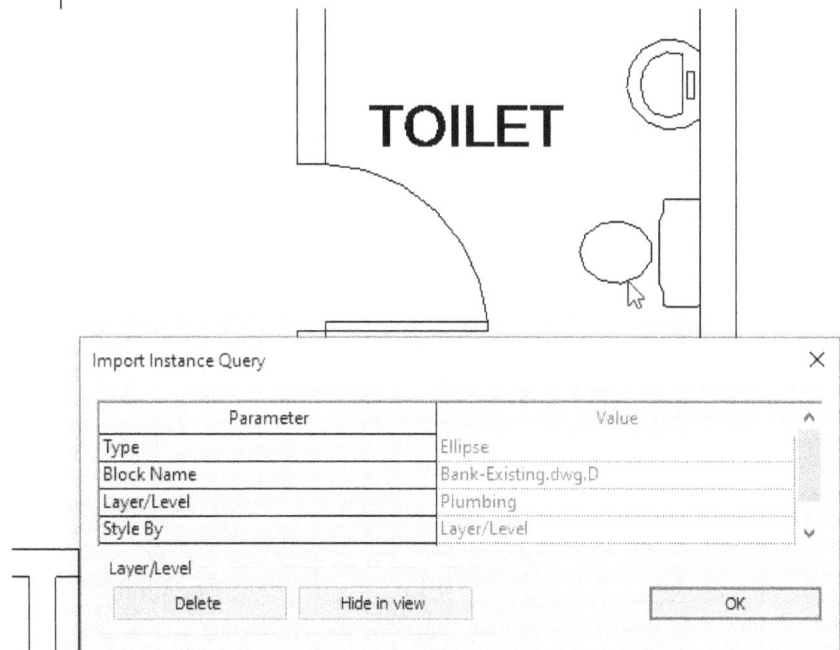

TOILET

Import Instance Query ✕

Parameter	Value
Type	Ellipse
Block Name	Bank-Existing.dwg.D
Layer/Level	Plumbing
Style By	Layer/Level

Layer/Level

| Delete | Hide in view | OK |

Figure 3–29

4. Click **Hide in View**. This and the other block are removed from the view.

5. Press <Esc> to end the query.

6. Type **VV** to open the Visibility/Graphic Overrides dialog box. Switch to the *Imported Categories* tab.

7. Click the "+" next to **Bank-Existing.dwg** to expand the layers. Toggle off the **Text** and **Furniture** layers. Click **OK**.

8. The cabinetwork of the tellers' booths is toggled off but the text still displays, as shown in Figure 3–30. Note that the text that was supposed to be on this layer is actually on a different layer.

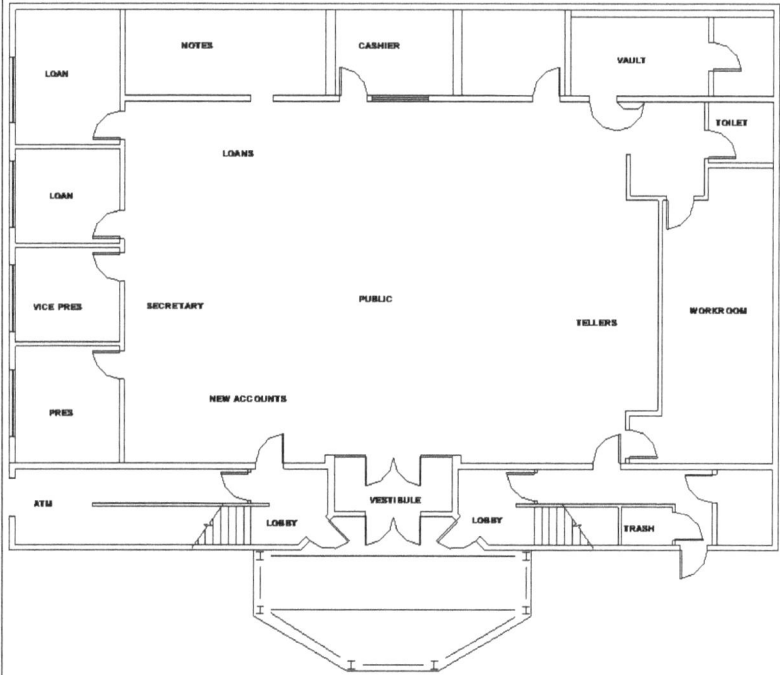

Figure 3–30

9. Select the linked CAD file and use ⛣ (Query) to find out which layer the text is on and hide it in the view.

10. Press <Esc> to end the query.

11. Elements on several layers are not required for this project. Select the linked CAD file in the project. In the *Modify | Bank-Existing.dwg* tab>Import Instance panel, click

⛣ (Delete Layers).

© 2020, ASCENT - Center for Technical Knowledge®

12. Select the layers **Header**, **Furniture**, and **Plumbing** in the dialog box, as shown in Figure 3–31, and click **OK**.

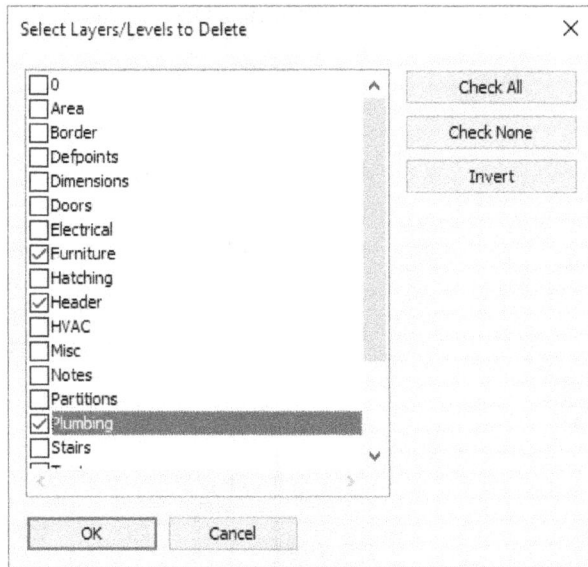

Figure 3–31

13. Save and close the project.

© 2020, ASCENT - Center for Technical Knowledge®

Practice 3c

Work with Vector Files - MEP

Practice Objectives

- Import an AutoCAD file into an Autodesk Revit project and use it as a basis to add elements for a hybrid drawing.
- Query elements in the imported file and delete extraneous layers.

In this practice, you will create a hybrid CAD/Autodesk Revit project for an addition to an existing building. You will link an AutoCAD file and an Autodesk Revit model into a project and add some Autodesk Revit elements, as shown in Figure 3–32. You will then query elements in an linked CAD file, toggle off layers, and delete layers from the file.

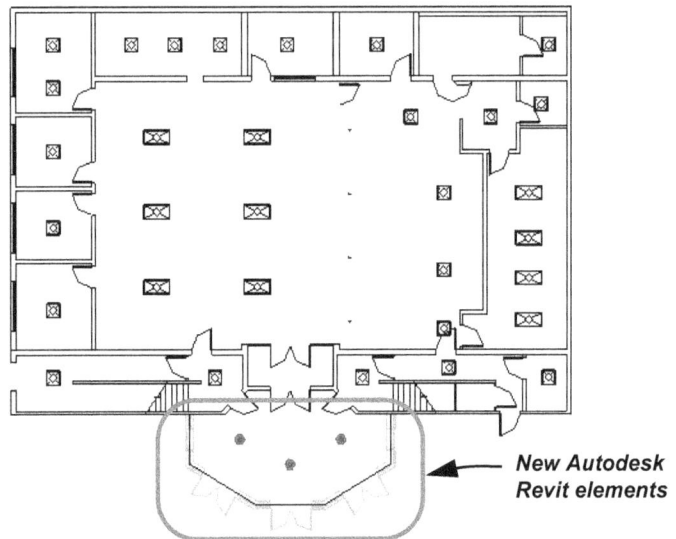

New Autodesk Revit elements

Figure 3–32

Task 1 - Import a CAD file.

1. Start a new project based on the Electrical or Systems template. (To access these templates, in the New Project dialog box, click **Browse...** and select the required template from the Autodesk Revit templates library.)

2. Save the project as **Bank Addition-MEP.rvt** in your practice files folder.

3. Open the Electrical>Lighting> **Floor Plans: 1- Lighting** view.

4. In the *Insert* tab>Link panel, click ⬛ (Link CAD).

© 2020, ASCENT - Center for Technical Knowledge®

5. In the Link CAD dialog box, in the practice files folder, select the AutoCAD drawing file **Bank-MEP.dwg** and set the following options:

   - Select **Current View Only**
   - *Colors*: **Black and White**
   - *Layers:* **All**
   - *Import Units:* **Auto-Detect**
   - Select **Correct lines that are slightly off axis**
   - *Positioning*: **Auto - Origin to Internal Origin**

6. Click **Open**.

7. Switch to an elevation view. No elements are in that view—the imported information is 2D only. Switch to **Floor Plans: Lighting 2**. You will not see the linked file because it was linked in **Floor Plans: Lighting 1** with **Current View Only** selected.

8. Switch back to the **Floor Plans: 1 - Lighting** view.

9. Link in the Autodesk Revit model **Bank-Addition-A.rvt** from your practice files folder using **Auto - Internal Origin to Internal Origin** positioning.

10. Open the Electrical>Lighting>Ceiling Plans>**1 - Ceiling Elec** view. The linked Autodesk Revit elements display in this view but the imported CAD elements do not.

11. Add several new lights in the new entry area similar to that shown in Figure 3–33. (This example uses pendant lights placed on the ceiling face.)

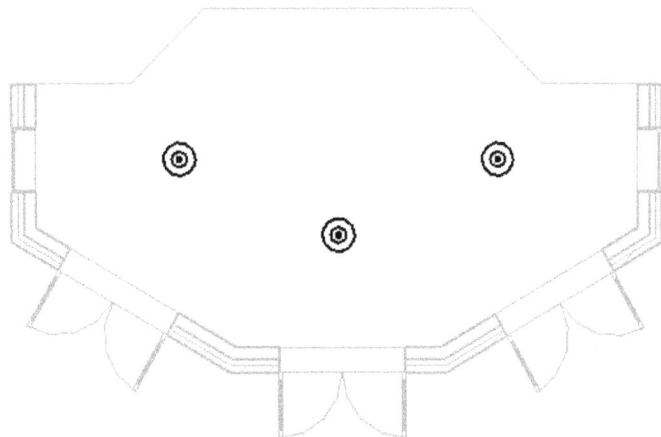

Figure 3–33

12. Verify that in the *Modify | Place Fixture* tab>Placement panel,

    ⬚ (Place on Face) is selected.Switch to the **Elevations (Building Elevations): North- Elec** view. You should see the Autodesk Revit objects in the view.

13. Save the project.

Task 2 - Query and modify the visibility of elements in the linked CAD file.

---

1. Return to the **Floor Plans: 1 - Lighting** view.

2. Select the linked CAD file. In the *Modify | Bank-MEP.dwg* tab>Import Instance panel, click ⬚ (Query).

3. Select one of the lighting fixtures. It is a block from AutoCAD on the layer **E-LITE-EQPM**, as shown in Figure 3–34. Click **OK**.

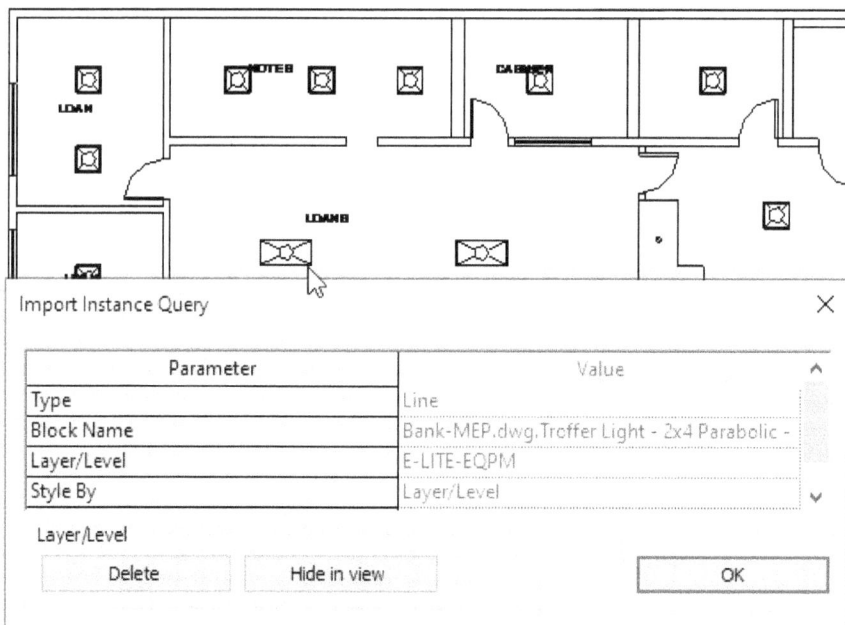

Figure 3–34

4. Select one of the elements in the toilet room. It is also a block on layer **Plumbing**. Click **Hide in view**. This and the other block are removed from the view.

5. Press <Esc> to end the query.

© 2020, ASCENT - Center for Technical Knowledge®

6. Type **VV** to open the Visibility/Graphic Overrides dialog box. Switch to the *Imported Categories* tab.

7. Click the "+" next to **Bank-MEP.dwg** to expand the layers. Toggle off the **Text** and **Furniture** layers. Click **OK**.

8. The cabinetwork of the tellers' booths is toggled off but the text still displays, as shown in Figure 3–35. Note that the text that was supposed to be on this layer, is actually on a different layer.

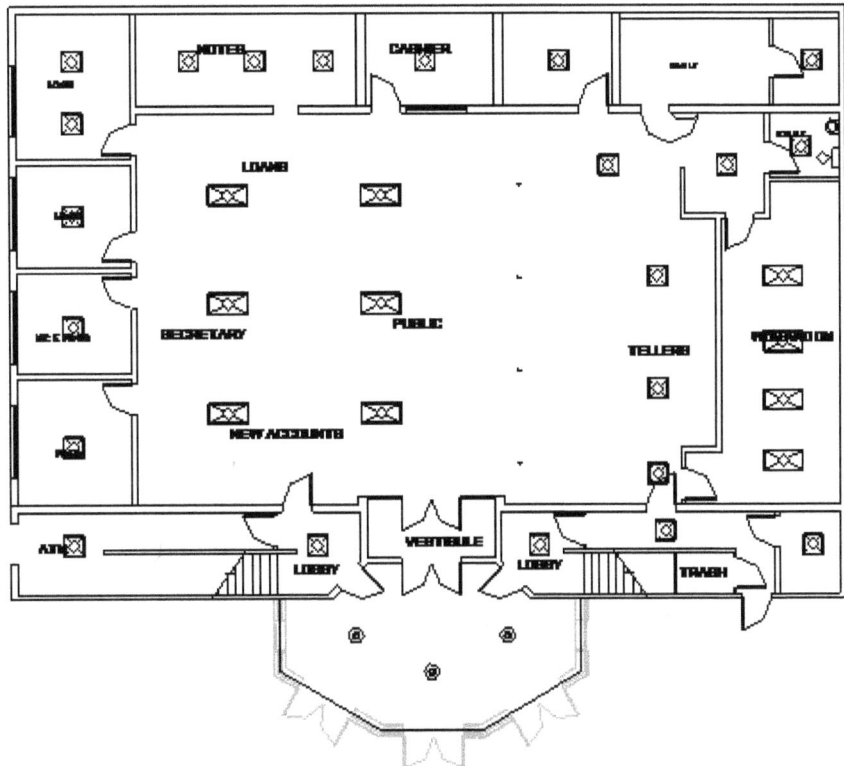

Figure 3–35

9. Select the linked CAD file and use ⌐ (Query) to find out which layer the text is on and hide it in the view.

10. Press <Esc> to end the query.

11. Elements on several layers are not required for this project. Select the linked CAD file in the project. In the Import Instance panel, click ⌐ (Delete Layers).

12. Select the layers **Header**, **Furniture**, and **Plumbing** in the dialog box, as shown in Figure 3–36, and click **OK**.

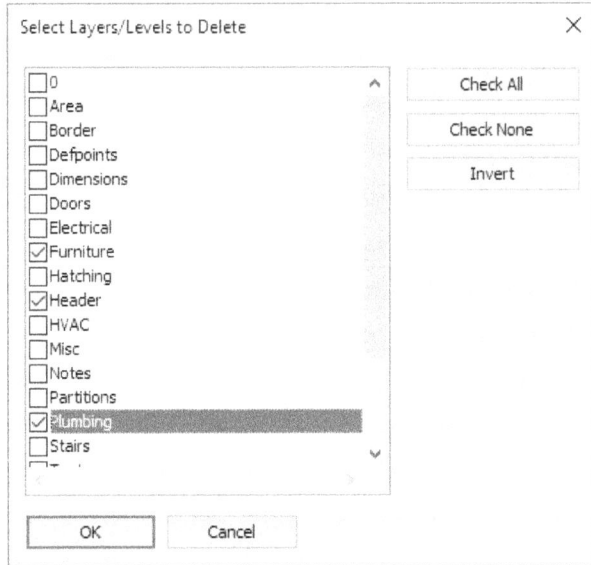

Figure 3–36

13. Save and close the project.

© 2020, ASCENT - Center for Technical Knowledge®

3.3 Importing and Linking Raster Image and PDF Files

Raster images are made up of pixels or dots in a file that create a picture. For example, a raster file is created when you scan a blueprint and then import or link it into Autodesk Revit to reference or trace. Another type of raster file is a PDF. Frequently used with text files, vector programs including Autodesk Revit and AutoCAD can also create PDF files that can be imported and linked into Revit, as shown in Figure 3–37.

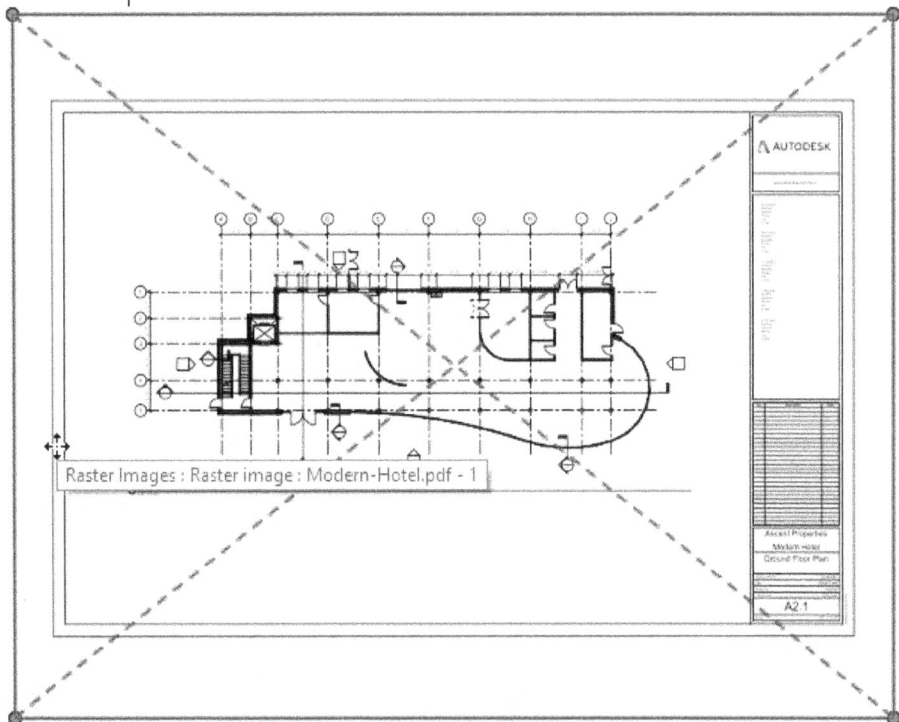

Raster Images : Raster image : Modern-Hotel.pdf - 1

Figure 3–37

- Link a PDF or raster image into a 2D view if you need to reference a file that will be updated throughout the project cycle and to keep the project's file size from increasing when importing files.

- Linked PDFs or raster images can be scaled, rotated, and moved just like an imported PDF or raster image. Any changes made to the PDF or raster image will update when you open your project that it is linked into.

- You cannot link PDFs or raster images while modifying/creating a family in the Family Editor.

Importing/ Linking Raster Image Files

A logo used in a title block is often a raster image made in a graphics program, as shown in Figure 3–38. You can add raster images to any 2D view, including sheet files. They can be used as a background view or as part of the final drawing. Imported or linked images are placed behind model objects and annotations.

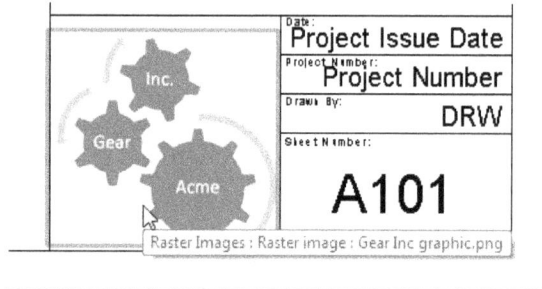

Figure 3–38

How To: Import and Link a Raster Image

To...	Then...
Import an image file	In the *Insert* tab>Import panel, click (Import Image).
Link an image file	In the *Insert* tab>Link panel, click (Link Image).

1. In the Import Image or Link Image dialog box, select the image you want to insert. You can insert .bmp, .jpg, .jpeg, .png, and .tif files.
2. Click **Open**. Four blue dots and an "x" illustrate the default size of the image file, as shown on the left in Figure 3–39. Click on the screen to place the image. It displays with the shape handles still visible, as shown on the right in Figure 3–39.

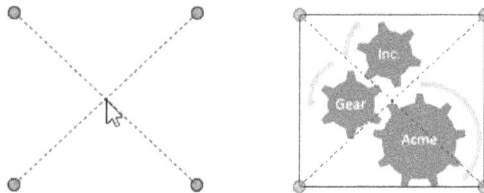

Figure 3–39

3. Drag the shape handles to resize the graphic, as needed.

© 2020, ASCENT - Center for Technical Knowledge®

Editing Raster Files

Select an imported/linked image to make changes. Once it is selected, you can resize the image as you did when you first inserted it or in Properties, specify *Width* and *Height* values.

- Select **Lock Proportions** in the Options Bar to ensure that the length and width resize proportionally to each other when you adjust the size of an image.

- Use the standard modification tools to **Move**, **Copy**, **Rotate**, **Mirror**, **Array**, and **Scale** images. Images can also be grouped together into Detail Groups.

- The Foreground/Background status can also be set in the Options Bar and in Properties, as shown in Figure 3–40.

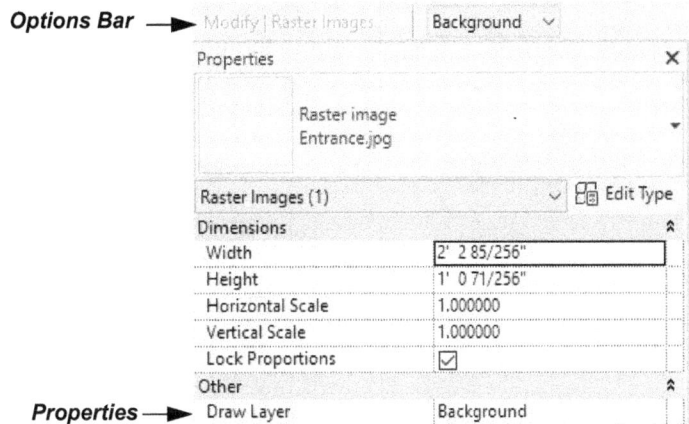

Figure 3–40

- From the *Modify | Raster Images* tab>Arrange panel, use the Arrange tools, as shown in Figure 3–41, to move images to the front or back of other images or objects.

- You can snap to edges of images, as shown in Figure 3–42.

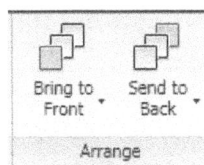

Figure 3–41

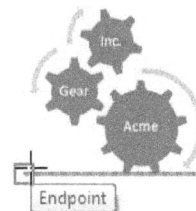

Figure 3–42

Importing/ Linking PDF Files

PDF files are often created for sharing information with people that do not have the original program and when you do not want anyone to change the original information. They can also be used as underlays when the original information includes vector data.

How To: Import and Link a PDF File

To...	Then...
Import a PDF file	In the *Insert* tab>Import panel, click (Import PDF).
Link a PDF file	In the *Insert* tab>Link panel, click (Link PDF).

1. In the Import PDF or Link PDF dialog box, navigate to the location where the PDF file is stored, select it, and click **Open**.
2. In the Import PDF or Link PDF dialog box (Figure 3–43 shows the Import PDF dialog box), select the page you want to import and click **OK**.

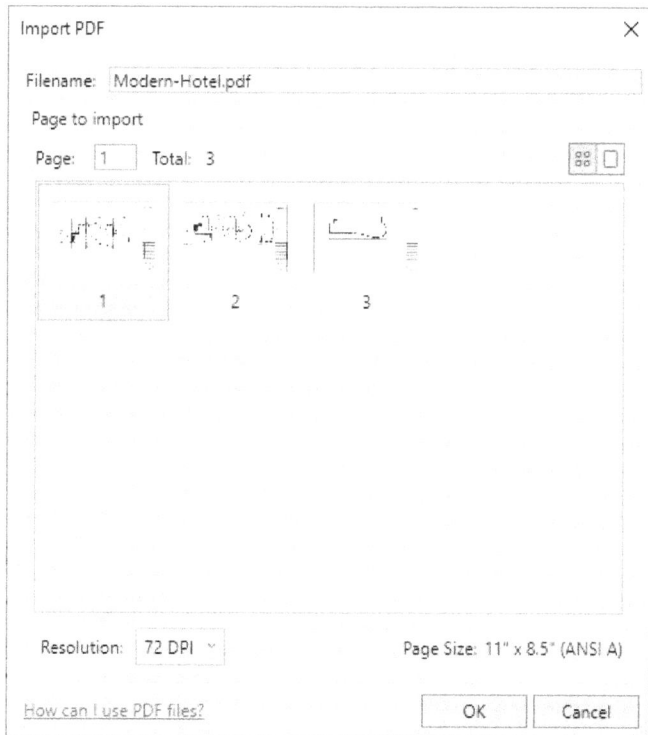

Figure 3–43

- Only one page can be imported/linked at a time, but you can import/link additional pages by repeating the process.

© 2020, ASCENT - Center for Technical Knowledge®

3. In Properties, you can specify the size and scale of the image, as shown in Figure 3–44.

- If the PDF comes from a vector source, you can also choose to enable snaps and trace over the elements in the PDF.

- The Foreground/Background status can also be set in the Options Bar and in Properties.

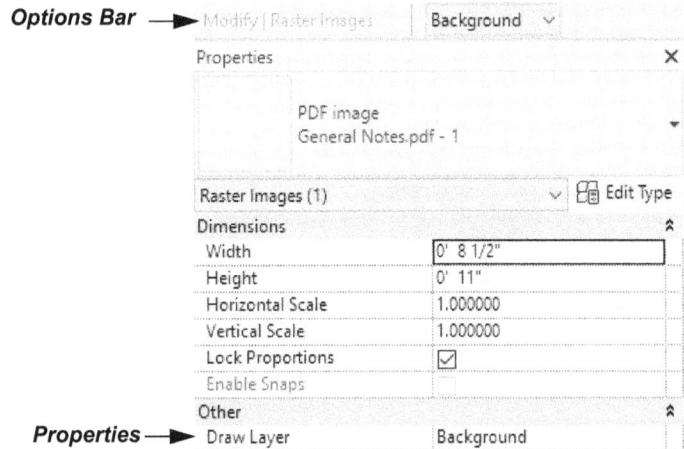

Figure 3–44

Managing Images and PDFs

Both images and PDFs can be modified from within the Manage Links dialog box, from either the *PDF* or *Images* tab.

- You can click **Add...** to add another PDF or image, **Place Instance** to place another instance of the selected PDF or image, or **Show** to open the project view that the PDF or image is in. You can also **Reload From...**, **Reload**, **Unload**, and **Remove** a PDF or image.

- If you have linked a PDF or image, you can change it to be imported instead within the Manage Links dialog box by selecting the link name and clicking the **Import** button.

- Every PDF and image instance is saved. If you delete it in a project view, it will remain in the Manage Links dialog box. You must open the Manage Links dialog box, select the PDF or image, and click **Remove** to delete it from the project.

- You can select more than one instance of PDFs or images within the Manage Links dialog box to reload or remove.

How To: Manage PDFs and Image files

1. In the *Insert* tab>Link panel, click ⬛ (Manage Links), or select the image or PDF and from the *Modify* contextual tab>Image panel, click ⬛ (Manage Links) to open the Manage Links dialog box, as shown in Figure 3–45.
2. Click on the *PDF* or *Images* tab to view the files.
   - Select a PDF or image to modify or remove it from the project.

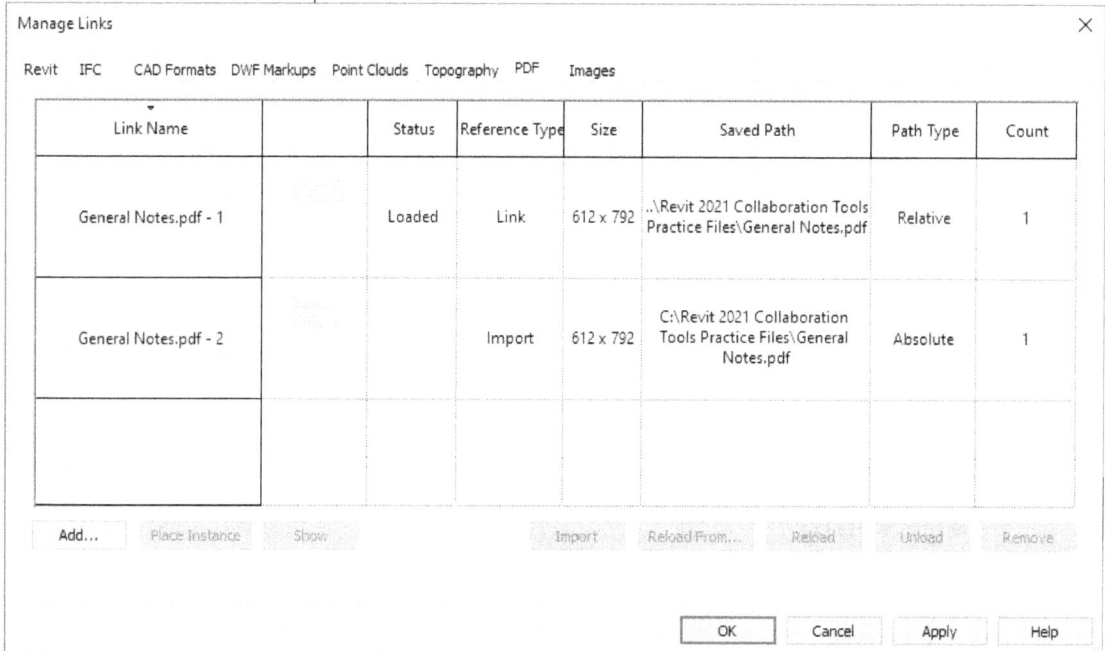

Manage Links   ✕

Revit   IFC   CAD Formats   DWF Markups   Point Clouds   Topography   PDF   Images

Link Name		Status	Reference Type	Size	Saved Path	Path Type	Count
General Notes.pdf - 1		Loaded	Link	612 x 792	..\Revit 2021 Collaboration Tools Practice Files\General Notes.pdf	Relative	1
General Notes.pdf - 2			Import	612 x 792	C:\Revit 2021 Collaboration Tools Practice Files\General Notes.pdf	Absolute	1

Add...   Place Instance   Show   Import   Reload From...   Reload   Unload   Remove

OK   Cancel   Apply   Help

Figure 3–45

© 2020, ASCENT - Center for Technical Knowledge®

Practice 3d | Import Image and PDF Files

Practice Objectives

- Add a rendered raster image to a sheet.
- Add a multi-page PDF to a sheet.

In this practice, you will add a rendered image of a new entrance to a sheet and add a multi-page PDF with General Notes to the same sheet, as shown in Figure 3–46.

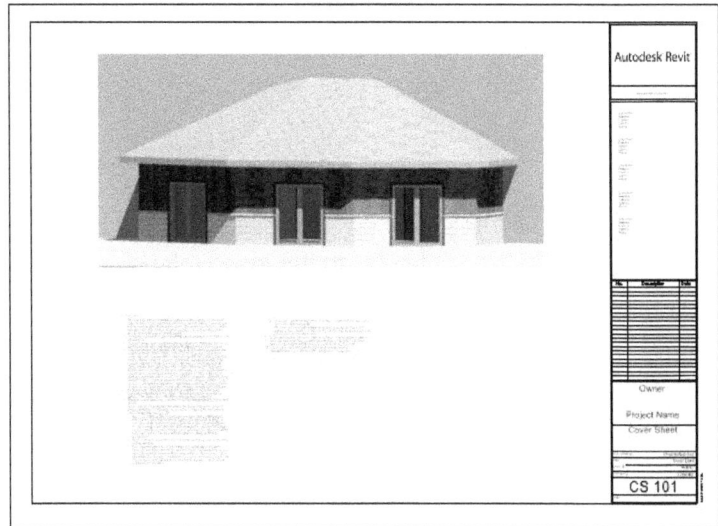

Figure 3–46

Task 1 - Add a PDF and image to a project file.

1. From the practice files folder, open **Bank-Addition-A.rvt**

2. In the Project Browser, expand the *Sheets (all)* node and open **CS 101 - Cover Sheet**.

3. In the *Insert* tab>Link panel, click 🖼 (Link Image). Select the image file **Entrance.jpg** (from your practice files folder) and place it on the sheet.

4. Move and resize it so that it fits on the sheet, as shown in Figure 3–47.

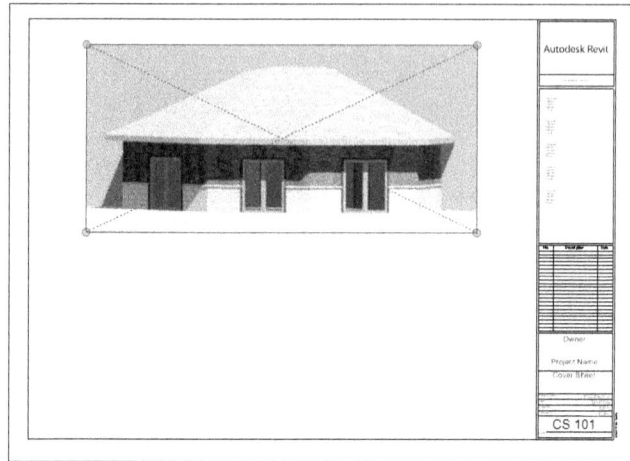

Figure 3–47

5. In the *Insert* tab>Import panel, click (Import PDF).

6. In the Import PDF dialog box, navigate to the practice files folder, select **General Notes.pdf**, and click **Open**.

7. In the Import PDF dialog box, select *Page* **1,** as shown in Figure 3–48, and click **OK**.

Figure 3–48

© 2020, ASCENT - Center for Technical Knowledge®

8. Place the text below the image, as shown in Figure 3–49.

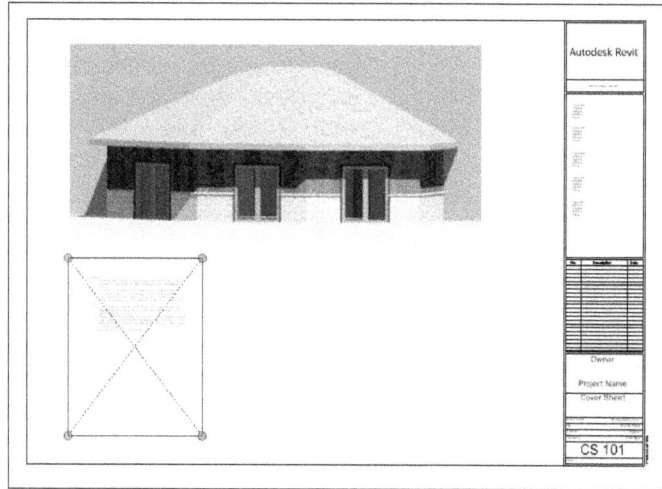

Figure 3–49

9. Repeat the process and add page 2 beside page 1.

Task 2 - Manage the linked image file.

1. Select the image and from the *Modify | Raster Images* tab>Image panel, select (Manage Links).

2. In the Manage Links dialog box, from the *Images* tab, note that the Entrace.jpg's *Reference Type* is **Link**, as shown in Figure 3–50.

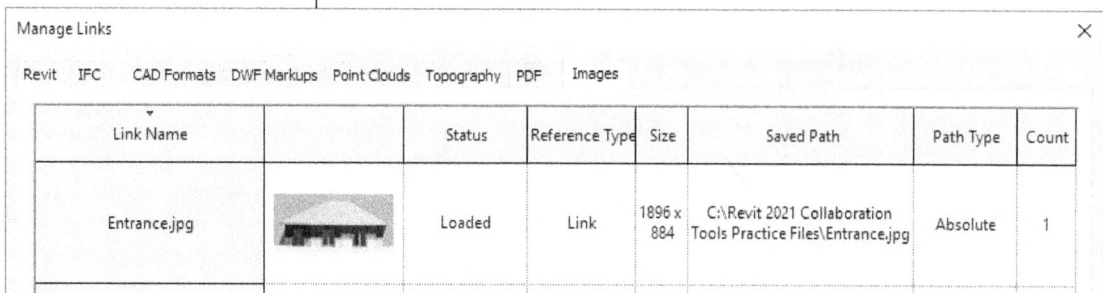

Link Name		Status	Reference Type	Size	Saved Path	Path Type	Count
Entrance.jpg		Loaded	Link	1896 x 884	C:\Revit 2021 Collaboration Tools Practice Files\Entrance.jpg	Absolute	1

Figure 3–50

3. Select the image and click the **Import** button at the bottom of the dialog box. The image's *Reference Type* is now set to **Import**.

4. Save and close the project.

3.4 Exporting Files

If your company uses multiple CAD programs or works with consultants who use other CAD programs, prepare your Autodesk Revit files so that the other programs can use them as well. The Autodesk Revit software provides ways to export Autodesk Revit vector data to CAD formats, DWF/DWFx, Images and Animations, Reports, FBX, gbXML, IFC (Industry Foundation Classes), and ODBC databases, as shown in Figure 3–51.

Scroll down the Export list to see additional options.

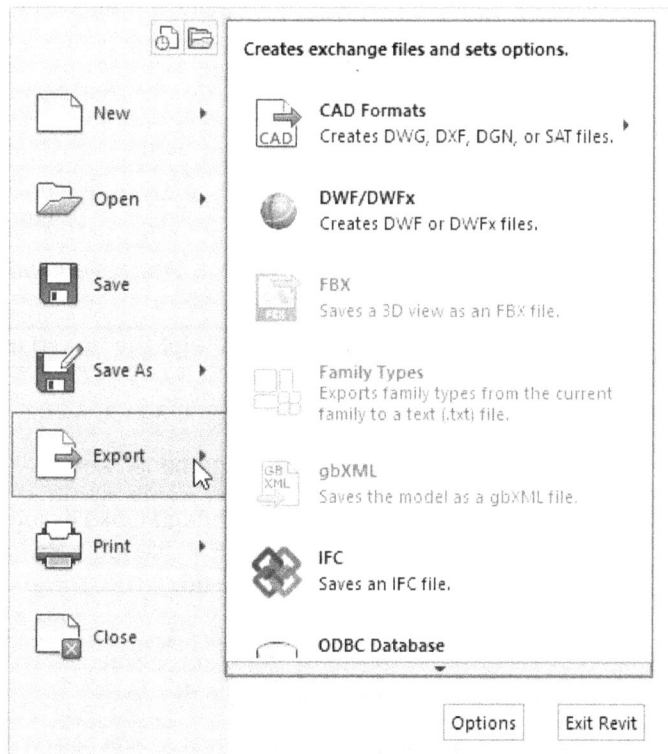

Figure 3–51

- Find out if the users for which you are exporting need a 2D or 3D view. You can export any view, but only 3D views export the entire building model; other views create 2D files.

- Text character size, location, and other text related properties is rendered faithfully when exported to other CAD file formats.

© 2020, ASCENT - Center for Technical Knowledge®

Export Types

- **CAD Formats:** Exports projects to AutoCAD DWG or DXF, MicroStation DGN, or ASIC SAT files for 3D modeling.

- **DWF/DWFx:** Exports views and sheets to DWF or DWFx files to be used in Autodesk® Design Review for review and redlining.

- **FBX:** Exports 3D files for Autodesk® MotionBuilder®, as well as Autodesk® Maya®, Autodesk® 3ds Max®, and Viz plug-ins. You must be in a 3D view for this to display.

- **Family Types:** Exports family type information to a text (.txt) file that can be imported into a spreadsheet program to verify that all of the parameters for each type are correct. You must be in a family file for this to display.

- **gbXML:** Exports model information that can be used in other programs for energy or load analysis.

- **IFC:** Exports the Autodesk Revit model to Industry Foundation Class objects. These can be used by CAD programs that do not use RVT file formats. It uses established standards for typical objects in the building industry. For example, an Autodesk Revit wall element translates to an IfcWall object. Additional mapping for specialty items can be set up.

- **ODBC Database:** Exports Autodesk Revit information to an Open Database Connectivity database file. It creates tables of the model element types and instances, levels, rooms, key schedules, and assembly codes.

- **Images and Animations:** Exports walkthroughs, solar studies, and images.

- **Reports:** Exports information from Schedules and Room/Area. Schedules are exported as delimited text files that can be imported into a spreadsheet. You must be in a schedule view to export. Room/Area reports are saved as HTML files.

- **Options:** Sets up the options for Export Setups for DWG/DXF, DGN, and IFC options.

- **NWC:** (Autodesk Navisworks or Navisworks NWC Export Utility installs only) If you have Autodesk Navisworks 2021 or the Navisworks NWC Export Utility 2021 installed, you will see the option to export to an NWC file type.

Exporting CAD Format Files

Exporting Autodesk Revit Projects to various CAD file formats is a common need in collaboration with consultants and engineers. Using this process, you can export individual views or sheets, or sets of views or sheets to DWG, DXF, DGN, and SAT files. You can also create and save sets of views/sheets.

- To improve performance and file size of the exported file, you will want to use Visibility/Graphic Overrides to turn off objects that are not being seen in the view you are exporting.

- Use a section box or crop region to minimize elements outside the region.

- Reduce the amount of detail by setting the view's detail level to Coarse or Medium.

How To: Export a CAD Format File

1. If you are exporting only one view, open the view you want to export. If you are exporting the model, open a 3D view.

2. In the *File* tab, expand (Export), click (CAD Formats), and select the type of format you want to export as shown in Figure 3–52.

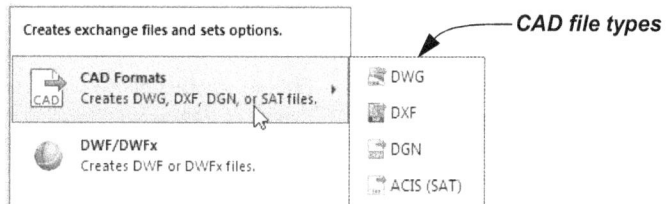

Figure 3–52

- The examples in this section show the process for DWG files. It is the same for other types of files.

3. The Export CAD Formats dialog box displays, as shown in Figure 3–53.

© 2020, ASCENT - Center for Technical Knowledge®

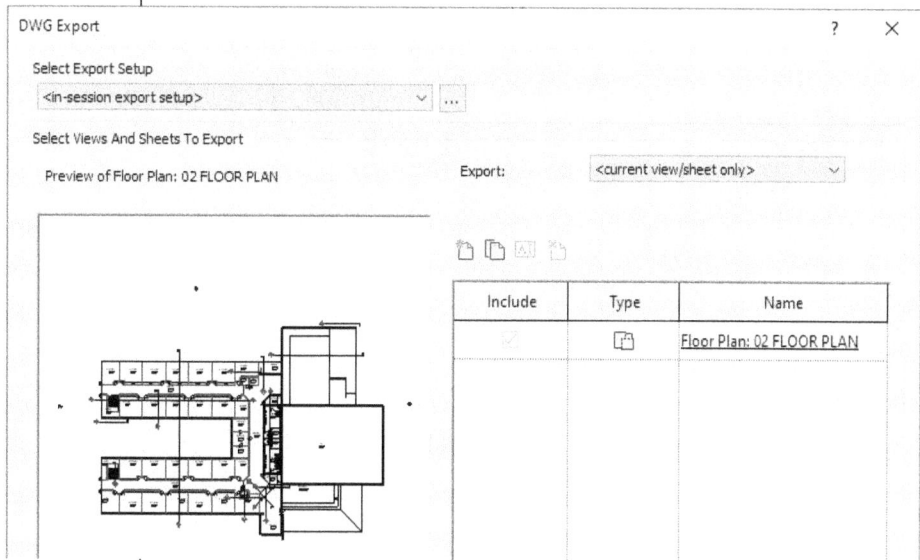

Figure 3–53

4. If you have an existing export setup, you can select it from the drop-down list as shown in Figure 3–54, or click

   [...] (Modify Export Setup) to create a new one.

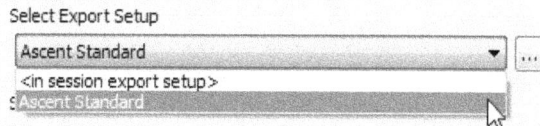

Figure 3–54

5. Select the view(s) you want to export from the Export drop-down list as shown in Figure 3–55.

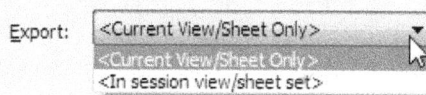

Figure 3–55

- To export only the active view, select **<Current View/ Sheet Only>**.

- To export any views or sheets that are open in the session of the Autodesk Revit software, select **<In session view/sheet set>**.

- To export a predefined set of views or sheets, select the name from the list if it is available. You can create new sets of views and sheets to export.

6. When everything is set up correctly, click **Next....**
7. In the Export CAD Formats - Save to Target Folder dialog box, select the folder location and name. If you are exporting to DWG or DXF, select the version in the Files of type drop-down list.
8. Click **OK.**

- The Project Base Point of the Autodesk Revit project becomes the 0,0 coordinate point in other CAD formats.

How To: Create an Export Setup

1. In the DWG, DXF, or DGN Export dialog box, next to the Select Export Setup list, click ⌐…⌐ (Modify Export Setup) or in the *File* tab, expand ⌐➡ (Export), scroll down to ✎ (Options), expand it, and select ☰ (Export Setups DWG/DXF) or ⌐ (Export Setups DGN).
2. The Modify DWG/DXF or Modify DGN Export Setup dialog box contains all of the elements and types you can export. You can select an existing Layer standard provided with the program (as shown in Figure 3–56), or create a new one.

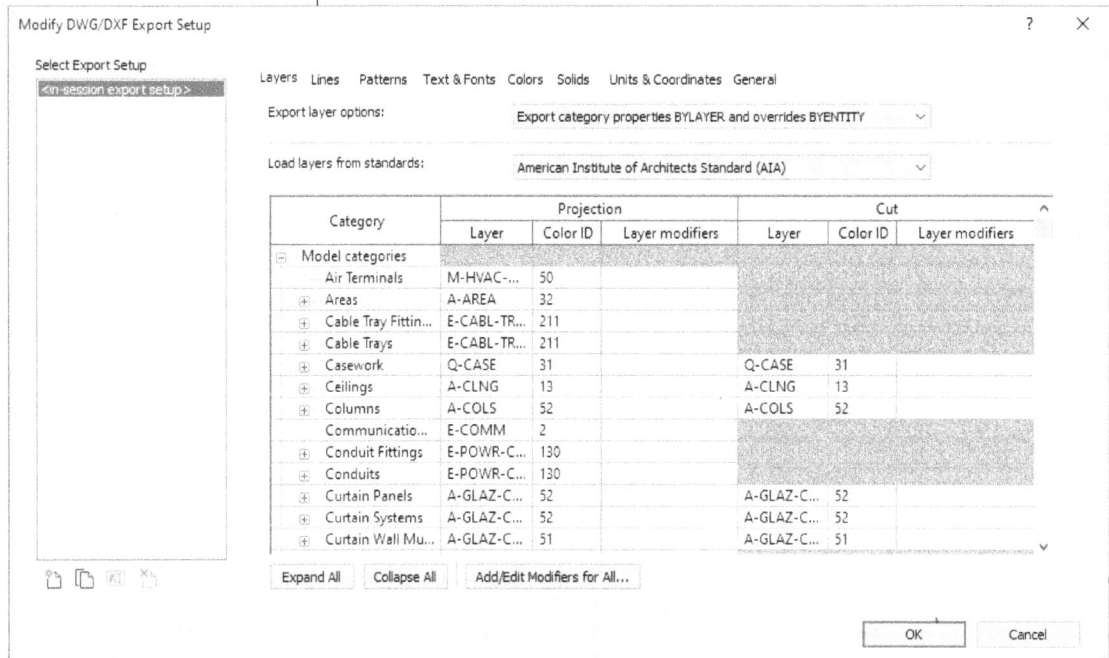

Figure 3–56

© 2020, ASCENT - Center for Technical Knowledge®

3. Select each of the tabs and apply the appropriate information.

- In the *Layers* tab, map the Categories in the Autodesk Revit software to the Layers (or Levels).
- In the *Lines*, *Patterns*, and *Text & Fonts* tabs map the styles required.
- In the *Colors* tab, select to export either Index colors (255 colors) or True color (RGB values).
- In the *Solids* tab (3D views only), select to export to either Polymesh or ACIS solids.
- In the *Units & Coordinates* tab, specify what unit type one DWG unit is and the basis for the coordinate system.
- In the *General* tab, you can set up how the rooms and room boundaries are exported, what to do with any non-plottable layers, how scope boxes, reference planes, coincident lines, and unreferenced view tags are handled, how views on sheets and links are treated, and which version of the DWG file format to use.

- Export setups can be created in a template file or shared between open projects using Transfer Project Standards.

How To: Create a New Set of Views/Sheets to Export

1. Start the appropriate Export CAD Formats command.

2. In the Export CAD Formats dialog box, click (New Set).
3. In the New Set dialog box, type a name and click **OK**.

4. The tab displays with the new set active and additional information, as shown in Figure 3–57.

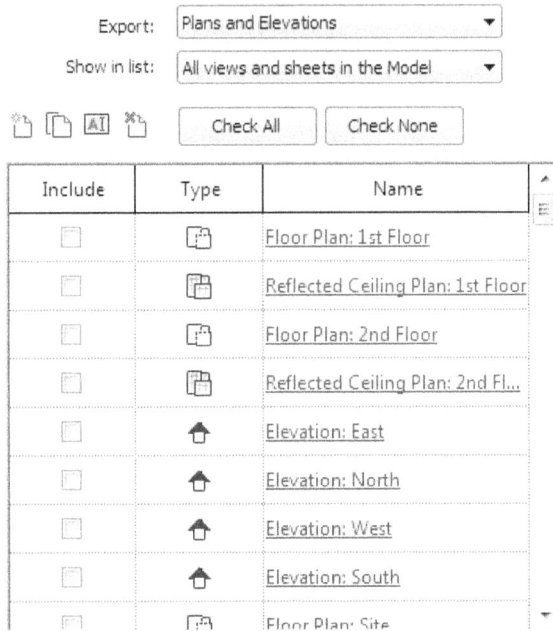

| Export: | Plans and Elevations ▼ |
| Show in list: | All views and sheets in the Model ▼ |

📄 📋 A1 📄 | Check All | Check None |

Include	Type	Name
☐	🗂	Floor Plan: 1st Floor
☐	🗂	Reflected Ceiling Plan: 1st Floor
☐	🗂	Floor Plan: 2nd Floor
☐	🗂	Reflected Ceiling Plan: 2nd Fl...
☐	⬆	Elevation: East
☐	⬆	Elevation: North
☐	⬆	Elevation: West
☐	⬆	Elevation: South
☐	🗂	Floor Plan: Site

Figure 3–57

5. Use *Show in List* to limit the number of items that display in the table.
6. Select the views and/or sheets that you want to export from the project.
   - Use **Check all** or **Check none** to aid in selection.
7. When you finish with the set, continue the export process.

Exporting to DWF

Exporting DWF/DWFx (Design Web Format) files gives you a safe and easy way to share Autodesk Revit project information without sending the actual file. For example, a client does not have to have the Autodesk Revit software on their machine to view the file and they cannot make any changes directly to it. DWF/DWFx files are also much smaller than project files and are therefore easier to email or post on a website. DWF/DWFx files can include element data that can be viewed in Autodesk Design Review.

© 2020, ASCENT - Center for Technical Knowledge®

The process of exporting a DWF file is similar to CAD Format exports. You can export individual views or sheets, as shown in Figure 3–58, or you can create sets of multiple views/sheets by clicking on ⬚ (New Set) and selecting from all the views/sheets in the project.

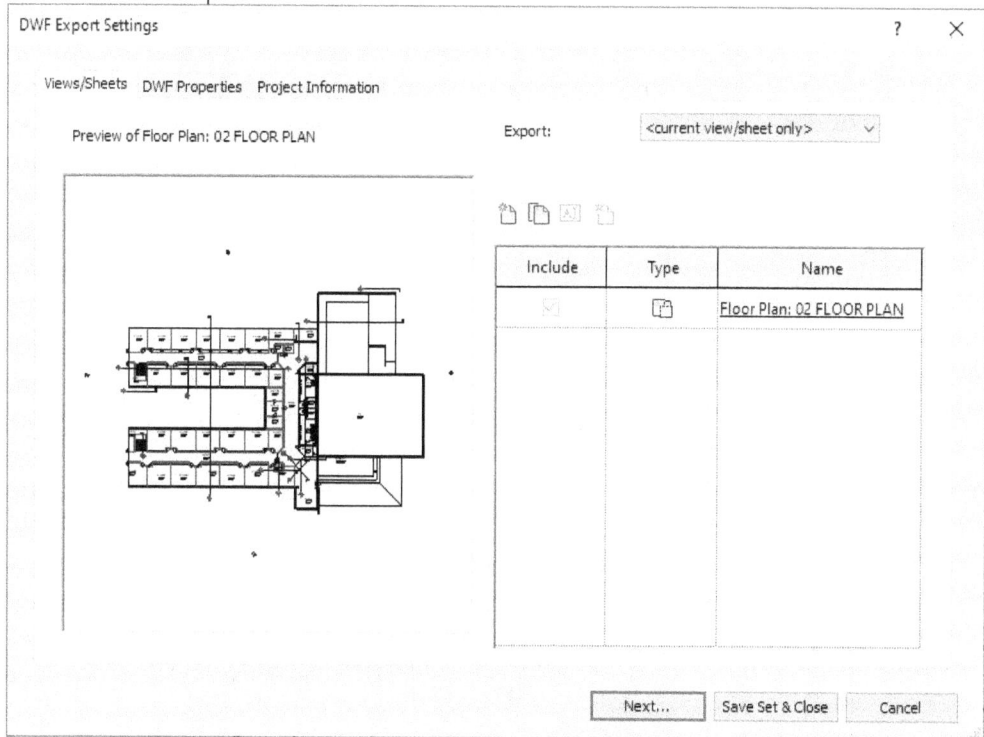

Figure 3–58

- In the *DWF Properties* tab, set up the export object data, the graphics settings, and print setup.

- The *Project Information* tab, shown in Figure 3–59, can be updated and included in a DWF export.

	DWF Export Settings	? ✕
	Views/Sheets DWF Properties Project Information	

Parameter	Value
Organization Name	
Organization Description	
Building Name	
Author	
Project Issue Date	Issue Date
Project Status	Project Status
Client Name	Owner
Project Address	## Street
Project Name	Project Name
Project Number	Project Number
Route Analysis Settings	Edit...

Figure 3–59

- Files can be exported to the DWF or DWFx format.

- You can mark up (redline) DWF/DWFx files using other programs. The markups can then be linked back into the Autodesk Revit project, using the 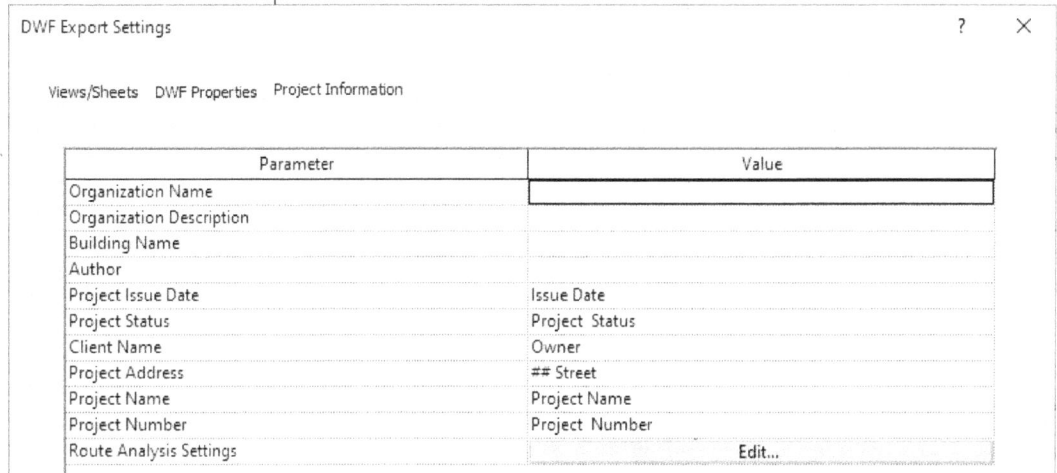 (DWG Markup) command so the original user can make the changes noted.

- Textures, line patterns, line weights, and text are included in 3D DWF exports.

© 2020, ASCENT - Center for Technical Knowledge®

Practice 3e

Export Files - All Disciplines

Practice Objective

- Export views to AutoCAD drawing files and DWF viewing files.

In this practice, you will export several views to AutoCAD drawing files and to DWF files, as shown in Autodesk Design Review in Figure 3–60.

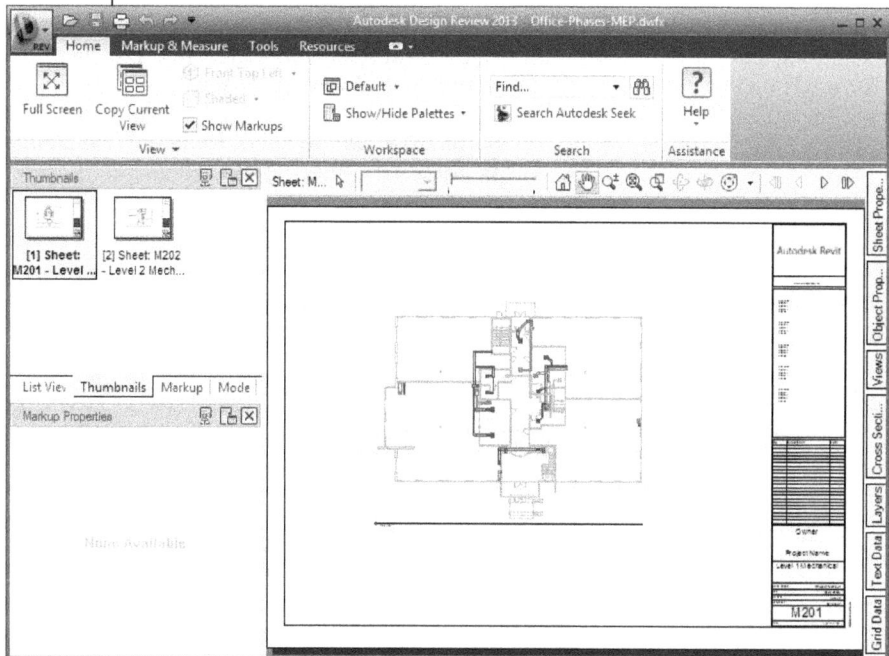

Figure 3–60

Task 1 - Set up and export a set of 2D views to a DWG file.

1. In the practice files folder, open the **Office Phases** project that matches your discipline.

   - The views shown in this practice use the original version of **Office Phases-MEP.rvt**. Your practice file will vary according to the project you select and the work that has been done in the file.

2. In the *File* tab, expand ⬚ (Export), expand ⬚ (CAD Formats), and click ⬚ (DWG).

3. In the DWG Export dialog box, in the *Select Export Setup* area, click ⬚ (Modify Export Setup).

4. In the Modify DWG/DXF Export Setup dialog box, *Layers* tab, *Load layers from standards* list, select the standard you are most likely to use.

5. In the *Text & Fonts* tab for *Text behavior when exported*, select **Preserve visual fidelity**.

6. Scroll down in the list of fonts and map *Arial* to **Arial Narrow**, as shown in Figure 3–61.

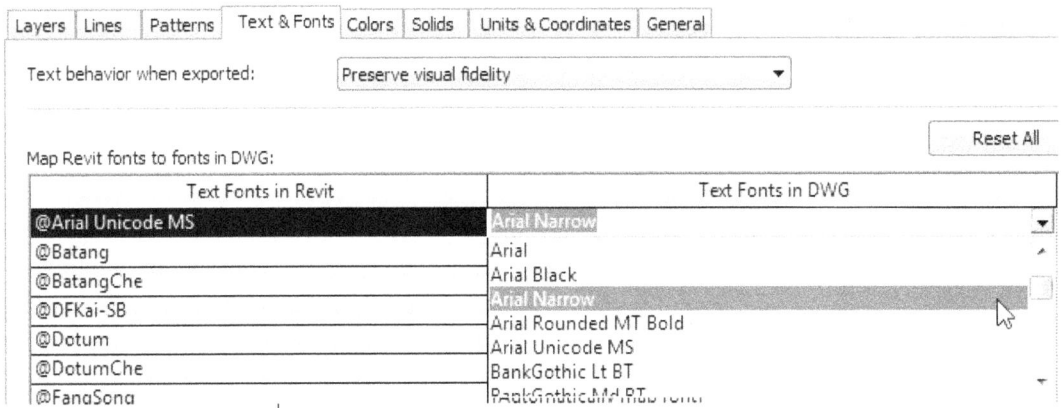

| Layers | Lines | Patterns | Text & Fonts | Colors | Solids | Units & Coordinates | General |

Text behavior when exported: Preserve visual fidelity ▼

Reset All

Map Revit fonts to fonts in DWG:

Text Fonts in Revit	Text Fonts in DWG
@Arial Unicode MS	Arial Narrow ▼
@Batang	Arial
@BatangChe	Arial Black
@DFKai-SB	Arial Narrow
@Dotum	Arial Rounded MT Bold
@DotumChe	Arial Unicode MS
@FangSong	BankGothic Lt BT
	BankGothicMd BT ...

Figure 3–61

7. In the *General* tab, select **Export rooms, spaces and areas as polylines**. Click **OK**.

8. In the DWG Export dialog box, click ⬚ (New Set).

9. In the New Set dialog box, type the name **Plans** and click **OK**.

© 2020, ASCENT - Center for Technical Knowledge®

10. Select at least two floor/structural plan views, as shown in Figure 3–62.

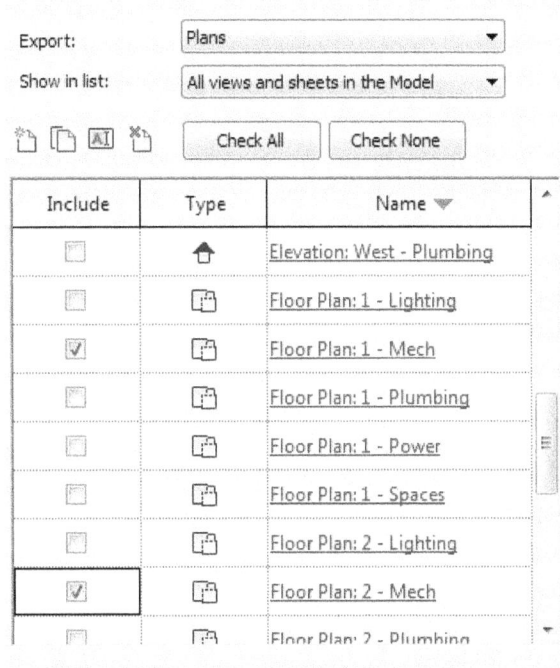

Export:	Plans ▼
Show in list:	All views and sheets in the Model ▼

🗋 🗐 AI 🗎 | Check All | Check None |

Include	Type	Name ▼
☐	🏠	Elevation: West - Plumbing
☐	🗗	Floor Plan: 1 - Lighting
☑	🗗	Floor Plan: 1 - Mech
☐	🗗	Floor Plan: 1 - Plumbing
☐	🗗	Floor Plan: 1 - Power
☐	🗗	Floor Plan: 1 - Spaces
☐	🗗	Floor Plan: 2 - Lighting
☑	🗗	Floor Plan: 2 - Mech
☐	🗗	Floor Plan: 2 - Plumbing

Figure 3–62

11. Click **Next...**.

12. In the Export CAD Formats - Save to Target Folder dialog box, set the *Save In:* to the practice files folder. Set the *Files of Type:* to **AutoCAD 2018 DWG Files (*.dwg)**.

13. Set the *Naming* to **Automatic-Long (Specify prefix)** and type **Plans** in the *File name/Prefix* field.

14. Click **OK**. The software generates DWG files for the each selected view using the setup you defined.

Task 2 - Export a 3D view to AutoCAD.

---

1. Switch to a 3D view from the 3D Views section in the Project Browser.

2. In the *File* tab, expand 🗗 (Export), expand 📇 (CAD Formats), and click 🖼 (DWG Files).

---

3. In the DWG Export dialog box, set *Export:* to **<Current View/Sheet only>**, as shown in Figure 3–63.

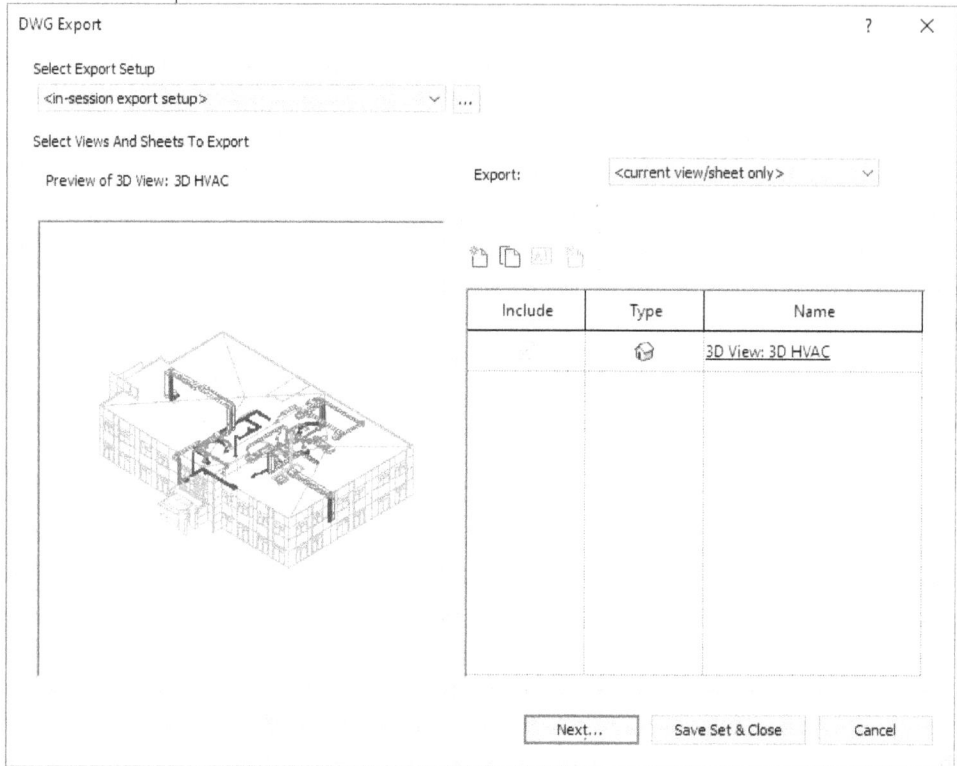

Figure 3–63

4. Click **Next...**. In the Export CAD Formats - Save to Target Folder dialog box, type a file name, and click **OK**.

5. If you have access to AutoCAD, you can open the files to see the exported geometry or view them in Windows Explorer, as shown in Figure 3–64 in the Extra Large Icons view.

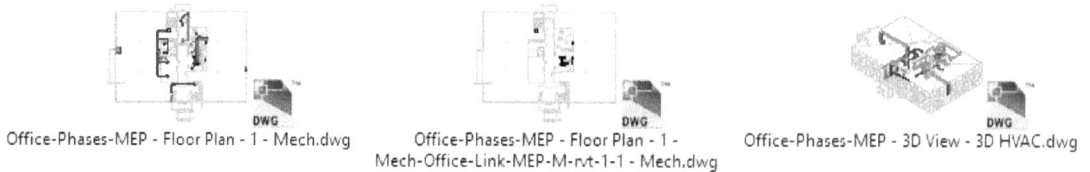

Office-Phases-MEP - Floor Plan - 1 - Mech.dwg

Office-Phases-MEP - Floor Plan - 1 - Mech-Office-Link-MEP-M-rvt-1-1 - Mech.dwg

Office-Phases-MEP - 3D View - 3D HVAC.dwg

Figure 3–64

© 2020, ASCENT - Center for Technical Knowledge®

Task 3 - Export to DWF.

1. In the *File* tab, expand [Export icon] (Export) and click

   [icon] (DWF/DWFx).

2. In the DWF Export Settings dialog box, click [icon] (New Set).

3. In the New Set dialog box, type the name **Sheets** and click **OK**.

4. Change the *Show in list:* to **Sheets in the Model** and select the sheets, as shown in Figure 3–65.

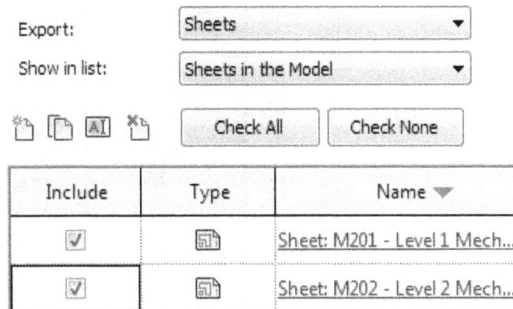

Include	Type	Name ▼
☑	📄	Sheet: M201 - Level 1 Mech...
☑	📄	Sheet: M202 - Level 2 Mech...

Figure 3–65

5. Switch to the *DWF Properties* tab and verify that **Element properties** is selected.

6. Click **Next...**.

7. In the Export DWF - Save to Target Folder dialog box, type in the *File name/prefix*: **Sheets**. Note that **Combine selected views and sheets into a single dwf file** is selected by default and grayed out because the *Naming:* is set to **Manual (Specify file name)**.

8. Click **OK**.

9. If you have Autodesk Design Review, you can open and view the file.

10. If you have time, create a 3D DWF of the model and view the file.

11. Save and close all open files.

3.5 Exporting for Energy Analysis

Green buildings and energy analysis are now a major component of design. Creating an energy-efficient building requires understanding of how lighting, heating, cooling, and other structures interact with the site, spaces, and materials used. For example, heating and cooling a 3-story space in a cold climate is very different from heating and cooling a room with a low ceiling in a desert area. The seasons and time of day also impact energy consumption, as shown in the shadow study in Figure 3–66.

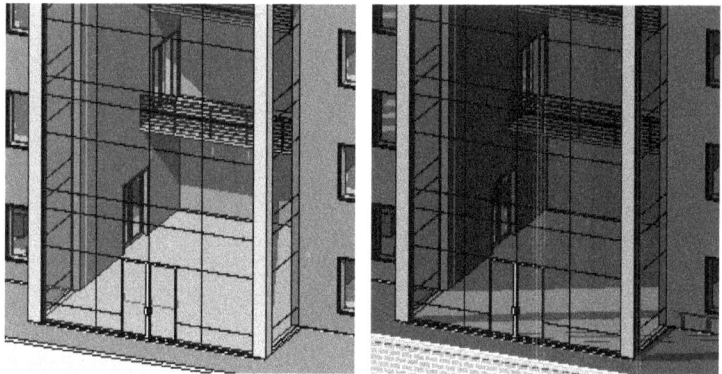

Figure 3–66

Numerous programs do this type of analysis. Autodesk Revit projects are Building Information Models (BIM). Therefore, instead of time-consuming hand-takeoff, you can export Autodesk Revit projects to a gbXML file that can then be imported into the analysis program.

- gbXML stands for <u>G</u>reen <u>B</u>uilding <u>E</u>xtensible <u>M</u>arkup <u>L</u>anguage. It is a standard used to transfer building information from a CAD BIM model to an engineering analysis tool.

- Engineering analysis tools include Green Building Studio, HVAC manufacturer programs (such as Trane or Carrier), and the United States Department of Energy's simulation tool.

© 2020, ASCENT - Center for Technical Knowledge®

- **Subscription-Only Feature**. You can enable the energy model directly in the Autodesk Revit software and run energy simulations in the cloud using Autodesk Green Building Studio and Insight web-based services. This can be done early in a project using either the conceptual mass elements or the building elements without the spaces in place. This does not require exporting to gbXML The results are hosted in the cloud and you can compare results from different runs of the program.

Preparing a Project for Energy Analysis

Using the Export to gbXML tool enables you to send information from the energy analytical model based on the energy settings (subscription-only) or the volumes in the model identified by room (architecture) or spaces (MEP).

This topic covers exporting using the volumes of rooms and spaces.

- To prepare a project to export for gbXML you need to verify room height properties and ensure that the volume, as well as the area, is being calculated.

- All interior spaces, including plenums and chases, larger than the Sliver Space Tolerance need to have a room/space element placed in them for accurate analysis.

- For more information on preparing an MEP project for energy analysis, see the ASCENT guide *Autodesk Revit: Fundamentals for MEP.*

How To: Set Up Room Properties for Volumes

1. In the *Architecture* tab>Room & Area panel, click on the title to expand the options, and click (Area and Volume Computations).

2. In the Area and Volume Computations dialog box, in the *Computations* tab, select **Areas and Volumes**, as shown in Figure 3–67, so that room volumes are calculated.

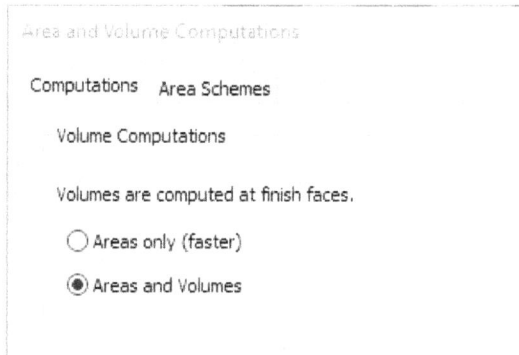

Area and Volume Computations

Computations   Area Schemes

   Volume Computations

   Volumes are computed at finish faces.

    ○ Areas only (faster)

    ◉ Areas and Volumes

Figure 3–67

3. Click **OK** to close the dialog box
4. Add rooms to the project that define the spaces and areas for the energy analysis.
5. Modify the room properties so that **Upper Limit** and **Limit Offset** describe the height of the room, as shown in Figure 3–68.

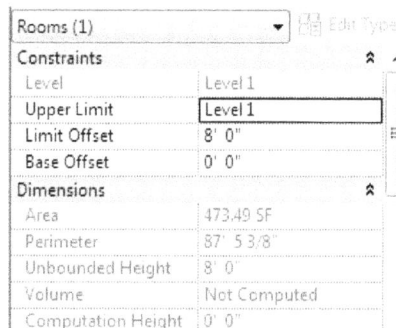

Rooms (1)	▼	Edit Type
Constraints		≫ ^
Level	Level 1	
Upper Limit	Level 1	
Limit Offset	8' 0"	≡
Base Offset	0' 0"	
Dimensions		≫
Area	473.49 SF	
Perimeter	87' 5 3/8"	
Unbounded Height	8' 0"	
Volume	Not Computed	
Computation Height	0' 0"	

Figure 3–68

© 2020, ASCENT - Center for Technical Knowledge®

Exporting to gbXML

When you start the export process, you can modify the Project Information and ensure that the rooms and analytical surfaces display as expected. The program calculates the inner room volumes, analytical room models, shading surfaces, openings, and more.

How To: Export a File to gbXML

1. Open a 3D view of the model.

2. In the *File* tab, expand ⬚ (Export) and click ⬚ (gbXML).
3. In the Export gbXML dialog box, select **Use Room/Space Volumes** and click **OK**.
4. The Export gbXML dialog box, as shown in Figure 3–69, displays with a 3D view of the room volumes and information on the *General* and *Details* tabs.

In this example only one floor of rooms has been created for clarity.

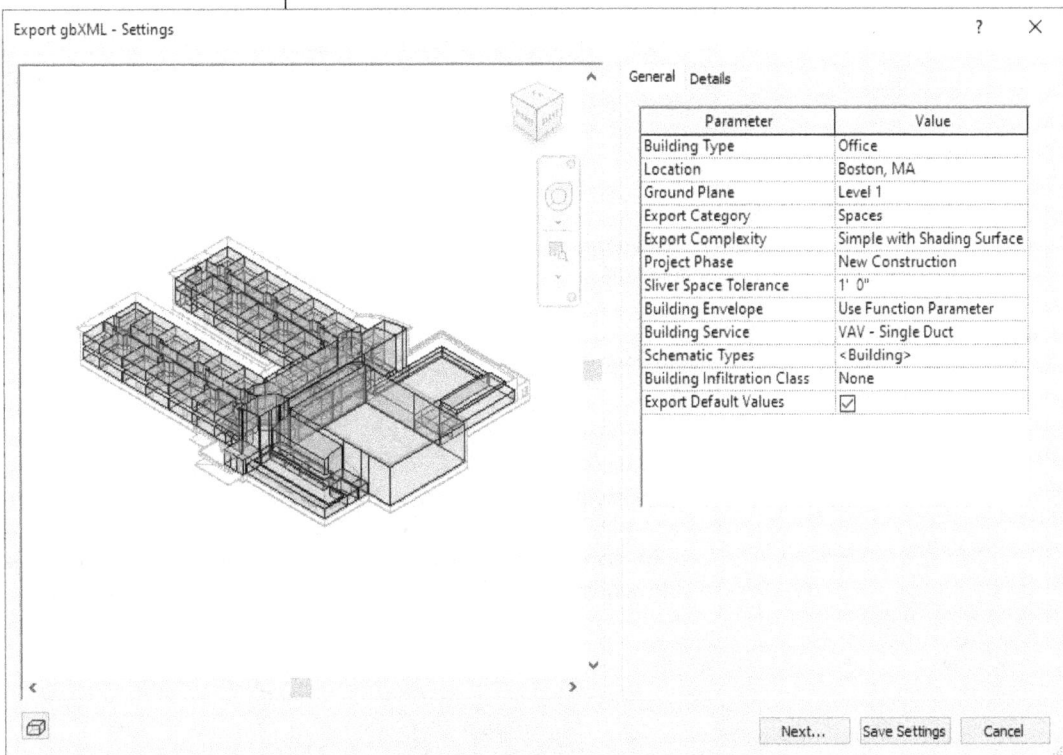

Export gbXML - Settings

General   Details

Parameter	Value
Building Type	Office
Location	Boston, MA
Ground Plane	Level 1
Export Category	Spaces
Export Complexity	Simple with Shading Surface
Project Phase	New Construction
Sliver Space Tolerance	1' 0"
Building Envelope	Use Function Parameter
Building Service	VAV - Single Duct
Schematic Types	<Building>
Building Infiltration Class	None
Export Default Values	☑

Next...   Save Settings   Cancel

Figure 3–69

5. In the *General* tab, verify or apply the Project Information parameters, including how much complexity you want to export, as shown in Figure 3–70.

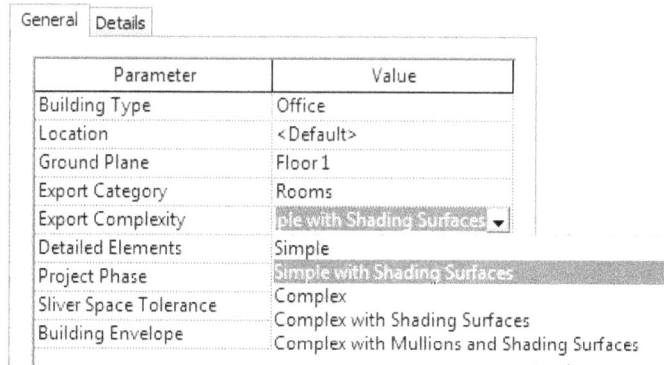

Parameter	Value
Building Type	Office
Location	<Default>
Ground Plane	Floor 1
Export Category	Rooms
Export Complexity	ple with Shading Surfaces ▼
Detailed Elements	Simple
Project Phase	Simple with Shading Surfaces
Sliver Space Tolerance	Complex
Building Envelope	Complex with Shading Surfaces
	Complex with Mullions and Shading Surfaces

Figure 3–70

6. Select the *Details* tab and expand the levels to see the rooms for each level. Icons beside the room name show if the room has been able to be calculated, as shown in Figure 3–71.

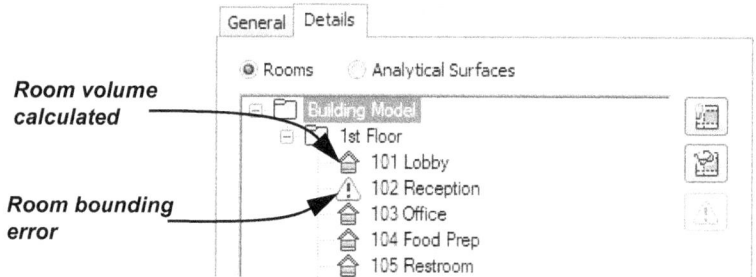

Figure 3–71

7. To view an error, click on the room name and then click

⚠ (Show Related Warnings). The warning dialog box, as shown in Figure 3–72, outlines the cause for the warning.

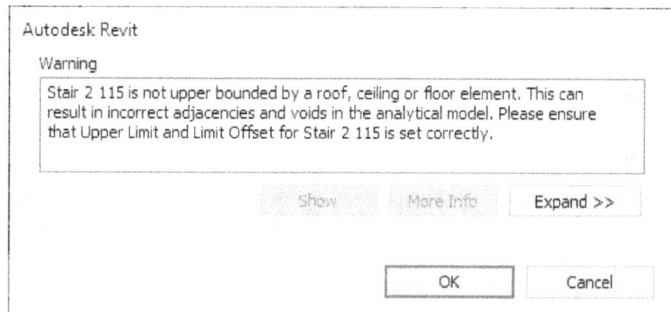

Figure 3–72

© 2020, ASCENT - Center for Technical Knowledge®

8. To see visual information about the room, select the room name and click ⬚ (Highlight) to highlight the room in the 3D view, or click ⬚ (Isolate) to toggle off all the display of the other rooms in the 3D view.

   • Click the icons again to toggle them off.

9. Select **Analytical Surfaces** to see the surface calculation planes, as shown in Figure 3–73.

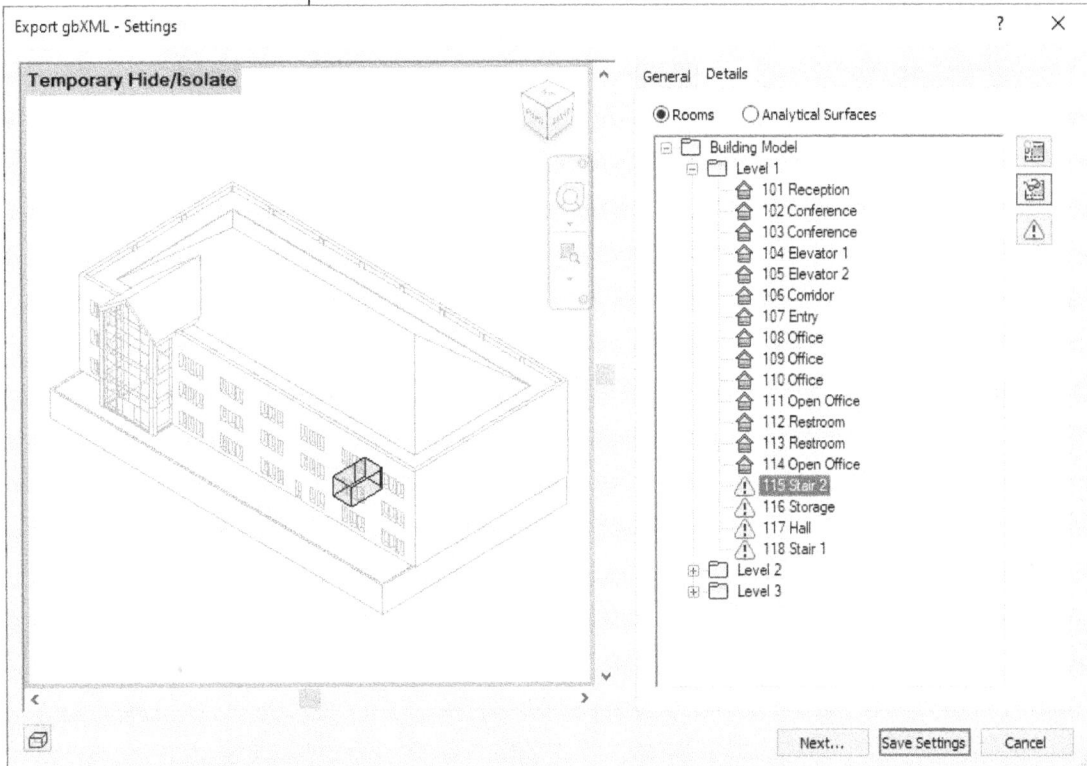

Figure 3–73

10. If you need to make changes to the model, click **Save Settings** to return to the model.
11. Run **Export gbXML** again and test the model. When you are ready to continue with the export, click **Next...**.
12. In the Export gbXML - Save to Target Folder dialog box, select the folder location and name for the file, and then click **Save**.

13. The resulting .XML file can then be imported into an energy analysis program.

The beginning of the .XML file contains project information about the building, including its location and type. Each room is then listed with its name, description, area, volume, and coordinate points (as shown in Figure 3–74).

```xml
<?xml version="1.0" encoding="UTF-8" ?>
<gbXML temperatureUnit="F" lengthUnit="Feet" areaUnit="SquareFeet" volumeUnit="CubicFeet" useSIUnitsForResults="false"
    xmlns="http://www.gbxml.org/schema" version="0.37">
  <Campus id="cmps-1">
    <Location>
      <Name>Boston, MA, USA</Name>
      <Latitude>42.358300</Latitude>
      <Longitude>-71.060300</Longitude>
    </Location>
    <Building id="bldg-1" buildingType="Office">
```

Figure 3–74

© 2020, ASCENT - Center for Technical Knowledge®

Practice 3f

Export for Energy Analysis

Practice Objectives

- Prepare a project with room heights and locations.
- Test the gbXML export and identify issues that need to be corrected.
- Resolve the issues and export the project to gbXML.

In this practice, you will modify room heights, as shown in Figure 3–75. You will also run the **Export to gbXML** command, investigate errors, and then correct the errors by adding ceilings and changing the room limits. You will then export the file to gbXML.

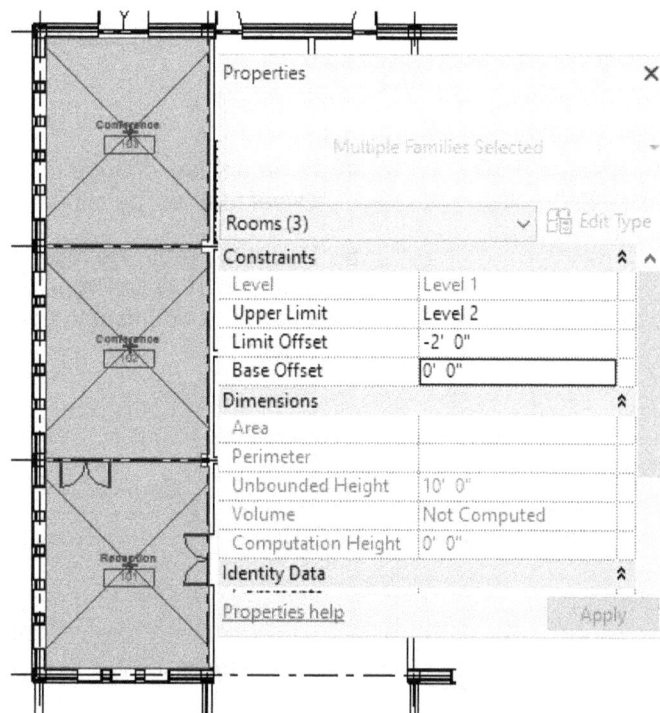

Figure 3–75

Task 1 - Prepare the project for export to gbXML.

1. In the practice files folder, open the project **Midrise-Energy-A.rvt**.

2. Open the Floor Plans: **Level 1 - Rooms** view.

3. Select the room **Entry 107**, as shown in Figure 3–76.

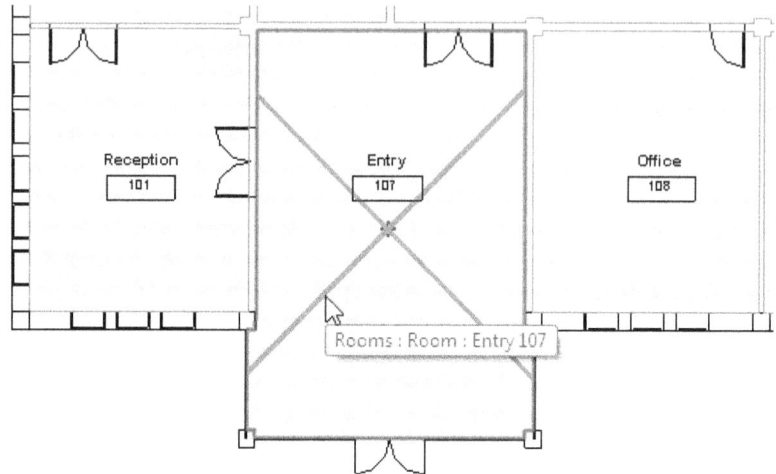

Figure 3–76

4. In Properties, change the *Upper Limit* to **Roof** and the *Limit Offset* to **0'-0"**, as shown in Figure 3–77.

5. Select the room **Reception 101** and two conference rooms (102 and 103). In Properties, set the *Upper Limit* to **Level 2** and the *Limit Offset* to (negative) **-2'-0"**, as shown in Figure 3–78.

Figure 3–77

Figure 3–78

- The level-to-level distance is 12'-0"; therefore, this creates 10'-0" ceilings in these rooms.

- In Properties, note that the *Volume* is listed as **Not Computed**.

© 2020, ASCENT - Center for Technical Knowledge®

6. In the *Architecture* tab>Room & Area panel, click on the title to expand the options and click (Area and Volume Computations).

7. In the Area and Volume Computations dialog box, in the *Computations* tab, select **Areas and Volumes**, as shown in Figure 3–79, so that room volumes are calculated.

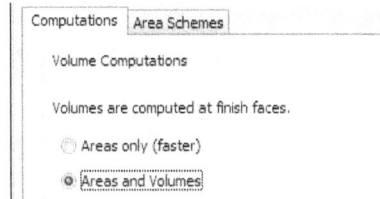

Figure 3–79

8. Click **OK** to close the dialog box.

9. Select one of the rooms and view the *Volume* that displays in Properties.

10. Press <Esc> to clear the selection.

11. Save the project.

Task 2 - Test the export to gbXML.

1. Open the default 3D view.

2. In the *File* tab, expand (Export) and click (gbXML).

3. In the Export gbXML dialog box, select **Use Room/space Volumes** and click **OK**.

4. In the Export gbXML dialog box, in the *General* tab, set the *Building Type* to **Office** from the list.

5. Click in the *Value* of the **Location** option and click

   ⬚ (Browse). In the Location Weather and Site dialog box, select a location for the building using the Internet Mapping Service and nearby weather station (as shown in Figure 3–80) and click **OK**.

6. In the Export to gbXML dialog box, switch to the *Details* tab and expand Level 1, as shown in Figure 3–81.

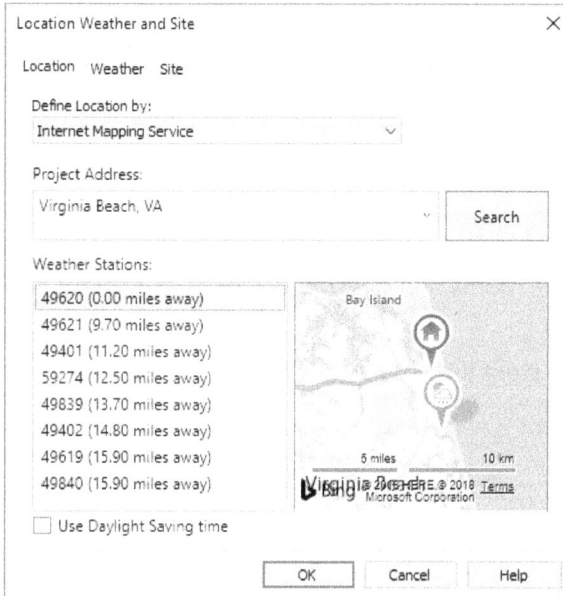

Figure 3–80

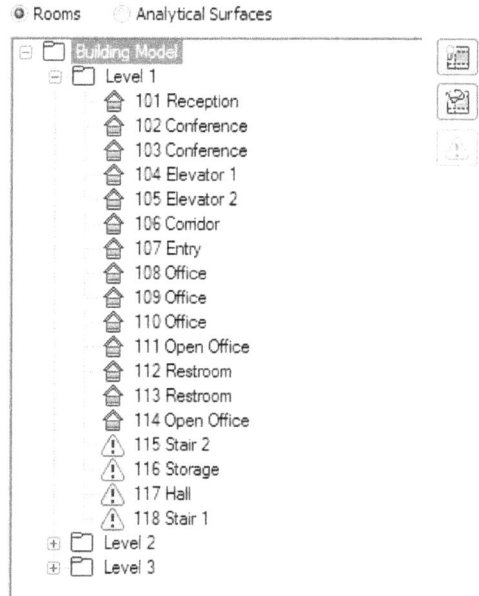

Figure 3–81

7. Select the room **115 Stair 2** and click ⚠ (Show Related Warnings). The warning displays as shown in Figure 3–82.

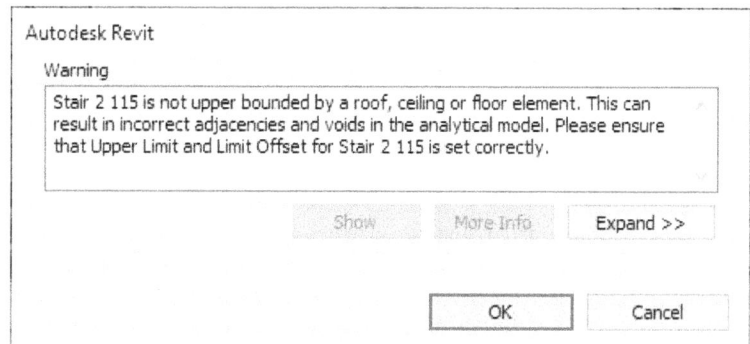

Figure 3–82

© 2020, ASCENT - Center for Technical Knowledge®

8. Select the other rooms with warnings on the first floor and display their warnings. In this case, all of the rooms that are not computed correctly are missing a boundary (such as a roof, ceiling, or floor).

9. Use ⬛ (Isolate) to identify the room locations, as shown in Figure 3–83.

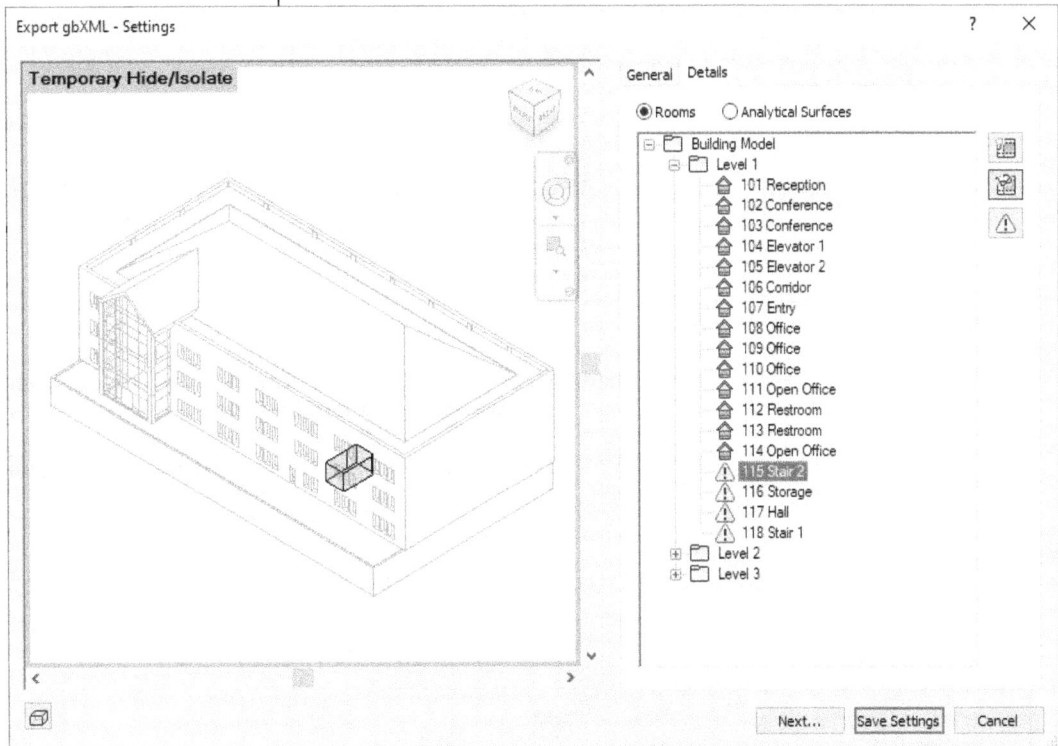

Figure 3–83

10. Click **Save Settings** to close the Export gbXML dialog box and return to the model to modify it.

Task 3 - Make changes to the model.

1. Open the Ceiling Plans: **Level 1** view.

2. Add ceilings to rooms **Hall 117** and **Storage 116** using the **Compound Ceiling: GBW on Mtl. Stud** type and a *Height Offset From Level* of **8'-0"**, as shown in Figure 3–84.

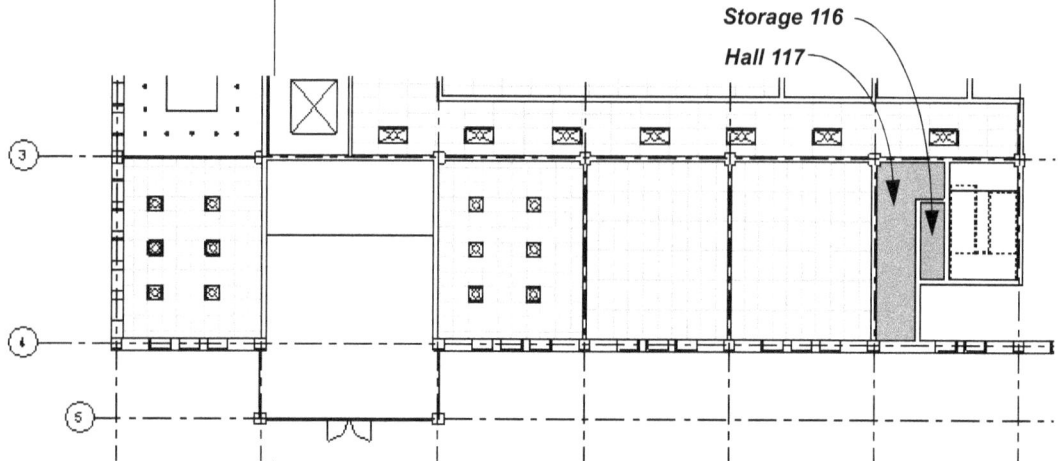

Figure 3–84

3. Open the Floor Plans: **Level 1 - Rooms** view. Select both of the stair room elements, as shown in Figure 3–85.

4. In Properties change the *Upper Limit* to **Roof** and the *Limit Offset* to **0'-0"**.

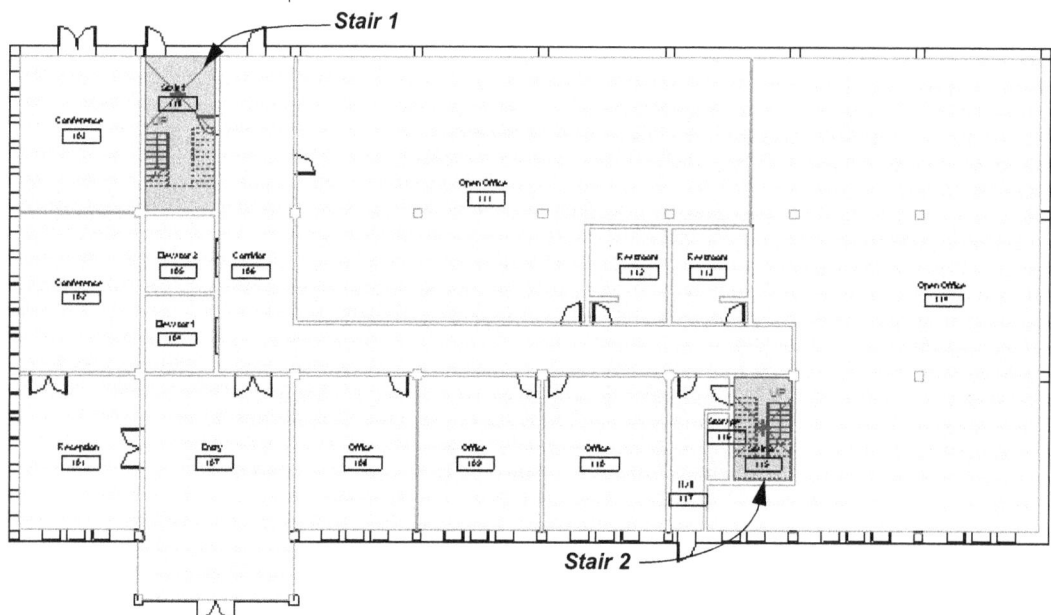

Figure 3–85

5. Save the project.

© 2020, ASCENT - Center for Technical Knowledge®

Task 4 - Rerun the export to gbXML.

1. Return to a 3D view.

2. Start the **Export to gbXML** command again using the room/space volumes method.

3. Switch to the *Details* tab and expand **Level 1**. All the rooms on Level 1 should now be ready to export (as shown in Figure 3–86), with the two stair rooms isolated.

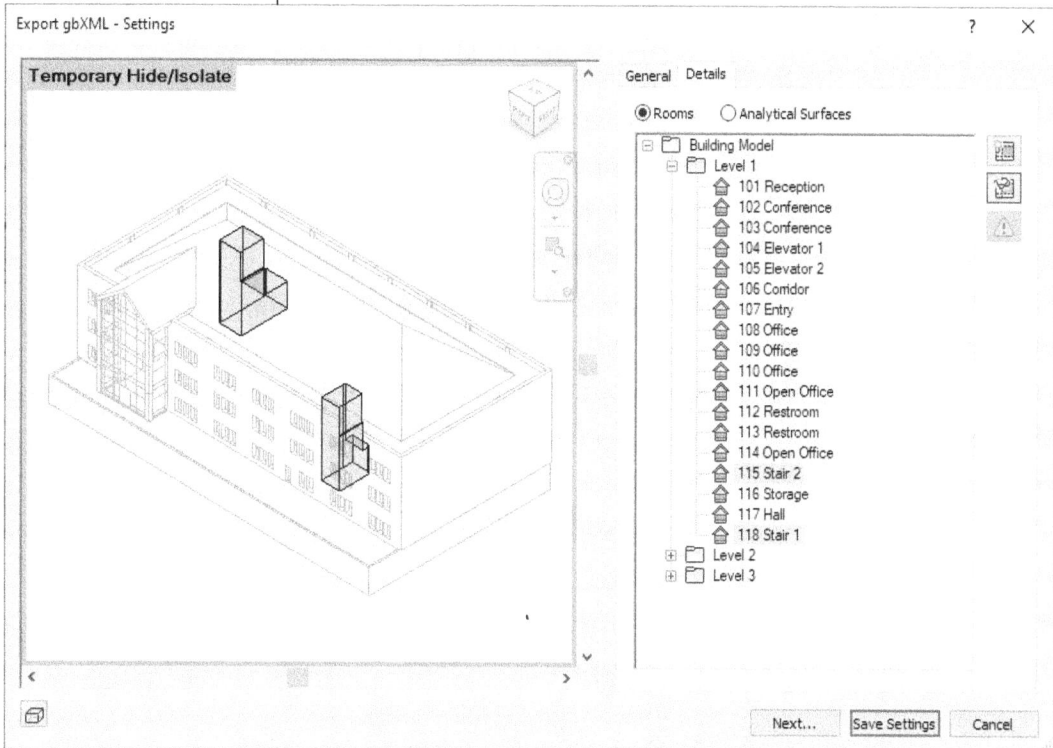

Figure 3–86

4. Click **Next...**.

5. In the Export gbXML - Save to Target folder dialog box, specify the practice files folder as the location for the file and click **Save**.

6. You can now import the resulting .XML file into an energy analysis program, or view it with Windows Explorer.

7. If you have time, you can fix the problems on Levels 2 and 3 and run the export to gbXML again.

Chapter Review Questions

1. Which of the following types of vector files can you import into the Autodesk Revit software? (Select all that apply.)

   a. DGN

   b. DWG

   c. DOC

   d. DXF

2. Which of the following settings can be specified before you import AutoCAD files or Microstation files into a project?

   a. Color to Line Weight

   b. Text and Dimension Styles

   c. Units

   d. Patterns

3. Once a vector file is imported into an Autodesk Revit project, can you change the visibility of elements in the imported instance?

   a. Yes

   b. No

4. When you explode an imported instance of a vector file, what type of elements would notes change to?

   a. Note Blocks

   b. Lines and Arcs

   c. Text

   d. Groups

© 2020, ASCENT - Center for Technical Knowledge®

5. Which of the following can you use to modify a raster image, such as the one shown in Figure 3–87? (Select all that apply.)

Figure 3–87

a. Delete portions of the graphic.

b. Resize it by dragging the corners.

c. Query the information inside the graphic.

d. Change the foreground/background status.

6. Which of the following settings can be specified when you export a project to DWG/DXF? (Select all that apply.)

a. Line Weight to Color

b. Text

c. Units

d. Patterns

7. (Optional) What elements MUST be in an architectural project before exporting to gbXML for energy analysis?

a. Ceilings

b. Floors

c. Rooms

d. Roofs

Command Summary

Button	Command	Location
Vector Files		
	Coordination Model	• **Ribbon**: *Insert* tab>Link panel
	Delete Layers	• **Ribbon**: *Modify	[imported file name]* tab>Import Instance panel
	Explode	• **Ribbon**: *Modify	[imported file name]* tab>Import Instance panel
	Full Explode	• **Ribbon**: *Modify	[imported file name]* tab>Import Instance panel>Explode
	Import CAD	• **Ribbon**: *Insert* tab>Import panel
	Link CAD	• **Ribbon**: *Insert* tab>Link panel
	Partial Explode	• **Ribbon**: *Modify	[imported file name]* tab>Import Instance panel>Explode
	Query	• **Ribbon**: *Modify	[imported file name]* tab>Import Instance panel
	Scale	• **Ribbon**: *Modify* tab>Modify panel
Raster Files		
	Bring Forward	• **Ribbon**: *Modify	Raster Images* tab>Arrange panel
	Bring to Front	• **Ribbon**: *Modify	Raster Images* tab>Arrange panel
	Import Image	• **Ribbon**: *Insert* tab>Import panel
	Import PDF	• **Ribbon**: *Insert* tab>Import panel
	Link Image	• **Ribbon**: *Insert* tab>Link panel
	Link PDF	• **Ribbon**: *Insert* tab>Link panel

© 2020, ASCENT - Center for Technical Knowledge®

	Manage Images	• **Ribbon**: *Insert* tab>Import panel
	Send Backward	• **Ribbon**: *Modify	Raster Images* tab>Arrange panel>
	Send to Back	• **Ribbon**: *Modify	Raster Images* tab>Arrange panel

Exporting

	ACIS (SAT)	• *File* tab: Expand Export>CAD Formats
	Building Site	• *File* tab: Expand Export
	CAD Formats	• *File* tab: Expand Export
	DGN	• *File* tab: Expand Export>CAD Formats
	DWF/DWFx	• *File* tab: Expand Export
	DWG	• *File* tab: Expand Export>CAD Formats
	DXF	• *File* tab: Expand Export>CAD Formats
	Export	• *File* tab
	Export Setups DGN	• *File* tab: Expand Export>Options
	Export Setups DWG/DWF	• *File* tab: Expand Export>Options
	Family Types	• *File* tab: Expand Export
	FBX	• *File* tab: Expand Export
	gbXML	• *File* tab: Expand Export
	IFC	• *File* tab: Expand Export
	IFC Options	• *File* tab: Expand Export>Options

	Images and Animations	• *File* tab: Expand Export
	Mass Model gbXML	• *File* tab: Expand Export
	ODBC Database	• *File* tab: Expand Export
	Options	• *File* tab: Expand Export
	Reports	• *File* tab: Expand Export

© 2020, ASCENT - Center for Technical Knowledge®

Project Team Collaboration

Project team collaboration happens on many levels in a firm and between disciplines. When you have a very large project with more than one person working on that project at one time, you need to enable worksharing, then create and use worksets. Worksets enable you to work in one part of a project while someone else is working in another part of the same project. Not everyone needs to know how to create a central model or set up worksets, but everyone needs to learn how to work with them.

Learning Objectives in This Chapter

- Understand worksharing workflow and definitions.
- Set up worksets in a project.
- Place elements in worksets.
- Create a central model.
- Create and open a local file based on the central model.
- Control workset visibility by view.
- Synchronize a local file with the central model.
- Set the active workset and work in the local file.
- Request and approve permission to edit elements.
- Temporarily enable the display of worksets.
- Close the workshared project correctly.
- Investigate tips for using worksets.

- The methodologies covered in this chapter focus on using server-based tools within Autodesk Revit. If you are using BIM 360 to access files, you can still use most of the processes covered in this chapter, such as setting up worksets. To learn more about BIM 360, refer to the ASCENT guide *Autodesk®️ BIM 360™️: Fundamentals.*

4.1 Introduction to Worksharing

NOTE: *All images in the upcoming sections refer to users as "User1" or "User2". In your working environment, you will see your unique Revit username in these dialog boxes.*

Autodesk® Revit® projects include the entire building model in one file. A process called *worksharing* is used when the file needs to be separated into logical components (as shown in Figure 4–1) without losing the connection to the whole. The main component of worksharing is worksets.

Worksharing gives multiple team members who are connected on the same network the ability to co-author a single project model (one RVT file).The appropriate team member creates a central model and worksets. Team members open and work in a local copy of the central model that is linked back to the central model through saving and synchronizing.

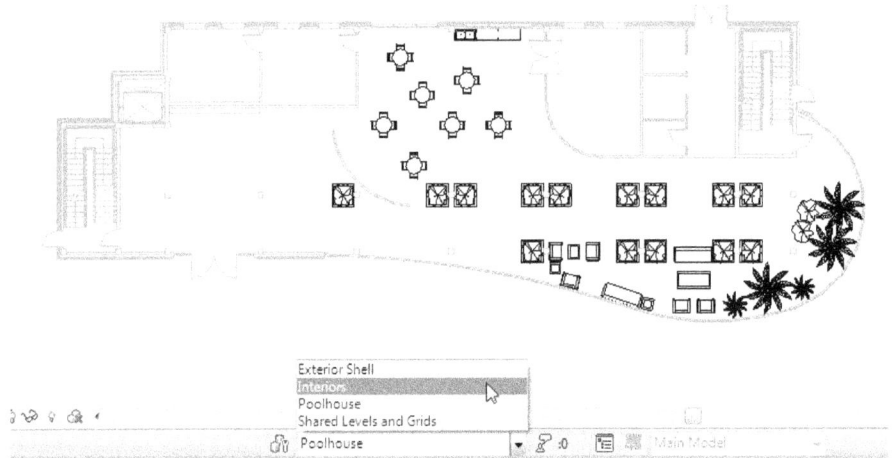

Figure 4–1

A workshared project consists of one central model (also known as a central file) and individual models for each user known as local files, as shown in Figure 4–2. Each team member will work in their local file and use a function called *synchronizing with central* to send and receive updates with the central model.

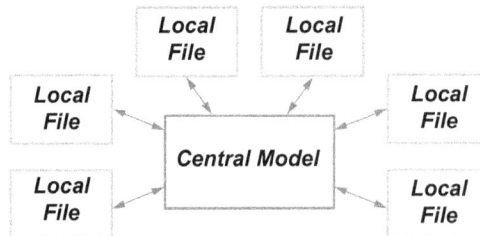

Figure 4–2

© 2020, ASCENT - Center for Technical Knowledge®

- The central model is created by the BIM manager, project manager, or project lead, and is stored on a server or in the cloud, enabling multiple user access.

Collaborate Tab

The tools found in the *Collaborate* tab, shown in Figure 4–3, are designed to help you and your team work more effectively in a workshared environment. Many of these tools are also available in the Quick Access Toolbar and Status Bar.

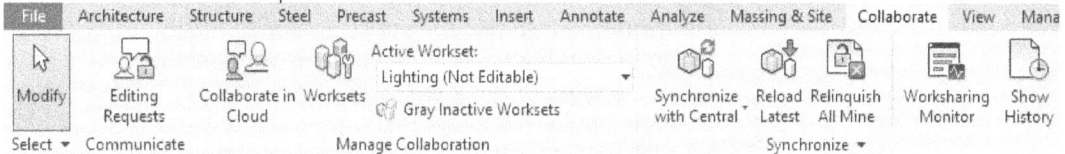

Figure 4–3

Worksharing Definitions

Worksharing: This is a functionality that, when enabled, allows multiple members of the team to access a project stored in one centralized location, which gives multiple users the ability to work on the same project simultaneously.

Workshared file: This is a project that has worksets enabled. If the project has no worksets enabled, it is called a *non-workshared file*.

Workset: This is a collection of elements that are related geometrically, parametrically, or by location within an overall project that are subdivided so they can be worked on while isolated from the rest of the model. When worksharing is enabled, worksets are automatically activated and the *Workset1* and *Shared Grids and Levels* worksets are added to the project by default.

Central model: Also called the central file, this is the main project file that is stored on a local network that all users can access. Using a central model is called *file-based worksharing*. The central model stores workset and element information in the project and is the file to which everyone saves and synchronizes their changes. The central model updates all the local files with the latest model information. This file should not be edited directly.

Local file: This is a copy of the central model that is saved to your local computer. This is the file that you modify and work in. As you work, you save the file locally and synchronize it with the central model.

Element borrowing: This refers to the process of modifying items in the project that are not part of the workset you have checked out. This either happens automatically (if no one else has checked out a workset) or specifically, when you request to have control of the elements (if someone else has a workset checked out).

Active workset: The workset that displays in the Status Bar is the active workset. Any new elements that are added will be placed on this workset. As you work, you will change the active workset accordingly.

Relinquish: This releases or returns a checked-out workset so that others can work on the elements within that workset. If you do not release or relinquish your checked-out worksets, other users will get a warning that they cannot edit the workset until you relinquish it, and they are given the option to request to borrow the workset. **Relinquish All Mine** allows you to relinquish worksets without synchronizing to the central model.

Reload Latest: This updates your local file without you needing to synchronize with the central model.

General Process of Worksharing and Worksets

1. Wait for the appropriate team member to enable worksharing, set up worksets, and create the central model.
2. Create a local file from the central model.
3. Work in your local file and select the worksets that you need to work on by verifying the active workset.
   - Work in your local model by adding, deleting, and modifying elements.
   - You may need to request to borrow elements in worksets that are currently checked out by other team members.
4. Save the local file as frequently as you would save any other project.
5. Synchronize the local file with the central model several times a day or as required by company policy or project status.
   - This reloads any changes from the central model to your local file and vice versa.
   - If the option to **Save Local File before and after synchronizing with central** is checked, your local file will be saved, but it is always recommended to save the local file yourself every time you synchronize to the central model.

© 2020, ASCENT - Center for Technical Knowledge®

4.2 Enabling Worksharing

Once it has been established that a project will need to be worksharad, a designated person will enable worksharing, create worksets, and create the central model. The central model will be placed in a shared centralized network location and each user will create their own local file to work from. The central model will host all updated information for the project so that it can be distributed to each user as it is updated.

How To: Enable Worksharing

1. Open an existing project that will become your workshared file or start a new project.
2. In the *Collaborate* tab>Manage Collaboration panel, click ▣ (Collaborate).

   - If this file has never been saved or if changes have been made and not yet saved, the Collaborate - Revit Model Not Saved dialog box will display, as shown in Figure 4–4. Select **Save the model and continue**.

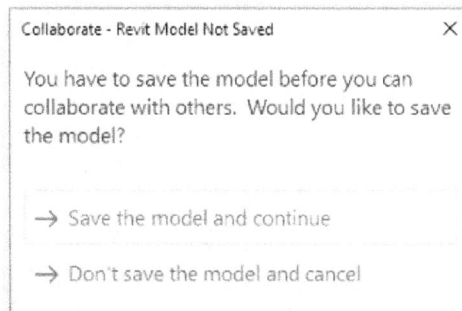

Collaborate - Revit Model Not Saved	✕

   You have to save the model before you can collaborate with others. Would you like to save the model?

   → Save the model and continue

   → Don't save the model and cancel

   Figure 4–4

   - The model needs to be saved to a shared network location for everyone to access it.

3. In the Collaborate dialog box, select **Within your network**, as shown in Figure 4–5. Then, click **OK**.

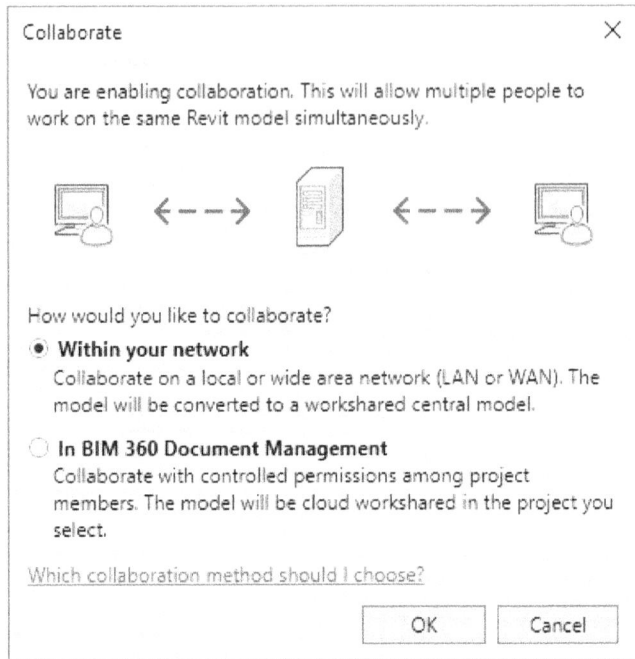

Figure 4–5

4. Once worksharing is enabled, default worksets will be created in the model.

*   Worksharing in the cloud can be done through BIM 360 Document Management, but this guide focuses on collaborating within your local area network. For BIM 360, refer to the ASCENT guide *Autodesk*® *BIM 360™: Fundamentals*.

© 2020, ASCENT - Center for Technical Knowledge®

4.3 Setting Up Worksets

After a project has worksharing enabled, worksets need to be created. Individual worksets are subsets of a project with only specific elements available to view or edit per team member. Worksets are created in the Worksets dialog box, as shown in Figure 4–6. There are four categories of worksets: User-Created, Families, Project Standards, and Views.

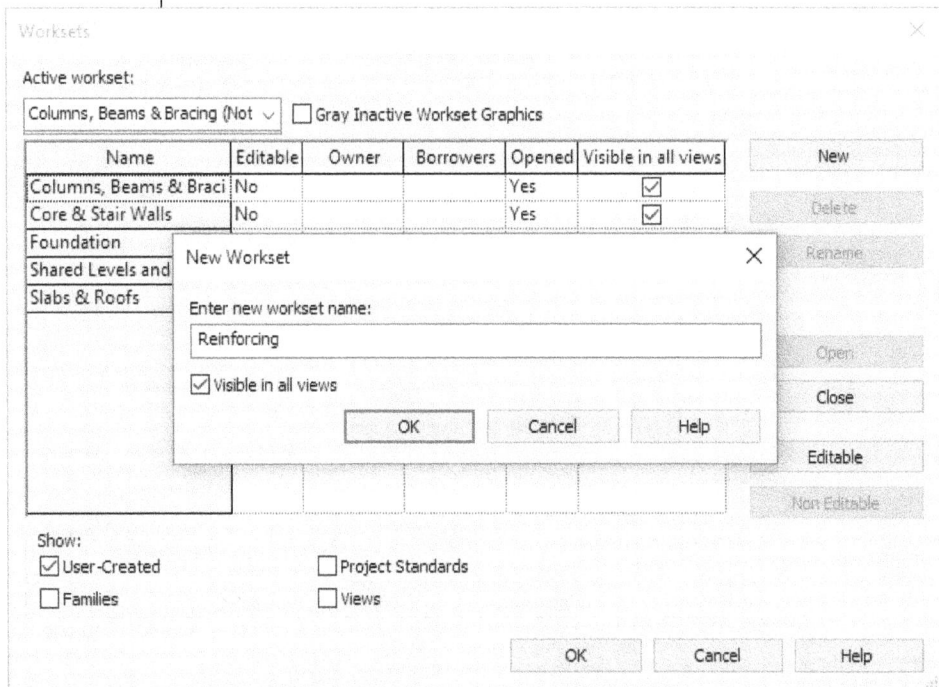

Figure 4–6

- It is important to have one user start a project and develop most of the views, families, and other settings before sharing.

- If you have multiple buildings in a project, use linking to show the relationships between the buildings. Each Revit model can have its own worksets.

- Determining how to divide a project into worksets depends on the complexity of the project, the need to be able to load only parts of the model, and the need to control visibility by workset.

- If your company's BIM standards are to primarily check out worksets rather than borrowing on the fly, dividing the project depends on the different tasks to be done and the number of people working on the project. See "Best Practices for Worksharing" on page 91.

- User-Created worksets should be based on areas of the building that can be worked on when isolated from the rest of the model, such as the exterior shell, building core, or certain sections of the building that can be worked on by a single user at a time.

- You can also have worksets for electrical, site, and structural work that are not visible to other users, and separate worksets for linked Autodesk Revit files.

How To: Create Worksets

1. In the *Collaborate* tab>Manage Collaboration panel, click

    (Worksets). Alternatively, in the Status Bar, click

    (Worksets).

    - Two default User-Created worksets are created: *Shared Levels and Grids* and *Workset1*.
    - Four categories of worksets are created by default, as described below:

Workset Category	Definition
User-Created	User-Created worksets are used to divide the overall model into collections of elements that are related, usually geometrically, so that the elements can be edited by a user as if they were isolated from the rest of the model.
Families	Each family type loaded into a project will have its own workset. This prevents type changes from being made to a family that is also being used by another user, even if you are using separate worksets. Family worksets cannot be renamed or deleted.
Project Standards	Project Standards are overall project settings, such as system family types (walls, ceilings, roofs, etc.), filters, fill patterns, line styles, materials, or text types. Project Standards worksets help keep these things consistent while multiple people are working on a collaborated model and allow more than one user to work with them at the same time.
Views	Every view that exists in a project will also have its own workset, which allows for any annotation or drafting elements to be placed in the View workset rather than in a workset with model elements. This happens automatically, so there is no need to specify the correct workset when you are placing annotation elements.

© 2020, ASCENT - Center for Technical Knowledge®

2. In the Worksets dialog box, click **New** and type a name for the workset in the New Workset dialog box, as shown in Figure 4–7.

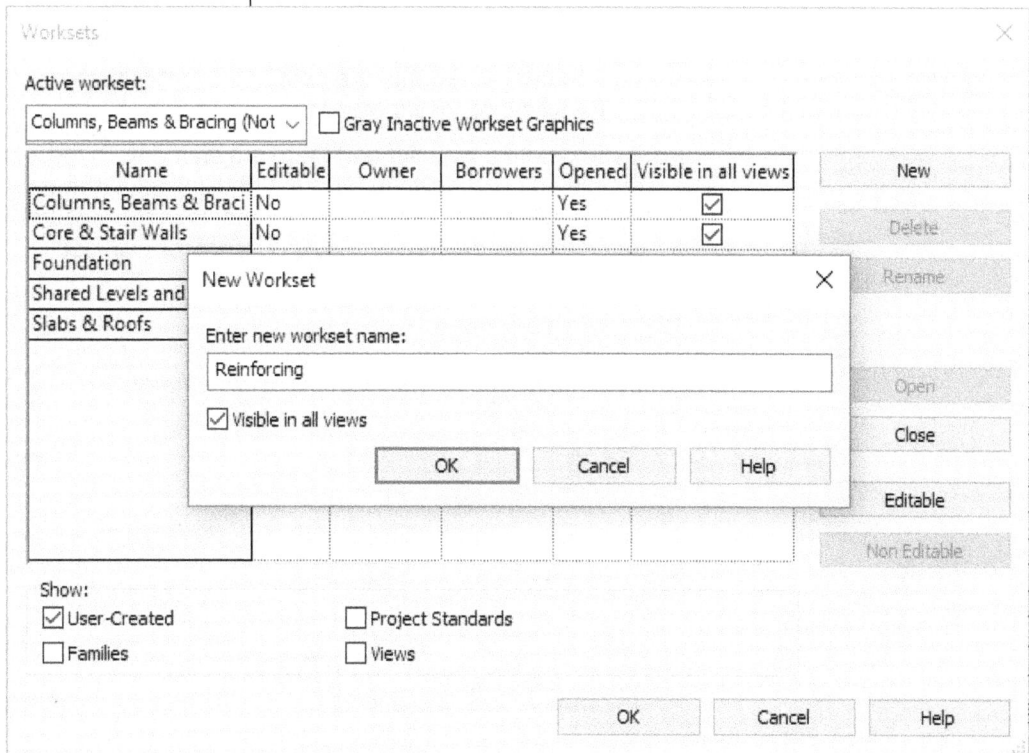

Figure 4–7

- As they are created, the worksets are open and editable by the person who set them up.

- Select or clear the **Visible in all views** option, as needed. For example, a workset showing the exterior of the building is required in all views, while a furniture layout is only required in specific views.

3. Click **OK**.
4. Continue to create new worksets, as needed.
5. Set the *Active workset*. This designates which workset will be active, meaning any new elements added to the project will be part of this workset.

- Selecting the **Gray Inactive Workset Graphics** check box allows users to have a visual understanding of which elements in a project are active and inactive by graying out inactive worksets.

- The new worksets are automatically made **Editable**.

- You can change existing workset names in the Worksets dialog box. Select the workset and click **Rename**.

  - You can rename the default Workset1 workset.
  - You cannot rename the default Project Standards, Families, or Views worksets.

- If you delete a workset and there are elements in the workset, the dialog box shown in Figure 4–8 displays, prompting you to choose what to do with any elements in the workset. They can either be deleted or moved to another workset.

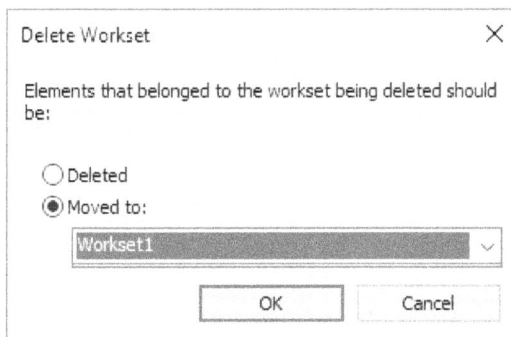

Figure 4–8

- To rename or delete a workset, it must first be made editable.

  - The Workset1, Project Standards, Families, and Views worksets cannot be deleted.

6. Click **OK** to close the dialog box.

© 2020, ASCENT - Center for Technical Knowledge®

Placing Elements in Worksets

When you are working with an existing model that has worksharing enabled and worksets created, you will want to place existing building elements into the appropriate worksets. For example, move any furniture already in a project to a furniture workset, as shown in Figure 4–9.

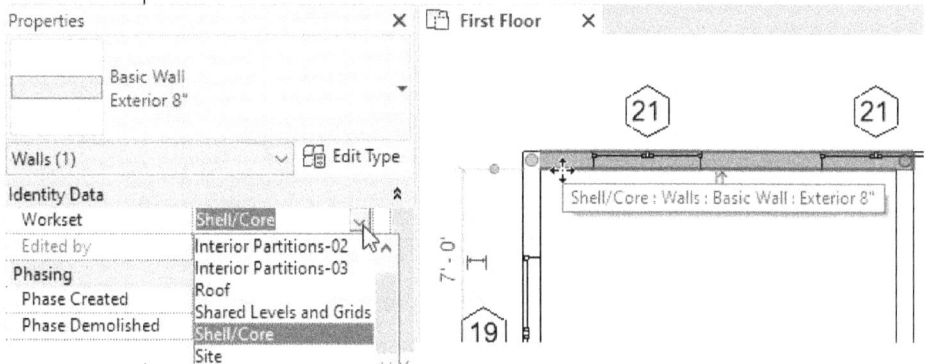

Figure 4–9

- Worksets can span levels; therefore, you can select elements on each level and move them into the appropriate workset.

- Whatever elements are not moved will remain in the default workset, which is Workset1.

How To: Move Elements to the Appropriate Worksets

1. Open a view that displays the elements you need to move to a different workset.
2. Select the element(s).
3. In Properties, change the *Workset* parameter to the workset in which you want the elements to be, as shown above in Figure 4–9.

- You can select multiple types of building elements and move them to a workset. However, you will need to filter out any annotation elements, such as views and tags, that are automatically assigned to the related View workset.

- Curtain wall subcomponents (grids, mullions, and panels) must be filtered out of a selection set. Select just the base curtain wall element when you want to move it to a workset.

- If you have added elements to a workset that is not visible in the current workset, the elements do not display in the view. If you need elements to be visible, open the Visibility/Graphic Overrides dialog box. Select the *Worksets* tab and modify the *Visibility Setting* for the worksets you want to be visible in the current view, as shown in Figure 4–10.

Worksets	Visibility Setting
Exterior Shell	Use Global Setting (Visible)
Furniture	Use Global Setting (Visible)
Plumbing	Use Global Setting (Not Visible)
Shared Levels and Grids	Use Global Setting (Visible)

Figure 4–10

Hint: Setting a Starting View

To save time when opening a complex model with worksharing activated, you can specify a *starting view*. This could be a cover sheet or a drafting view with information about the project. The idea is that the contents of the starting view are simple elements rather than model elements.

- To set the starting view, in the *Manage* tab>Manage Project panel, click ⬚ (Starting View). In the Starting View dialog box, select the view name, as shown in Figure 4–11.

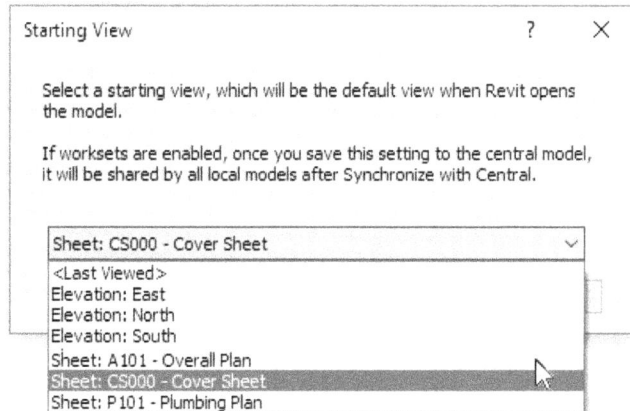

Starting View   ?   ✕

Select a starting view, which will be the default view when Revit opens the model.

If worksets are enabled, once you save this setting to the central model, it will be shared by all local models after Synchronize with Central.

Sheet: CS000 - Cover Sheet ⌄
<Last Viewed>
Elevation: East
Elevation: North
Elevation: South
Sheet: A101 - Overall Plan
Sheet: CS000 - Cover Sheet
Sheet: P101 - Plumbing Plan

Figure 4–11

© 2020, ASCENT - Center for Technical Knowledge®

4.4 Create a Central Model

The central model keeps track of available worksets and coordinates the changes made in each one with the rest of the worksets. It needs to be accessible to all team members, but should not be worked in directly. The central model maintains a connection to all local files and distributes updated information when a user syncs or reloads latest.

How To: Create a Central Model

1. In the workshared project's *File* tab, click 🖫 (Save As)> 📑 (Project).
2. In the Save As dialog box, navigate to the network location and click the **Options...** button.
3. In the File Save Options dialog box, **Make this a Central Model after save** is selected and grayed out (as shown Figure 4–12) because worksets have been enabled and the next step is to create the central model. Click **OK**.

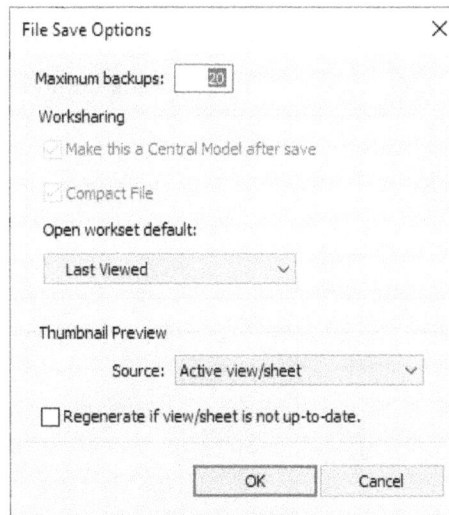

Figure 4–12

4. In the Quick Access Toolbar or the *Collaborate* tab>Synchronize panel, click ⬡ (Synchronize and Modify Settings).

5. In the Synchronize with Central dialog box, select **User-created Worksets** so that worksets you checked out are relinquished and available to everyone, as shown in Figure 4–13. You can also add a comment. Click **OK**.

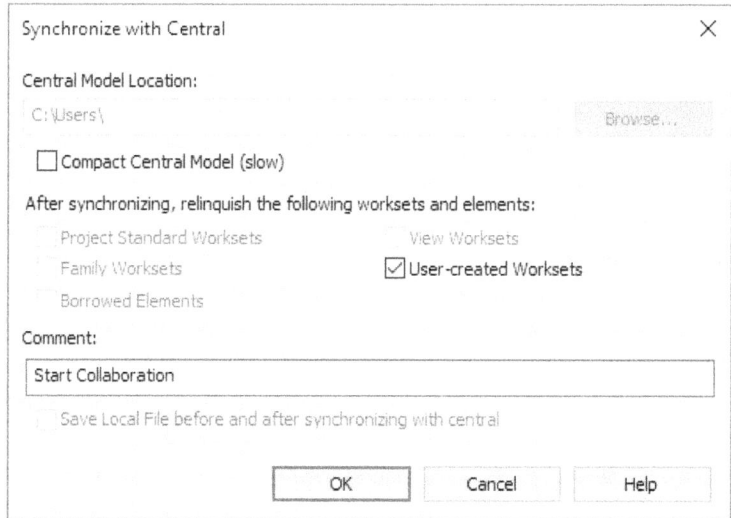

Synchronize with Central	×

Central Model Location:

C:\Users\   Browse...

☐ Compact Central Model (slow)

After synchronizing, relinquish the following worksets and elements:

☐ Project Standard Worksets   ☐ View Worksets

☐ Family Worksets   ☑ User-created Worksets

☐ Borrowed Elements

Comment:

Start Collaboration

☐ Save Local File before and after synchronizing with central

OK   Cancel   Help

Figure 4–13

6. Close the central model.

© 2020, ASCENT - Center for Technical Knowledge®

Practice 4a

Set Up a Workshared File - Architectural

Practice Objectives

- Enable worksharing on an existing project.
- Set up worksets and move existing elements to the worksets.
- Create a central model.

In this practice, you will set up a workshared file from an existing project, create worksets, move building elements to different worksets, and create a central model.

Task 1 - Set up a workshared file.

1. In the practice files folder, open **Midrise-A.rvt**.

2. In the *Collaborate* tab>Manage Collaboration panel, click 🖳 (Collaborate).

3. In the Collaborate dialog box, select **Within your network** and click **OK**.

4. In the *Collaborate* tab>Manage Collaboration panel or in the Status Bar, click 👥 (Worksets).

Owner "User1" will differ
for each user and will be
your Revit username,
found in Options in the
General pane.

5. In the Worksets dialog box, rename Workset1 to **Exterior**,
    then create the new worksets shown in Figure 4–14. The
    Visible in all views option should be off for all new worksets,
    except for **Vertical Circulation** and **Plumbing Fixtures**.

    *   When you have an existing project and you are creating
        worksets, you want to rename Workset1 to something that
        the project has a majority of. For example, an
        architectural project will have a lot of walls, doors, and
        windows; therefore, you would want all the elements to
        start out in this workset instead of trying to pick all the
        elements individually to put in the appropriate workset.

Worksets

Active workset:

Vertical Circulation				☑ Gray Inactive Workset Graphics	

Name	Editable	Owner	Borrowers	Opened	Visible in all views
Exterior	Yes	User1		Yes	☑
Furniture Level 1	Yes	User1		Yes	☐
Interior Level 1	Yes	User1		Yes	☐
Interior Level 2	Yes	User1		Yes	☐
Plumbing Fixtures	Yes	User1		Yes	☑
Shared Levels and Grids	Yes	User1		Yes	☑
Vertical Circulation	Yes	User1		Yes	☑

Figure 4–14

6. Verify that the *Active workset* is **Exterior**. Select **Gray
    Inactive Workset Graphics** and click **OK** to close the
    Worksets dialog box.

7. If prompted to change the active workset, click **No**. Elements
    on the Shared Levels and Grids workset and the
    view-specific room tags are grayed out. Everything in the
    Exterior workset displays in black.

    *   Note which workset shows as active either in the
        Collaborate tab>Manage Collaboration panel>Active
        Workset or in the Status Bar.

Task 2 - Move building elements to worksets.

---

1. In the **Floor Plans: Level 1** view, select all of the interior

    walls, columns, and doors. Use ⌧ (Filter) to remove other
    items from the selection set. Ensure that you do not select
    any exterior doors, rooms, room tags, and especially the
    curtain wall door.

© 2020, ASCENT - Center for Technical Knowledge®

2. In Properties, change the *Workset* for the selected elements to **Interior Level 1**. The items should be removed from the view if you toggled off the **Visible by default** option when you created the workset.

3. Repeat the same procedure to move the furniture and furniture systems to the **Furniture Level 1** workset.

4. Repeat the same procedure and move the elevators (Specialty Equipment), stairs, and railing to the **Vertical Circulation** workset, and the bathroom items to the **Plumbing Fixtures** workset. These elements are still visible but grayed out, as shown in Figure 4–15.

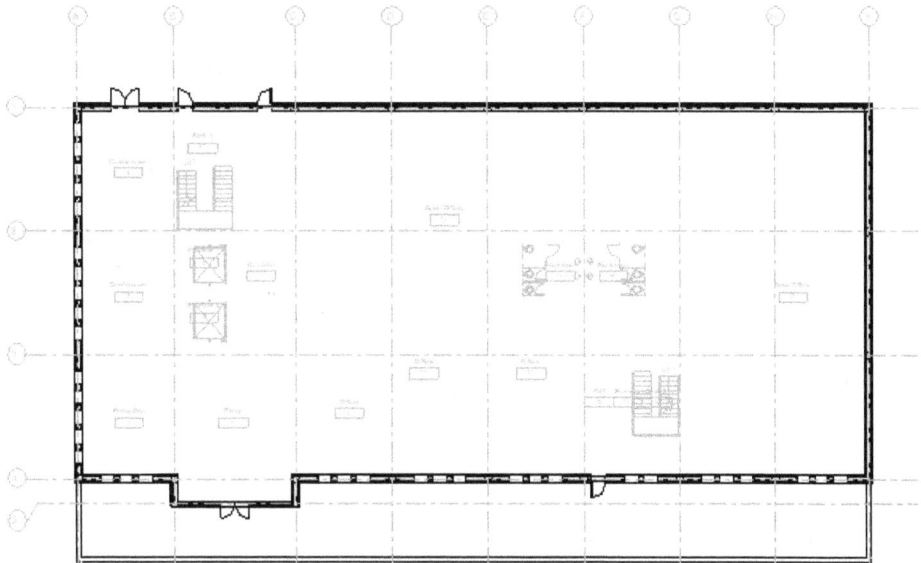

Figure 4–15

Task 3 - Create a central model.

1. In the *File* tab, expand (Save As) and click (Project).

2. Click **Options...** and verify that **Central file** is checked.

- The **Make this a Central Model after save** option is selected but grayed out. This project must become the central model because you have initiated worksets. Click **OK** to close the dialog box.

For this practice, you will be saving to your local drive, but central models must always be saved to a network location.

3. Name the file **Midrise-A.rvt** and be sure that you are saving it within your practice files folder. Click **Save**.

4. In the Status Bar, click ⚙ (Worksets). All of the files are now *Editable* with your username listed as the *Owner*, as shown in Figure 4–16.

Name	Editable	Owner	Borrowers	Opened	Visible in all views
Exterior	Yes	User1		Yes	☑
Furniture Level 1	Yes	User1		Yes	☐
Interior Level 1	Yes	User1		Yes	☐
Interior Level 2	Yes	User1		Yes	☐
Plumbing Fixtures	Yes	User1		Yes	☑
Shared Levels and Grids	Yes	User1		Yes	☑
Vertical Circulation	Yes	User1		Yes	☑

Figure 4–16

5. Click **OK** to close the dialog box.

6. In the *Collaborate* tab>Synchronize panel, click

   ⚙ (Synchronize and Modify Settings). In the Synchronize with Central dialog box, select the option to relinquish **User-created Worksets** so that they are available to everyone, as shown in Figure 4–17.

Since no local file has been created from this model, the "Save Local File before and after synchronizing with central" option is grayed out.

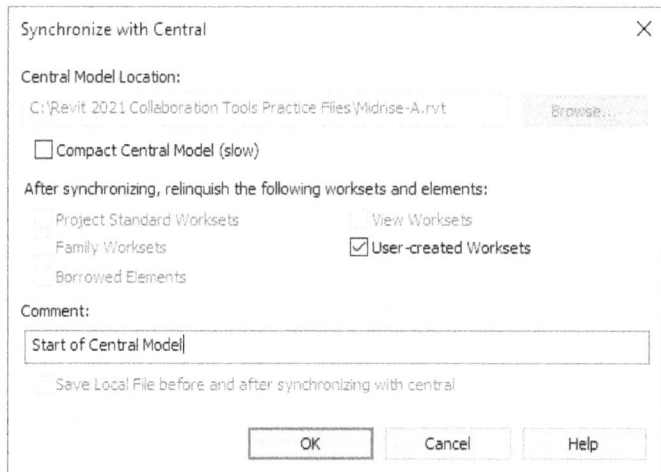

Figure 4–17

7. Click **OK** to synchronize with central and close the file.

© 2020, ASCENT - Center for Technical Knowledge®

Practice 4b

Set Up a Workshared File - Structural

Practice Objectives

- Enable worksharing on an existing project.
- Set up worksets and move existing elements to the worksets.
- Create a central model.

In this practice, you will set up a workshared file from an existing project, set up worksets, move elements to different worksets, and create a central model.

Task 1 - Set up a workshared file.

1. In the practice files folder, open **Bon-Air-Office-S.rvt**.

2. In the *Collaborate* tab>Manage Collaboration panel, click ⬚ (Collaborate).

3. In the Collaborate dialog box, select **Within your network** and click **OK**.

4. In the *Collaborate* tab>Manage Collaboration panel or in the Status Bar, click ⬚ (Worksets).

5. In the Worksharing dialog box, rename Workset1 as **Columns, Beams & Bracing** and click **OK**.

   - When you have an existing project and you are creating worksets, you want to rename Workset1 to something that the project has a majority of. For example, a structural project will have a lot of columns, beams, and bracing; therefore, you would want all the elements to start out in this workset instead of trying to pick all columns, beams, and bracing to put in the appropriate workset.

Owner "User1" will differ for each user and will be your Revit username, found in Options in the General pane.

6. In the Worksets dialog box, create the new worksets shown in Figure 4–18. The **Visible in all views** option should be off for all new worksets. (The Shared Levels and Grids workset has already been created.)

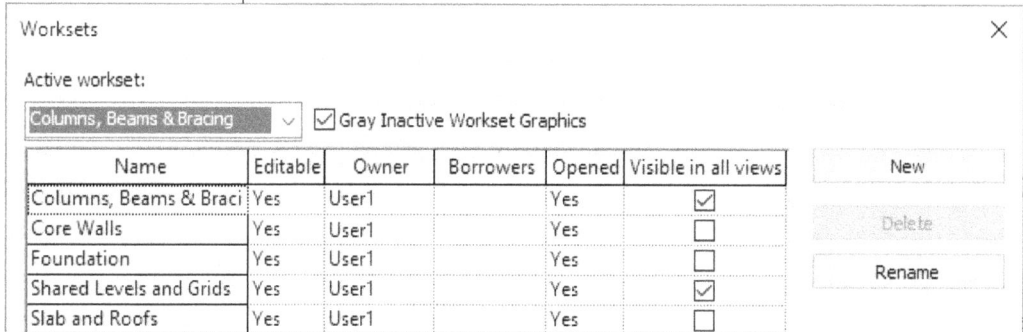

Worksets							✕
Active workset:							
Columns, Beams & Bracing ⌄	☑ Gray Inactive Workset Graphics						
Name	Editable	Owner	Borrowers	Opened	Visible in all views	New	
Columns, Beams & Braci	Yes	User1		Yes	☑		
Core Walls	Yes	User1		Yes	☐	Delete	
Foundation	Yes	User1		Yes	☐		
Shared Levels and Grids	Yes	User1		Yes	☑	Rename	
Slab and Roofs	Yes	User1		Yes	☐		

Figure 4–18

7. Verify that the *Active workset* is **Columns, Beams & Bracing**. Select **Gray Inactive Workset Graphics** and click **OK** to close the Worksets dialog box.

8. If prompted to change the active workset, click **No** because you want to keep the active workset as Columns, Beams & Bracing and not the last workset you created.

   • Note which workset shows as active either in the *Collaborate* tab>Manage Collaboration panel>Active Workset or in the Status Bar.

9. Open the **Structural Plans: Level 1** view. Elements in the Shared Levels and Grids workset and the view-specific view and section markers are grayed out. Everything else is black because they are in the Columns, Beams & Bracing workset that was formerly named Workset1.

Task 2 - Move building elements to worksets.

1. Open the **Elevations (Building Elevation): East** view.

2. Select all of the elements from Level 1 down to the lowest footing, as shown in Figure 4–19.

© 2020, ASCENT - Center for Technical Knowledge®

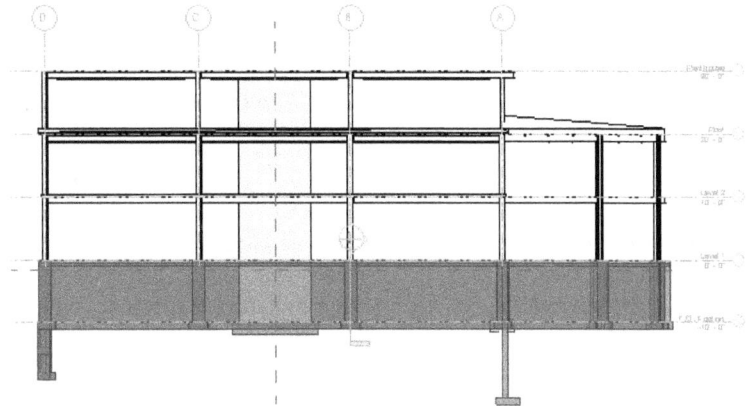

Figure 4–19

3. In Properties, change the workset for the selected elements to **Foundation**. Use ▽ (Filter) to remove slab edges. (The elements should be removed from the view if you toggled off the **Visible in all views** option when you created the workset.)

- Although you are changing the workset for the wall foundations, analytical wall foundations do not automatically follow and it is not possible to manually change their workset. When starting a project from scratch, as would typically be the case, it is important to set the right workset before creating the wall foundations.

4. In the East Elevation, select everything in the view. Use ▽ (Filter) to only select the slabs (floors) and roofs. Move them to the **Slabs & Roofs** workset. Ensure that you include the slab edge.

5. Repeat the procedure by opening the appropriate views and moving the elevator walls to the **Core Walls** workset.

Task 3 - Create a central model.

1. In the *File* tab, expand ⊞ (Save As) and click ⊡ (Project).

For this practice, you will be saving to your local drive, but central models must always be saved to a network location.

2. In the Save As dialog box, click **Options...**. The **Make this a Central Model after save** option is selected but grayed out. This project must become the central model because you have initiated worksets. Click **OK** to close the dialog box.

3. Name the file **Bon-Air-Office-S.rvt** and be sure that you are saving it within your practice files folder. Click **Save**.

4. Click 🔧 (Worksets). All of the files are listed as *Editable* with your username listed as the *Owner*, as shown in Figure 4–20.

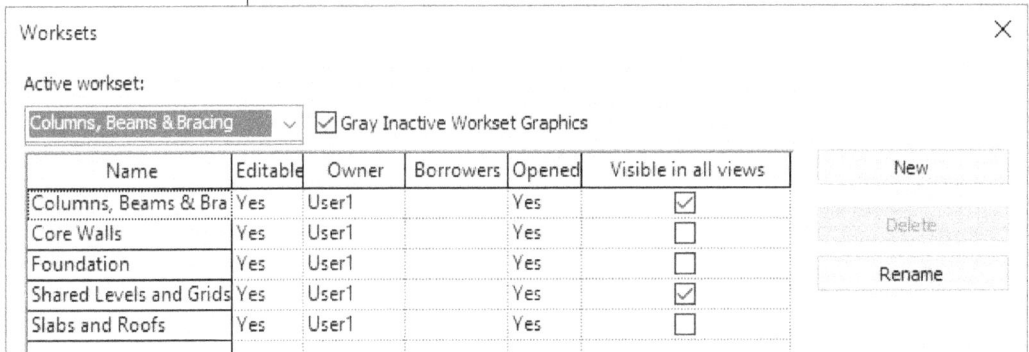

Worksets						
Active workset:						
Columns, Beams & Bracing ▾	☑ Gray Inactive Workset Graphics					
Name	Editable	Owner	Borrowers	Opened	Visible in all views	New
Columns, Beams & Bra	Yes	User1		Yes	☑	
Core Walls	Yes	User1		Yes	☐	Delete
Foundation	Yes	User1		Yes	☐	Rename
Shared Levels and Grids	Yes	User1		Yes	☑	
Slabs and Roofs	Yes	User1		Yes	☐	

Figure 4–20

5. Click **OK** to close the dialog box.

6. Click 🔄 (Synchronize and Modify Settings). In the Synchronize with Central dialog box, select the option to relinquish **User-created Worksets** so that they are available to everyone, as shown in Figure 4–21.

© 2020, ASCENT - Center for Technical Knowledge®

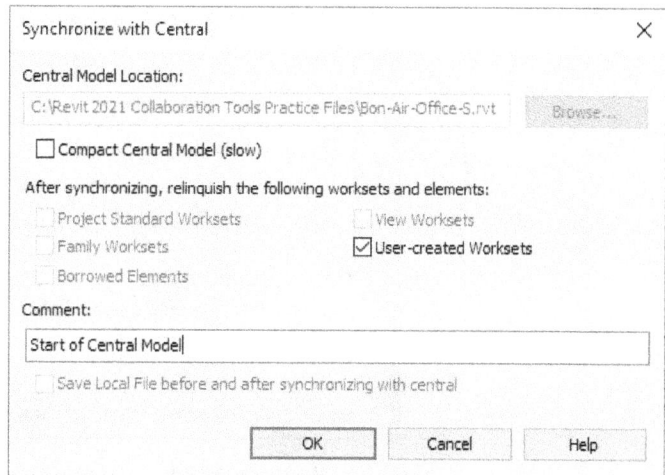

Figure 4–21

7. Click **OK** to synchronize with central and close the file.

Practice 4c | Set Up a Workshared File - MEP

Practice Objectives

- Enable worksharing on an existing project.
- Set up worksets and move existing elements to the worksets.
- Create a central model.

In this practice, you will set up a workshared file from an existing project, set up worksets, move building elements to different worksets, and create a central model.

Task 1 - Set up a workshared file.

1. In the practice files folder, open **Olethe-Building-MEP.rvt**.

2. In the *Collaborate* tab>Manage Collaboration panel, click ⬚ (Collaborate).

3. In the Collaborate dialog box, select **Within your network** and click **OK**.

4. In the *Collaborate* tab>Manage Collaboration panel or in the Status Bar, click ⬚ (Worksets).

5. In the Worksets dialog box, rename Workset1 to **HVAC** (the majority of the existing elements, which are ducts and duct fittings, need to be in this workset).

    - When you have an existing project and you are creating worksets, you want to rename Workset1 to something that the project has a majority of. For example, a mechanical project will have a lot of ducts and duct fittings; therefore, you would want all the elements to start out in this workset instead of trying to pick all elements individually to put in the appropriate workset.

© 2020, ASCENT - Center for Technical Knowledge®

Owner "User1" will differ for each user and will be your Revit username, found in Options in the General pane.

6. In the Worksets dialog box, create the new worksets shown in Figure 4–22. The **Visible in all views** option should be off for all new worksets, except for **Architectural Link**.

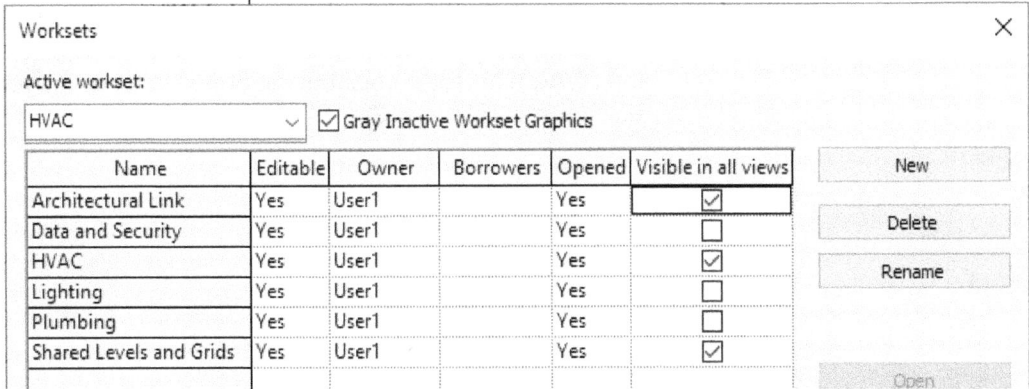

Worksets   ×

Active workset:

HVAC   ∨   ☑ Gray Inactive Workset Graphics

Name	Editable	Owner	Borrowers	Opened	Visible in all views	
Architectural Link	Yes	User1		Yes	☑	New
Data and Security	Yes	User1		Yes	☐	Delete
HVAC	Yes	User1		Yes	☑	
Lighting	Yes	User1		Yes	☐	Rename
Plumbing	Yes	User1		Yes	☐	
Shared Levels and Grids	Yes	User1		Yes	☑	
						Open

Figure 4–22

7. Verify that the active workset is **HVAC**. Select the **Gray Inactive Workset Graphics** option and click **OK** to close the Worksets dialog box.

8. If prompted to change the active workset, click **No** to keep the HVAC workset active.

   • Note which workset shows as active either in the *Collaborate* tab>Manage Collaboration panel>Active Workset or in the Status Bar.

Task 2 - Move building elements to worksets.

1. In the 3D view, select some of the ducts and equipment. In Properties, you can see that the *Workset* is **HVAC**.

2. Select the linked architectural model. It is also set to HVAC. Change the *Workset* to **Architectural Link**.

   • If the link is not selected, in the Status Bar, click

       (Select Links) to toggle it on.

3. Open the Electrical>Lighting>Floor Plans>**1-Lighting** view.

4. Select all of the lighting fixtures and move them to the **Lighting** workset. The elements are removed from the view because the Lighting workset is set to not visible.

5. Open the Mechanical>Plumbing>Floor Plans>**1-Plumbing** view and move the plumbing fixtures to the **Plumbing** workset. These elements are also removed from the view because the Plumbing workset is set to not visible.

6. Open the Coordination>MEP>Floor Plans>**1 - MEP** view.

7. Open the Worksets dialog box and make the Lighting and Plumbing worksets visible. Click **OK**. The view displays with the HVAC workset in color but the other worksets grayed out, as shown in Figure 4–23.

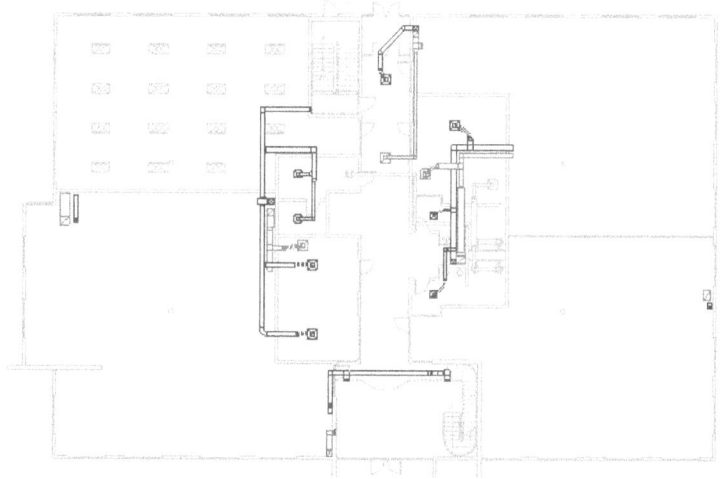

Figure 4–23

Task 3 - Create a central model.

1. In the *File* tab, expand (Save As), and click (Project).

For this practice, you will be saving to your local drive, but central models must always be saved to a network location.

2. In the Save As dialog box, click **Options...**. The **Make this a Central Model after save** option is selected but grayed out. This project must become the central model because you have initiated worksets. Click **OK** to close the dialog box.

3. Make sure the name is **Olethe-Building-MEP.rvt** and that you are saving it within your practice files folder. Click **Save**.

4. Click (Worksets). All of the files are now *Editable* with your username listed as the *Owner*. Clear **Visible in all views** for Lighting and Plumbing, as shown in Figure 4–24.

© 2020, ASCENT - Center for Technical Knowledge®

Name	Editable	Owner	Borrowers	Opened	Visible in all views
Architectural Link	Yes	User1		Yes	✓
Data and Security	Yes	User1		Yes	
Electrical	Yes	User1		Yes	
HVAC	Yes	User1		Yes	✓
Lighting	Yes	User1		Yes	
Plumbing	Yes	User1		Yes	
Shared Levels and Grids	Yes	User1		Yes	✓

Figure 4–24

5. Click **OK** to close the dialog box.

6. Click ⬡ (Synchronize and Modify Settings). In the Synchronize with Central dialog box, select the option to relinquish **User-created Worksets** so that they are available to everyone, as shown in Figure 4–25.

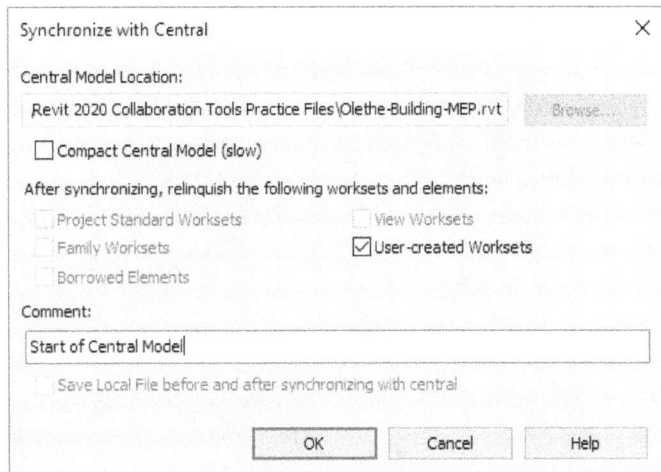

Figure 4–25

7. Click **OK** to synchronize with central and close the file.

4.5 Create a Local File from a Central Model

After a central model has been saved to a shared local network location, you will use the Open dialog box to create a local copy, as shown in Figure 4–26. Doing this creates a link between your local file and the central model.

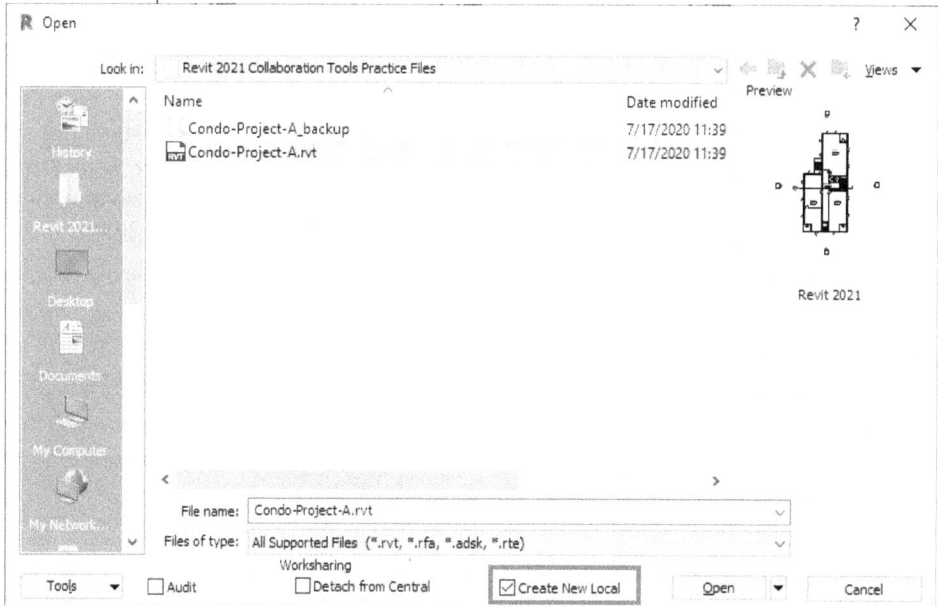

Figure 4–26

- You always work directly in your local file and synchronize your changes to the central model.

- Synchronizing to central will also update your local file with any changes from other users working on the project.

© 2020, ASCENT - Center for Technical Knowledge®

Hint: Notifications and Default File Location

In the *File* tab, click **Options**. In the Options dialog box, in the *General* tab, you can set reminders to save and synchronize the local file with the central model, as shown in Figure 4–27.

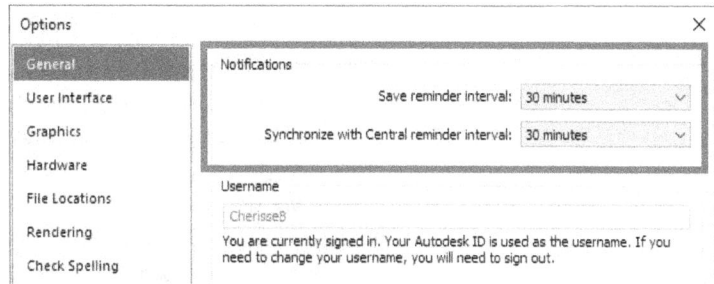

Figure 4–27

- This pane is also where your local file pulls your username from.

In the *File Locations* tab, set the *Default path for user files*, as shown in Figure 4–28.

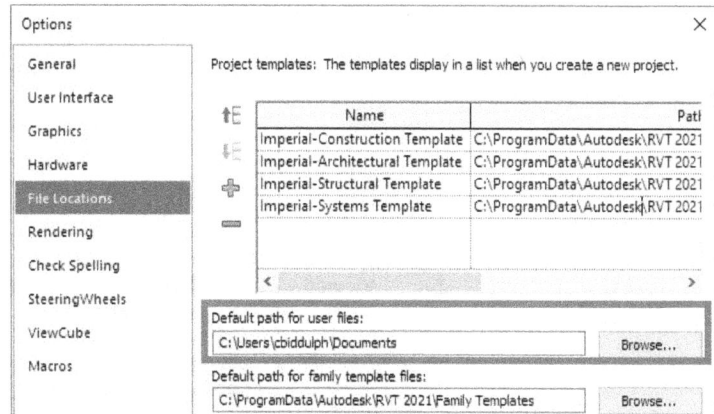

Figure 4–28

- This pane is also where you set the location for project template files, family template files, and point cloud files.

How To: Create a Local File

1. From the Quick Access Toolbar, click 📂 (Open).
2. In the Open dialog box, navigate to the central model and verify that **Create New Local** (shown previously in Figure 4–26) is checked.

   There are two other options available in the Open dialog box:

   - **Detach from Central:** Opens the file and detaches it from the central model. This should only be done by the administrator of the central model.
   - **Audit:** Scans and fixes corrupt elements in a model when working with workshared files.

3. Click **Open**. You can also expand the **Open** button for other options, as shown in Figure 4–29 and explained in the following table.

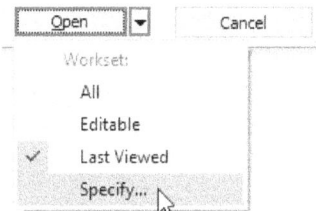

Figure 4–29

All	Opens all worksets.
Editable	Opens all worksets that are editable (not checked out by someone else).
Last Viewed	Opens the worksets that were viewed the last time you saved the local file. This is the default setting after the local file has been saved once.
Specify	Opens the Opening Worksets dialog box (once you click **Open**), where you select the worksets you want opened or closed.

If you select **Specify...** and click **Open**, the Opening Worksets dialog box displays, as shown in Figure 4–30, where you can do the following:

- Select the name of the workset(s) and click **Close** if a workset is opened and you want it closed.
- Select the name of the workset(s) and click **Open** if a workset is closed and you want it opened.
- Select more than one workset by holding <Ctrl> or <Shift>.
- Select all of the worksets by pressing <Ctrl>+<A>.

© 2020, ASCENT - Center for Technical Knowledge®

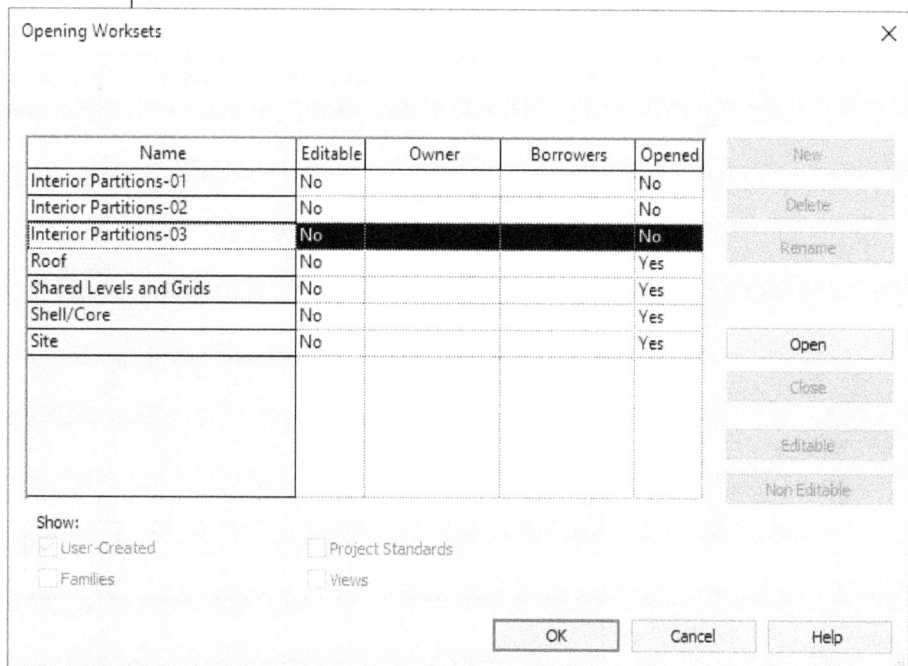

Name	Editable	Owner	Borrowers	Opened
Interior Partitions-01	No			No
Interior Partitions-02	No			No
Interior Partitions-03	No			No
Roof	No			Yes
Shared Levels and Grids	No			Yes
Shell/Core	No			Yes
Site	No			Yes

Opening Worksets ✕

New
Delete
Rename

Open
Close
Editable
Non Editable

Show:
☑ User-Created ☐ Project Standards
☐ Families ☐ Views

OK   Cancel   Help

Figure 4–30

4. Click **OK** in the Opening Worksets dialog box after making your selections.
5. A copy of the project is created. It will have the same name as the central model with your Autodesk Revit username added to the end.
6. From the *Collaborate* tab>Synchronize panel, expand the Synchronize with Central drop-down list and select

   ⬡ (Synchronize and Modify Settings).

7. In the Synchronize with Central dialog box, verify that the *Central Model Location* path is correct and that **Save Local File before and after synchronizing with central** is checked, as shown in Figure 4–31. You can add a comment if needed.

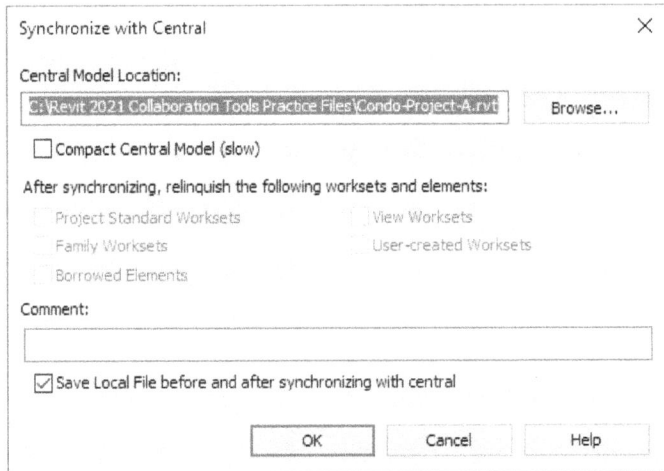

Figure 4–31

8. Click **OK** to close the dialog box.

- After your local file is created, you will not open the central model again unless a new local file is needed. You will always work from your local file.

- Save the local file as frequently as you would save any other project.

- Synchronize the local file with the central model several times a day or as required by company policy or project status.

  - If your company policy is to create a new local file daily or weekly, when you open the central model with **Create New Local** checked, you will get the Duplicate name dialog box. Click **Overwrite existing copy**, as shown in Figure 4–32, to continue.

© 2020, ASCENT - Center for Technical Knowledge®

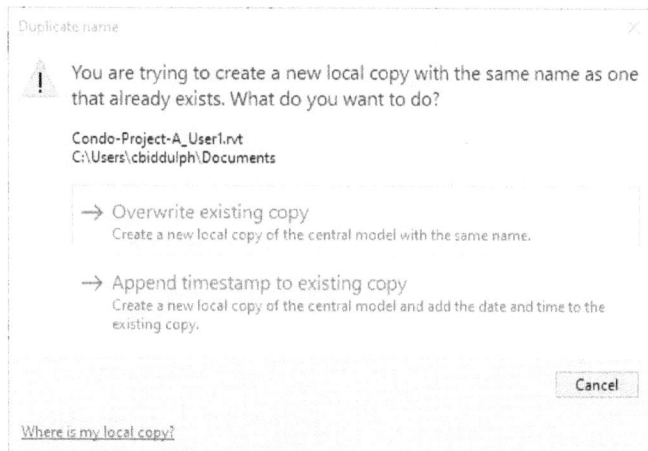

Figure 4–32

- **Append timestamp to existing copy** creates a new local file but adds the date and time to the end of the file name in your local file location, as shown in Figure 4–33.

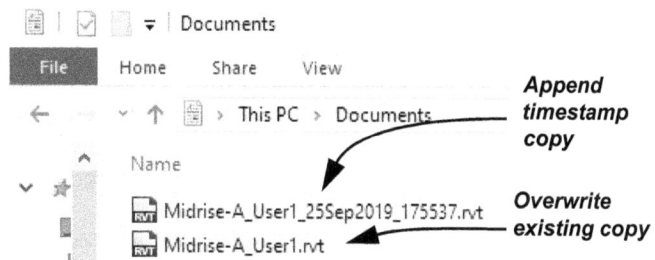

Figure 4–33

- When you open a local file, select only the worksets you need to open. Limiting the number of worksets speeds up the opening and saving process and frees up elements for other project team members to edit.

Saving and Synchronizing Your Local File

To save your local file, you can click ▣ (Save) in the Quick Access Toolbar. You can also make sure that within the Synchronize with Central dialog box, you have the check box selected for **Save Local File before and after synchronizing with central**, as shown in Figure 4–34.

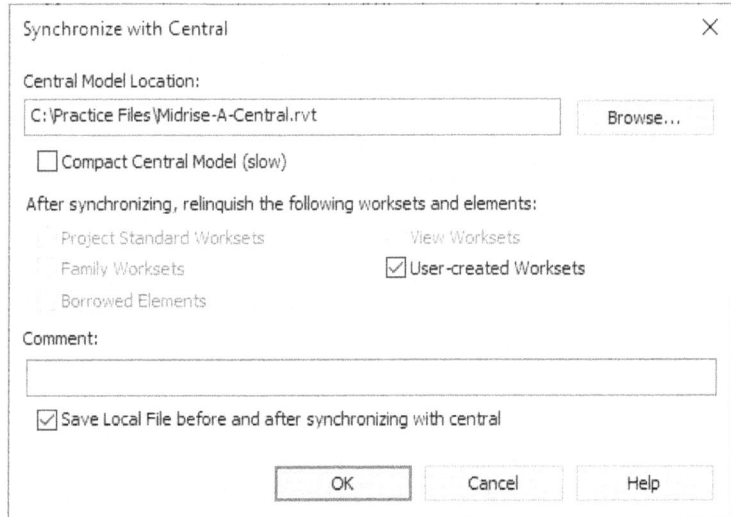

Figure 4–34

- Save the local file frequently (every 15 to 30 minutes).

- Synchronize to the central model periodically (every hour or two) or after you have made major changes to the project. At the end of the day, make sure you synchronize with central and relinquish worksets.

Synchronizing to the Central Model

There are two methods for synchronizing to the central model. In the Quick Access Toolbar or *Collaborate* tab>Synchronize panel, expand ⬡ (Synchronize with Central) and click ⬡ (Synchronize Now) or ⬡ (Synchronize and Modify Settings). The last-used command is active if you click the top-level icon.

© 2020, ASCENT - Center for Technical Knowledge®

- **Synchronize Now:** Updates the central model and then the local file with any changes to the central model since the last synchronization without prompting you for any settings. It automatically relinquishes elements borrowed from any workset but retains worksets used by the current user.

- **Synchronize and Modify Settings:** Opens the Synchronize with Central dialog box so you can set the options for relinquishing worksets and elements, add comments, and specify to save the file locally before and after synchronization.

- Always keep **Save Local File before and after synchronizing with central** checked to ensure your local copy is up to date with the latest changes from the central model.

- When you close a local file without saving to the central model, you are prompted to do so, as shown in Figure 4–35.

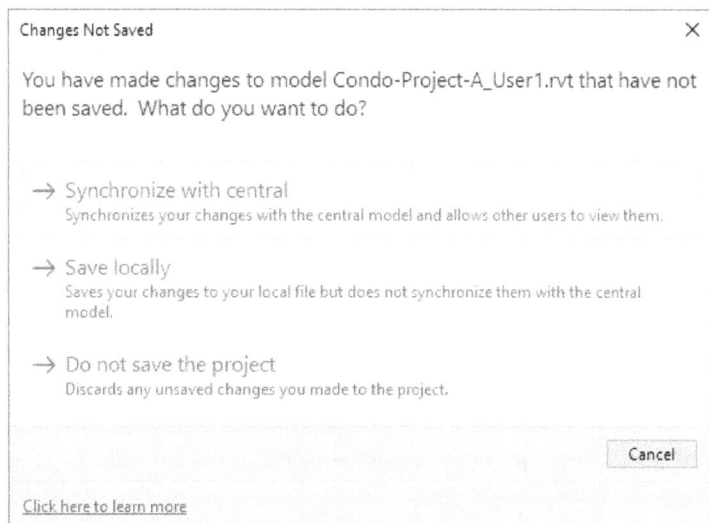

Figure 4–35

4.6 Working in a Workshared File

The key to successfully working in a workshared project is coordinating and communicating with the other members of your team. However, the majority of the work you will do in a workshared project will be no different than any other project. Only check out worksets that you need to work in (as shown in Figure 4–36) and borrow elements as you work.

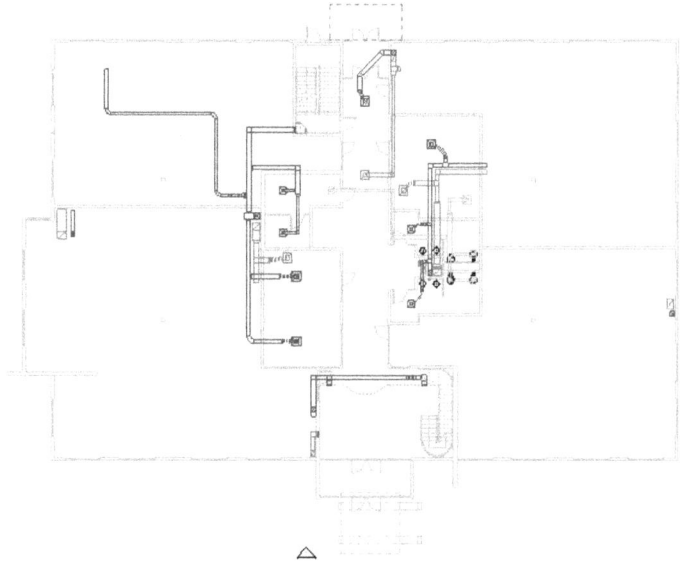

Figure 4–36

When new elements are added to the project, they are placed in the active workset, as shown in Figure 4–37. It is therefore important to set the active workset correctly before adding new elements. Not doing so can result in visibility and permissions-related issues.

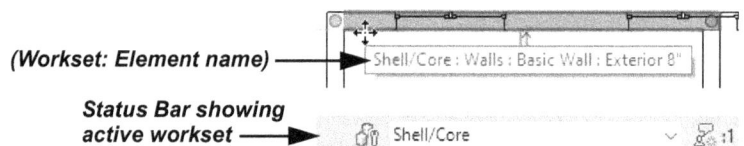

(Workset: Element name) ⟶ | Shell/Core : Walls : Basic Wall : Exterior 8"

Status Bar showing active workset ⟶ Shell/Core

Figure 4–37

© 2020, ASCENT - Center for Technical Knowledge®

How To: Set the Active Workset

1. Open your local file.
2. In the Status Bar (or *Collaborate* tab>Manage Collaboration panel), expand the *Active Workset* list and select a workset, as shown in Figure 4–38.

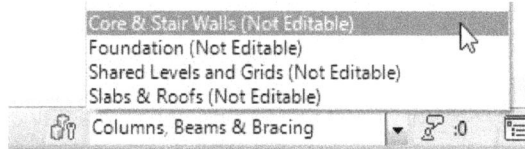

Figure 4–38

- It does not matter if the workset says **(Not Editable)**; you can still add elements to it. **Not Editable** means that you have not checked out the workset but are working on the basis of borrowing elements.

- You can gray out inactive worksets in a view to easily distinguish between active and inactive worksets, as shown in Figure 4–39. In the *Collaborate* tab>Manage Collaboration panel, toggle (Gray Inactive Workset Graphics) on. You can also select **Gray Inactive Workset Graphics** in the Worksets dialog box.

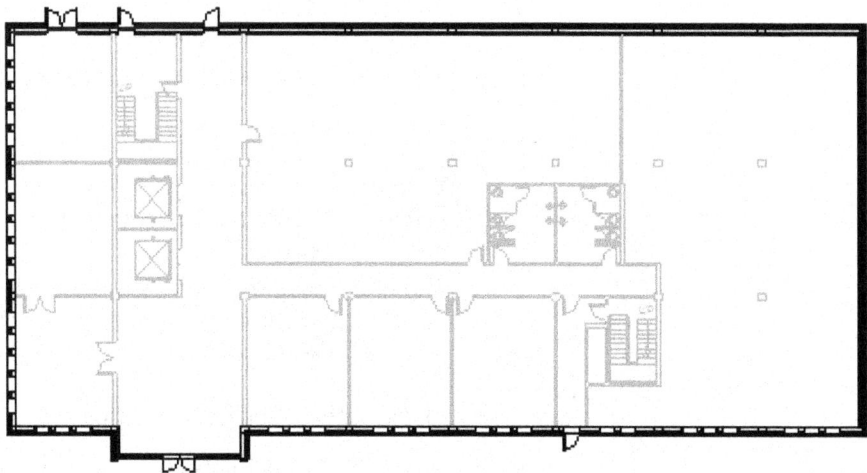

Figure 4–39

Hint: Worksharing Monitoring

Worksharing monitoring displays information about the workshared model you are working in or have opened, as shown in Figure 4–40. It shows you who is working in the project, if there are any issues, if your local file is up to date, and information about requests for borrowing elements. You can also set up options on what information you would like displayed in desktop notifications that appear above your computer's system tray (Date and Time). You can click on the History icon to display the action from all team members working in the project.

Click to open the Central File History dialog box

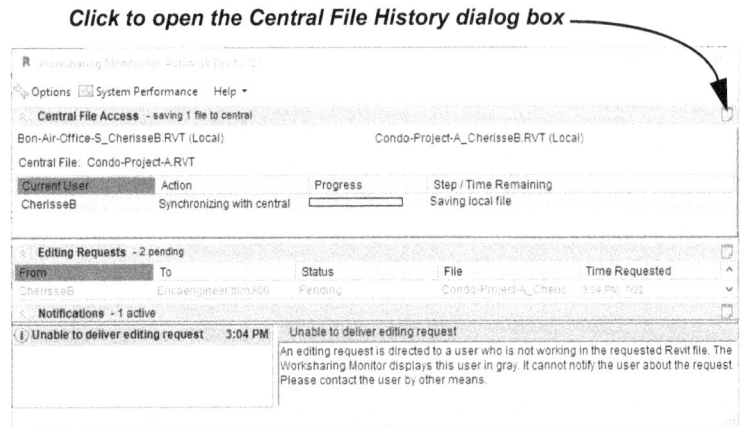

Figure 4–40

- From the *Collaborate* tab>Synchronize panel, click
  (Worksharing Monitor).

  - You can open System Performance to monitor your computer's resources, like hard drive space, memory, and CPU load.
  - The Worksharing Monitor for Autodesk Revit 2021 dialog box needs to remain open while you work in order to receive desktop notifications.

- To specify notification options, click (Options).

  - Worksharing Monitor options include General, Central File Access, Editing Request, and Notifications.

© 2020, ASCENT - Center for Technical Knowledge®

Editing Elements in Worksets

There are two different ways to edit elements in worksets.

- **Borrow elements:** If you *borrow* the elements as you make changes, no one has to wait for permission to make modifications. After the interior wall is moved (as shown in Figure 4–41), it will show that you have borrowed the workset that the element is on (as shown in Figure 4–42). This method allows others to modify elements on the same workset without requesting permission. This can speed up the work if you have a fairly small group of people working on the project, especially when there is some overlap between the purposes of the users or when the project has only been divided into a few worksets.

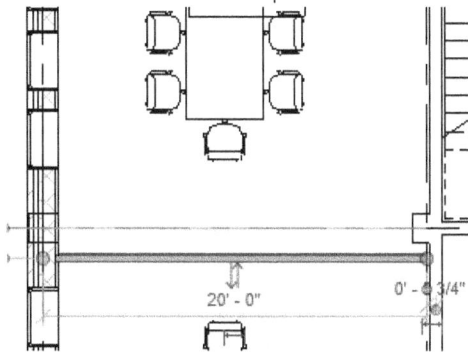

Figure 4–41

Worksets

Active workset:

Interior Level 1 (Not Editable) ⌄   ☐ Gray Inactive Workset Graphic

Name	Editable	Owner	Borrowe	Opened
Exterior	No			Yes
Furniture	No			Yes
Interior Level 1	No		User2	Yes
Plumbing	No			Yes
Shared Levels and Grids	No			Yes
Vertical circulation	No			Yes

Figure 4–42

Check with your project coordinator to see which method your office uses.

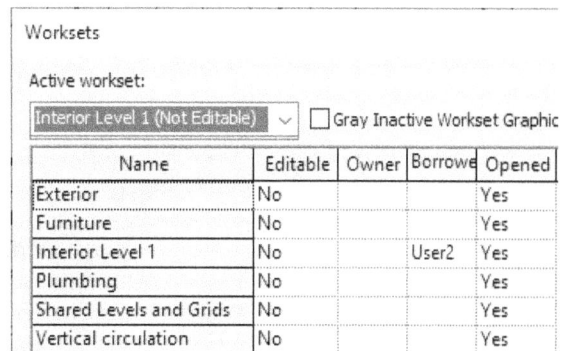

- **Check out a workset:** When you *check out* a specific workset and make it editable, no one else can modify elements in that workset without placing a request to borrow an element.

Borrowing Elements

When you select an element and see the **Make element editable** icon, as shown in Figure 4–43, it means that you have not checked out that particular workset or that you are not currently borrowing the element.

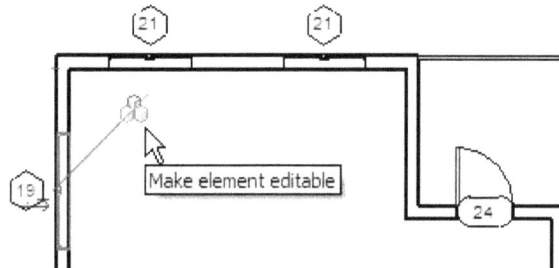

Figure 4–43

- It is not necessary to click the icon; simply proceed to edit the element.

  - If you modify the element and it enables you to do so, then no one else has that workset checked out and you were given automatic permission to modify this element.
  - If someone else has borrowed the element or checked out the workset to which it belongs, you are prompted to request permission to edit the element.

How To: Check Out Worksets

You can also open the Worksets dialog box from the Status Bar.

1. In the *Collaborate* tab>Manage Collaboration panel, click

   (Worksets).

2. In the Worksets dialog box, select **Yes** in the *Editable* column next to the workset name that you want to check out and edit, as shown in Figure 4–44. More than one workset can be checked out and made editable at a time, but ensure that you only check out the ones that you really need.

© 2020, ASCENT - Center for Technical Knowledge®

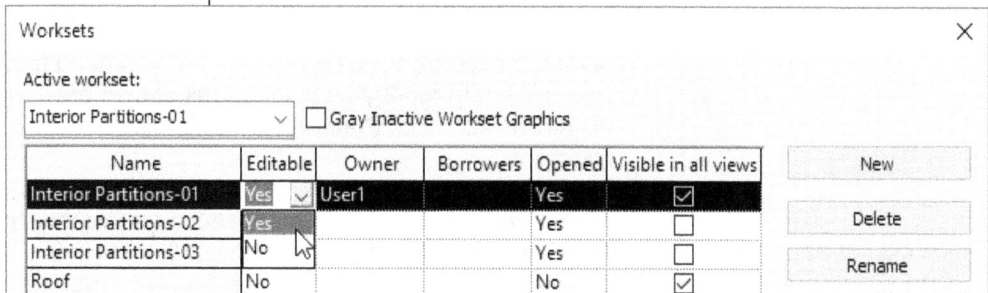

Figure 4–44

3. Select an **Active workset** in the drop-down list. You can also set the active workset from the list in either the Manage Collaboration panel or Status Bar.
4. Click **OK**.

• When editing elements, you can control which ones can be picked by selecting the **Editable Only** option in the Options Bar, as shown in Figure 4–45. If **Editable Only** is selected, you can only select items that are available in the editable worksets or those which you borrowed. If it is cleared, you can select anything.

Figure 4–45

Permissions to Edit

If you try to edit an element that is owned by someone else, an alert box opens stating that you cannot edit the element without their permission, as shown in Figure 4–46. First, you must request an edit. Second, the owner of the workset either grants or denies the request. If the request is granted, update your local file and you will have control of the element until you relinquish it.

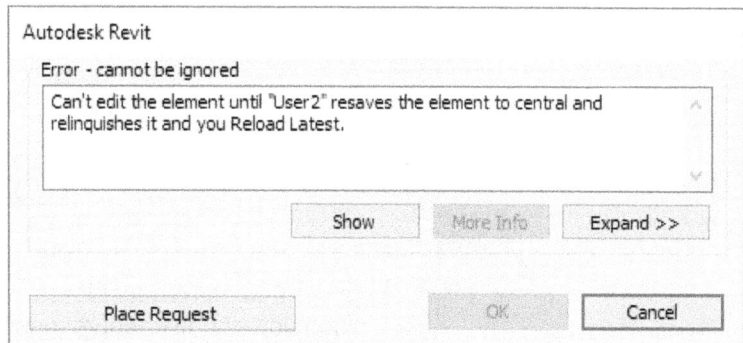

Figure 4–46

How To: Request an Edit

1. When the alert box opens stating that you need to have permission to modify an element (as shown previously in Figure 4–46), click **Place Request** to ask to borrow the element.

2. An alert box opens stating the request has been made, as shown in Figure 4–47. If you expect a quick reply, leave the message in place. If you want to continue working, click **Close** and cancel out of the alert box. The request is still active.

Figure 4–47

How To: Grant or Deny an Editing Request

1. When a user sends an editing request for an element you are currently borrowing or which belongs to a workset that you have checked out (editable), an alert displays, as shown in Figure 4–48.

Figure 4–48

2. In the Editing Request Received dialog box, click **Show** to zoom into the element requested, **Grant** to allow the other user to modify the element, or **Deny** to stop the other user from modifying the element.

© 2020, ASCENT - Center for Technical Knowledge®

3. If you do not respond right away to the editing request, you can always access it again. In the *Collaborate* tab> Synchronize panel, click 🖾 (Editing Requests) or in the Status Bar, click 🖾 (Editing Requests). The information in the Status Bar includes the number of requests outstanding, as shown in Figure 4–49.

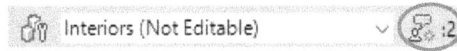

Figure 4–49

4. In the Editing Requests dialog box, as shown in Figure 4–50, select the pending request. Click on the date.

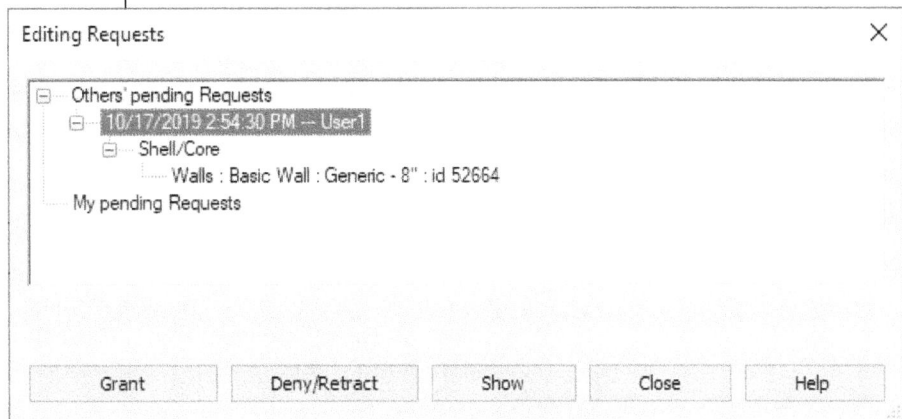

Figure 4–50

- When you select the editing request date, the elements included in the request are highlighted in the project. Click **Show** to zoom in on the elements, if needed.

5. Click **Grant** to enable the other user to make the changes or **Deny/Retract** to deny the request. (The original user can also retract the request with this button.) You can also grant the request by saving the entire workset back to the central model and relinquishing the items.

Applying an Editing Request

When an editing request is granted, a confirmation alert box opens in the program of the user who requested it, as shown in Figure 4–51. Close the alert box.

Once a request is granted, you can make modifications to the element without having to request to edit the feature, although the icon still displays.

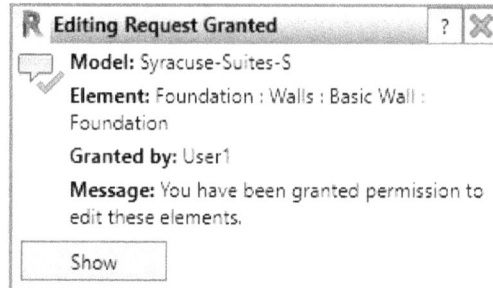

Figure 4–51

- If the requesting user canceled out of the Edit Request dialog box, when they are notified that they have permission, they can click ⬡ (Reload Latest) or type **RL** to make the ownership modification.

- If the Error dialog box is still open, the Editing Request Placed dialog box displays that the request has been granted, as shown in Figure 4–52. Click **Close** and the element is modified.

An additional note "Reload Latest is required to edit the elements" might display in the dialog box depending on what the other user did with the borrowed elements.

Figure 4–52

Editing Request Frequency

To control the frequency of updates to editing requests (and worksharing display modes), in the Options dialog box, in the *General* tab, move the slider bar between *Less Frequent* and *More Frequent*, as shown in Figure 4–53.

© 2020, ASCENT - Center for Technical Knowledge®

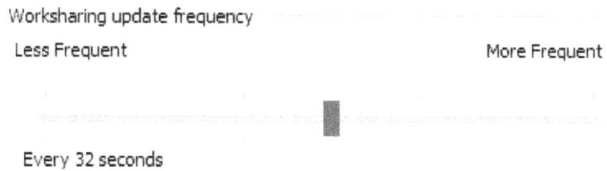

Worksharing update frequency

Less Frequent   More Frequent

Every 32 seconds

Figure 4–53

- If the bar is moved to the far side of *Less Frequent*, it changes to manual and updates only when you borrow elements or synchronize with the central model. This can improve the performance of the program but also causes the other user to wait until you receive the request.

Relinquishing Worksets

After you have been working with borrowed elements or have checked out worksets, you should return them to the central model when you are finished. In the Quick Access Toolbar or *Collaborate* tab>Synchronize panel, click (Synchronize and Modify Settings). The Synchronize with Central dialog box displays, as shown in Figure 4–54. In this dialog box, select the worksets and/or borrowed elements you want to relinquish. Only those which you have ownership of are available.

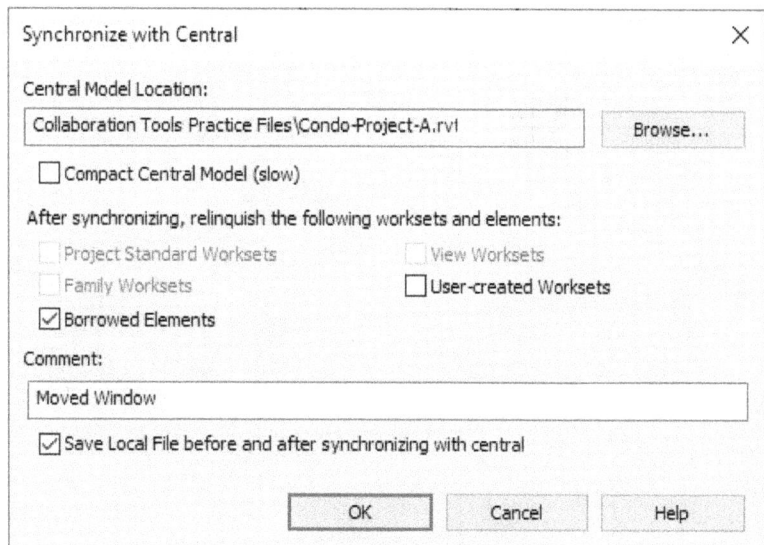

Synchronize with Central   ×

Central Model Location:

Collaboration Tools Practice Files\Condo-Project-A.rvt   Browse...

☐ Compact Central Model (slow)

After synchronizing, relinquish the following worksets and elements:

☐ Project Standard Worksets   ☐ View Worksets
☐ Family Worksets   ☐ User-created Worksets
☑ Borrowed Elements

Comment:

Moved Window

☑ Save Local File before and after synchronizing with central

[OK]   [Cancel]   [Help]

Figure 4–54

Synchronize with Central Options

Adding comments at key points and for significant changes in the project is useful in case the project backup needs to be restored in the future.

- The **Borrowed Elements** option will be selected by default. This relinquishes any elements you borrowed from another workset.

- Select the **Save Local File before and after synchronizing with central** option to save extra steps.

- Periodically, use the **Compact Central Model (slow)** option when you save to the central model. This reduces the file size, but also increases the time required to save.

- You can add comments to the central model for others to see. To view the comments, in the *Collaborate* tab>Synchronize panel, click ⬚ (Show History) and select the central model whose history you want to view. The History dialog box displays with the *Date/Time Stamp*, *Modified by*, and *Comments* columns populated with information, as shown in Figure 4–55.

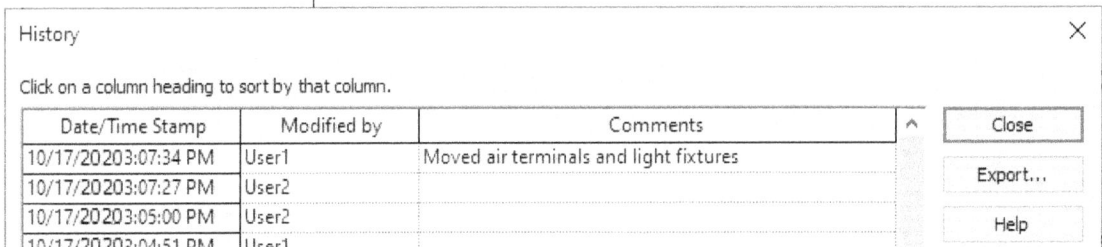

Date/Time Stamp	Modified by	Comments	
10/17/2020 3:07:34 PM	User1	Moved air terminals and light fixtures	
10/17/2020 3:07:27 PM	User2		
10/17/2020 3:05:00 PM	User2		
10/17/2020 3:04:51 PM	User1		

Figure 4–55

© 2020, ASCENT - Center for Technical Knowledge®

4.7 Visibility and Display Options with Worksharing

While using worksets, there are certain display tools to help you as you work. Worksets can be toggled off and on in the Visibility/Graphic Overrides dialog box. You can use the Worksharing Display settings to graphically differentiate by color, such as indicating the Owners of different elements or the elements that need to be updated.

Controlling Workset Visibility

Not all worksets need to be visible in every view. For example, the exterior shell of a building should display in most views, but interior walls or the site features only need to be displayed in related views. The default workset visibility is controlled when the workset is first created, but can be managed in the Visibility/Graphic Overrides dialog box, as shown in Figure 4–56.

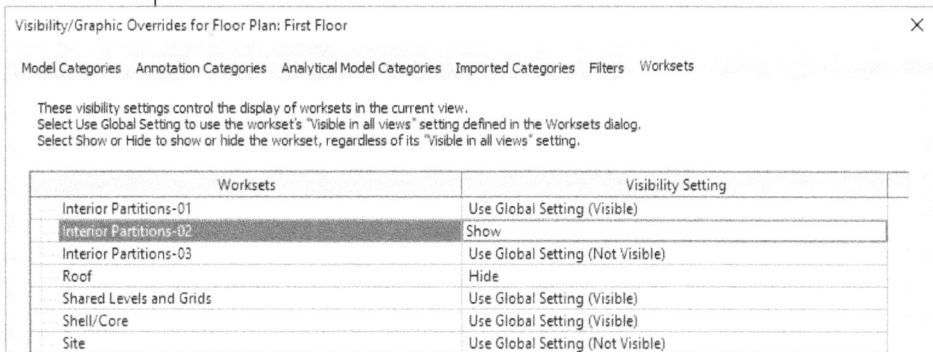

Visibility/Graphic Overrides for Floor Plan: First Floor   ×

Model Categories   Annotation Categories   Analytical Model Categories   Imported Categories   Filters   Worksets

These visibility settings control the display of worksets in the current view.
Select Use Global Setting to use the workset's "Visible in all views" setting defined in the Worksets dialog.
Select Show or Hide to show or hide the workset, regardless of its "Visible in all views" setting.

Worksets	Visibility Setting
Interior Partitions-01	Use Global Setting (Visible)
Interior Partitions-02	Show
Interior Partitions-03	Use Global Setting (Not Visible)
Roof	Hide
Shared Levels and Grids	Use Global Setting (Visible)
Shell/Core	Use Global Setting (Visible)
Site	Use Global Setting (Not Visible)

Figure 4–56

How To: Change the Visibility of Worksets

1. Type **VV** or **VG** to open the Visibility/Graphic Overrides dialog box.

2. Select the *Worksets* tab. Modify the *Visibility Setting* for each workset, as required. Changing the setting to **Show** or **Hide** only impacts the current view.

3. Click **OK** to close the dialog box.

- Worksets marked with an asterisk (*) have not been opened in this session of the Autodesk Revit software and are therefore not visible in any view.

Limiting the number of worksets speeds up the process of opening and saving the file. It is recommended that you close a workset that is not required rather than change its visibility.

- Closing worksets toggles off element visibility in all views. It also saves more computer memory than just toggling off the display of worksets.

- The *Worksets* tab in the Visibility/Graphic Overrides dialog box is only available when worksets have been enabled.

- These overrides can also be set up in a view template.

Worksharing Display Options

A handy way to view the status of elements in worksharing is to set the Worksharing Display. For example, when you set the Worksharing Display to Worksets, as shown in Figure 4–57, the elements in each workset are highlighted in a different color.

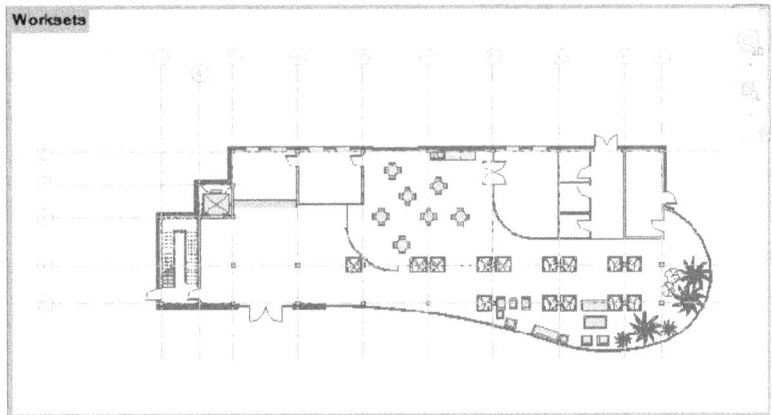

Figure 4–57

There are several types of worksharing displays: Checkout Status, Owners, Model Updates, and Worksets. You can access them in the Status Bar, as shown in Figure 4–58.

Figure 4–58

- As you hover the cursor over elements in a view with Worksharing Display selected, information about the element displays, depending on the type you selected (as shown in Figure 4–59).

© 2020, ASCENT - Center for Technical Knowledge®

Toggling on Gray Inactive Worksets while using Worksharing Display might change the display status of elements in two tones of the same color.

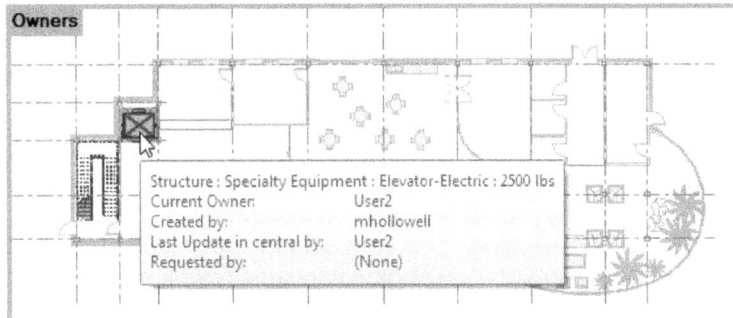

Structure : Specialty Equipment : Elevator-Electric : 2500 lbs
Current Owner: User2
Created by: mhollowell
Last Update in central by: User2
Requested by: (None)

Figure 4–59

- You can modify the colors in the Worksharing Display Settings dialog box, as well as select which items you want to display, as shown in Figure 4–60.

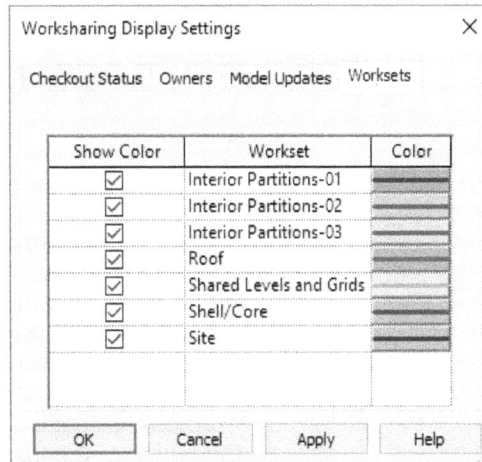

Worksharing Display Settings

Checkout Status   Owners   Model Updates   Worksets

Show Color	Workset	Color
☑	Interior Partitions-01	
☑	Interior Partitions-02	
☑	Interior Partitions-03	
☑	Roof	
☑	Shared Levels and Grids	
☑	Shell/Core	
☑	Site	

OK   Cancel   Apply   Help

Figure 4–60

4.8 Worksharing and Linked Models

NOTE: *All images in the upcoming sections refer to users as "User1" or "User2". In your working environment, you will see your unique Revit username in these dialog boxes.*

When you are working in a workshared project, each linked model should be in a separate workset. For example, before linking in a structural model, specify and set the appropriate workset, as shown in Figure 4–61. When you open a local file, you can specify which worksets you want to display, as shown in Figure 4–62.

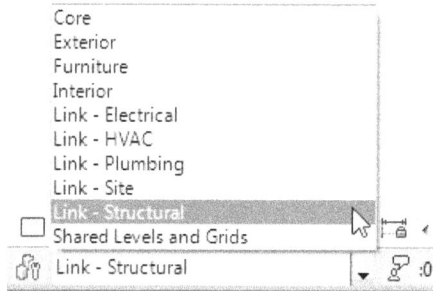

Figure 4–61

Figure 4–62

The same is true if you are linking in a model that has been workshared. You can control which worksets are open and which worksets display. In this case, the worksets from the linked model are not available for modification or use in the host project (which might have its own worksets).

* Remember that limiting the number of worksets you open and display speeds up the process of opening and saving the file. It is recommended that you close a workset that is not required rather than change its visibility. When working with linked files, you can also close them, as shown in Figure 4–63.

Worksets

Active workset:

Structural link ⌄ ☐ Gray Inactive Workset Graphics

Name	Editable	Owner	Borrowe	Opened	Visible in all views
Exterior Shell	Yes	User1		Yes	☑
HVAC link	Yes	User1		No	☐
Plumbing link	Yes	User1		No	☐
Shared Levels and Grids	Yes	User1		Yes	☑
Structural link	Yes	User1		Yes	☑

Figure 4–63

© 2020, ASCENT - Center for Technical Knowledge®

Managing Links in Local Files

When you open a local file that includes linked models set up in separate worksets, you can choose to unload each link for just yourself or for all users. In the Manage Links dialog box, as shown in Figure 4–64, select the link and in the *Unload* area, select either **For all users** or **For me**.

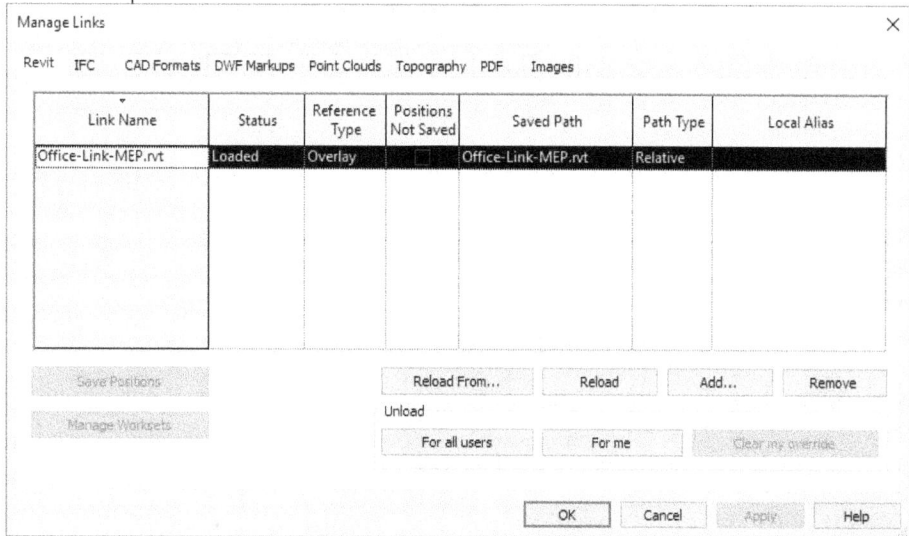

Figure 4–64

- If you unload for all users, the link will still be available but will be unloaded by default anytime someone else opens a local file. You will need to place a request to reload it if the original person that unloaded the link has not relinquished it.

- If you unload a link just for yourself, this action is remembered when you synchronize with the central model. If you want to reload the link, select it and click **Clear my override**.

Managing Worksets in Linked Models

Linked models that include worksets can be managed at two levels. You can load and unload the entire link or you can open and close the individual worksets in the linked model. For example, you might want the Site workset turned on in some views but not in others, as shown in Figure 4–65.

- Worksets can also be set as visible in some views and not visible in other views.

Figure 4–65

How To: Open and Close Worksets in a Linked Model

1. Open the Manage Links dialog box.
2. In the Manage Links dialog box, select the link that includes worksets, as shown in Figure 4–66, and click **Manage Worksets**.

© 2020, ASCENT - Center for Technical Knowledge®

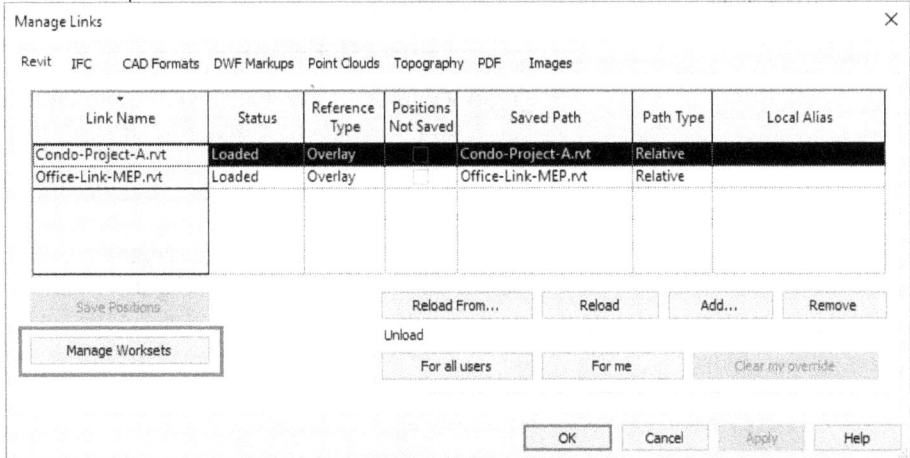

Figure 4–66

- The **Manage Worksets** button will be grayed out if there are no worksets associated with a link.

3. In the Manage Worksets for Link dialog box, select the workset(s) you want to close and click **Close** or the workset(s) you want to open and click **Open**. For example, in Figure 4–67, the linked Roof and Site worksets have been closed.

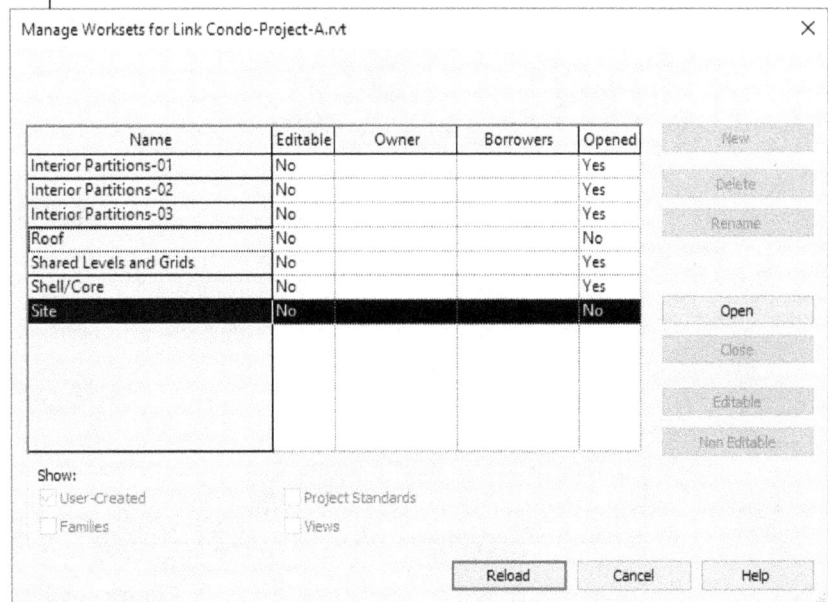

Figure 4–67

4. Click **Reload** and the link displays only the worksets that are opened.

How To: Change the Visibility of Worksets in a Linked Model

1. Type **VV** to open the Visibility/Graphic Overrides dialog box.
2. Click on the *Revit Links* tab. This tab only displays if there are links in the project.
3. In the *Display Settings* column, beside the link, click **<By Host View>**.
4. In the RVT Link Display Settings dialog box, in the *Basics* tab, select **Custom**, as shown in Figure 4–68.

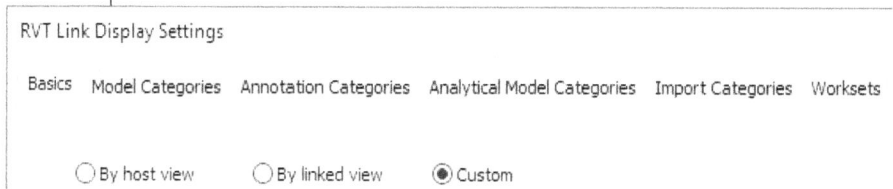

RVT Link Display Settings

Basics   Model Categories   Annotation Categories   Analytical Model Categories   Import Categories   Worksets

◯ By host view   ◯ By linked view   ◉ Custom

Figure 4–68

5. Select the *Worksets* tab and set the *Worksets* to **<Custom>**. This enables you to modify the visibility of individual worksets as needed. For example, in Figure 4–69, the **Interior Partitions** worksets are cleared, indicating that they are not visible in the current view.

   - Worksets that display with **(Closed)*** do not display in any view.

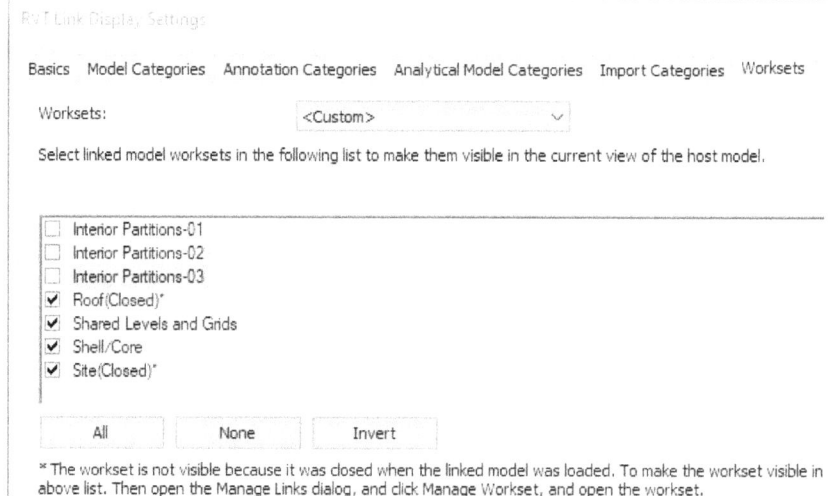

RVT Link Display Settings

Basics   Model Categories   Annotation Categories   Analytical Model Categories   Import Categories   Worksets

Worksets: <Custom>

Select linked model worksets in the following list to make them visible in the current view of the host model.

☐ Interior Partitions-01
☐ Interior Partitions-02
☐ Interior Partitions-03
☑ Roof(Closed)*
☑ Shared Levels and Grids
☑ Shell/Core
☑ Site(Closed)*

All	None	Invert

* The workset is not visible because it was closed when the linked model was loaded. To make the workset visible in above list. Then open the Manage Links dialog, and click Manage Workset, and open the workset.

Figure 4–69

6. Click **OK** to close the dialog boxes.

© 2020, ASCENT - Center for Technical Knowledge®

Practice 4d

Working in a Workshared Project - Architectural

Practice Objectives

- Work in pairs to simulate a worksharing environment.
- Update an existing central model for use in the practice.
- Create a local file of the central model from each copy of the software.

In this practice, you will need to work in pairs to simulate a worksharing environment. On your individual machines, User1 and User2 will each create a local file and select specific worksets to open in each project, as shown in Figure 4–70. One user within the pair will create the central model.

*A video called **Intro to Worksharing.mp4** is located in the practice files Videos folder.*

- Instructors: You will need to create a shared network folder for students to work in pairs to simulate the work environment.
- Students: If this is self-paced training and you are not able to work in pairs or save a central model to a shared network location, videos are available in the practice files *Videos* folder for each of the tasks in Practice 4d.

"User1" and "User2" are referenced throughout the practice but you will see your unique Revit username instead.

Worksets

Active workset:

Interior Partitions-01 ⌄   ☐ Gray Inactive Workset Graphics

Name	Editable	Owner	Borrowers	Opened	Visible in all v
Interior Partitions-01	Yes	User1		Yes	☑
Interior Partitions-02	No			Yes	☐
Interior Partitions-03	No			Yes	☐
Roof	No			No	☑
Shared Levels and Grids	No			Yes	☑
Shell/Core	No			Yes	☑
Site	No			No	☐

Figure 4–70

This practice uses a project that has been subdivided into worksets. To simulate a worksharing environment, work in groups of two. To keep the practices simple, the terms "User1" and "User2" will be used to indicate which user is to do certain tasks.

- **User1** updates the central model and focuses on the interiors of the condo units.

- **User2** focuses on the exterior and core.

Task 1 - Update the central model.

A video called
Task1.mp4 *is located in the practice files Videos folder.*

1. **User1**, in the Quick Access Toolbar, click 🖿 (Open). In the practice files folder, open **Condo-Project-A.rvt**.

2. Alert boxes about a Copied Central Model and Cannot find Central Model display. Read and then close the alert boxes.

3. In the *File* tab, expand 🖫 (Save As) and click 🖳 (Project).

4. In the Save As dialog box, click **Options...**.

A central model needs to be repathed if it has been relocated. You will typically not have to do this in a work environment, but will need to do it for this practice to work.

5. In the File Save Options dialog box, select **Make this a Central Model after save** and then click **OK**.

6. Verify that the name is still set to **Condo-Project-A.rvt**, navigate to the shared network folder location and click **Save**.

- If the Workset File Already Exists dialog box displays, click **Yes** to replace the existing file.

7. Close the project.

Task 2 - Create the local file for User1.

A video called
Task2.mp4 *is located in the practice files Videos folder.*

1. **User1** continues working within Revit.

2. In the Quick Access Toolbar, click 🖿 (Open). In the practice files folder, open **Condo-Project-A.rvt**.

- Do not select central models from the startup screen, as that opens the central model itself. Instead, use the Open command to create a new local file.

3. Verify that **Create New Local** is selected and click **Open**, as shown in Figure 4–71.

© 2020, ASCENT - Center for Technical Knowledge®

File name:	Condo-Project-A|.rvt	
Files of type:	All Supported Files (*.rvt, *.rfa, *.adsk, *.rte)	

Worksharing

☐ Audit   ☐ Detach from Central   ☑ Create New Local   <u>O</u>pen

Figure 4–71

4. The file opens and displays the name
   Condo-Project-A_User1.rvt at the top of the interface.

   - Note what the file name is at the top of your Revit user
     interface. It should have the file name with your unique
     username at the end.

5. In the *Collaborate* tab>Manage Collaboration panel or in the
   Status Bar, click 🔄 (Worksets).

6. In the Worksets dialog box, do the following, as shown in
   Figure 4–72:

   - Set the *Active workset* to **Interior Partitions-01**.
   - For **Interior Partitions-01**, set *Editable* to **Yes** and select
     Visible in all views.
   - Select the worksets **Roof** and **Site**. Click **Close** so that
     the worksets are not open in this session.

Worksets   ✕

Active workset:

| Interior Partitions-01 ⌄ | ☐ Gray Inactive Workset Graphics |

Name	Editable	Owner	Borrowers	Opened	Visible in all views	
Interior Partitions-01	Yes	User1		Yes	☑	New
Interior Partitions-02	No			Yes	☐	Delete
Interior Partitions-03	No			Yes	☐	
Roof	No			No	☑	Rename
Shared Levels and Grids	No			Yes	☑	
Shell/Core	No			Yes	☑	
Site	No			No	☐	Open
						Close
						Editable
						Non Editable

Show:
☑ User-Created   ☐ Project Standards
☐ Families   ☐ Views

| OK | Cancel | Help |

Figure 4–72

7. Click **OK** to finish.

8. In the Quick Access Toolbar, click 💾 (Save) to save the local file.

Task 3 - Create the local file for User2.

*A video called **Task3.mp4** is located in the practice files Videos folder.*

1. **User2**, in the Quick Access Toolbar, click 📂 (Open), navigate to the shared network folder location and select the file **Condo-Project-A.rvt**. Verify that **Create New Local** is selected.

2. Click the arrow next to **Open** and select **Specify...** in the drop-down list, as shown in Figure 4–73.

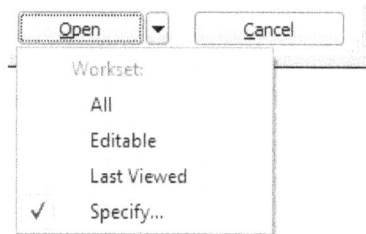

Figure 4–73

3. Click **Open** to open the project.

4. In the Opening Worksets dialog box, select the three **Interior Partitions** worksets and click **Close** so that these worksets are not opened in this session, as shown in Figure 4–74.

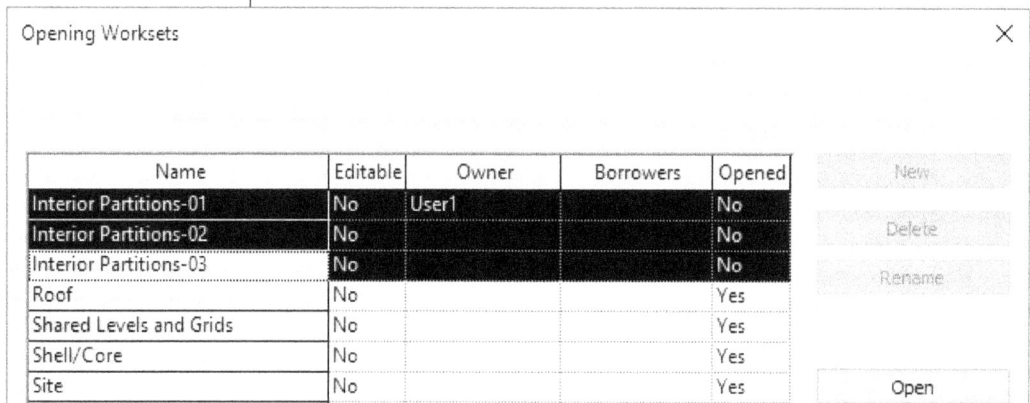

Name	Editable	Owner	Borrowers	Opened
Interior Partitions-01	No	User1		No
Interior Partitions-02	No			No
Interior Partitions-03	No			No
Roof	No			Yes
Shared Levels and Grids	No			Yes
Shell/Core	No			Yes
Site	No			Yes

Figure 4–74

© 2020, ASCENT - Center for Technical Knowledge®

5. Click **OK** to finish.

The local file name should be Condo-Project-A_your unique username.rvt.

- Note what the file name is at the top of your Revit user interface. It should have the file name with your unique username at the end.

6. Save the local file. Keep the file open.

Task 4 - Add and modify elements in worksets.

*A video called **Task4.mp4** is located in the practice files Videos folder.*

1. **User1,** in your local file for Condo-Project-A, verify that you are in the **Floor Plans: First Floor** view.

2. Zoom in on Unit 1C and add several walls using an interior wall type with the *Height* set to **Second Floor**. Include one that butts up against an existing window, as shown in Figure 4–75. A warning displays, noting that the insert conflicts with the joined wall.

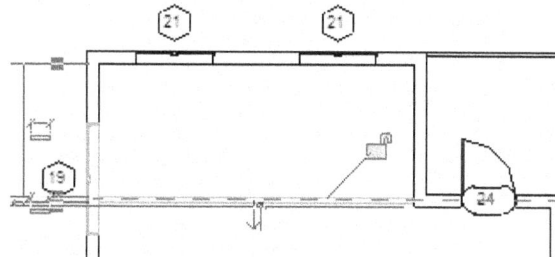

Figure 4–75

3. Close the warning.

4. Click ![cursor] (Modify) and select the window. It has an icon connected to it, as shown in Figure 4–76, indicating that it belongs to another workset. Click the **Make element editable** icon.

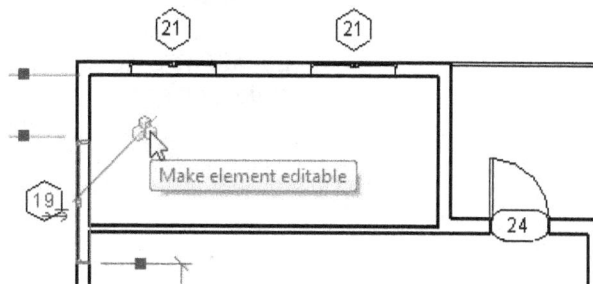

Figure 4–76

5. Move the window so it does not conflict with the wall.

6. Open the Worksets dialog box. **User1** will be noted as the *Owner* of the **Interior Partitions-01** workset and a *Borrower* of the **Shell/Core** workset, as shown in Figure 4–77.

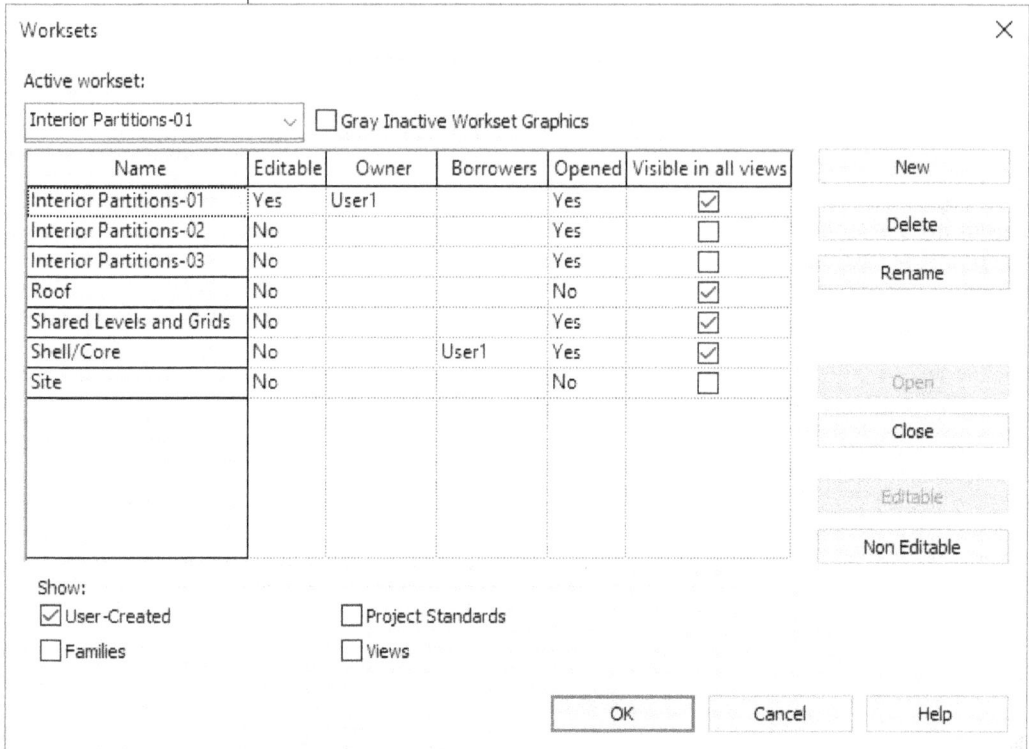

Worksets						✕

Active workset:

Interior Partitions-01 ⌄	☐ Gray Inactive Workset Graphics

Name	Editable	Owner	Borrowers	Opened	Visible in all views	
Interior Partitions-01	Yes	User1		Yes	☑	New
Interior Partitions-02	No			Yes	☐	Delete
Interior Partitions-03	No			Yes	☐	Rename
Roof	No			No	☑	
Shared Levels and Grids	No			Yes	☑	
Shell/Core	No		User1	Yes	☑	
Site	No			No	☐	Open
						Close
						Editable
						Non Editable

Show:
☑ User-Created   ☐ Project Standards
☐ Families   ☐ Views

OK	Cancel	Help

Figure 4–77

7. Click **OK** to close the dialog box.

8. In the *Collaborate* tab>Synchronize panel or in the Quick Access Toolbar, click ⬡ (Synchronize and Modify Settings) to open the Synchronize with Central dialog box. The **Borrowed Elements** option should be selected. Add a comment about moving the window and select the **Save Local File before and after synchronizing with central** option, as shown in Figure 4–78.

© 2020, ASCENT - Center for Technical Knowledge®

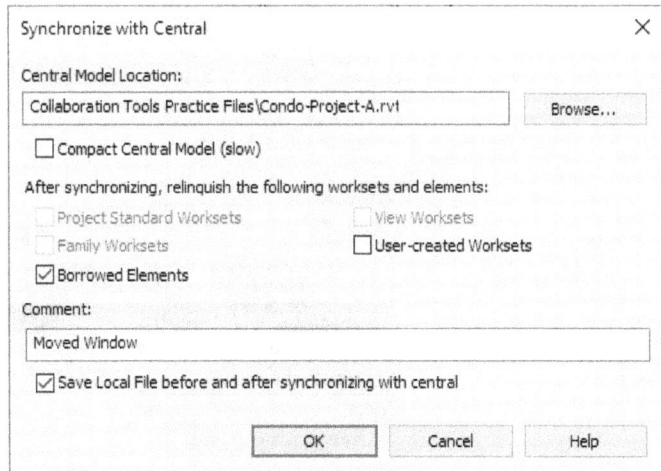

Synchronize with Central   ✕

Central Model Location:

Collaboration Tools Practice Files\Condo-Project-A.rvt   Browse...

☐ Compact Central Model (slow)

After synchronizing, relinquish the following worksets and elements:

☐ Project Standard Worksets   ☐ View Workset

☐ Family Worksets   ☐ User-created Worksets

☑ Borrowed Elements

Comment:

Moved Window

☑ Save Local File before and after synchronizing with central

OK   Cancel   Help

Figure 4–78

9. Click **OK**.

Task 5 - Check out a workset.

*A video called **Task5.mp4** is located in the practice files Videos folder.*

1. **User2**, open the **Floor Plans: First Floor** view if it is not already open. None of the changes show in the local file.

2. In the *Collaborate* tab>Synchronize panel, click (Reload Latest or type **RL**. The window location changes but you might not see the new walls if that workset is not open and visible.

3. Click (Worksets) to open the dialog box.

4. In the *Visible in all views* column, select the check box for **Interior Partitions-01**, if it is not already showing. Make sure the *Opened* column for **Interior Partitions-01** is set to **Yes**.

5. Select **Shell/Core** in the *Active workset* drop-down list and make it editable (select **Yes** in the *Editable* column). The *Owner* should display as **User 2**, as shown in Figure 4–79.

Worksets

Active workset:

| Shell/Core | ⌄ | ☐ Gray Inactive Workset Graphics |

Name	Editable	Owner	Borrowers	Opened	Visible in all views
Interior Partitions-01	No	User1		Yes	☑
Interior Partitions-02	No			Yes	☐
Interior Partitions-03	No			Yes	☐
Roof	No			Yes	☑
Shared Levels and Grids	No			Yes	☑
Shell/Core	Yes	User2		Yes	☑
Site	No			Yes	☐

Figure 4–79

6. Click **OK** to close the dialog box.

7. Move door number 5 in Unit 1A down in the wall so that it is no longer opposite to door number 6.

8. In the Quick Access Toolbar, click 🖫 (Save) to save the local file.

9. **User1**, type **RL** (Reload Latest). There are no new changes to load, as shown in Figure 4–80, because User2 has not saved back to the central model. Close the dialog box.

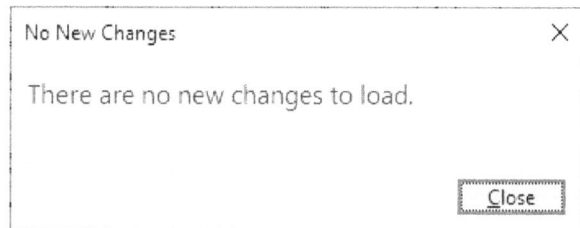

No New Changes	✕
There are no new changes to load.	
	Close

Figure 4–80

10. **User2** will click 📷 (Synchronize Now). This saves the changes to the central model without relinquishing the Shell/Core workset.

© 2020, ASCENT - Center for Technical Knowledge®

Task 6 - Request permission to edit.

A video called **Task6.mp4** is located in the practice files Videos folder.

1. **User1**, type **RL** (Reload Latest) again. This time, the door moves in response to the change made in the central model.

2. Try to move the door back where it was. This time, an error message displays that cannot be ignored, as shown in Figure 4–81. **User2** has made the Shell/Core workset editable. Therefore, other users cannot edit elements in it without permission.

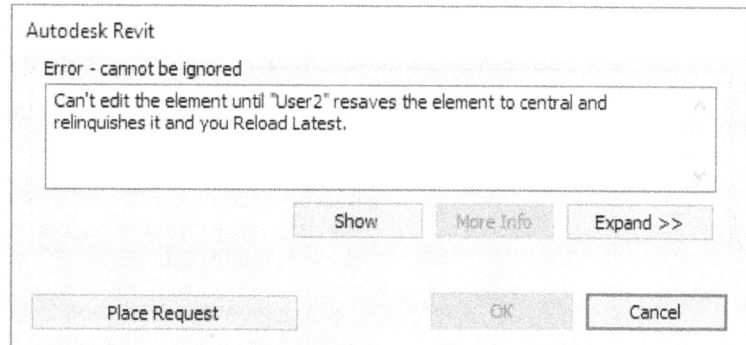

Figure 4–81

3. Click **Place Request**. The Editing Request Placed dialog box opens. Leave it open.

4. **User2** now has an alert box displayed, as shown in Figure 4–82.

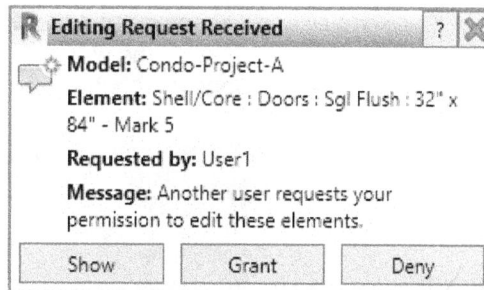

Figure 4–82

5. Hover the cursor over the **Show** button to highlight the door. Move the dialog box out of the way if needed to see the door.

6. Click on **Grant** to give the other user permission to modify the placement of this door. By doing this, you enable the other user full control over this one element in the workset.

7. **User1** will get an Editing Request Granted dialog box, as shown in Figure 4–83.

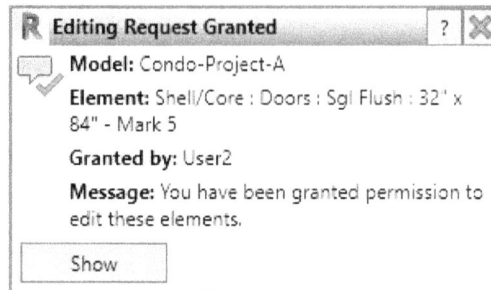

Figure 4–83

8. Close the Editing Request Granted dialog box. Because your request was granted, the door moves.

9. Move the door again to exactly where you want it. This time, you are not prompted to ask to move the door because you are still borrowing it.

10. Try to move another door. You do not have permission to move this door. Click **Cancel** rather than place the request. The door returns to its original location.

Task 7 - View information about the worksets.

---

*A video called **Task7.mp4** is located in the practice files Videos folder.*

1. **User1,** in the View Control Bar, expand the Worksharing Display and click ⚏ (Owners). Different colors highlight the elements and their respective owners. Hover the cursor over one of the walls to display information about the owner, as shown in Figure 4–84.

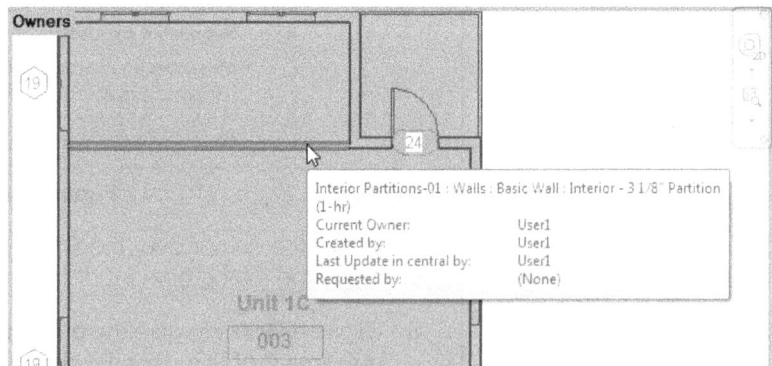

Figure 4–84

• The color on your display might be different.

2. Zoom out so you can see the full floor plan.

3. Click ⬡ (Synchronize and Modify Settings) and relinquish **User-created Worksets** and **Borrowed Elements.**

4. The new interior walls once displayed as owned by **User1** are now not in color and the door that was borrowed returns to the original owner **User2**.

5. Toggle the Worksharing Display off.

6. Save the local file.

7. **User2**, click ⬡ (Synchronize Now). The door moves to the location where **User1** moved it. When you save to the central model, it also reloads the latest changes.

8. Close the project. When the Editable Elements dialog box opens, as shown in Figure 4–85, click **Relinquish elements and worksets**.

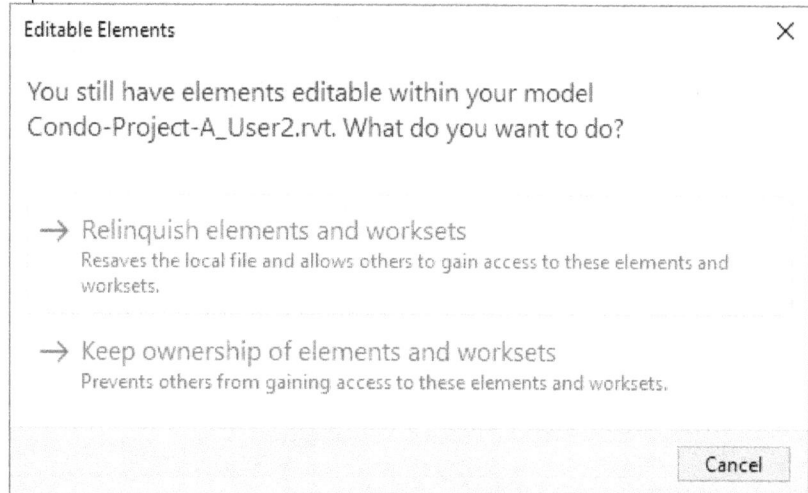

Editable Elements   ✕

You still have elements editable within your model
Condo-Project-A_User2.rvt. What do you want to do?

→ Relinquish elements and worksets
   Resaves the local file and allows others to gain access to these elements and
   worksets.

→ Keep ownership of elements and worksets
   Prevents others from gaining access to these elements and worksets.

                                                                   Cancel

---

Figure 4–85

9. **User1**, close the project and synchronize with central.

Practice 4e

Working in a Workshared Project - Structural

Practice Objectives

- Work in pairs to simulate a worksharing environment.
- Update an existing central model for use in the practice.
- Create a local file of the central model from each copy of the software.

In this practice, you will need to work in pairs to simulate a worksharing environment. On your individual machines, User1 and User2 will each create a local file and select specific worksets to open in each project, as shown in Figure 4–86. One user within the pair will create the central model.

*A video called **Intro to Worksharing.mp4** (Architectural) is located in the practice files Videos folder.*

- Instructors: You will need to create a shared network folder for students to work in pairs to simulate the work environment.
- Students: If this is self-paced training and you are not able to work in pairs or save a central model to a shared network location, Architectural videos are available in the practice files *Videos* folder for each of the tasks for Practice 4d for your reference.

"User1" and "User2" are referenced throughout the practice but you will see your unique Revit username instead.

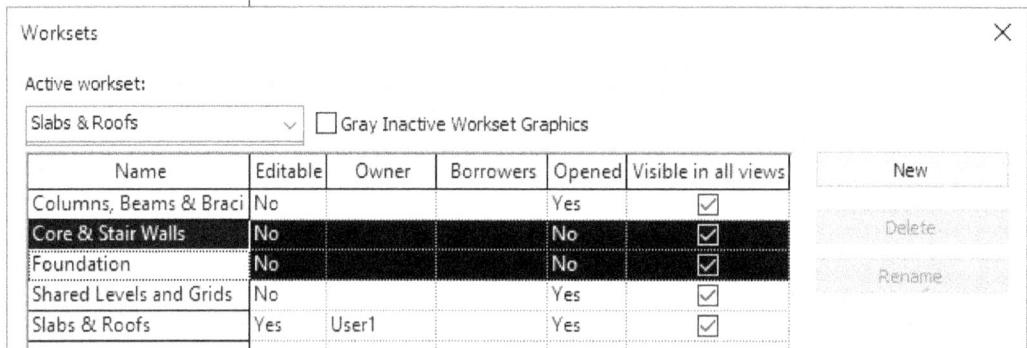

Worksets								✕

Active workset:

Slabs & Roofs	⌄	☐ Gray Inactive Workset Graphics				

Name	Editable	Owner	Borrowers	Opened	Visible in all views	New
Columns, Beams & Braci	No			Yes	☑	
Core & Stair Walls	No			No	☑	Delete
Foundation	No			No	☑	Rename
Shared Levels and Grids	No			Yes	☑	
Slabs & Roofs	Yes	User1		Yes	☑	

Figure 4–86

This practice uses a project that has been subdivided into worksets. To simulate a worksharing environment, work in groups of two. To keep the practices simple, the terms "User1" and "User2" will be used to indicate which user is to do certain tasks.

© 2020, ASCENT - Center for Technical Knowledge®

- **User1** updates the central model and focuses on the floor slabs.
- **User2** focuses on the core and stair walls.

Task 1 - Update the central model.

A video called
Task1.mp4
(Architectural) is located in the practice files Videos folder.

1. **User1**, in the Quick Access Toolbar, click � (Open). In the practice files folder, open **Syracuse-Suites-S.rvt**.

2. Alert boxes about a Copied Central Model and Cannot find Central Model display. Read and then close the alert boxes.

3. In the *File* tab, expand 💾 (Save As) and click 🗒 (Project).

4. In the Save As dialog box, click **Options...**.

A central model needs to be repathed if it has been relocated. You will typically not have to do this in a work environment, but will need to do it for this practice to work.

5. In the File Save Options dialog box, select **Make this a Central Model after save** and then click **OK**.

6. Verify that the name is still set to **Syracuse-Suites-S.rvt** and then click **Save**.

   - If the Workset File Already Exists dialog box displays, click **Yes** to replace the existing file.

7. Close the project.

Task 2 - Create the local file for User1.

A video called
Task2.mp4
(Architectural) is located in the practice files Videos folder.

1. **User1** continues working within Revit.

2. In the Quick Access Toolbar, click 📂 (Open). In the practice files folder, open **Syracuse-Suites-S.rvt**.

   - Do not select central models from the startup screen as it opens the central model directly. Instead, use the **Open** command and create a new local file.

3. Verify that **Create New Local** is selected and click **Open**. A file with the name **Syracuse-Suites-S_User1.rvt** is opened.

   - Note what the file name is at the top of your Revit user interface. It should have the file name with your unique username at the end.

4. In the *Collaborate* tab>Manage Collaboration panel or in the Status Bar, click 👥 (Worksets).

5. In the Worksets dialog box, make **Slabs & Roofs** the Active workset. Set *Editable* to **Yes** and select **Visible in all views** for this workset. Select the **Core & Stair Walls** and **Foundation** worksets. Click **Close** so the worksets are not open in this session, as shown in Figure 4–87.

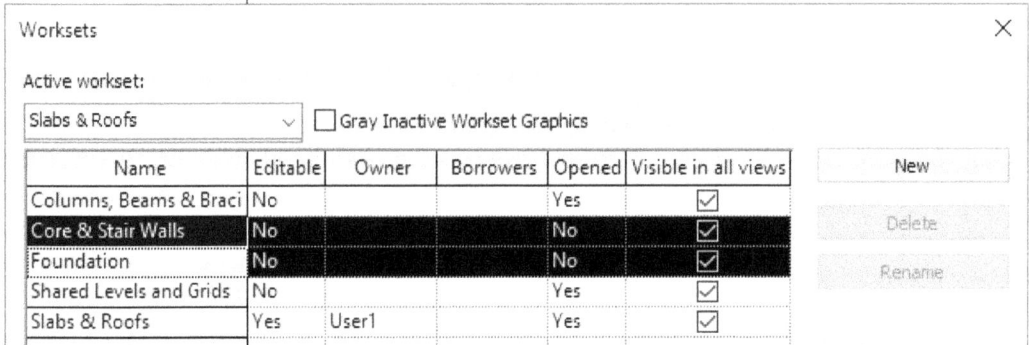

Active workset:						
Slabs & Roofs ⌄		☐ Gray Inactive Workset Graphics				
Name	Editable	Owner	Borrowers	Opened	Visible in all views	New
Columns, Beams & Braci	No			Yes	☑	
Core & Stair Walls	No			No	☑	Delete
Foundation	No			No	☑	
Shared Levels and Grids	No			Yes	☑	Rename
Slabs & Roofs	Yes	User1		Yes	☑	

Figure 4–87

6. Click **OK** to finish.

7. In the Quick Access Toolbar, click 💾 (Save) to save the local file.

Task 3 - Create the local file for User2.

A video called
Task3.mp4
(Architectural) is located in the practice files Videos folder.

1. **User2**, in the Quick Access Toolbar, click 🗁 (Open) and select the file **Syracuse-Suites-S.rvt**. Verify that **Create New Local** is selected, click the arrow next to **Open**, and select **Specify...** in the drop-down list, as shown in Figure 4–88.

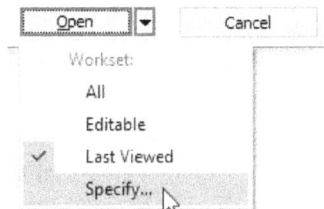

Open ▾	Cancel
Workset:	
All	
Editable	
✓ Last Viewed	
Specify...	

Figure 4–88

2. Click **Open** to open the project.

3. In the Opening Worksets dialog box, select the **Columns, Beams & Bracing** and **Slabs & Roofs** worksets and click **Close** so these worksets are not opened in this session, as shown in Figure 4–89.

© 2020, ASCENT - Center for Technical Knowledge®

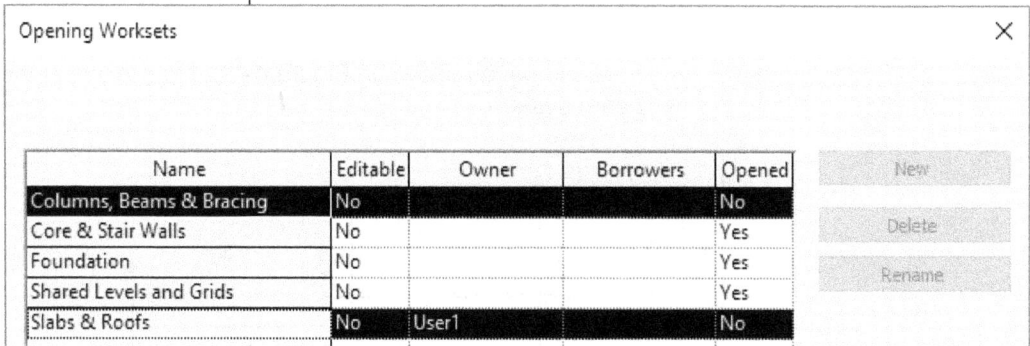

Name	Editable	Owner	Borrowers	Opened
Columns, Beams & Bracing	No			No
Core & Stair Walls	No			Yes
Foundation	No			Yes
Shared Levels and Grids	No			Yes
Slabs & Roofs	No	User1		No

Figure 4–89

4. Click **OK** to finish.

   • Note what the file name is at the top of your Revit user interface. It should have the file name with your unique username at the end.

5. Save the local file.

Task 4 - Add and modify elements in worksets.

A video called ***Task4.mp4*** *(Architectural) is located in the practice files Videos folder.*

1. **User1**, in your local file for **Syracuse-Suites-S**, open the **Structural Plans: 1ST FLOOR** view.

2. Zoom in on the beam system between grids 6 and 7 and C and D. Stay far enough out so that you can see the edge of the building, as shown in Figure 4–90. Do not select the beam system.

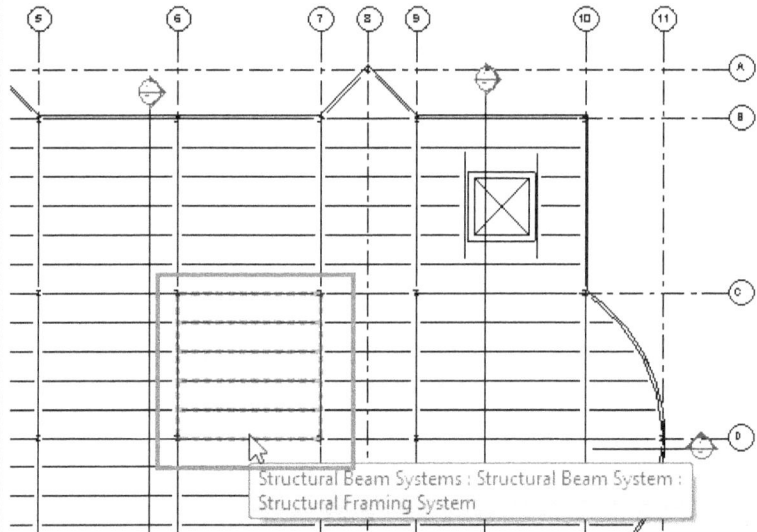

Structural Beam Systems : Structural Beam System : Structural Framing System

Figure 4–90

3. Select the second beam from the top and type **UP** to unpin it from the beam system. Move it up so that the distance between the beams is larger, as shown in Figure 4–91.

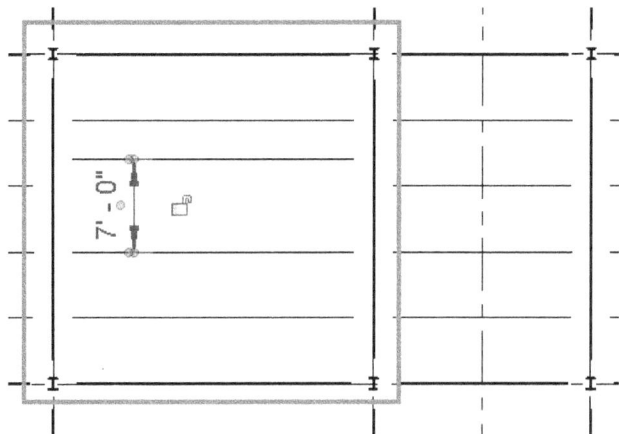

7' - 0"

Figure 4–91

4. Hover the cursor over the edge of the building and press <Tab> until the floor is highlighted. Select the floor.

© 2020, ASCENT - Center for Technical Knowledge®

5. In the *Modify | Floors* tab>Mode panel, click ⬜ (Edit Boundary).

6. In the Draw panel, click ⌐ (Boundary Line) and draw a rectangle, as shown in Figure 4–92, to add a new opening in the floor. Move the opening inside the framing system between two beams, as shown in Figure 4–92. An exact location is not required for this practice.

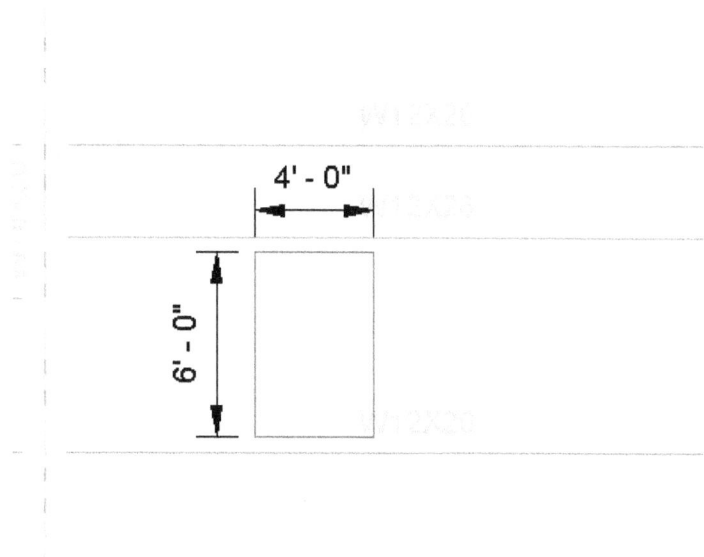

Figure 4–92

7. Click ✔ (Finish Edit Mode).

8. In the *Collaborate* tab>Manage Collaboration panel, in the Active Workset drop-down list, select the **Columns, Beams & Bracing** workset to make it the active workset. It should be listed as **(Not Editable)**.

9. In the *Structure* tab>Structure panel, click 🡥 (Beam).

10. In the Type Selector, verify that the selected beam is **W-Wide Flange: W12x26**. In the Options Bar, set the *Structural Usage* to **Joist** and clear the **Chain** option, as shown in Figure 4–93.

Figure 4–93

11. Add two beams to frame the new opening on the unsupported sides, as shown in Figure 4–94.

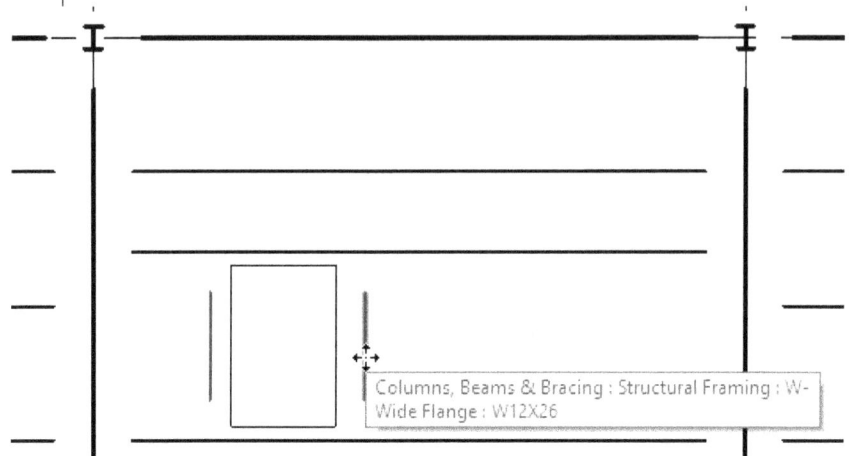

Columns, Beams & Bracing : Structural Framing : W-Wide Flange : W12X26

Figure 4–94

12. Click ⌖ (Modify) to end the Beam command.

13. In the *Collaborate* tab>Manage Collaboration panel or in the Status Bar, click 🗂 (Worksets).

14. In the Worksets dialog box, **User1** is noted as the *Owner* of the **Slabs & Roofs** workset and as a *Borrower* of **Columns, Beams & Bracing**, as shown in Figure 4–95.

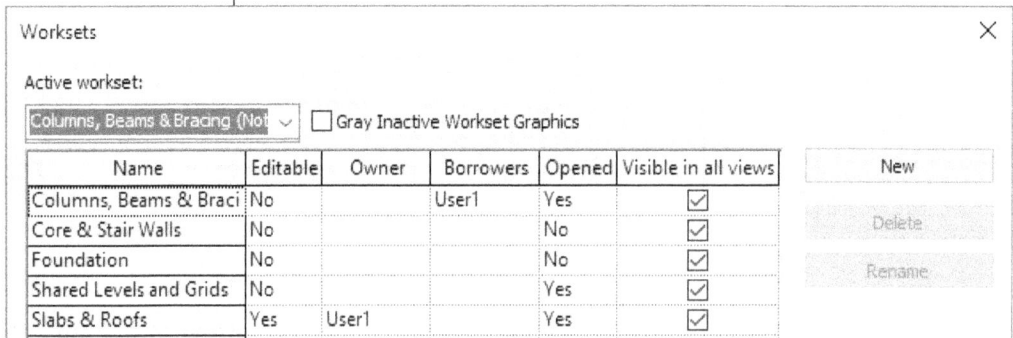

Name	Editable	Owner	Borrowers	Opened	Visible in all views	
Columns, Beams & Braci	No		User1	Yes	☑	New
Core & Stair Walls	No			No	☑	Delete
Foundation	No			No	☑	Rename
Shared Levels and Grids	No			Yes	☑	
Slabs & Roofs	Yes	User1		Yes	☑	

Worksets

Active workset:

Columns, Beams & Bracing (Not ⌄) ☐ Gray Inactive Workset Graphics

Figure 4–95

15. Close the dialog box.

16. In the Quick Access Toolbar, click 🔄 (Synchronize and Modify Settings).

© 2020, ASCENT - Center for Technical Knowledge®

17. In the Synchronize with Central dialog box, the **Borrowed Elements** option should be selected. Add a comment about adding an opening to the first floor slab and select the **Save Local File before and after synchronizing with central** option, as shown in Figure 4–96.

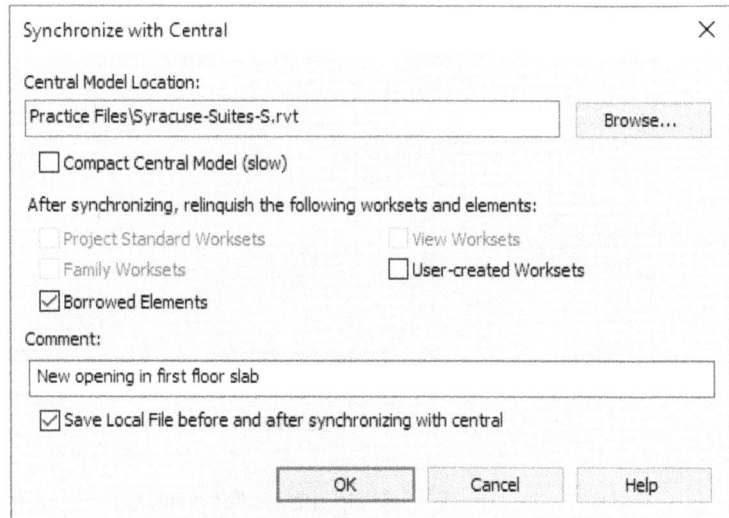

Synchronize with Central	✕

Central Model Location:

Practice Files\Syracuse-Suites-S.rvt	Browse...

☐ Compact Central Model (slow)

After synchronizing, relinquish the following worksets and elements:

☐ Project Standard Worksets   ☐ View Worksets

☐ Family Worksets   ☐ User-created Worksets

☑ Borrowed Elements

Comment:

New opening in first floor slab

☑ Save Local File before and after synchronizing with central

[OK]   [Cancel]   [Help]

Figure 4–96

18. Click **OK** to finish synchronizing.

Task 5 - Check out a workset.

A video called
Task5.mp4
(Architectural) is located in the practice files Videos folder.

1. **User2**, in the local Syracuse-Suites-S file, open the **Structural Plans: 1ST FLOOR** view if it is not already open. None of the changes display in the local file yet.

2. In the Status Bar, click 🗇 (Worksets).

3. In the Worksets dialog box, open the **Columns, Beams & Bracing** and **Slabs & Roofs** worksets by setting the *Opened* column to **Yes**, as shown in Figure 4–97. Click **OK**.

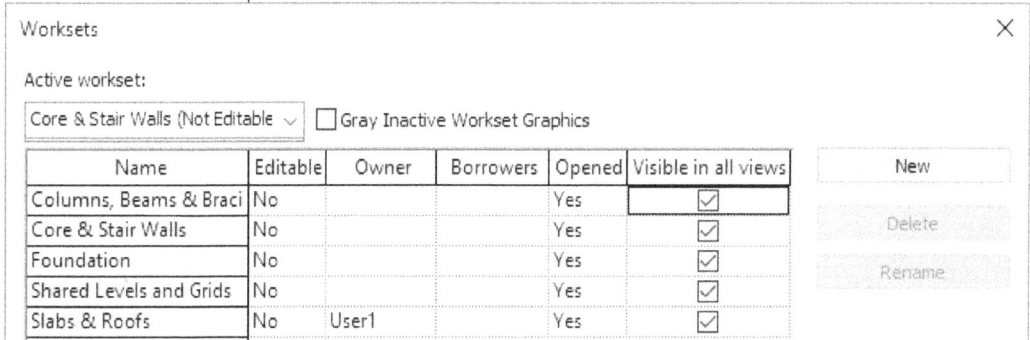

Worksets						✕

Active workset:

Core & Stair Walls (Not Editable ∨) ☐ Gray Inactive Workset Graphics

Name	Editable	Owner	Borrowers	Opened	Visible in all views	
Columns, Beams & Braci	No			Yes	☑	New
Core & Stair Walls	No			Yes	☑	Delete
Foundation	No			Yes	☑	Rename
Shared Levels and Grids	No			Yes	☑	
Slabs & Roofs	No	User1		Yes	☑	

Figure 4–97

4. In the **Structural Plans: 1ST FLOOR** view, you can now see the beams and other elements, but the changes are still not displayed.

5. In the *Collaborate* tab>Synchronize panel, click ⬡ (Reload Latest) or type **RL**. The new opening and joists display.

6. Open the Worksets dialog box.

7. In the Worksets dialog box, select **Core & Stair Walls** in the list of worksets and make it **Editable**. The *Owner* should change to **User2**, as shown in Figure 4–98.

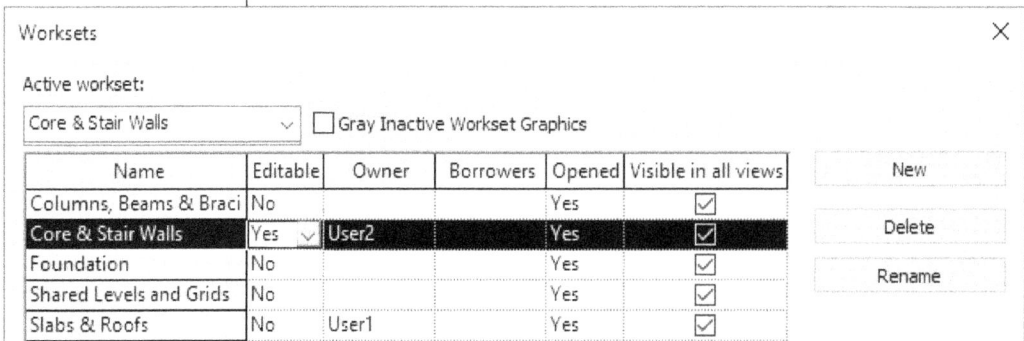

Worksets						✕

Active workset:

Core & Stair Walls   ∨ ☐ Gray Inactive Workset Graphics

Name	Editable	Owner	Borrowers	Opened	Visible in all views	
Columns, Beams & Braci	No			Yes	☑	New
Core & Stair Walls	Yes ∨	User2		Yes	☑	Delete
Foundation	No			Yes	☑	Rename
Shared Levels and Grids	No			Yes	☑	
Slabs & Roofs	No	User1		Yes	☑	

Figure 4–98

8. Click **OK**.

9. Zoom in on the elevator in the upper right of the building.

© 2020, ASCENT - Center for Technical Knowledge®

10. Move the core's north wall approximately **1'-0"** up.

11. In the Quick Access Toolbar, click 🖫 (Save) to save the local file.

12. **User1**, type **RL** (**Reload Latest**). There are no new changes to load because User2 has not saved back to the central model.

13. **User2** will click 🖼 (Synchronize Now). This saves the changes to the central model without relinquishing the Core & Stair Walls workset.

Task 6 - Request permission to edit.

A video called ***Task6.mp4*** *(Architectural) is located in the practice files Videos folder.*

1. **User1**, open the Worksets dialog box.

2. Select **Core & Stair Walls** in the list of worksets and click **Open**. Click **OK** to exit the dialog box.

3. Type **RL** (**Reload Latest**) again. This time, the core wall moves in response to the change made by **User2**.

4. Try to move the core wall back to its previous position. An error message opens that cannot be ignored. **User2** has made the Core & Stair Walls workset editable. Therefore, no one else can edit elements in it without permission, as shown in Figure 4–99.

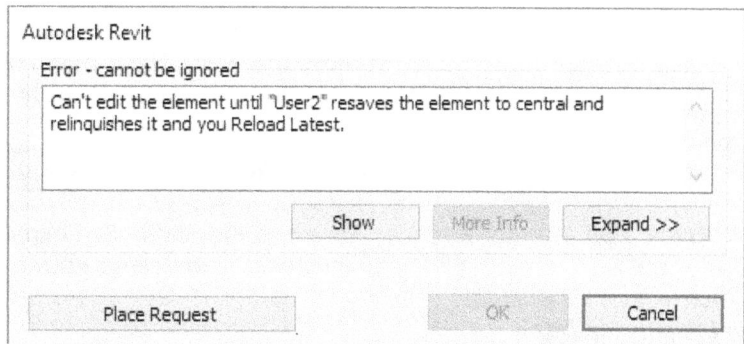

Autodesk Revit

Error - cannot be ignored

Can't edit the element until "User2" resaves the element to central and relinquishes it and you Reload Latest.

| Show | More Info | Expand >> |

| Place Request | OK | Cancel |

Figure 4–99

5. Click **Place Request**. The Editing Request Placed dialog box opens. Leave it open.

6. **User2** now has an alert box displayed, as shown in Figure 4–100.

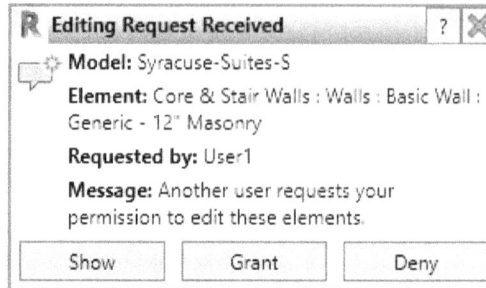

Figure 4–100

7. Hover the cursor over the **Show** button to highlight the wall. (Move the box out of the way as required to display the modified wall.)

8. Click **Grant** to give **User1** permission to modify the placement of this core wall. By doing so, you enable the other user to have full control over this one element in the workset.

9. **User1** will get an Editing Request Granted dialog box.

10. Close the Editing Request Granted dialog box. Because your request was granted, the core wall moves.

11. Move the core wall again. This time, you are not prompted to ask permission to move the core wall because you are still borrowing it.

12. Try to move another core wall. You do not have permission to move this wall. Click **Cancel** rather than place the request. The core wall returns to its original location.

Task 7 - View information about the worksets.

A video called
Task7.mp4
(Architectural) is located in the practice files Videos folder.

1. **User1**, in the Status Bar, expand the Worksharing Display, and select **Owners**, as shown in Figure 4–101.

© 2020, ASCENT - Center for Technical Knowledge®

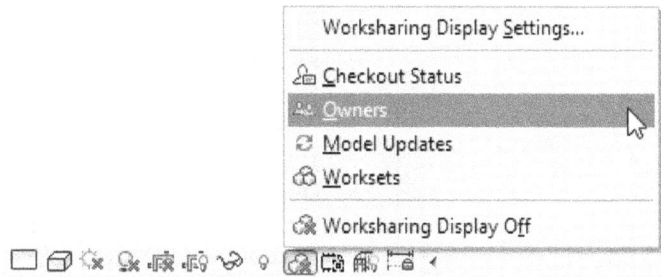

Figure 4–101

2. The view displays in color showing the two owners. Different colors highlight the elements and their respective owners, as shown in Figure 4–102. Hover the cursor over one of the walls to display information about the owner.

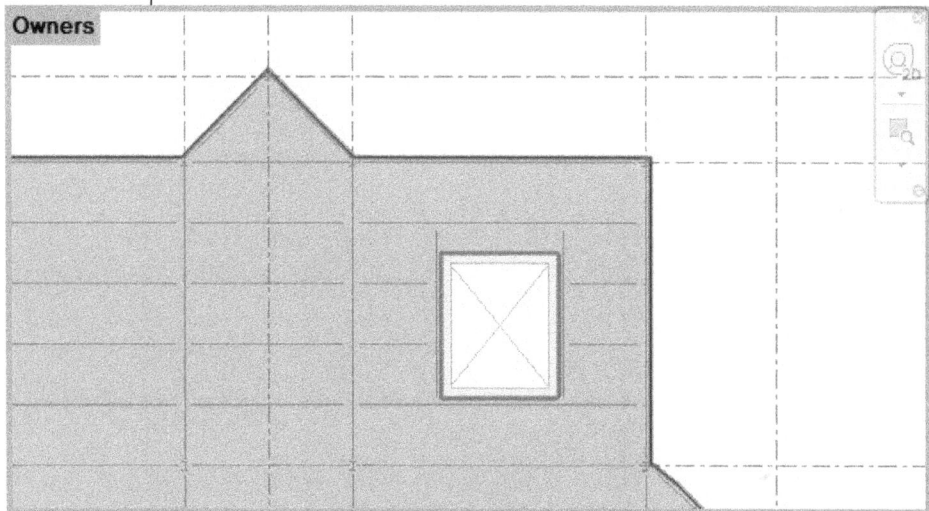

Figure 4–102

3. Open the Worksets dialog box. The owner of Core & Stair Walls is listed as **User2**, but **User1** is also listed as a borrower. Click **Cancel**.

4. Toggle the Worksharing Display off and zoom out to see the full building.

5. In the *Collaborate* tab>Manage Collaboration panel, click

   (Gray Inactive Worksets) to gray out the elements that you cannot modify without requesting permission. This also grays out the core walls, although you have a right to edit the wall that you borrowed.

6. Click ⬡ (Synchronize and Modify Settings) and verify that all of the worksets will be relinquished before clicking **OK**.

7. Close the project.

8. **User2**, click ⬡ (Synchronize Now). The core wall moves to the location selected by **User1**. When you sync with the central model, it also reloads the latest changes.

9. Close the project. When the Editable Elements dialog box opens, select **Relinquish elements and worksets**.

© 2020, ASCENT - Center for Technical Knowledge®

Practice 4f

Working in a Workshared Project - MEP

Practice Objectives

- Work in pairs to simulate a worksharing environment.
- Update an existing central model for use in the practice.
- Create a local file of the central model from each copy of the software.

In this practice, you will need to work in pairs to simulate a worksharing environment. On your individual machines, User1 and User2 will each create a local file and select specific worksets to open in each project, as shown in Figure 4–103. One user within the pair will create the central model.

*A video called **Intro to Worksharing.mp4** (Architectural) is located in the practice files Videos folder.*

- Instructors: You will need to create a shared network folder for students to work in pairs to simulate the work environment.
- Students: If this is self-paced training and you are not able to work in pairs or save a central model to a shared network location, Architectural videos are available in the practice files *Videos* folder for each of the tasks for Practice 4d for your reference.

"User1" and "User2" are referenced throughout the practice but you will see your unique Revit username instead.

Worksets

Active workset:

HVAC ⌄ ☐ Gray Inactive Workset Graphics

Name	Editable	Owner	Borrowers	Opened	Visible in all views
Data and Security	No			No	☑
Electrical	No			No	☑
Fire Safety	No			Yes	☑
HVAC	Yes	User1		No	☑
Lighting	No			No	☑
Linked Architectural	No			Yes	☑
Plumbing	No			No	☑
Shared Levels and Grids	No			Yes	☑

Figure 4–103

This practice uses a project that has been subdivided into worksets. To simulate a worksharing environment, work in groups of two. To keep the practices simple, the terms "User1" and "User2" will be used to indicate which user is to do certain tasks.

- **User1** updates the central model and focuses on the HVAC portion of the project.

- **User2** focuses on the lighting portion of the project.

Task 1 - Update the central model.

A video called Task1.mp4 (Architectural) is located in the practice files Videos folder.

1. **User1**, in the Quick Access Toolbar, click 🖾 (Open). In the practice files folder, open **Elementary-School-MEP.rvt**.

2. Alert boxes about a Copied Central Model and Cannot find Central Model display. Read and then close the alert boxes.

3. In the *File* tab, expand 🖫 (Save As) and click 🖽 (Project).

4. In the Save As dialog box, click **Options...**.

A central model needs to be repathed if it has been relocated. You will typically not have to do this in a work environment, but will need to do it for this practice to work.

5. In the File Save Options dialog box, select **Make this a Central Model after save** and then click **OK**.

6. Verify that the name is still set to **Elementary-School-MEP.rvt** and then click **Save**.

7. When the Workset File Already Exists dialog box displays, click **Yes** to replace the existing file.

8. Close the project.

Task 2 - Create the local file for User1.

A video called Task2.mp4 (Architectural) is located in the practice files Videos folder.

1. **User1**, in the Quick Access Toolbar, click 🖾 (Open). In the practice files folder, open **Elementary-School-MEP.rvt**.

   - Do not select central models from the startup screen as it opens the central model directly. Instead, use the **Open** command and create a new local file.

2. Verify that **Create New Local** is selected and click **Open**.

3. In the *Collaborate* tab>Manage Collaboration panel or in the Status Bar, click 🕼 (Worksets).

© 2020, ASCENT - Center for Technical Knowledge®

4. In the Worksets dialog box, make **HVAC** the Active workset. Set *Editable* to **Yes** and select **Visible in all views** for this workset.

5. Select all the other worksets except **Linked Architectural** and **Shared Levels and Grids**. Click **Close** so that the worksets are not open in this session, as shown in Figure 4–104.

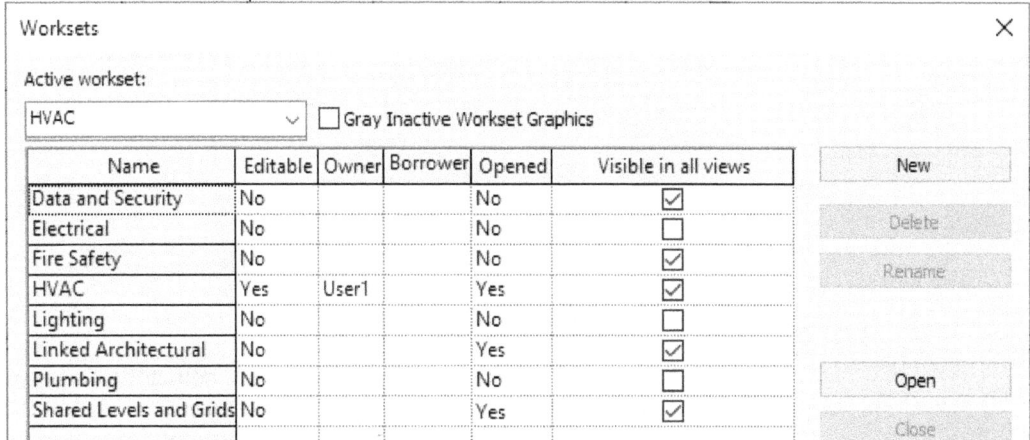

Worksets								✕

Active workset:

HVAC ⌄ ☐ Gray Inactive Workset Graphics

Name	Editable	Owner	Borrower	Opened	Visible in all views		
Data and Security	No			No	☑		New
Electrical	No			No	☐		Delete
Fire Safety	No			No	☑		
HVAC	Yes	User1		Yes	☑		Rename
Lighting	No			No	☐		
Linked Architectural	No			Yes	☑		
Plumbing	No			No	☐		Open
Shared Levels and Grids	No			Yes	☑		Close

Figure 4–104

6. Click **OK** to finish.

7. In the Quick Access Toolbar, click ▣ (Save) to save the local file.

8. Keep the file open.

Task 3 - Create the local file for User2.

A video called
Task3.mp4
(Architectural) is located in the practice files Videos folder.

1. **User2**, in the Quick Access Toolbar, click 📂 (Open) and select the file **Elementary-School-MEP.rvt**. Verify that **Create New Local** is selected, click the arrow next to **Open**, and select **Specify...** in the drop-down list, as shown in Figure 4–105.

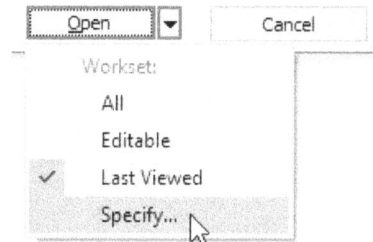

Figure 4–105

2. Click **Open** to open the project.

3. In the Opening Worksets dialog box, select the **Data and Security**, **Fire Safety**, **HVAC**, and **Plumbing** worksets and click **Close** so that these worksets are not opened in this session, as shown in Figure 4–106.

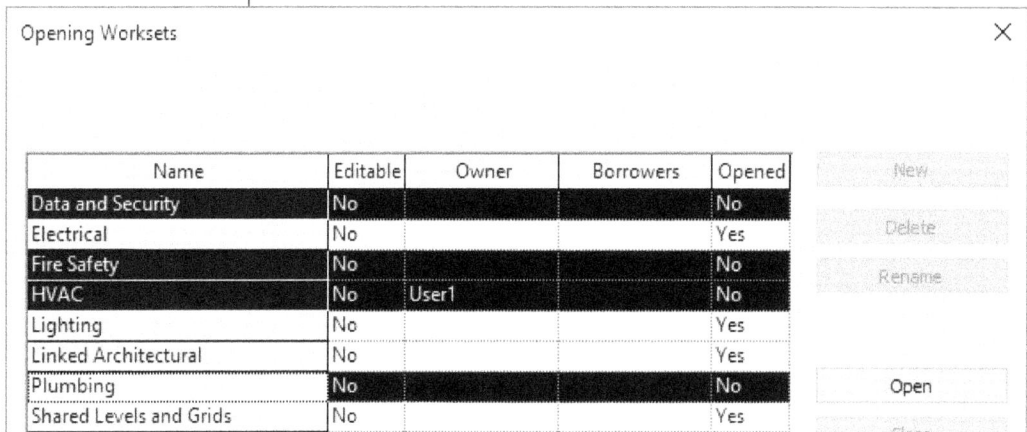

Name	Editable	Owner	Borrowers	Opened
Data and Security	No			No
Electrical	No			Yes
Fire Safety	No			No
HVAC	No	User1		No
Lighting	No			Yes
Linked Architectural	No			Yes
Plumbing	No			No
Shared Levels and Grids	No			Yes

Figure 4–106

4. Click **OK** to finish.

5. Save the local file and keep it opened.

© 2020, ASCENT - Center for Technical Knowledge®

Task 4 - Add and modify elements in worksets.

A video called
Task4.mp4
(Architectural) is located in the practice files Videos folder.

1. **User1**, in your local file for **Elementary-School-MEP**, open the Coordination>MEP>**Ceiling Plans:01 RCP** view.

2. Zoom in on the lower left classroom. You should see elements related to HVAC. (If you do not, open the Worksets dialog box and ensure that the HVAC workset is opened.)

3. Move the second row of air terminals one ceiling grid to the left, similar to that shown in Figure 4–107. Reattach the flex duct, if required.

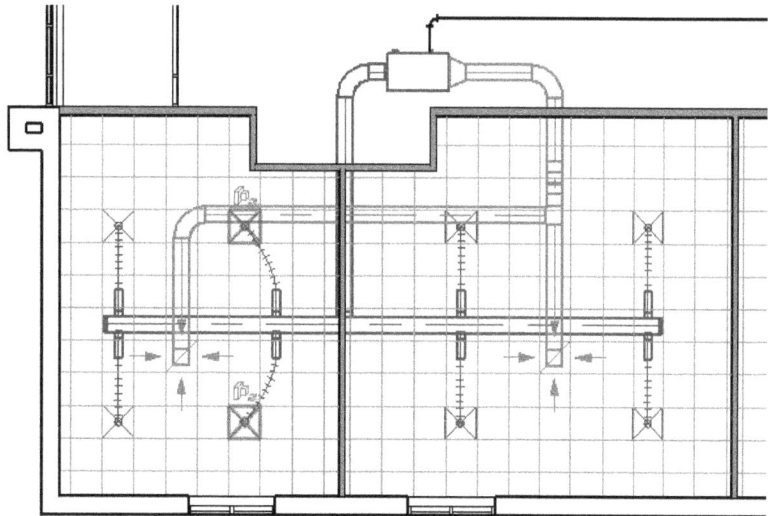

Figure 4–107

4. Open the Worksets dialog box and select the Lighting workset. Open it and make it visible in all views. Click **OK**. Now the air terminals are on top of the lights.

5. Select one of the lighting fixtures. It has an icon connected to it, as shown in Figure 4–108, indicating that it belongs to another workset. Click the icon to make the element editable.

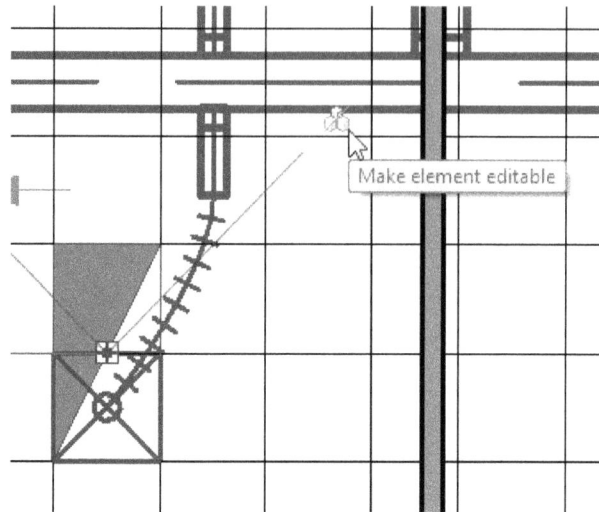

Figure 4–108

6. Move the lighting fixture so it does not conflict with the air terminal.

7. Open the Worksets dialog box. **User1** is noted as the *Owner* of the **HVAC** workset and a *Borrower* of the **Lighting** workset, as shown in Figure 4–109.

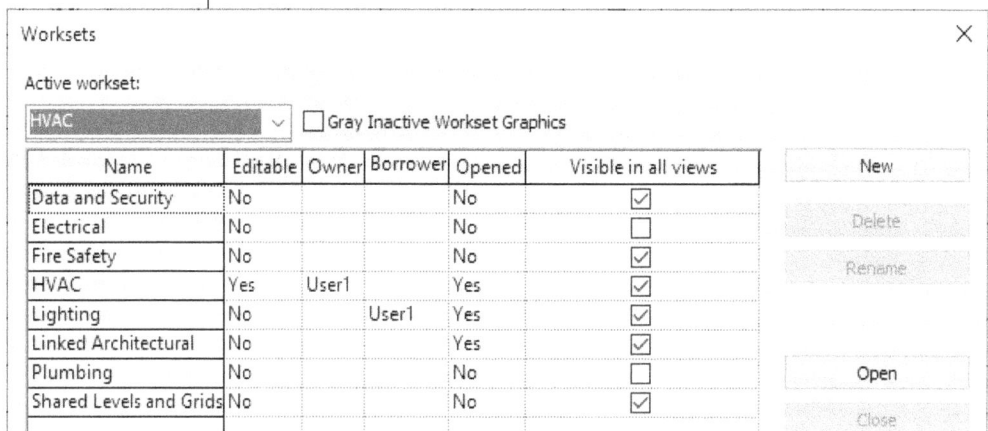

Name	Editable	Owner	Borrower	Opened	Visible in all views
Data and Security	No			No	☑
Electrical	No			No	☐
Fire Safety	No			No	☑
HVAC	Yes	User1		Yes	☑
Lighting	No		User1	Yes	☑
Linked Architectural	No			Yes	☑
Plumbing	No			No	☐
Shared Levels and Grids	No			No	☑

Figure 4–109

8. Click **OK** to close the dialog box.

© 2020, ASCENT - Center for Technical Knowledge®

9. In the *Collaborate* tab>Synchronize panel or the Quick Access Toolbar, click ⬡ (Synchronize and Modify Settings) to open the Synchronize with Central dialog box, as shown in Figure 4–110. The **Borrowed Elements** option should be selected. Add a comment about moving the air terminals and light fixtures and select **Save Local File before and after synchronizing with central**. Click **OK**.

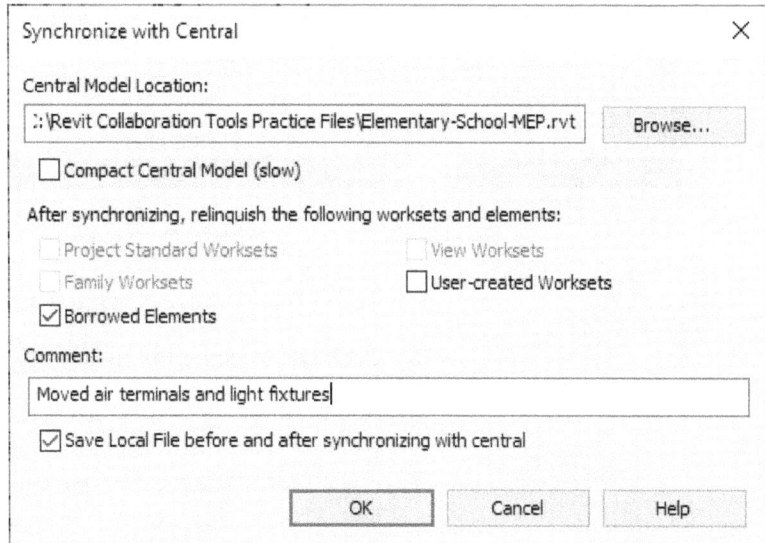

Synchronize with Central   ✕

Central Model Location:

:.\Revit Collaboration Tools Practice Files\Elementary-School-MEP.rvt	Browse...

☐ Compact Central Model (slow)

After synchronizing, relinquish the following worksets and elements:

☐ Project Standard Worksets   ☐ View Worksets

☐ Family Worksets   ☐ User-created Worksets

☑ Borrowed Elements

Comment:

Moved air terminals and light fixtures

☑ Save Local File before and after synchronizing with central

OK	Cancel	Help

Figure 4–110

Task 5 - Check out a workset.

A video called
Task5.mp4
*(Architectural) is located
in the practice files
Videos folder.*

1. **User2**, open the Coordination>MEP>**Ceiling Plans: 01 RCP** view in your local file. Neither the HVAC elements nor the changes show in the local file.

2. In the *Collaborate* tab>Synchronize panel, click ⬡ (Reload Latest or type **RL**. The light fixture location changes but you do not see the air terminals because that workset is not open.

3. Click ⬡ (Worksets) to open the dialog box and open the HVAC workset. Verify that it is **Visible in all views**.

4. Select **Lighting** in the *Active workset* drop-down list and make it editable (select **Yes** in the *Editable* column). The *Owner* should display as **User2**, as shown in Figure 4–111.

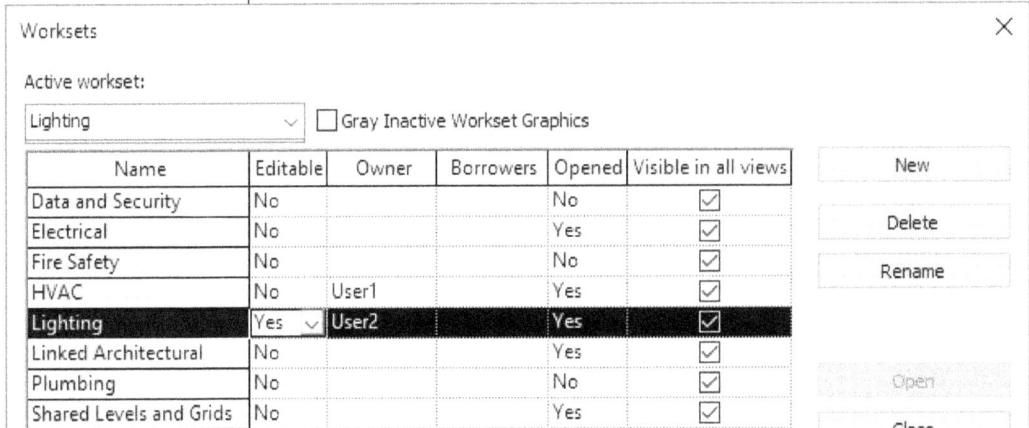

Worksets						✕

Active workset:

Lighting	☐ Gray Inactive Workset Graphics

Name	Editable	Owner	Borrowers	Opened	Visible in all views	
Data and Security	No			No	☑	New
Electrical	No			Yes	☑	Delete
Fire Safety	No			No	☑	
HVAC	No	User1		Yes	☑	Rename
Lighting	Yes	User2		Yes	☑	
Linked Architectural	No			Yes	☑	
Plumbing	No			No	☑	Open
Shared Levels and Grids	No			Yes	☑	Close

Figure 4–111

5. Click **OK** to close the dialog box.

6. Add another lighting fixture in the room.

7. In the Quick Access Toolbar, click 🖫 (Save) to save the local file.

8. **User1**, type **RL** (Reload Latest). There are no new changes to load, as shown in Figure 4–112, because User2 has not saved back to the central model. Close the dialog box.

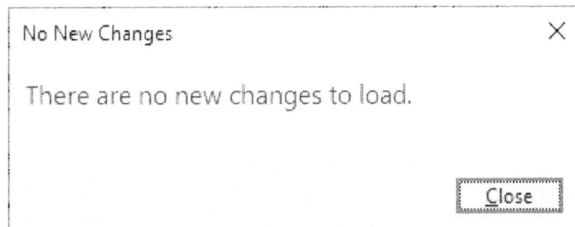

No New Changes	✕

There are no new changes to load.

Close

Figure 4–112

9. **User2** will click ⬡ (Synchronize Now). This saves the changes to the central model without relinquishing the Lighting workset.

© 2020, ASCENT - Center for Technical Knowledge®

A video called
Task6.mp4
(Architectural) is located in the practice files Videos folder.

Task 6 - Request permission to edit.

1. **User1**, type **RL** (Reload Latest) again. This time, the new lighting fixture displays because it was saved to the central model.

2. Try to move one of the lighting fixtures. This time, an error message displays that cannot be ignored, as shown in Figure 4–113. **User2** has made the Lighting workset editable. Therefore, no one else can edit elements in it without permission.

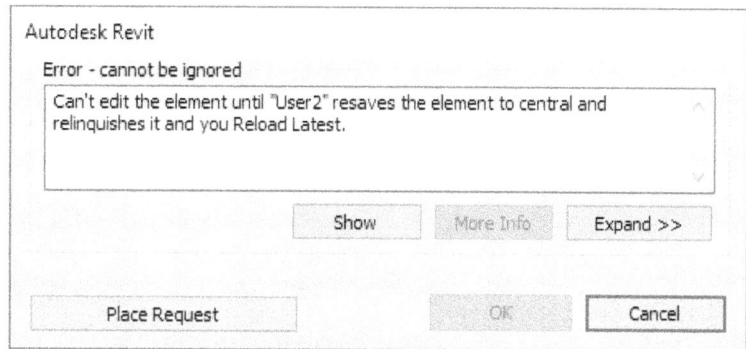

Autodesk Revit

Error - cannot be ignored

Can't edit the element until "User2" resaves the element to central and relinquishes it and you Reload Latest.

| | Show | More Info | Expand >> |

| Place Request | | OK | Cancel |

Figure 4–113

3. Click **Place Request**. The Editing Request Placed dialog box opens. Leave it open.

4. **User2** now gets an alert box display, as shown in Figure 4–114.

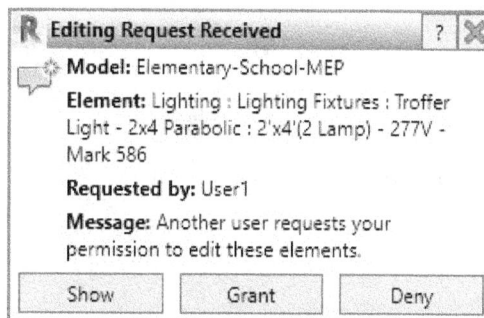

Editing Request Received ? ✖

Model: Elementary-School-MEP

Element: Lighting : Lighting Fixtures : Troffer Light - 2x4 Parabolic : 2'x4'(2 Lamp) - 277V - Mark 586

Requested by: User1

Message: Another user requests your permission to edit these elements.

| Show | Grant | Deny |

Figure 4–114

5. Hover the cursor over the **Show** button to highlight the lighting fixture. (Move the dialog box out of the way if needed to see the modified lighting fixture.)

6. Click **Grant** to give **User1** permission to modify the placement of this lighting fixture. By doing so, you enable the other user to have full control over this element in the workset.

7. **User1** will get an Editing Request Granted dialog box, as shown in Figure 4–115.

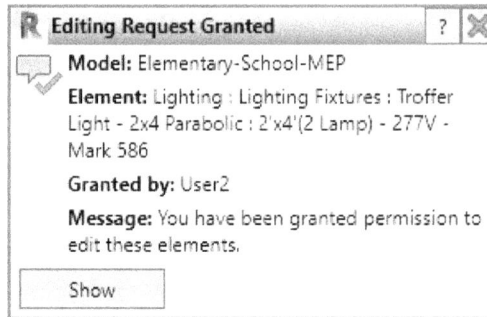

Figure 4–115

8. Close the Editing Request Granted dialog box. Because your request was granted, the lighting fixture moves.

9. Move the lighting fixture again to exactly where you want it. This time, you are not prompted to ask to move the element because you are still borrowing it.

10. Try to move another lighting fixture. You do not have permission to move this or any others. Click **Cancel** rather than place the request. The lighting fixture returns to its original location.

Task 7 - View information about the worksets.

A video called
Task7.mp4
(Architectural) is located in the practice files Videos folder.

1. In the View Control Bar, expand the Worksharing Display and click (Owners). Different colors highlight the elements and their respective owners. Hover the cursor over one of the elements to display the information about the owner, as shown in Figure 4–116.

© 2020, ASCENT - Center for Technical Knowledge®

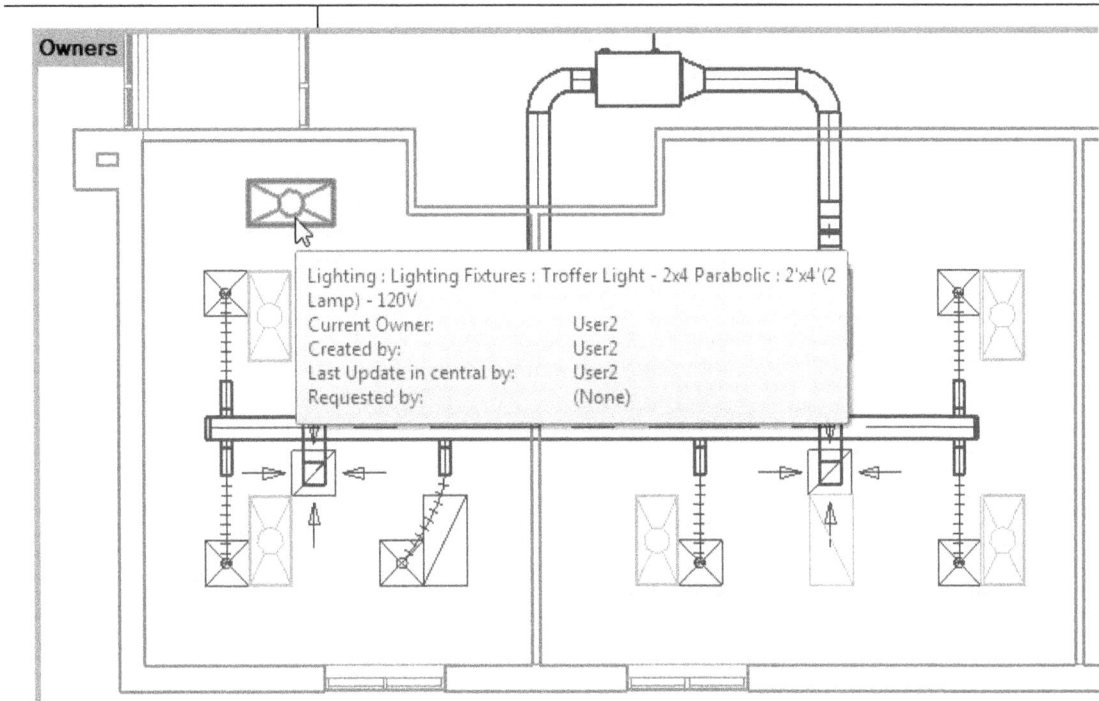

Lighting : Lighting Fixtures : Troffer Light - 2x4 Parabolic : 2'x4'(2 Lamp) - 120V
Current Owner: User2
Created by: User2
Last Update in central by: User2
Requested by: (None)

Figure 4–116

- The color on your display might be different.

2. Click ⬡ (Synchronize and Modify Settings) and relinquish **User-created Worksets** and **Borrowed Elements.**

3. Toggle the Worksharing Display off and zoom out to see the full building.

4. Save the local file.

5. **User2**, click ⬡ (Synchronize Now). The lighting fixture moves to the location where **User1** moved it. When you save to the central model, it also reloads the latest changes.

6. Close the project. When the Editable Elements dialog box opens, as shown in Figure 4–117, click **Relinquish elements and worksets**.

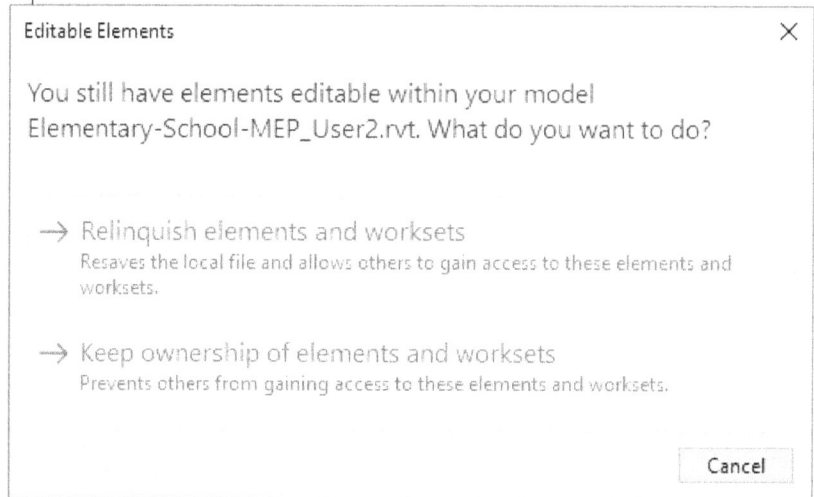

Editable Elements   ✕

You still have elements editable within your model
Elementary-School-MEP_User2.rvt. What do you want to do?

⟶ Relinquish elements and worksets
Resaves the local file and allows others to gain access to these elements and worksets.

⟶ Keep ownership of elements and worksets
Prevents others from gaining access to these elements and worksets.

                                                    Cancel

Figure 4–117

7. Close the project.

© 2020, ASCENT - Center for Technical Knowledge®

4.9 Best Practices for Worksharing

Working with Company Policies

There are different practices regarding the frequency of synchronizing with the central model. Some companies ask users to synchronize before lunch and at the end of the day. Other companies require users to synchronize every 30 to 60 minutes. As the file size gets larger, synchronizing more often prevents the loss of data and also makes the synchronization finish quicker than if there are several hours worth of work to synchronize. However, there can be many reasons to change this frequency or to do additional synchronizations at specific points in time. They are:

- Major or critical changes to the project, such as moving an elevator core, reorienting the building on the site, etc.

- Users working in close proximity inside the model, to reduce permission issues.

When users need to leave their work for an hour or more (for lunch or a meeting or at the end of the day), it is best to synchronize and relinquish all. Then, upon returning, they should create a new local file (with a new name if you want the previous file saved as a backup). This ensures their file is up to date and eliminates the update time.

Tips for Using Worksets

Working with the Local File

- Be selective about which worksets you open. Avoid opening worksets that are not required for the work you are doing in the project. Limiting the number of worksets that will be opened with the file speeds up the process of opening and saving the file.

- Close unused views on a regular basis.

- Use a Starting View that is a drafting view, 2D plan, or elevation view. The Autodesk Revit software only loads into memory what it displays, so this saves memory the next time the file is opened. This can also be used before plotting to increase the amount of available RAM.

- If you have been away from an active project for some time, it is better to create a new local file rather than depend on the **Reload Latest** command to update your current local file for you.

- If you are not sure what workset to put certain elements in, you can use *Workset1* or a specific temporary workset to put them in until the decision can be finalized.

- Restart the software before performing memory-intensive operations, such as printing an entire document set.

Saving to the Central Model

- Stagger syncing to the central model among users so that they are not saving concurrently.

- Type **RL** (Reload Latest) to update your copy of the project without changing the central model. This saves time by eliminating the need to reload as part of the **Synchronize and Modify Settings** command.

- Periodically synchronize with the central model using the **Compact File** option. This takes longer to save, but frees up more memory.

- If you get an error, such as *Unable to Save* or *File not found*, you might have run out of memory. Close the major worksets and view so that the Autodesk Revit software releases some of the virtual memory that can be used to then save the file.

Requesting Edits

- Enable elements, not worksets, whenever possible. The Autodesk Revit software automatically borrows the unowned elements without user intervention. This saves time by not having to request an edit in the first place.

- Communicate with the team members working on a project to avoid working on the same elements at the same time.

Tips for Creating Worksets

Worksets and the Team

- Assign one person to enable worksharing and create worksets and the central model.

© 2020, ASCENT - Center for Technical Knowledge®

- Create your project team structure to correspond with the new way of working with the building model. For example, architects and engineers do much of the work directly without needing an intern or drafter to create working drawings until the later parts of a project.

- Divide worksets according to components of a building rather than drawing types (such as plans, elevations, and sections), as these are created automatically.

- Key considerations when determining how to divide a project into worksets include the ability to load only those worksets that are required at the time and the ability to control visibility by worksets.

- As the project progresses, more worksets can be added.

- Using worksets does not negate the need for good team communication. You still need to have scheduling and planning meetings.

- Be sure that everyone knows which part of the model they are responsible for.

- File sharing should be a tool that is used in the workflow of the project; it should not be something that is disruptive.

Creating Worksets

- A multi-floor building does not need to have a workset for each floor until you are working on the floor-specific layouts.

- If you have a project with a large floor plate that needs to be divided by match lines to fit on sheets, you should divide the various parts of the building into separate worksets.

- If you have imported files into a project, each import should be in a separate workset that is not visible by default. They should also be closed when not in use.

- Every linked file should be in a separate workset not visible by default. They should also be closed when not in use.

- Worksets cannot be included in templates.

Default Workset Visibility

- As you create worksets, you should set the visibility. For example, the exterior and core of a building should be visible in all views, but furniture layouts or tenant partitions only need to be visible in specific views.

- Set up a standard for typical workset visibility designations. There are always exceptions, but working with the standard first is simpler.

Ending the Day

IMPORTANT: When you have finished working on the project for the day, you need to save, synchronize to central, and relinquish all borrowed and user-created worksets. If you are working on a project with other people, you need to relinquish all your worksets when closing a project so they can edit them if needed.

- When you close a project, if you did not relinquish elements and all worksets when you saved to the central model, the alert shown in Figure 4–118 will display.

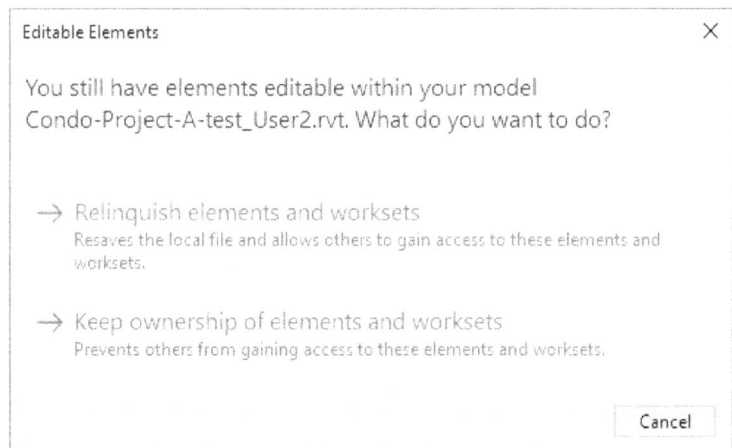

Editable Elements	×

You still have elements editable within your model Condo-Project-A-test_User2.rvt. What do you want to do?

→ Relinquish elements and worksets
Resaves the local file and allows others to gain access to these elements and worksets.

→ Keep ownership of elements and worksets
Prevents others from gaining access to these elements and worksets.

Cancel

Figure 4–118

© 2020, ASCENT - Center for Technical Knowledge®

- To relinquish worksets without saving to the central model, in the *Collaborate* tab>Synchronize panel, click ⬜ (Relinquish All Mine).

Do not delete any files in these directories.

- The backup directory for central models and local files, as shown in Figure 4–119, holds information about the editability of worksets, borrowed elements, and workset/element ownership. If required, you can restore the backup directory. In the *Collaboration* tab>Synchronize panel, click ⬜ (Restore Backup).

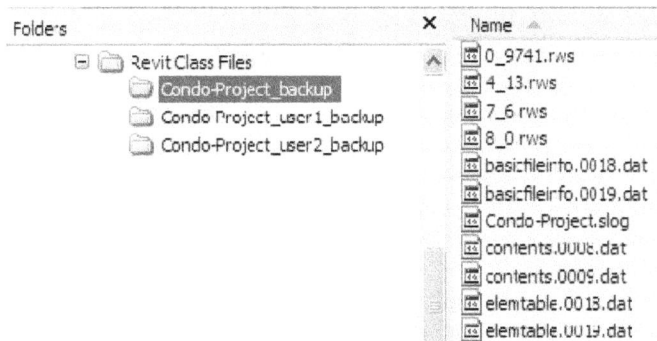

Folders	×	Name ▲
⊟ 📁 Revit Class Files	^	🗎 0_9741.rws
📁 Condo-Project_backup		🗎 4_13.rws
📁 Condo-Project_user1_backup		🗎 7_6.rws
📁 Condo-Project_user2_backup		🗎 8_0.rws
		🗎 basicfileinfo.0018.dat
		🗎 basicfileinfo.0019.dat
		🗎 Condo-Project.slog
		🗎 contents.0008.dat
		🗎 contents.0009.dat
		🗎 elemtable.0013.dat
		🗎 elemtable.0019.dat

Figure 4–119

Chapter Review Questions

1. When setting up a project to be workshared, which of the following is performed first?

   a. Use Save As and, in Options, select **Make this a Central Model** after save.

   b. Start the project using a Central Model template.

   c. Use the Collaborate tool to enable worksharing, then use the **Worksets** command and add worksets.

   d. All of the grids and levels need to be in place.

2. Where should a central model be located?

   a. On your computer.

   b. On the company server.

   c. On each of the computers used by the team.

3. When you want to update the work that you have done and receive any changes others have made, but you do not want to change anything else, which command do you use?

   a. (Synchronize and Modify Settings)

   b. (Synchronize Now)

   c. (Relinquish All Mine)

   d. (Reload Latest)

4. Where should a local file be located?

   a. On the project manager's computer.

   b. On the company server.

   c. On each team member's computer.

© 2020, ASCENT - Center for Technical Knowledge®

5. What do you need to do so that any new elements you add are placed in a particular workset?

   a. Gray out inactive worksets so you know not to work in them.

   b. Make the workset editable.

   c. Set the workset as active.

   d. Create a new workset.

6. When selecting an element to edit, the icon shown in Figure 4–120 displays. What do you need to do?

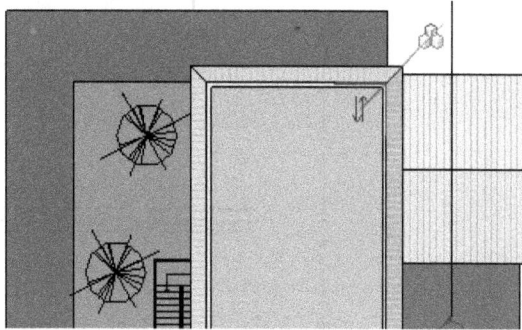

Figure 4–120

   a. You can either edit the element without checking it out if it is not owned by someone else or place a request to edit it if it is owned by someone else.

   b. Click the icon and an error dialog box displays indicating that you cannot edit the element.

   c. Click the icon and an error dialog box displays indicating that you cannot edit the element, but you can request permission to edit it.

   d. Click the icon and a dialog box displays granting you permission to edit the element.

7. You have the most recent updates from the central model but some elements in a workset are not displaying, as shown in Figure 4–121. Which of the following should you do? (Select all that apply.)

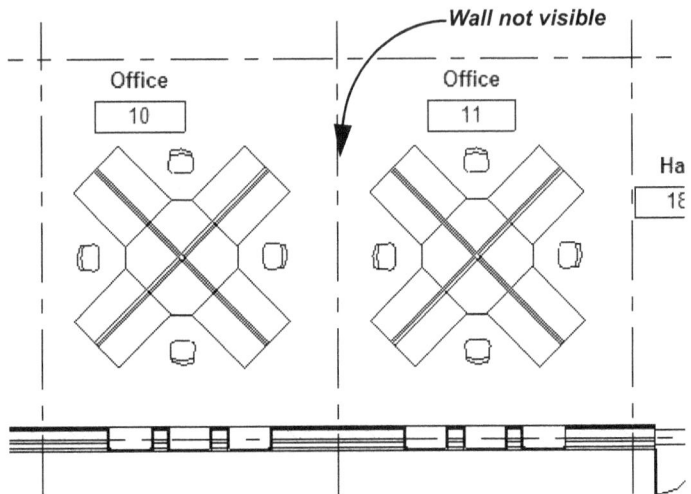

Figure 4–121

a. In the Visibility/Graphic Overrides dialog box, change the Visibility Setting of the workset to **Visible**.

b. In the Worksets dialog box, request permission to edit.

c. Set the workset as active.

d. In the Status Bar, change the Worksharing Display.

e. In the Worksets dialog box, verify if the workset is open.

© 2020, ASCENT - Center for Technical Knowledge®

Command Summary

Button	Command	Location
	Collaborate	• **Ribbon**: *Collaborate* tab>Manage Collaboration panel
	Editing Requests	• **Ribbon**: *Collaborate* tab>Synchronize panel • **Status Bar**
	Gray Inactive Worksets	• **Ribbon**: *Collaborate* tab>Manage Collaboration panel
	Owners (Display)	• **Status Bar**: expand Worksharing Display Off
	Relinquish All Mine	• **Ribbon**: *Collaborate* tab>Synchronize panel
	Reload Latest	• **Ribbon**: *Collaborate* tab>Synchronize panel • **Shortcut**: RL
	Restore Backup	• **Ribbon**: *Collaborate* tab>Synchronize panel
	Show History	• **Ribbon**: *Collaborate* tab>Synchronize panel
	Synchronize and Modify Settings	• **Quick Access Toolbar** • **Ribbon**: *Collaborate* tab>Synchronize panel>expand Synchronize with Central
	Synchronize Now	• **Quick Access Toolbar** • **Ribbon**: *Collaborate* tab>Synchronize panel>expand Synchronize with Central
	Worksets	• **Ribbon**: *Collaborate* tab>Manage Collaboration panel>Worksets • **Status Bar**
	Worksets (Display)	• **Status Bar**: expand Worksharing Display Off
	Worksharing Display Off	• **Status Bar**

© 2020, ASCENT - Center for Technical Knowledge®

Additional Information

When you are working with links in Autodesk® Revit®, several additional features can help you with some specific situations, such as copying elements from a link into the host project, converting links into groups (or groups into links), and acquiring or publishing coordinates between linked files.

Learning Objectives in This Appendix

- Copy individual items from a linked file into the host file.
- Convert links into groups and groups into links.
- Publish coordinates of the host project to linked models.
- Acquire coordinates from a linked model for a host project.
- Select named locations for multiple instances of linked models in a host project.

A.1 Linked Model Conversion

There are times when you require information stored in a linked file that is brought into your host file. The information required might be about one or more individual elements or an entire link. A link can be converted to a group by binding it to the project. The group becomes a part of the project and does not update if the original file is modified. You can also convert a group to a link, which creates a new project file containing the elements of the group. Links and groups display differently when selected, as shown in Figure A–1.

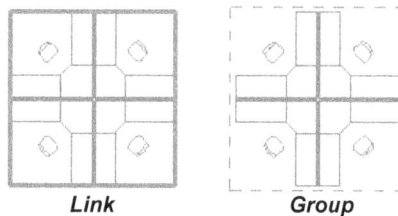

Link   Group

Figure A–1

How To: Copy Individual Elements in a Linked File to the Host File

1. Select an individual element in a linked model by moving the cursor over the element and pressing <Tab>.
2. When the element you want to use highlights, click on it.
3. In the *Modify | RVT Links* tab>Clipboard panel, click

    (Copy to the Clipboard).

4. Click (Paste from Clipboard) to insert the individual element into the project, as shown in Figure A–2.

Individual items in a linked model can be copied into the host project or into another project file.

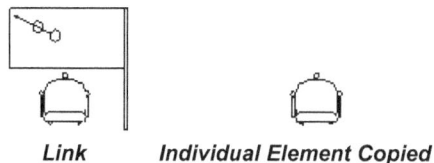

Link   *Individual Element Copied*

Figure A–2

- This is not the same as copying and monitoring elements.

© 2020, ASCENT - Center for Technical Knowledge®

How To: Convert a Link to a Group

1. Select the link. In the *Modify | RVT Links* tab>Link panel, click
   ⬚ (Bind Link).
2. The Bind Link Options dialog box opens, as shown in Figure A–3. Select the items that you want to include and click **OK**.

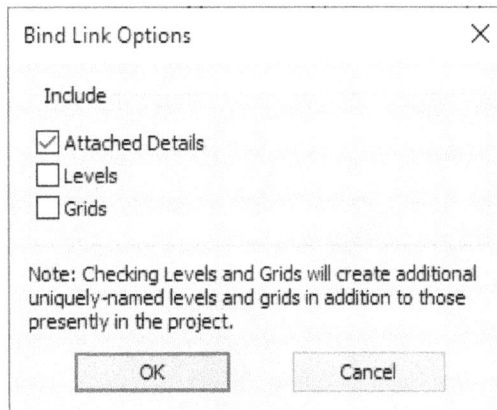

Bind Link Options   ✕

Include

☑ Attached Details
☐ Levels
☐ Grids

Note: Checking Levels and Grids will create additional uniquely-named levels and grids in addition to those presently in the project.

| OK | Cancel |

Figure A–3

- An alert box might open, warning you about duplicate types. The types in the current project override the types in the linked project.

- If there is an existing group with the same name as the link in the project, an alert box opens, as shown in Figure A–4.

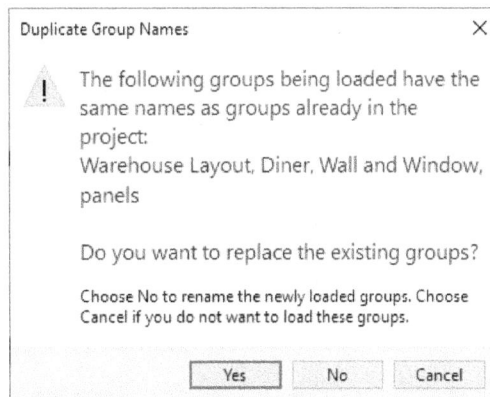

Duplicate Group Names   ✕

⚠ The following groups being loaded have the same names as groups already in the project:
Warehouse Layout, Diner, Wall and Window, panels

Do you want to replace the existing groups?

Choose No to rename the newly loaded groups. Choose Cancel if you do not want to load these groups.

| Yes | No | Cancel |

Figure A–4

How To: Convert Groups to Links

1. Select the group(s) you want to convert. You can select multiple copies, but they must be the same group.
2. In the *Modify | Model Groups* tab>Group panel, click [icon] (Link).
3. In the Convert to Link dialog box, select the method for converting the group, as shown in Figure A–5.

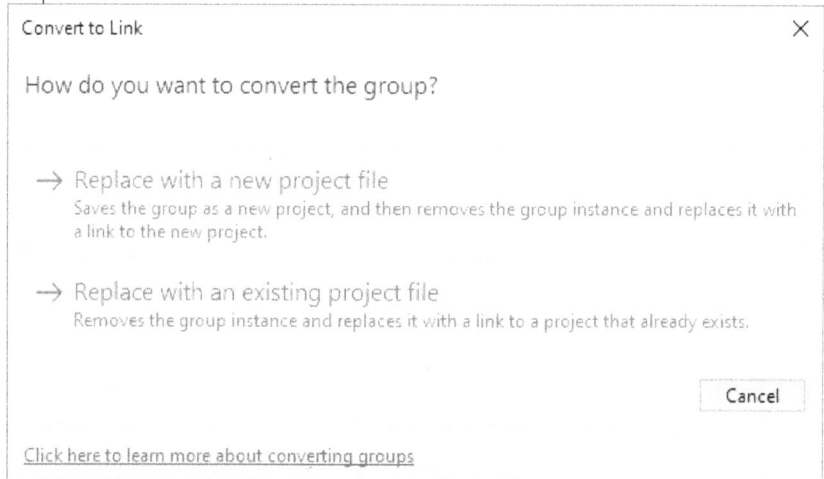

Convert to Link   ✕

How do you want to convert the group?

→ Replace with a new project file
   Saves the group as a new project, and then removes the group instance and replaces it with
   a link to the new project.

→ Replace with an existing project file
   Removes the group instance and replaces it with a link to a project that already exists.

                                                                    Cancel

Click here to learn more about converting groups

Figure A–5

4. When you select **Replace with a new project file,** the Save Group dialog box displays. Navigate to the appropriate folder, name the group (the default is the same as the group name), and click **Save**.

   - Select **Include attached detail groups as views** when you have both a model group and detail group together.

5. When you select **Replace with an existing project file,** the Open dialog box displays. Navigate to the appropriate folder, select the file you want to use to replace the selected group and click **Open**.

© 2020, ASCENT - Center for Technical Knowledge®

A.2 Shared Positioning

Each project created in the Autodesk Revit software has a set of internal coordinates that are only used by that project. As long as you are working in a stand-alone project, you do not need to reference these coordinates. However, if you are linking projects together, you might want to have one coordinate system that is referenced throughout the connected projects. This is when you need to share coordinates.

- Shared Sites can be specified in the Properties of the linked model, as shown in Figure A–6.

The Project Base Point, typically visible in a site plan, establishes the coordinate system.

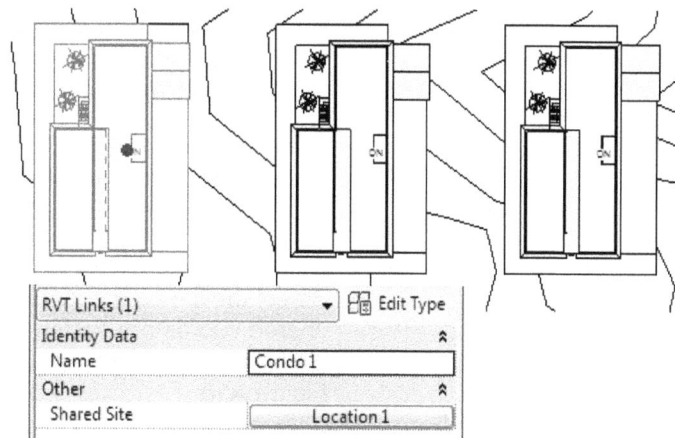

Figure A–6

- Linked models that share coordinates can be created in the Autodesk Revit software or a combination of files created in the Autodesk Revit software and DWG and DXF files created in the AutoCAD software.

- Within the host model, you can display linked models' coordinates by turning on the Internal Origin from the *Site* area of the Visibility/Graphic Overrides dialog box. Linked model coordinates will be grayed out in the view, as shown in Figure A–7.

Figure A–7

- Shared coordinates should only be derived from one file. You can acquire coordinates from a linked project or drawing or publish them from the host project to the other files.

Publishing and Acquiring Coordinates

Shared coordinates are often used with site plans to which multiple buildings are linked. The buildings can all be different or can be copies of the same project, such as in an apartment complex. The site project typically controls the coordinates.

- If you are working in the site project, you can select the links and publish the coordinates to them.

- If you are working in a building project, you can acquire the coordinates from the site project.

- Typically, the architectural project acquires the coordinates from a site project and then the other disciplines link the architectural model into their projects using Origin to Origin or **Project Base Point to Project Base Point**.

How To: Publish Coordinates to Linked Models

1. Open the host project that has the coordinates you want to use and contains the linked models.
2. In the *Manage* tab>Project Location panel, expand

   (Coordinates) and click (Publish Coordinates).
3. Select the linked model to which you want to publish the shared coordinate system. The Location Weather and Site dialog box opens with the *Site* tab active, as shown in Figure A–8.

Click (Location) in the Manage tab>Project Location panel to open the dialog box at any time.

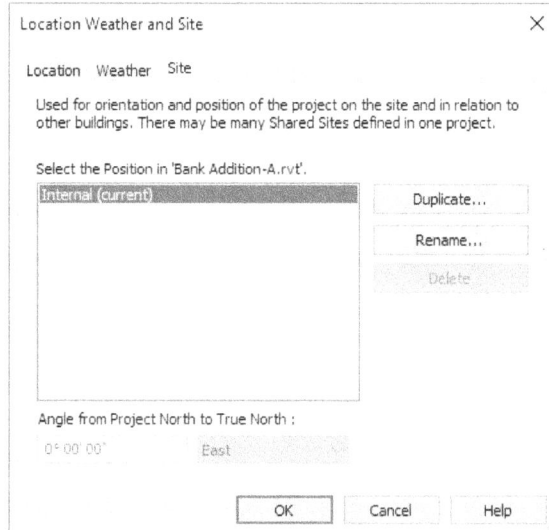

Figure A–8

4. The Internal named location of the linked model is the default. Click **Rename...** to give the default location a different name. Click **Duplicate...** to create a new name for the instance location. Each instance of the linked model should have a differently named location.

5. Select the location that you want to use and click **OK**.

6. You are still in the command and can select another linked project to which to publish the coordinates or press <Esc> to end the command.

• You only need to publish coordinates to a linked model once. However, you can use this method on multiple instances to create the named locations.

How To: Save the Modifications to the Linked Model

When the coordinates have been published, they still need to be saved to the linked model.

1. In the *Manage* tab>Manage Project panel, click ⬚ (Manage Links).

2. In the Manage Links dialog box, select the *Revit* tab.

3. A checkmark displays in the *Positions Not Saved* column, as shown in Figure A–9, indicating that the published coordinates have not yet been saved to the linked model.

Linked File	Status	Reference Type	Positions Not Saved
Townhouse.r	Loaded	Overlay	☑

Figure A–9

4. Select the name in the *Linked File* column and click **Save Positions**.

5. In the Location Position Changed dialog box shown in Figure A–10, select the method that you want to use.

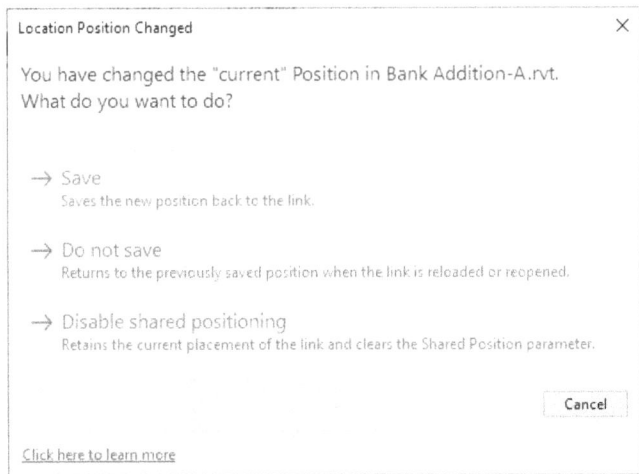

Figure A–10

6. If you selected **Save**, the **Positions Not Saved** option is cleared in the Manage Links dialog box

7. Click **OK** to close the dialog box.

• If you make a change to the location or save the project before managing the links, you are prompted to make a selection in the same dialog box.

Acquiring Coordinates

If you are working in a project with linked models and want to use the coordinates from one of the linked models rather than from the host project, you can acquire the coordinates, as shown in Figure A–11. For example, you might have a drawing site plan that was created in the AutoCAD software linked to a project created in the Autodesk Revit Architecture software and want to use the coordinates from the DWG file.

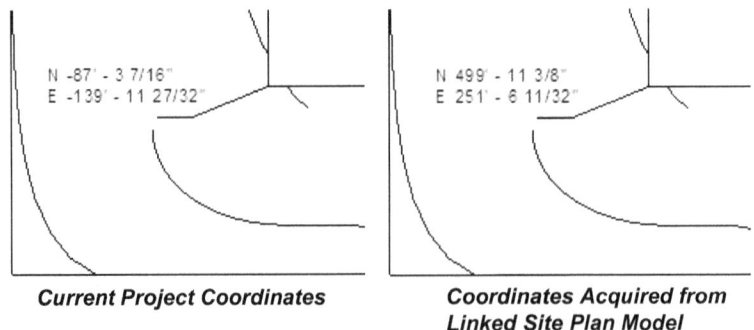

Current Project Coordinates *Coordinates Acquired from Linked Site Plan Model*

Figure A–11

© 2020, ASCENT - Center for Technical Knowledge®

To maintain a consistent geographic location between models, you can use the GIS coordinates stored in a linked DWG file that includes a Geographic Marker, as shown in AutoCAD in Figure A–12. When you acquire the coordinates from the linked DWG, these are shared with the Revit project.

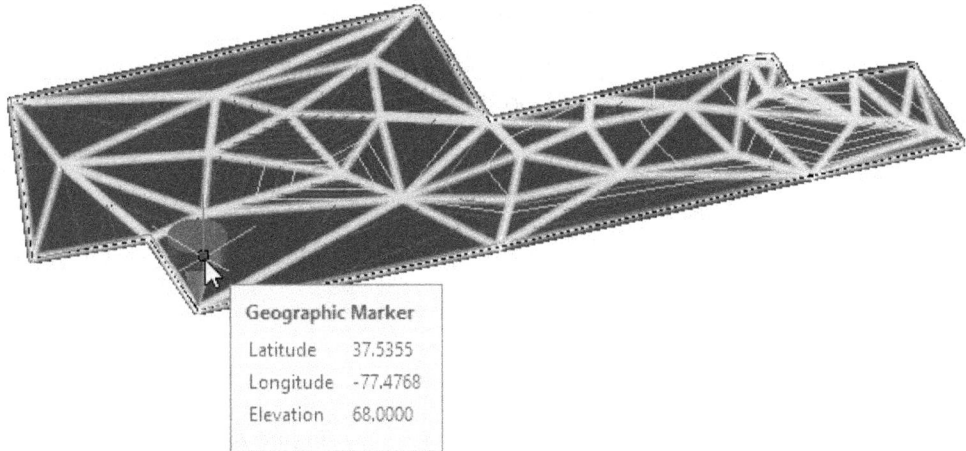

Geographic Marker

Latitude	37.5355
Longitude	-77.4768
Elevation	68.0000

Figure A–12

When you acquire coordinates from a Geographic Marker, as shown in Figure A–13, the Autodesk Revit model updates to show the real-world position of the model, which improves energy analysis.

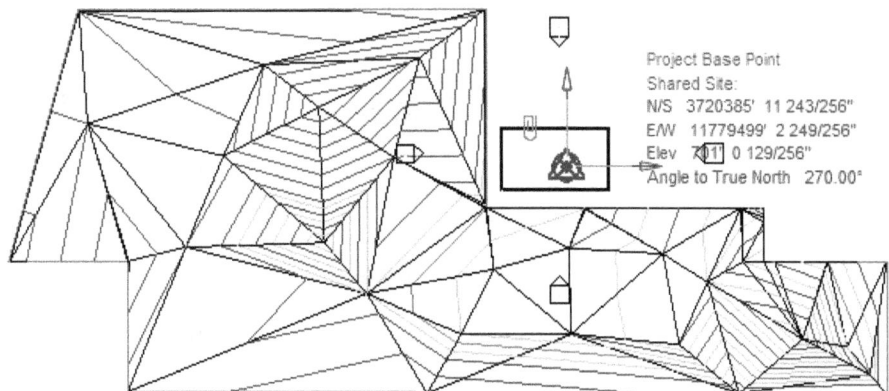

Project Base Point
Shared Site:
N/S 3720385' 11 243/256"
E/W 11779499' 2 249/256"
Elev 7011 0 129/256"
Angle to True North 270.00°

Figure A–13

How To: Acquire Coordinates from a Linked Project

1. In the *Manage* tab>Project Location panel, expand

   ⌐ (Coordinates) and click ⌐ (Acquire Coordinates).
2. Select a linked model from which to acquire the shared coordinate system. The current project now uses the new coordinates.

   - If successfully acquired, you will receive an Acquired Coordinates Succeed message, as shown in Figure A–14.

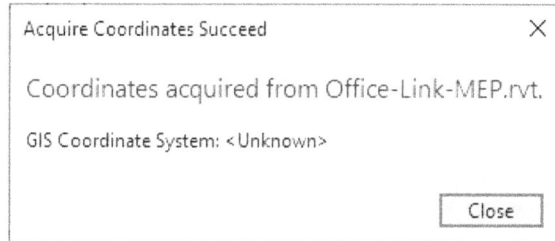

Figure A–14

   - If you move or rotate a linked instance after it has been shared and saved, a Warning box opens as shown in Figure A–15. You can click **Save Now** to save the position or click **OK** to continue working in the project. You can save the linked model later using the Manage Links dialog box.

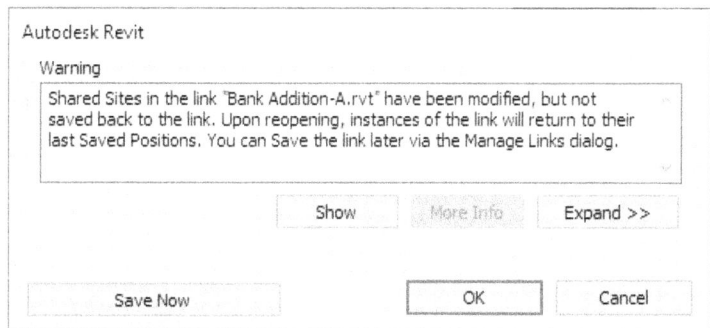

Figure A–15

Selecting Locations

It is possible to select locations for multiple instances of linked models using the **Publish Coordinates** command. Another way of specifying locations is to use the Properties of the linked model. If you have not already published coordinates to the linked project, you are prompted to reconcile the link before proceeding. Through Properties, you can move a linked instance to a new location, record the current position to a named location, or stop sharing the location of the linked instance.

How To: Select or Specify a Named Location for a Linked Model

1. Select the linked model.
2. In Properties, next to *Shared Site*, click **<Not Shared>**.
3. If the linked model is already reconciled, the Select Location dialog box opens, as shown in Figure A–16.

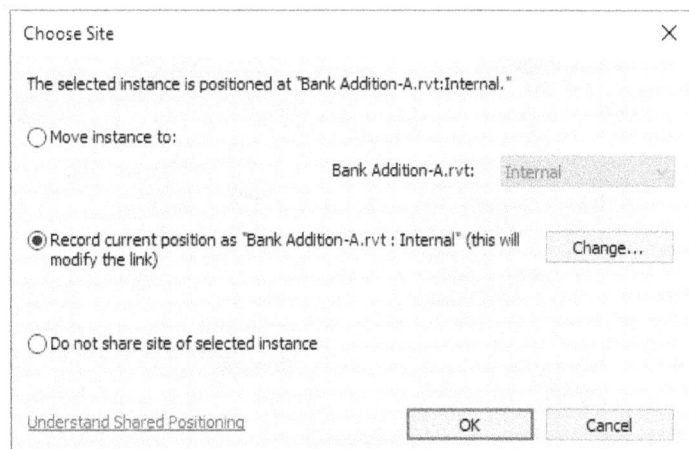

Figure A–16

- You can move the instance to an existing named location. Select **Move instance to:** and select the location from the list.
- If you do not want to select a named location, select **Do not share location of selected instance**.

- If you need to create a new named location, select **Record current position…** and click **Change…**. The Location Weather and Site dialog box opens, in which you can create a new named location as shown in Figure A–17. Make the new location current.

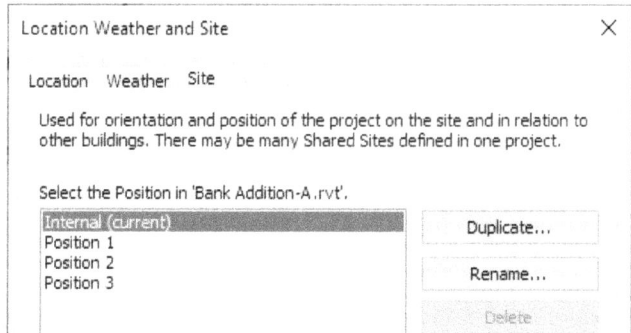

Figure A–17

4. Click **OK** to close the dialog box.
5. The value of the **Shared Site** option is now the new location name, as shown in Figure A–18.

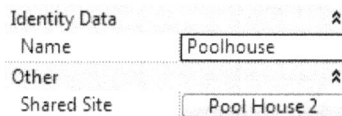

Figure A–18

Hint: Identifying Coordinates

To identify a coordinate point: in the *Manage* tab>Project Location panel, expand (Coordinates) and click

 (Report Shared Coordinates). The cursor icon displays. Move it over a point on the project and click on it. The Shared Coordinates display in the Options Bar, as shown in Figure A–19.

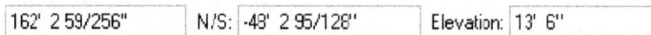

Figure A–19

- To move the project to new coordinates, change the Project Base Point or click (Specify coordinates at point).

© 2020, ASCENT - Center for Technical Knowledge®

Reconciling Links

When you select a linked model and in Properties, select **Shared Site**, and the link has not been reconciled with the host project, the Share Coordinates dialog box opens, as shown in Figure A–20.

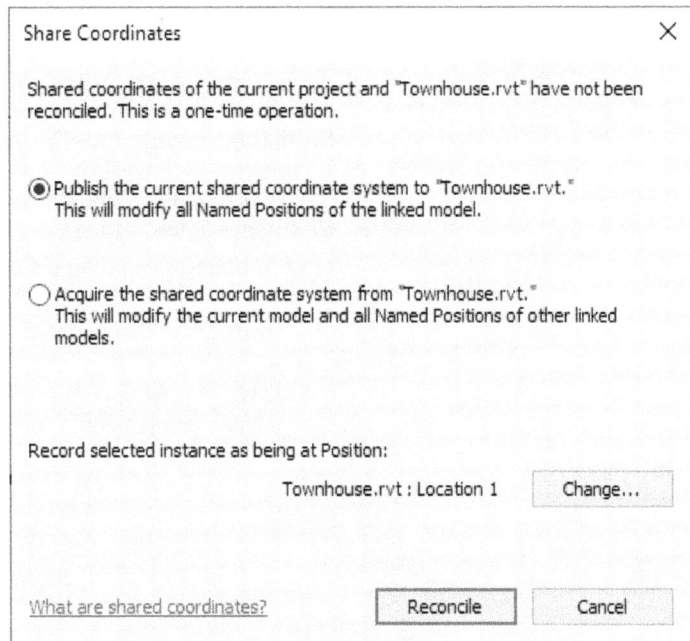

Figure A–20

- This only occurs the first time you select a file that does not share coordinates. If you select other instances of the same link, this dialog box does not open.

How To: Reconcile Links

1. In the Share Coordinates dialog box, select **Publish** or **Acquire**.
2. Click **Change...** to record the location of the instance.
3. In the Location Weather and Site dialog box, specify the named location and click **OK**.
4. In the Share Coordinates dialog box, click **Reconcile**.

Resetting Shared Coordinates

When you need to re-establish coordinates from a linked model, you can reset the shared coordinates. Resetting the shared coordinates will break the relationship between models that have shared coordinates. This will only affect the host model and not the linked files. When resetting, you eliminate the position of the GIS coordinate and reset the true north angle to zero.

How To: Reset the Shared Coordinates

1. From the *Manage* tab>Project Location panel, expand

   (Coordinates) and click (Reset Shared Coordinates).
2. Select the linked model.
   - A message will display, as shown in Figure A–21.

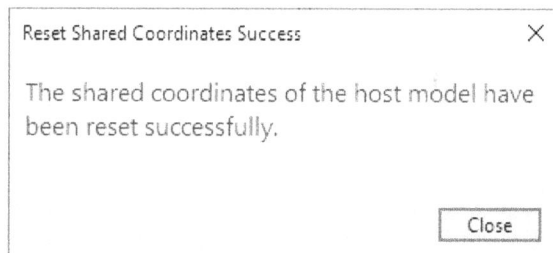

Reset Shared Coordinates Success	✕
The shared coordinates of the host model have been reset successfully.	
	Close

   Figure A–21

Practice A1

Shared Positioning

Practice Objectives

- Link a model to a site host project multiple times.
- Publish coordinates and share locations.
- Test different locations.

In this practice, you will link a project to a site multiple times, publish coordinates, and share locations. You will also test different locations using shared coordinates, as shown in Figure A–22.

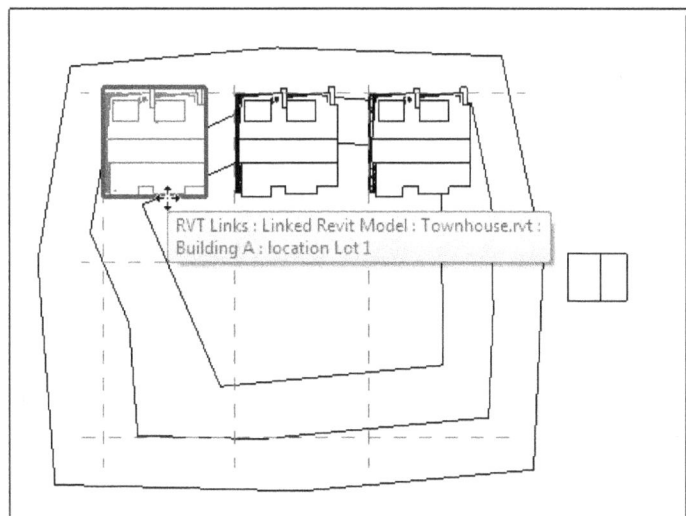

Figure A–22

Task 1 - Link a model to a site multiple times.

1. In the practice files folder, open **Townhouse-Site.rvt**.

2. In the *Insert* tab>Link panel, click 🖳 (Link Revit).

3. In the Import/Link RVT dialog box, select **Townhouse.rvt** with the *Positioning:* set to **Auto - Internal Origin to Internal Origin**. Type **ZA** to zoom out and see the linked model.

4. Move the link so that the upper left corner meets the intersection of the two reference planes, as shown in Figure A–23.

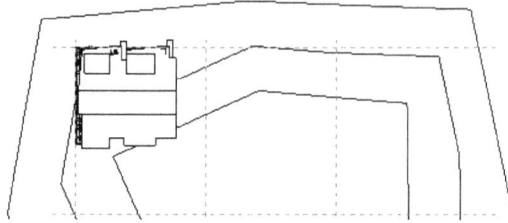

Figure A–23

5. Copy the link to the other two reference plane intersections, as shown in Figure A–24.

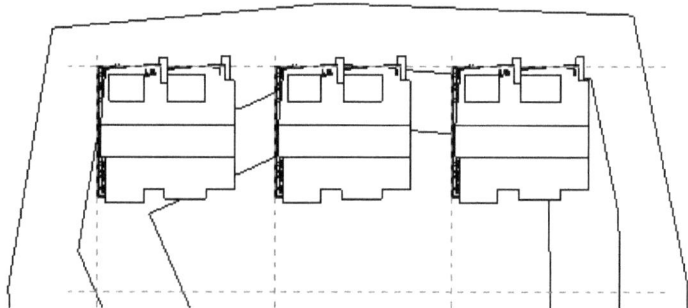

Figure A–24

6. Select the first link. In Properties, set the value of the *Name* to **Building A**, as shown in Figure A–25. Do not modify the **Shared Site** at this time.

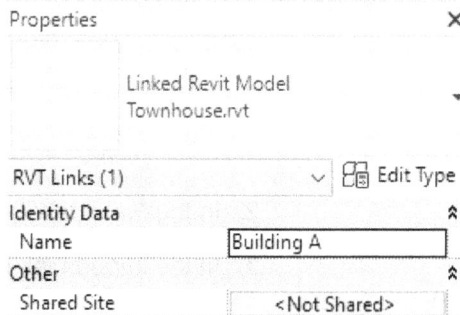

Figure A–25

7. Repeat the process with the other two instances of the linked model. Name them **Building B** and **Building C**.

© 2020, ASCENT - Center for Technical Knowledge®

Task 2 - Publish coordinates and share locations.

1. In the *Manage* tab>Project Location panel, expand
   (Coordinates) and click (Publish Coordinates).

2. Select **Building A**.

3. In the Location Weather and Site dialog box, in the *Site* tab, click **Rename...**. Rename the location as **Lot 1**, as shown in Figure A–26.

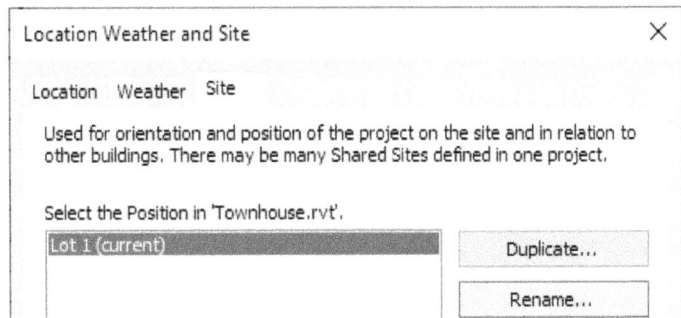

Location Weather and Site ✕

Location   Weather   Site

Used for orientation and position of the project on the site and in relation to other buildings. There may be many Shared Sites defined in one project.

Select the Position in 'Townhouse.rvt'.

| Lot 1 (current) | Duplicate... |
| | Rename... |

Figure A–26

4. Click **OK** and click (Modify) to end the command. (You could continue using the **Publish Coordinates** command to assign named locations to the other instances of the link, but the next steps show you how to do it using Properties.)

5. Select **Building B**. In Properties, next to *Shared Site*, click **<Not Shared>**

6. Select **Record current position...** and click **Change...**

7. Click **Duplicate...** to create a new named location named **Lot 2**, then click **OK**.

8. Click **OK** twice to close the dialog boxes. The *Shared Site* is now set to **Lot 2**.

9. Repeat the process with the third link.

10. In the *Manage* tab>Manage Project panel, click (Manage Links).

11. In the Manage Links dialog box, select the *Revit* tab.

12. The **Positions Not Saved** option is selected in the list (as shown in Figure A–27) indicating that the published coordinates have not been saved to the linked model.

Linked File	Status	Reference Type	Positions Not Saved
Townhouse.r	Loaded	Overlay	☑

Figure A–27

13. Select the *Link Name* **Townhouse.rvt** and click **Save Positions**.

14. In the Location Position Changed dialog box shown in Figure A–28, select **Save**.

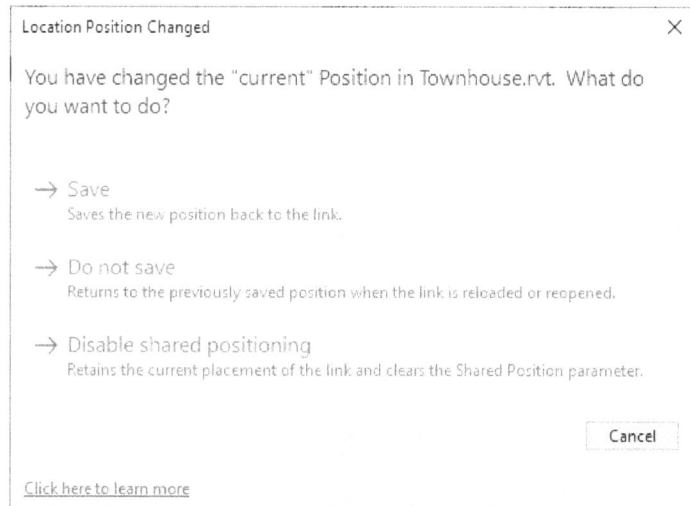

Location Position Changed   ✕

You have changed the "current" Position in Townhouse.rvt. What do you want to do?

→ Save
Saves the new position back to the link.

→ Do not save
Returns to the previously saved position when the link is reloaded or reopened.

→ Disable shared positioning
Retains the current placement of the link and clears the Shared Position parameter.

Cancel

Click here to learn more

Figure A–28

15. The **Positions Not Saved** option is cleared. Click **OK** to close the Manage Links dialog box.

16. Zoom out to see the entire site.

17. Do not close the project.

© 2020, ASCENT - Center for Technical Knowledge®

Task 3 - Test different locations.

1. In the practice files folder, open **Poolhouse.rvt**.

2. In the *Manage* tab>Project Location panel, click

   ⊕ (Location).

3. In the Location Weather and Site dialog box, in the *Site* tab, three named locations are listed in addition to the **Internal** location, as shown in Figure A–29. These were created when the model was previously linked to the host site project.

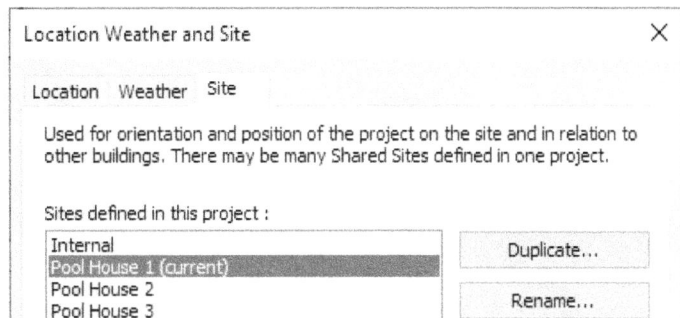

Location Weather and Site   ✕

Location   Weather   Site

Used for orientation and position of the project on the site and in relation to other buildings. There may be many Shared Sites defined in one project.

Sites defined in this project :

Internal	Duplicate...
Pool House 1 (current)	
Pool House 2	Rename...
Pool House 3	

Figure A–29

4. Close the dialog box, close the project, and verify that you are in the **Townhouse-Site.rvt** project.

5. In the *Insert* tab>Link panel, click 📄 (Link Revit).

6. Select the **Poolhouse.rvt** project. Set the *Positioning:* to **Auto - By Shared Coordinates**, as shown in Figure A–30, and click **Open**.

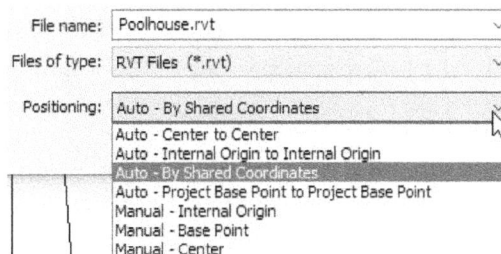

File name: Poolhouse.rvt

Files of type: RVT Files (*.rvt)

Positioning: Auto - By Shared Coordinates
Auto - Center to Center
Auto - Internal Origin to Internal Origin
Auto - By Shared Coordinates
Auto - Project Base Point to Project Base Point
Manual - Internal Origin
Manual - Base Point
Manual - Center

Figure A–30

7. In the Location Weather and Site dialog box, in the *Site* tab, select one of the named locations and click **OK**. The pool house is automatically inserted at that location.

8. Select the pool house.

9. In Properties, click the button next to *Shared Site*.

10. In the Choose Site dialog box, select **Move Instance to:** and select one of the other named locations in the list, as shown in Figure A–31. Click **OK**.

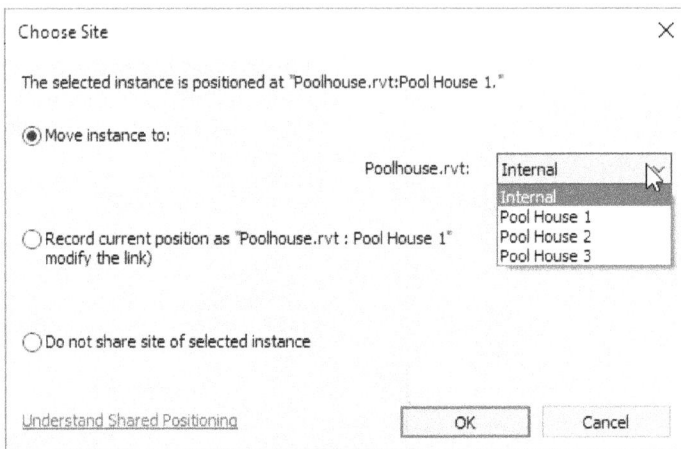

Figure A–31

11. The pool house moves to the named location. The three locations are shown in Figure A–32.

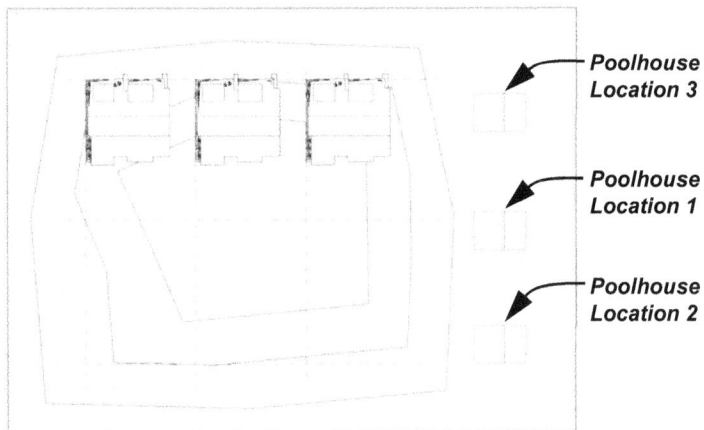

Figure A–32

12. Save and close the project.

© 2020, ASCENT - Center for Technical Knowledge®

Command Summary

Button	Command	Location
Groups and Links		
	Bind Link	• **Ribbon**: *Modify	Revit Link* tab>Link panel
	Link	• **Ribbon**: *Modify	Revit Link* tab>Link panel
Shared Coordinates		
	Acquire Coordinates	• **Ribbon**: *Manage* tab>Project Location panel>expand Coordinates
	Coordinates	• **Ribbon**: *Manage* tab>Project Location panel
	Location	• **Ribbon**: *Manage* tab>Project Location panel
	Publish Coordinates	• **Ribbon**: *Manage* tab>Project Location panel>expand Coordinates
	Report Shared Coordinates	• **Ribbon**: *Manage* tab>Project Location panel>expand Coordinates
	Reset Shared Coordinates	• **Ribbon**: *Manage* tab>Project Location panel>expand Coordinates
	Specify Coordinates at Point	• **Ribbon**: *Manage* tab>Project Location panel>expand Coordinates

© 2020, ASCENT - Center for Technical Knowledge®

Index

© 2020, ASCENT - Center for Technical Knowledge®

www.ingramcontent.com/pod-product-compliance
Lightning Source LLC
Chambersburg PA
CBHW082107220326
41598CB00066BA/5643